INTERPERSONAL COMMUNICATION:

PRAGMATICS OF HUMAN RELATIONSHIPS

INTERPERSONAL COMMUNICATION:
PRAGMATICS OF HUMAN RELATIONSHIPS

B. Aubrey Fisher
University of Utah

Random House
New York

Consulting Editor: Lloyd Drecksel, University of Utah

Thanks are due to Jerry L. Buley, Arizona State University; Laura Stafford, Ohio State University; and Sally Widenmann Yoerks, University of California, Santa Barbara, who read the manuscript in progress and offered many helpful suggestions.

First Edition
98765432
Copyright © 1987 by Random House, Inc.

Library of Congress Cataloging-in-Publication Data

Fisher, B. Aubrey, 1937–1986
  Interpersonal communication.

  Bibliography: p.
  Includes index.
  1. Interpersonal communication.   2. Interpersonal relations.   3. Communication—Psychological aspects.
I. Title.
BF637.C45F56   1987   158′.2   86-20999
ISBN 0-394-34111-2

Manufactured in the United States of America

Cover design by Katharine Urban

TO IRVING FELDMAN

—Whoever He Is
—Wherever He May Be

PREFACE

The title of this book, *Interpersonal Communication: Pragmatics of Human Relationships*, is intended to demonstrate the equivalence of the two key terms, "interpersonal communication" and "human relationships," which are virtually synonymous. To communicate is to relate, and to participate in communication is to participate in a relationship. Communication is "the fourth *R*"—*relating*. It is a subject no less basic than reading, writing, and arithmetic. Then why are so many of us literate in reading and writing our language, literate in adding, subtracting, multiplying, and dividing numbers, while at the same time we are functional illiterates in our interpersonal relationships?

All around us are signs that we are living in a relationally "sick" society. Interpersonal relationships are floundering. Divorce rates are high, which is surprising in light of the fact that so many couples live together without getting married. Palimony suits (which demand "divorce" settlements in the absence of any marriage) are not uncommon. The lyrics of a recent country song asked, "Doesn't anybody ever stay together anymore?" We can buy a sophisticated computer for less than $20 and hold it in the palm of the hand. We can put a receiving dish in our backyard and watch programs on our own television set from a satellite orbiting thousands of miles above the earth. We live in a glorious high-tech society, but the "state of the art" human relationship is one that breaks up after only a short time.

This book is about literacy—"relational literacy." In other words, it is about the basic skills of interpersonal communication. It is about what people actually do when they communicate with one another in face-to-face interaction—the *pragmatics* of human relationships. It is about people relating with people in the only way they can, through interpersonal communication. It focuses on the evolutionary process of *creating* human relationships through acting toward and with each other. It is about how people *negotiate* the definitions of their relationships through the process of interpersonal communication. It is about the process of understanding how human relationships evolve and it is about developing the skills of interpersonal communication on the basis of that understanding.

This book is divided into four parts, the first three of which—"The Context," "The Individual," and "The Relationship"—comprise the fundamental elements of interpersonal communication and human relationships. Some scholars have referred to these as three levels of understanding: the "cultural-normative" level, the "individual-psychological" level, and the "interpersonal-behavioral" level. All three levels are necessary for understanding human relationships. They are best understood as three concentric circles or three boxes of descending size nested within one another.

The "context" (cultural-normative level) is the largest box. It "deals with the norms, roles, social rules, expectations and ideals that affect personal relationships" (LaGaipa, 1981, p. 72). The "individual" (individual-psychological level) is the smallest box and deals with the perceptions, self-concepts, and personalities of participants that can also affect interpersonal relationships. The "relationship" (interpersonal-behavioral level) is the middle-sized box nested within the context and containing the individuals nested within it. The relationship "includes various kinds of interpersonal events, particularly in face-to-face groups" (LaGaipa, 1981, p. 72) and is the central level of interpersonal communication.

Part 4, "Outcomes of Relationships," treats the subject of increasing the communicator's competence and satisfaction within the process of interpersonal communication and human relationships. To be truly competent or to develop skills in interpersonal communication requires having a repertoire of behaviors to contribute to the interaction and the ability to adapt them appropriately to the particular communicative situation and the particular stage of the relationship. Competence in and satisfaction with your interpersonal relationships, then, is more than a matter of knowing what to do. It is also knowing when to do it. To be competent is to adapt your behaviors so that you communicate appropriately. And that means behaving on the basis of a thorough understanding of the evolutionary process that is interpersonal communication and human relationships.

A fundamental premise underlying this book is viewing interpersonal communication as a *pattern* of interaction that defines the relationship and binds the individuals together. In this sense, then, communication is not something you *do* as much as it is something you *participate in*. No individual communicator can create *inter*action or define the *inter*personal relationship. An individual communicator *contributes* to the interaction. Together, two (or more) individuals can create the pattern of interaction and thus define their relationship. Hence, it is important that each participant in communication be able to *adapt* to the other person, to the context, to the particular type of relationship, and to the specific stage of that developing relationship.

When contributing to the pattern of interaction, each communicator enacts a behavior. That behavior will have consequences in terms of how it potentially affects the pattern of interaction and, hence, the relationship itself. Therefore, we will treat each behavior contributed to the interaction/relationship as a "strategy." Every strategy in interpersonal communication attempts to resolve some "issue" or topic question that, when answered, helps to define the interpersonal relationship. Developing your skills in interpersonal communication means using relational strategies that are appropriate to the issues in the conversation. When used appropriately and effectively, strategies resolve relational problems, manage relational conflict, answer relational issues, and negotiate relational definitions. Every participant in the process of interpersonal communication uses strategies. The competent communicator uses strategies appropriately.

Communication is a process. Relationship is a process. As people continue communicating, they continually define and redefine their relationship with each other. Hence, we say that a human relationship is constantly in a state of "becoming"— becoming something different from what it was. As a matter of fact, just living is a process. As people grow older and more relationally experienced, they change. And so do their relationships.

It has been suggested that the fluid life-styles we lead in our society call for three or four different mates over the course of a lifetime. The first mate should be a "lover" suited to the raptures of falling in love. The second should be a "friend" suited to the need for social support during the effort to build careers and family. The third should be a "companion" suited to the comfort and ease of later life, when loneliness may be a problem. The fourth should be a "second lover" suited to the desire and need to freshen and revitalize a stagnating relationship. The person with all four relationships is rich indeed. I am very wealthy in my relationships, for I have all four—lover, friend, companion, and mistress. Her name is Irene.

B. AUBREY FISHER

CONTENTS

CHAPTER 1

Introduction

[T]here are two main kinds of love: in the first, the heart beats faster, you can't eat, you tremble at the sight of each other.

That's puppy love, new love, romantic love.

The second kind is the love you have to work at: it's the deeper, stronger love between grown-ups who know that no matter how close they are, they will always be two separate beings.

When the romantic love goes, people shouldn't panic because it comes back. In waves or cycles. Like a fever.

—Alan Alda (1981)

Few people think of Alan Alda as an expert in communication theory. Most of us see him (and still do in syndicated reruns of *M*A*S*H*) as Hawkeye Pierce, the wisecracking, woman-chasing, gin-swilling master of one-liners who brought humor and pathos out of the tragedy of war. I may be, in fact, the only person in the world who considers Alan Alda an expert in communication theory. But anyone who saw this writer-director-actor's movie *Four Seasons* was treated to a crash course in interpersonal communication. The central concern of *Four Seasons* was interpersonal communication and relationships—how they grew and changed and developed, how they changed the individuals in the relationships, and how they persisted despite and because of the individuals who were in them. No, there's no doubt about it! Alan Alda (whether he knows it or not) is definitely an expert in communication.

This book is about interpersonal communication. It is also about human relationships. I shall attempt to illustrate how these two descriptive statements about this book are identical. That is, to say that this book is about interpersonal communication is synonymous with saying it is about human relationships. Let's begin by focusing on the term *interpersonal*. Interpersonal denotes a particular level of communication, a level that exists in the sociological hierarchy of communication. Now there are two different kinds of hierarchies: a vertical hierarchy and a "nested" hierarchy. You may already be thinking of a hierarchy in terms of a vertical ladder. The hierarchy of a university, for instance, might be visualized as administrative levels on the ladder—the university president at the top and (in descending order)

1

the vice president of academic affairs, the dean of the college, the departmental chair, the faculty member, and the student. (I guess this example places the student at the "bottom" of the ladder, but you can rest assured that your instructor isn't much higher up.) But when we discuss sociological levels of communication, we refer to a nested hierarchy and not the ladderlike vertical hierarchy.

To locate interpersonal communication within a nested hierarchy of communication, let's begin with the notion of "system"—specifically, a social system. Communication involves people who are engaged in the act or process of communicating. A social system may be as small as a single person or as large as an entire society. It may include a small group, such as the twelve people on a jury assigned the task of deciding the guilt or innocence of an accused person on trial. A social system may include an entire organization, such as your college or university with its many members engaged in instructional, service, maintenance, and research activities. It may be the mass audience of potential customers viewing a televised commercial that is urging them to buy a particular brand of laundry detergent. A communication system is, first of all, a social system comprising people. The number of people and the extent to which these people know each other varies widely from one system to another. But all communication systems, including systems of interpersonal communication, are social systems.

Now think of a series of concentric circles, each circle nested within a larger circle (see Figure 1–1). Each circle represents a system of communication that corresponds to a social system. The smallest possible social system is the individual human being, which can be called the system of *intra*personal communication. The intrapersonal system is thus a part of the *inter*personal communication system, but it is *only* a part of the system. The interpersonal system is a part of larger communication systems comprising groups, organizations, and societies.

Each one of these systems can be thought of as having a "culture" (with cultural beliefs, values, traditions, etc.) of its own, with subcultures nested within larger cultures. Our main interest in this book will be the "culture" of the interpersonal communication system. This system, as a part of larger cultures, will affect and be affected by groups, organizations, and societies of which it is a part. Similarly, the interpersonal communication system, as the larger culture for intrapersonal communication, will affect and be affected by the internal self (the feelings, emotions, beliefs, personality, and so forth) of each individual who is a part of it.

It is important to remember this nested hierarchy of communication systems as you continue reading this book. Be careful, though not to confuse the *intra*personal communication level with the system of *inter*personal communication. As a part of the system, the individual person may affect and be affected by interpersonal communication. But the individual is not and should never be considered to be the same thing as the system of interpersonal communication. Knowing everything there is to know about the individual participants will not enable you to define the system of interpersonal communication. Conversely, the larger cultures can affect and be affected by interpersonal communication, but they cannot and do not define the system of interpersonal communication. Interpersonal communication is a relationship between and among individual human beings and is, to a greater or lesser extent, different from the individuals who are its members and from the culture in which it exists.

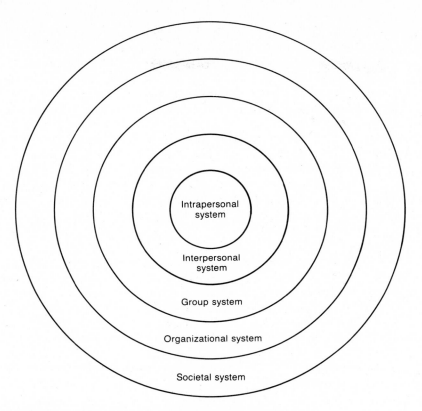

Figure 1-1. Nested Hierarchy of Communication Systems

ON RELATIONSHIP AND COMMUNICATION

Now we need to turn our attention to the nature of human relationships. Note that the title of this book is *Interpersonal Communication: Pragmatics of Human Relationships*. This book will take the point of view that the terms *interpersonal communication* and *human relationship* are synonyms. Your reaction to this statement is probably something on the order of "You've gotta be kidding!" But I'm not! The relationship you have with another person is so intertwined with the interpersonal communication you have with each other that the two terms are virtually synonymous. Let me illustrate this point. Each of the following statements, selected from a recent textbook in interpersonal communication, points out the lack of a clear distinction between "interpersonal communication" and "human relationship":

1. *Relationship is the* context *in which communication occurs.*
   Communicators are people who enter into relationships with other people. Without communication we would be unable to function. During the course of a single day we interact with others to share information and beliefs, exchange ideas and feelings, make plans, and solve problems. Sometimes this is done interpersonally, sometimes in a small group, and sometimes in a public forum.

However communication occurs, it is essential in helping to initiate, develop, control, and sustain our contact with others. (Gamble & Gamble, 1984, p. 4)

2. *Relationship is a* dimension *or* component *of communication.*

All people perception is concerned with what might be called relationship communication, since the meanings grow to a large extent from the notions we form about others while actively interacting with them. There is also, of course, a content aspect, and both are ever present. . . . Relevant areas of nonverbal communication are a large part of what was previously defined as relationship communication. (Ross & Ross, 1982, pp. 17, 163)

3. *Relationship is an* outcome *or* result *of communication.*

As individuals communicate, they create something new—a relationship. The relationship is both formed by communication and defined by communication. That is, the individuals come together by communicating with one another, and what happens to them thereafter is the result of their communication. (Phillips & Wood, 1983, p. 83).

3. *(Corollary) Communication is a* function *of a relationship.*

In the most basic sense, a relationship is formed whenever reciprocal data processing occurs, that is, when two or more individuals mutually take account of one another's verbal or nonverbal activities. This reciprocal data processing, which we can term interpersonal communication, is the means through which relationships of all types are initiated, develop, grow, and deteriorate. (Ruben, 1984, p. 249)

4. *Relationship is an* economic exchange *of costs and rewards which result from communication.*

Interpersonal communication is a symbolic process by which two people, bound together in a relationship, provide each other with resources or negotiate the exchange of resources. (Roloff, 1981, p. 30)

Now I do not want you, the reader, to get the impression that I am implying that any of these statements concerning communication and relationship is "wrong." To the contrary, every statement I have quoted above is absolutely correct. The human relationship is the context, the outcome or result, a function, and an economic exchange of interpersonal communication—and more. In fact, there seems to be no valid reason to assume any difference between the terms "relationship" and "interpersonal communication." Maintaining the distinction between them may be important when we are discussing other communication systems in the hierarchy, particularly intrapersonal communication. But at the interpersonal level of human communication, nothing seems to be gained (and, in fact, some real understanding may be lost) by keeping the two terms distinct. Therefore, we shall treat the terms as synonymous. To communicate with another person is to relate to that person. In fact, others have said (and I strongly agree) that study in communication is a fundamental part of a basic education—"the fourth R"—*relating.*

A "MODEL" OF COMMUNICATION

Virtually every textbook ever written about the subject of interpersonal communication has included a model, traditionally in the form of a visual or pictorial depiction of how communication happens. This book is no exception. Lest it be said that I am making fun of communication models per se, I must digress for a moment to explain my attitude toward them. Permit me to engage in a little self-disclosure (a concept to be discussed in more detail in Part II of this book). My present attitude toward communication models began developing when I was a student in a class whose instructor assigned everyone to devise an "original" model of communication. No big deal, I thought. Everyone has to devise his or her own model of communication in some class sooner or later. The "kicker" in this assignment, though, was that my instructor told us that we were not allowed to use any arrows. Resenting this unwarranted restriction on our creative efforts, I and most of my fellow students proceeded to create models by using substitutes for arrows. As I recall, I used a system of pulleys and ropes; my fellow classmates used caterpillar treads, conveyor belts, mathematical equations—in short, anything that would substitute for the arrowlike notion of transmitting and receiving messages.

It wasn't until much later that I discovered what my instructor in communication models was attempting to teach us. To represent pictorially a model of communication on a two-dimensional sheet of paper is to submit to the limitations of those geometric boundaries of length and width. Asking us to draw a model on two-dimensional paper without using arrows was the instructor's attempt, I now believe, to get his students to think about communication beyond these two dimensions. It is difficult, for example, to illustrate other dimensions, such as "depth" or "time," in a pictorial drawing.

Long after I was a student in that course, I came to prefer a verbal model, an explanatory model of communication that does not involve pictorial representation. Where is it written that communication models need to be visual drawings? After all, a model is only an analogy or metaphor that stands for something "real." And metaphors can be expressed in words as well as pictures. In this sense, and contrary to popular cliché, a few words are worth far more than a thousand pictures. The model that follows is, then, overly simplified because it is restricted to the limits of being a "picture," but it actually represents a much more complex definition— particularly in its omission of the fact that communication always comprises events that occur in time. The verbal model of communication (which is actually the remainder of this book) will illustrate that complexity.

Most models of interpersonal communication employ two people, a social grouping commonly known as a *dyad*. Of course, three people (or four or five or more) are also perfectly capable of engaging in interpersonal communication, of having a relationship. The model does not change at all with the addition of more individuals; it merely includes more people. My model, meant to illustrate the intrapersonal levels of communication within the relationship, personalizes the human components with typical human names—Alfred and Betty. The model thus possesses three elements: individuals (Alfred and Betty), relationship, and context. (See Figure 1–2.)

This model attempts to illustrate the nested hierarchy of communication systems. Alfred and Betty represent two intrapersonal systems, components of the relationship. The enveloping context represents the higher levels of groups, organizations, and societal cultures within which interpersonal communication occurs. It is important to note that the relationship exists *not* inside the heads of Alfred and Betty but *between* them. The relationship represents the bonds or connections that tie Alfred

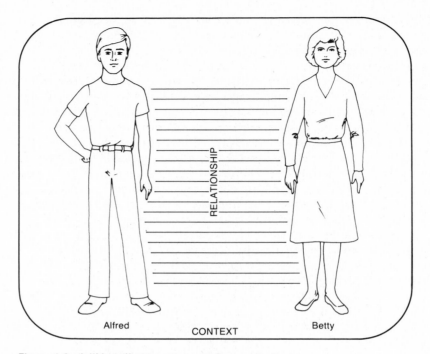

RELATIONSHIP

Alfred   CONTEXT   Betty

Figure 1-2. A "Model" of Interpersonal Communication

and Betty together. Interpersonal communication (the human relationship) thus lies outside and separate from the intrapersonal systems of Alfred and Betty and, conversely, inside and separate from the cultures in which the relationship between Alfred and Betty is nested. These, then, are the three elements of the model of interpersonal communication.

Interpersonal communication includes *individuals* who bring to communication their own idiosyncratic differences. The self of each communicator can influence the relationship and be influenced by the relationship but, strictly speaking, is separate from it. The self does carry the residues (that is, the outcomes) of the relationship after the relationship ceases to exist. Each individual, even when not interacting with the friend, possesses a residue of that relationship internalized in the form of an emotional response, a memory, a perceptual definition of that relationship. Further, that internalized residue of the relationship is reactivated and subject to change when communication (the relationship) occurs again later. Within every relationship, then, is a self and one or more "others," each of whom also has a self.

The *relationship* exists between the individual participants. The relationship, though, is not a "thing" but an event—more accurately, a series of connected events. All relationships are very sporadic. That is, we interact with even very close friends for, at most, only a few hours per day and not even every day. When Alfred and Betty are communicating (interacting) with each other, their relationship is actively occurring and can be said to exist. When they are not interacting, their relationship no longer actively exists except as a residual memory within the intrapersonal systems: Alfred's definition of his relationship with Betty and Betty's definition of her

People jointly create a relationship by their communication.
(Frank Siteman/The Picture Cube)

relationship with Alfred. But that memory is not the same thing as the relationship; it is only a residue, a footprint, a memory trace of the relationship. Like any residue, it erodes with time and no longer reflects contemporary reality.

Think back, if you can, of some childhood friend whom you have not seen for years. When I was a small child, I played constantly with Kay, the girl next door. We were best friends for years, but I moved away when I was six years old and have not seen nor heard about Kay for decades. My only image of her is that of a chubby preadolescent girl with blonde curly hair. Our relationship ceased to exist when we ceased communicating. The only thing left of that very close relationship is a residue which grows ever fainter with the passage of time. I'm quite sure Kay no longer resembles my memory of her. Furthermore, she may not even remember that we once were close friends. The relationship is gone; only individual memories (residues) of the relationship remain.

The relationship *is* the communication, the events of acting toward and with one another. And, of course, no one can avoid having a relationship. In the same sense of the axiomatic cliché that "one cannot not communicate," one cannot not relate. Whenever you (and the other) act or behave toward one another, you are relating to and with that other person. In fact, we might say that you are defining what your relationship with the other person is by the way you act toward and with that person. To illustrate, you would describe your relationship with a lover on the basis that your actions toward each other are loving actions. You describe your relationship with an acquaintance on the basis that you act in very superficial ways toward each other.

Your actions thus provide the basis for (in fact, are the same thing as) your definition of the interpersonal relationship. In this way, then, communication *occurs* more than it can be said to exist as a "thing." In other words, communication is an event or a series of events that occur in time. Like any event that occurs in time, it is over; it ceases to exist when the event is over. The only thing left of the event is a memory trace in your mind and in the mind of the other person.

But communication is not just your actions, what you do to create the relationship. Nor is it just what the other person does during the communication event. Communication is not merely actions toward another person; it is the *inter*action created by both your actions and the other's actions in concert with one another. Ray Birdwhistel (1959), a renowned expert in kinesics, more popularly known as "body language," has summarized this notion very well:

> An individual does not communicate; he engages in or becomes part of communication. He may move, or make noises . . . but he does not communicate. In a parallel fashion, he may see, he may hear, smell, taste, or feel—but he does not communicate. In other words, he does not originate communication; he participates in it. (p. 104)

The relationship between you and another person (your interpersonal communication) is created by your actions and the actions of the other person—by your actions in concert with the other's actions. Your actions isolated from the other person's actions are meaningless and can be interpreted only with great difficulty. Have you ever overheard someone talking on the telephone with an unknown caller? You hear only one side of the conversation, the actions of only one person in the interpersonal communication. Sometimes you can "fill in the blanks" and interpret what is going on in the conversation, but more often you really wonder what the conversation is about. Without hearing the actions of the person on the other end of the telephone conversation, you have difficulty in interpreting its meaning. You need the actions of both persons in the conversation to be able to understand the meaning of the entire conversation.

The actions of both members of the relationship, the *inter*personal communication or the *inter*actions, create what we have come to call a relationship. In the same sense as the cliché "It takes two to tango," a relationship is not something you "do" but something you enter into, become a part of. You, as an individual participant, don't define the relationship any more than an individual raindrop defines a whole thundershower. You are merely a part of the interpersonal communication system. Your actions, together with the coordinated actions of the other, combine to define the relationship.

The relationship can thus be thought of as the bonds that *connect* two or more people, and they exist *between* the people involved in the relationship. What are the bonds that tie people together in a relationship? Are they your feelings toward each other? Your common experiences? To the contrary, they are events—the actions of each person combined with the actions of the other. In other words, the relationship comprises not persons so much as events, the actions or behaviors of the persons involved in creating and maintaining the relationship. If these bonds are not to weaken and disintegrate, these events or actions must occur again and again over time.

Communication always occurs in some *context*. Although the context may include the physical environment (interaction in a public restaurant may be quite different from interaction of those same people in the front seat of a parked automobile), the more influential part of the context is social—the culture or society to which the individual people in the relationship belong. Cultural aspects include such influences on the relationship as social norms, rules, expectations, and even whether the participants are available for interaction.

The context certainly influences the human relationship, and that influence may be a constructive or a destructive one. That is, the context may function to encourage or discourage further development of the relationship and may serve to intensify or erode it. In a high school society, for example, students rarely date or have friendships with people outside their own subculture. Punks go with punks, rockers go with rockers, trendies go with trendies, preppies go with preppies, and so forth. Within their own culture, though, dating and friendships are encouraged.

The model of communication contains three nested elements: individual human beings, a relationship, and a context. In terms of the hierarchy of communication discussed earlier, these three elements can be thought of as intrapersonal, interpersonal, and cultural communication systems. Implied within this model is the element of time or process. That is, interpersonal communication itself comprises actions, behaviors, or events which, taken together, form *inter*action. Interpersonal communication, already defined as synonymous with human relationship, is also so closely linked with human interaction that we could use all three terms interchangeably.

A PRAGMATIC VIEW OF COMMUNICATION

This definition of relationship/communication/interaction, comprising actions or behaviors as a series of interconnected and coordinated events, reflects a particular view of communication—a pragmatic view. The term *pragmatics* in reference to human communication was probably first coined in 1967 with the publication of a book entitled *Pragmatics of Human Communication*, written by three psychiatrists and clinical psychologists, Paul Watzlawick, Janet Beavin, and Don Jackson. Sometimes known as the "interactional view" of human communication, pragmatics can be understood in terms of five general principles.

Why do you need to know these principles of communication pragmatics, you ask? The answer lies in the fact that the only way to improve or develop skills in interpersonal communication is to be both a *participant* in communication and an *observer* of communication at the same time. You can always learn how to communicate by engaging in communicating, but you will probably never become very proficient at it until and unless you know what you are doing. Jump in the pool, and you will start swimming. But until and unless you know what you're doing, you will be a dog-paddler all your life. In order to avoid dog-paddling your way through interpersonal communication, you need to understand the nature of the interpersonal communication process (as an observer) in order to develop your skills in interpersonal communication (as a participant). These, then, are the five principles of communication pragmatics that will help you to understand the process of interpersonal communication.

Principle #1: Behaviors (human actions) are the phenomena necessary for understanding communication. Underlying this principle is the axiom "One cannot not communicate." Even if you've never had a communication course before this one, you may have heard this axiom expressed. Simply put, this axiom focuses on behaviors (rather than the intrapersonal selves of the communicators) as being most central to interpersonal communication. It means that communication is behavior, and behavior has no opposite. You simply cannot not behave; even holding still and not moving a muscle is a form of behavior. Behavior (unlike emotions, feelings, beliefs, and other elements of the intrapersonal system) is accessible to other persons. You can never know what is going on inside another person, but you can always see and hear (and in some instances feel, taste, and smell) the behaviors of other persons.

When you engage in communication with another person, you will probably think it is important to discover the feelings and emotions of the other's intrapersonal system; but it is absolutely *necessary* for you to know the behaviors of the other person in order to gain even a minimal understanding of human communication. The other person's feelings, motivations, emotions, and so on—because they vary in the extent to which they affect the relationship—may or may not be important to your understanding of and participating in human communication. But behaviors or actions, both yours and those of your partner, are absolutely essential to your understanding.

A behavior is an event. Because it is an event, it occurs in time and cannot be "taken back." If you hit somebody in the face and break his nose, the event (and its consequences) have "occurred"; you can't roll back the clock and pretend it didn't happen. The most you can do is to attempt an additional behavior by saying, for example, "I'm so sorry. It was an accident." The new behavioral event (apologizing) does not change the previous behavioral event (face punching). It provides an additional event in the ongoing sequence of events. It thus becomes part of the sequence of events which may redefine the former event so that it may take on a different meaning. That is, you can change the semantic "reality" (your own personal and internalized meaning) of a behavior with subsequent behaviors, but you cannot change the pragmatic reality (its effects or consequences) of any behavioral event. In other words, you can apologize all you want, but the nose is still broken.

There is a familiar saying about communication that is relevant to this point about the connection between intentions and behaviors. It is quoted so often that I should remember it without difficulty. I never can. In fact, I had to copy it from a sign on my office bulletin board so that I could include it here: "I know you believe you understand what you think I said, but I'm not sure you realize that what you heard is not what I meant." This saying is typically used to show how the "meanings" that any one person has of reality are subject to the whims of perception. One person's understanding is not necessarily the same as another person's understanding. And the actual utterance that one person heard is not necessarily the same as the idea the other person intended to convey.

Perhaps an example would make this point clear. I say to you, "I come originally from South Dakota." You interpret my comment as saying that I was a farmer who couldn't wait to get out of "the sticks." You have a certain "meaning" of what "from South Dakota" entails. Your meaning of my comment is one meaning; it "belongs to" you. My meaning of my comment is another meaning; it "belongs to" me. I have never been a farmer, and I'm rather proud of my South Dakota heritage. Thus, you didn't hear what I intended. If these were the only two meanings, then interpersonal communication becomes a simple process of continuing to exchange messages so that "my" meaning gets closer to "your" meaning. Of course, we are not allowed to hope that our two meanings will be the same. The best we can hope for is some degree of "overlapping meanings."

Now consider that same saying within a pragmatic view. The utterance (behavior) occurred. Despite the intention (part of my intrapersonal system) which preceded the utterance and your understanding (also intrapersonal) of my utterance, neither of us can deny the fact that my utterance did in fact occur. And because it did occur, it will have consequences for the future interaction.

The saying embodies a certain pessimistic implication that individuals' perceptions will inevitably result in confusion, misunderstanding, and conflicts over meanings. If perceptual reality were that powerful, such pessimism would be well deserved and communication would be extraordinarily difficult, if not impossible. On the other hand, a pragmatic view accepts perceptual differences as a very normal part of the process of interpersonal communication. But misunderstanding or confusion of two different intrapersonal meanings is not really the point of the interpersonal relationship. Given the undeniable truth that intrapersonal perceptions will always be different, let's move on to the second principle of communication pragmatics.

Principle #2: The interpretation or definition of communicative behaviors is to be found in the patterns of how those behaviors interconnect with one another. A former colleague of mine used to delight in intentionally misinterpreting questions on standardized survey forms. For example, after the question asking about "marital status," he would write, "Shaky!" On a job placement information form, he once responded to the question "Minimum salary acceptable?" with a decisive "No!" The point is simply this. No single behavior isolated from the stream of interactional events is interpretable or definable unless one jumps to gross and probably inaccurate conclusions. But place that behavior within the interactional stream, and its meaning becomes clearer. (I have often wondered who read those survey forms and what they thought about the person who filled them out.)

An excellent example of the second principle of pragmatics is Bud Abbott and

Lou Costello's classic comedy routine "Who's on First?" If you are one of those rare persons who have not had the good fortune to have heard this routine, I will provide some necessary background. The premise of the dialogue centers on the unusual names of the players on a baseball team, so that the nickname of the first baseman is "Who," the second baseman is "What," and the third baseman is "I don't know." Abbott understands this principle; Costello does not. Thus, Abbott's "Who's on first" is a declarative statement identifying the first baseman by his nickname, but to Costello that same statement is a question asking for the identity of the first baseman. The humor of the dialogue, of course, requires a third interpretation, which comes from a pragmatic view of the entire interaction. We, the audience, are aware of Abbott's interpretation, Costello's "misinterpretation," and the "real" interpretation (it's a comedy routine), which necessarily incorporates both the individual interpretations.

Toward the end of the dialogue, Costello makes a final desperate effort to discover the first baseman's name. He creates a hypothetical situation in which he is the catcher in a game:

COSTELLO: Valentine gets up, and he bunts the ball. Now when he bunts the ball, me, being a good catcher, I'm gonna throw Valentine out at first base. So I pick up the ball and throw it to who?

ABBOTT: Now that's the first thing you've said right.

COSTELLO: I don't even know what I'm talking about!

ABBOTT: That's all you have to do.

COSTELLO: Just throw it to first base. Now who's got it?

ABBOTT: Naturally.

COSTELLO: If I throw the ball to first base, somebody's got to get it. Now who's got it?

ABBOTT: Naturally.

COSTELLO: Who has it?

ABBOTT: Naturally.

COSTELLO: Naturally? So I pick up the ball, and I throw it to Naturally.

ABBOTT: No! No! You throw the ball to first base, then Who gets it.

COSTELLO: Naturally.

ABBOTT: That's right.

COSTELLO: So I pick up the ball and I throw it to Naturally.

ABBOTT: No! You don't!

COSTELLO: I throw it to who?

ABBOTT: Naturally.

COSTELLO: That's what I'm saying.

ABBOTT: You're not saying that.

COSTELLO: I said I throw the ball to Naturally.

ABBOTT: You throw the ball to Who.

COSTELLO: Naturally.

ABBOTT: Well, say that.

COSTELLO: That's what I'm saying. I throw the ball to Naturally.

ABBOTT: You don't!

COSTELLO:	I throw it to who?
ABBOTT:	Naturally.
COSTELLO:	I'm saying it the same as you! I throw it to who?
ABBOTT:	Naturally.
COSTELLO:	Okay, I throw it to Naturally.
ABBOTT:	You don't.
COSTELLO:	Who did I throw it to?
ABBOTT:	Who.
COSTELLO:	Naturally.
ABBOTT:	That's right.

Costello's anguished "I'm saying it the same as you are!" is quite accurate. But he appears to see only the pattern in which "Naturally" is an answer to his interrogative "Who?" He does not see the alternative pattern of the declarative meaning of "Naturally," which is an accurate response to the statement that "Who" is playing first base. Abbott's interpretation is no more accurate than Costello's. After all, the "real" interpretation of the dialogue is that of a comedy routine, not a discussion of a particular baseball team. Of course, a realistic conversation would undoubtedly clarify this confusion of individual meanings within the intrapersonal systems, but then the dialogue wouldn't be funny. And "comedy routine" is the "true" meaning of this interaction. Significantly, the "true" meaning of the dialogue is quite independent from the perceived meaning of either individual. And that brings us to the third principle of the pragmatic view of human communication.

Principle #3: To discover the meaning or significance of the communicative patterns is to place them in some context. The third principle seems obvious on the face of it. We all know the problem of quoting out of context. Often, however, we tend to confuse contexts. Some soap opera fans are notorious for their rabid identification with the fictional characters and have been known to attack physically the actresses who play the villain roles (apparently every soap opera has at least one villainous female character) when they see them in real life. After the tragic death of Natalie Wood, CBS reportedly received hundreds of letters wondering why Robert Wagner and Stephanie Powers did not marry. After all, they obviously loved each other, as their characterizations of Jonathan and Jennifer Hart on the CBS series *Hart to Hart* proved. Naturally, these examples seem extreme because they involve confusing reality with obvious fiction. No normal person with normal intelligence, we think, would ever do such a thing. But confusing contexts and thereby creating different meanings is not always so obviously "wrong."

I personally have a reputation (well deserved, I might add) as a person who frequently (even habitually) engages in insulting and arguing behavior. My interaction with my closest friends frequently comprises mutual and reciprocated insults and fervent arguments. Such interaction is recreational conversation within the context of these friendships.

More than once, however, I have insulted someone whom I didn't know very well. I knew I was in trouble when I wasn't insulted in return and the conversation either terminated or became exceedingly polite. I was left with the residual memory of embarrassment. I was guilty of confusing the relational context of "friend" with

We can discover the significance of communication patterns only if we consider them in context.
(Susan Lapides/Design Conceptions)

that of "acquaintance," so that my insult was defined within the interactional pattern as a rude behavior (acquaintance) rather than as participation in ritual repartee (friend). In other words, the meaning of any interactional pattern varies with a variation in the relational context in which it occurs. The pattern (for example, "How are you?" "Fine.") that is insignificant in one context (two acquaintances meeting on the street) may be highly significant in another context (after a person has fallen off a 10-foot cliff).

Principle #4: To understand communication is to "make sense" of the communicative patterns retrospectively (that is, after they have occurred). Our Western culture has conditioned us to think in prospective (past to present to future) ways. We like to think in terms, for example, of causes and effects. We are not typically satisfied until we find causes for our behavior or the behavior of others. What caused me to act that way? Why did I say that? Why did he say those things about me? What can I do to make more money? Despite our tendency to seek causes for "why" events happen, we tend to derive the meanings of most (if not all) of our behaviors after the fact, after they occur, in the form of rationalization of retrospective sensemaking. We tend to seek (and invariably "discover") lofty motives for our good actions and reasonable justifications (or excuses) for our "less than good" actions. This fourth principle of the pragmatic view of communication does not imply that our meanings or definitions of communication are necessarily more correct when they occur after the fact but that retrospective sensemaking is what we typically do to define our behaviors and, hence, our relationships.

Some will scoff at this notion of retrospective sensemaking and point to actions that are directed toward some future goal. Such behavior, they will argue, is driven by some predetermined purpose—to attain the goal. The athlete trains to compete in the Olympics. The student works her way through school to be a lawyer. The sales representative practices his pitch to make the sale. Now don't get me wrong. I'm not denying the fact that much of our behavior may be directed toward some goal. But the meaning we ultimately have for our goal-directed behavior will eventually come from *re*defining our behaviors based on rationalizing or retrospectively making sense of the pattern of events after they have occurred. If the person achieves her goal, she will retrospectively make sense of it, perhaps by saying, "See? It was all worth it. I made it." She thus confirms her original definition. On the other hand, if she does not achieve her goal, she will still engage in retrospective sensemaking, perhaps by saying, "What a waste of time," or by redefining her goals—"I didn't really want to do that in the first place."

Several years ago I was the faculty adviser of a student who had decided at an early age to be an engineer. He took all the math courses he could take in high school and directed all his activities toward being an engineer. After a "D" in his first college math course, he discovered that he really didn't want to be an engineer after all. He redefined his goal, became a communication major, and appeared very satisfied when, upon graduation, he entered a management training program with a public utility firm. The goal, like any other part of one's definition of a pattern of events, is also subject to being redefined through retrospective sensemaking. As events change, so do goals.

Specifically in terms of communication, the pragmatic view suggests, for instance, that Alfred retrospectively looks back on his interaction with Betty and defines the relationship he has with her. Betty does her sensemaking of the relationship too. Our definitions of the relationships we have with others are derived retrospectively and continuously. Because we continue to make sense of the interaction after it has occurred, the meaning or definition we have of any relationship is constantly subject to change, often frequent change. And as the interaction continues, the events of the relationship accumulate and continue to change. But change is the essense of process. Communication is definitely a process and, in the sense that change is constantly occurring, can be said to be constantly *in process*.

Principle #5: A pragmatic view of communication involves asking different questions in order to acquire knowledge or understanding. What is the question we ask pragmatically about the meaning of behavior? We might ask, for example, "*What* does this behavior mean?" At this point in our discussion, however, we should already know that such a question is the wrong question to ask from a pragmatic view of human communication. We have no way of interpreting the meaning of a given behavior until we can see it within the pattern or stream of interaction. Behavior, to be meaningful interpersonally, involves finding how that behavior links with or connects with other behaviors in the stream of interaction or conversation. But even the definition of the interaction pattern is unclear until we place the entire interaction within some context, such as the cultural relationship of which this interaction pattern is a part.

The question we would be most likely to ask in a commonsense view of communication is "What do people mean by their behaviors?" This question, of course, is important and could be quite significant. Unfortunately it is important primarily for the *intra*personal communication system. In the context of the *inter*personal system of communication, it is not always appropriate. To discover what meanings people have for their own behaviors is to ask a question exclusive to the individual, the intrapersonal communication system. People's meanings are inside their heads. Another person can interpret those meanings, but only on the basis of some inference (filling in the blanks). Remember the line "What you heard is not what I meant." The answer to the question of what people mean by their behavior is vitally significant intrapersonally but not very informative if we want to understand the system of interpersonal communication and of human relationships.

The pragmatic question that informs us about the system of interpersonal communication is "*How* does behavior mean?" Albert Scheflen, in a 1974 book provocatively titled *How Behavior Means*, suggests that we should cease "asking what people mean by their behavior. This is an issue of focus; does one focus on people or on behavior forms?" (p. 204) Behaviors "fit together" with other behaviors in the familiar pattern of interaction: that interaction placed within a relational context serves to define that relationship. If you observe one person hitting another person hard on the shoulder with a clenched fist, the second person hitting back, followed by both persons laughing and then throwing their arms about each other, you could answer the question of *how* the hitting behavior takes on meaning in that relationship. You might come to the conclusion that "hitting behavior" serves as a greeting ritual for two rather close friends.

Granted, this particular kind of greeting ritual may not be typical of all friendships you observe, but your asking the "how" question leads you to looking (retrospectively, of course) for how one behavior meshes within the overall pattern of behaviors and thereby takes on meaning.

You might even go so far as to ask the participant *why* he hit the other person, and he would be likely to respond with "I don't know. We just do that whenever we haven't seen each other in a while." If you asked, "How did such a greeting get started?" he would be likely to respond, "I'm not sure; it just did. And we've been doing it ever since." In other words, it is not necessary for a thorough understanding of communication and relationship to know either the causes for relational behaviors or the individual meanings of those behaviors. You can gain a rather thorough understanding of any relationship, even of one in which you are a participant, by knowing how the behaviors are integrated with other behaviors to create the relationship. However, as later chapters will demonstrate, knowing how the intrapersonal communication systems operate, as well as how the interpersonal communication system operates, will provide an even deeper understanding of human relationships.

INTERPERSONAL COMMUNICATION AND COMMON SENSE

Some of the preceding discussion may be quite new to you. You may even disagree with some of it. Why? Because it doesn't "make sense" to you. After all, you already know a great deal about interpersonal communication. For one thing, you've had years of experience in this field. And years of experience with doing anything gives you some knowledge about it. Such knowledge, the kind gained from experience, is always worth more than "book knowledge" or "theory."

We usually refer to knowledge gained from experience as "common sense." It is acquired, consistent with a pragmatic view, from retrospectively making sense out of the experiences we have had. It is also called common sense because it is extremely "common." That is, such knowledge is widely believed; common sense is typical to a wide variety of people who believe it. In fact, we often refer to common sense when we begin a sentence with "Everybody knows that. . . ." Common sense is knowledge, to be sure. And it is often, but not necessarily, true. Common sense is powerful, too, not because it is true but because so many people believe it.

Nothing is particularly exceptional about commonsense knowledge, despite what we may think. Much of what we know as common sense is undoubtedly true; much is blatantly false. Some of it even contradicts other pieces of commonsense knowledge. The only remarkable thing about common sense is that we believe it so tenaciously and cling to our belief in it, sometimes in the face of overpowering evidence to the contrary. My reason for bringing up the topic of commonsense knowledge about human relationships is not to prove its truth or to disprove it. Rather, the purpose is to recognize what people *believe* to be true about human relationships and to understand how those beliefs function to affect how people form, develop, maintain, and terminate their relationships with one another.

The following is a partial listing of some commonsense "truths" concerning human relationships. I suspect that most of you will find these statements to make good sense:

1. Some people make friends easily; others don't.
2. Relationships vary widely and have different functions and purposes.
3. Some people possess qualities that make them more attractive to others.
4. You have to like yourself if others are going to like you.
5. Relationships (such as falling in love) just "happen" and don't require any special effort. They may happen even despite our efforts to resist them.
6. Liking and friendship are based on gut emotional reactions.
7. Good friends *really* communicate; people with relational problems talk but don't really communicate.
8a. People who have many things in common are more likely to become friends. (Birds of a feather flock together.)
8b. People who are very different from each other are more likely to become friends. (Opposites attract.)
9a. You are judged by the company you keep.
9b. You don't belong with that crowd; you're different.
10a. Absence makes the heart grow fonder.
10b. Out of sight, out of mind.

It would be a mistake to accept the above "truths" too literally. Each of the last three items (8, 9, and 10) includes statements that clearly contradict each other. Both "a" and "b" cannot be true; one of them must be false. On the other hand, item 2 doesn't seem to be very controversial at all. Who would deny that we all participate in many different relationships that are clearly dissimilar, and they certainly serve different functions for us. But remember that our use of commonsense "truths" about interpersonal communication is not to prove or disprove them but to realize that such "truths" are believed by most individuals who participate in social relationships and with whom we have relationships. To understand fully the phenomenon of interpersonal communication is to know how intrapersonal communication systems function to affect the interpersonal communication level (the subject of further discussion in Part Two of this book). And commonsense knowledge about human relationships is part of a typical person's intrapersonal system, at least in our culture.

One final word about commonsense knowledge: the effect that commonsense knowledge has on any given situation (including interpersonal communication situations) is hardly consistent. For one thing, we tend to explain away (to rationalize, to make sense of retrospectively) any instance that doesn't conform to common sense. We typically say, "It isn't true" or "That's just an exception to the rule" or "We don't know all the facts." Second, we also tend to use the same term to refer to different things. Take, for example, the relational term "friend." We use that same term to define many different kinds of relationships. For instance, we may use the term to define a close intimate relationship, as in "my best friend"; to define a relationship neither close nor intimate, as in "just a friend"; and to define a relationship denoted by interpersonal distance and rules of politeness, as in "I was just being friendly."

Hence, our commonsense knowledge about communication may or may not have a significant impact on how we participate in interpersonal communication. Perhaps the most significant impact of common sense is that it may get in the way of our participant-observer's understanding of the process of interpersonal communication. We should probably treat the commonsense knowledge that we already have about communication as something to be on the lookout for. If we recognize it as "merely common sense," it won't affect our understanding or the way we participate in interpersonal communication. If we assume that because it is common sense it must be true, we have taken a giant step backward in improving our interpersonal communication skills. From time to time in the following chapters, our discussions will point out some commonsense knowledge that gets in the way of our efforts to understand interpersonal communication.

As we shall soon discover, many of the terms used to describe interpersonal communication and interpersonal relationships are quite familiar and frequently used in our everyday speech. Because we use these terms so commonly to mean so many different things, their definitions just don't seem to "sit still." I shall attempt in subsequent chapters to be very careful about defining terms, so that I use them consistently and with the same meanings. For the most part, I will use a term as though it had a rather precise meaning. We should now be ready to embark on our exploration of interpersonal communication and human relationships.

PART 1

The Context of Communication

CHAPTER 2

The Nature of Context

A: A nice soft pillow filled up with down.
C: Up with down?
A: Certainly. See that pillow up there? It's down.
C: How can it be down if it's up there? . . .
A: That pillow is down, Costello. You get down off a duck's back.
C: That's a lie. I never even got up on a duck's back.
A: I didn't say you got up on a duck's back. I said you get down off a duck's back.
C: How can I get down off a duck if I never got on a duck?

> —Abbott and Costello discussing
> the nature of linguistic context

Several years ago the television networks aired a commercial which I remember as one of the most effective I have ever seen. It opened with an aerial view, ostensibly taken from a helicopter, of a huge parking lot surrounding a large factory-type warehouse. The grounds were filled with brand new trucks of all shapes, colors, and sizes—pickups, dump trucks, semis with trailers, ad infinitum. The viewer saw nothing but trucks and more trucks as the camera slowly circled the lot. The lines of trucks extended in every direction from the building in what appeared to be thousands, perhaps hundreds of thousands of trucks. As the impressive array of trucks unfolded before our eyes, the mellow voice of the announcer (which was audible above the "whap-whap" of helicopter rotors) related facts about the manufacturer of these trucks. We were told that one company and only one company had produced more trucks than General Motors, Dodge, Ford, Datsun, and every other truck manufacturing company combined; that despite day-to-day abuse of these trucks, an astonishing proportion (well over 90 percent, as I recall) were still in daily use even decades after they rolled off the assembly lines.

To say the least, my curiosity was aroused; I couldn't wait to discover who was making such outrageous claims for this product. As the camera pulled back (the helicopter supposedly increasing elevation), what should come into view but the foot and leg of a man (a studio technician) who towered over the trucks and the parking lot! Only then were we aware that the trucks were in miniature, the helicopter sounds were mere sound effects, and the commercial was on behalf of Tonka Toys!

That television commercial vividly represents the influence of the context on how one interprets the meaning of any phenomenon, object, or event. We are all aware of what it means to take something "out of context," lest we be guilty of misunderstanding. In one way, the advertisers who dreamed up the Tonka Toys commercial "cheated" the audience. They provided clues indicating a "false" context: the chopping background noise of helicopter blades and the slightly metallic amplification of the announcer's voice, simulating radio transmission. These clues led the viewer to believe that the TV camera was mounted in a helicopter rather than on a studio boom. The contextual clue of the normal-sized human being, which allowed the viewer to realize that the trucks were all toys, succeeded in "jarring" the viewer's interpretation with its abrupt shift of context. Only then did the viewers realize that they had "been had." The context is certainly a significant influence on how we interpret the meaning of any person, place, object, or event.

TYPES OF CONTEXT

Communication always and inevitably occurs within some context. And, like any interpretation, the meaning of communication (and hence the meaning of the relationship between people) is influenced by the context in which it occurs. But what precisely is the context of communication? A dictionary would tell us that the context is the environment, the physical surroundings of an event or object. But the physical surroundings are only part of the context. We already know that part of the context must include a social system (people) as well.

Generally speaking, we can probably think of context as being of two kinds: physical and social. A physical context includes physical objects and a social context includes people. Certainly, if something is included in the physical context of communication, it must be physically present when you are communicating. On the other hand, the social context may not be so easily observed. The physical context may include the U.S. flag standing in the corner or a *Time* magazine on the table. These are physical objects that are easily seen. Two people having a conversation in that physical context are also members of the social context of the American society and are subject to its influence, too. Remove the flag and magazine from the physical context and the social context of our national society remains, even though we may not be able to see it. An example might serve better to illustrate the nature of the physical and social contexts.

You are a student in a class dealing with interpersonal communication. This is your context, and it includes the room in which your class meets. If it is a typical classroom, it probably contains chairs with tablet-size arms on which to rest notebooks or textbooks. These chairs are probably not attached to the floor but arranged in rows and columns facing one end of the room. In the direction you are facing is probably a desk and chair and a chalkboard mounted on the wall. The instructor stands or sits at that end of the room and is the focal point of your visually directed attention. This classroom context strongly influences the communication, the relationship which occurs within its boundaries, often in subtle ways generally unnoticed but present nonetheless.

You will note that as a student, you are just another one of a group of people. And every member of the group of students has virtually the same orientation. You are all seated, facing the same direction, sitting on similar if not identical chairs, restricted in your actions, and submerged within a group identity of "audience." The instructor, however, is unique. The instructor has a desk and chair, may stand and roam the room, is the only person facing the other participants, has the power to control use of the chalkboard, may stand or sit behind the "barrier" of the desk, and can, from the standing position, "look down" on the seated audience. The context of the classroom itself clearly differentiates the instructor from the students (but not the students from one another).

Whether they choose to take advantage of it or not, instructors in traditional American classrooms are placed in a position of power. The physical context of the classroom itself identifies the instructor as having more power than the undifferentiated individuals in the group of students. The instructor stands; the students remain seated. The instructor can walk around; the students have only restricted movement. The instructor talks; the students listen. The instructor has a desk; the students have tablet-arm chairs. The instructor has a public chalkboard; the students have private notebooks. The physical context of the traditional classroom provides the instructor with a great deal of power. And as you well know, many instructors tend to exercise their classroom power with their actual behaviors, too.

Now the physical context doesn't "make" us behave in a certain way. The physical context of the classroom doesn't require that the instructor act like Julius Caesar. However, the physical context does provide us with a set of expectations which we often use to guide how we behave in the classroom. When you walk into a classroom on the first day, for example, do you sit at the desk or in one of the tablet-arm chairs? Why don't you stand at the front of the room and face the other people who are seated in chairs? But these are dumb questions. You know what the "rules" are on how to behave in the classroom. Well, some of those rules that guide your behavior come from the expectations you have about appropriate behavior on the basis of the physical context itself.

I once knew of a university instructor who broke the rules of the classroom context. On the first day of class he entered the classroom early and sat in one of the tablet-arm chairs. He wore casual clothes, often cutoffs and a T-shirt, and sat among the rest of the students until after the class bell had rung. After a few moments of grumbling by students about irresponsible instructors who were late for class, he walked to the front of the room and began lecturing as though nothing out of the ordinary had happened. The students were invariably shocked by this sudden reversal of roles, and nearly every one of them reacted negatively toward the instructor. I've lost track of this instructor in recent years, but I have always suspected that he may be producing television commercials for toy trucks!

The physical context of your classroom, described above, is but one aspect of your classroom environment. It comprises those cues that are available to your five senses (that is, what you see, hear, touch, smell, and taste). But your class also exists in a social context, which is made up of people. Your class exists, for example, within the context of the university. You are students, and your instructor is a member of the faculty of some college or university. The college itself is a part of the larger context of higher education. Your social role of student is a part of the culture of students within your college and higher education. Your course may be a part of a course of study in your major field or a course designed to liberalize your education beyond that of your major.

Your interpretation of and attitude toward this class is influenced by these elements of the social context. For example, students typically like courses in their major more than courses required to fulfill some liberal education requirement. Students typically like and elect to enroll in courses taught by instructors recommended by other students. I know I certainly did when I was a student, and I would wager money that your own student culture, with its active grapevine, is not significantly different. Furthermore, the social context of instructor and students and of students and students affects how you interpret the course content. Even though the physical context of the classrooms is similar, you undoubtedly feel closer to some instructors than to others. The degree to which you know and like other students in your class affects your assessment of the value of the course's subject matter. When you like the instructor and/or fellow students, you tend to feel that you learn more from that class. More importantly, you probably do learn more in a favorable social context.

These, then, are the two general types of contexts within which communication takes place: the physical context and the social context. The physical context exists as the physical surroundings in which the relationship takes place, while the social context comprises people rather than objects. Its influences are more subtle and reflect cultural or social beliefs, values, attitudes, norms, and roles. Moreover, you will typically communicate in only one physical context at a time (such as this particular classroom), but you are subject to the influences of several social contexts (your fellow students, your college, your social class, your national society, and so forth) at the same time.

LOCUS OF CONTEXTS

Sometimes, when one is attempting to understand *what* something is, it is valuable to know *where* that something is. In other words, knowing where to look for something is sometimes as important as knowing what to look for. The story is told of the drunk who was down on his hands and knees on the sidewalk under a street lamp, obviously searching for something. A passerby stopped and asked what he was looking for. The drunk replied, "I lost my keys and can't find them." The passerby, wanting to be helpful, fell to his hands and knees and joined in the search for the missing keys. After several minutes of fruitless hunting, the passerby asked, "Are you sure you lost your keys here?" "No," responded the drunk, "I dropped them in the alley back there." "Then why," the exasperated good Samaritan shouted, "are we looking for the keys on the sidewalk?" The innocent response: "Because there's more light over here."

The parable of the drunkard's search illustrates a number of important conceptual insights as well as an obvious and overlooked truism—that knowing what to look for won't help you find it unless you also know where to look. Because the physical context contains directly observable objects, the location of the physical context is

The social context of the relationship between this teacher and student consists of
"rules" for what is considered appropriate in their communication.
(Susan Lapides/Design Conceptions)

rarely a problem in interpersonal communication. But the social context contains
people and the influences of those people who make up a particular social system.
And those people are rarely physically present when interpersonal communication
takes place, even though their influences (cultural values, beliefs, norms, and so
forth) are certainly present when two people relate with each other.

The context of a relationship in the sense of a physical environment is easy to
find. The social context is often more difficult to locate. In a very real sense, it exists
outside the communicative event, outside the parameters of the relationship; but one
looks for the social context *within* each of the communicators. Therefore, the following
discussion of the location of contexts is generally concerned only with social contexts.

Each relational partner carries elements of the social context of the communicative
event into the relationship. As I stated previously, the students whose instructor
initially pretended to be a student resented his false role playing. Their expectations,
developed over years of experience in the culture of American education, separated
students from instructors. Upon entering a class, one is expected to perform in a
certain manner, as dictated by the cultural context of the American college. The
instructor violated those norms, and the students evaluated him negatively for having
done so. His students had apparently developed an "us and them" mentality regarding
students and faculty. Instructors were not meant to be privy to the private
conversations of students, especially those addressing the topic of tardy instructors.

Where does one look for the social context? Inside the heads of the participants
in the communicative event. A culture or society (and I'm using these two terms
almost interchangeably to refer to an organized social system), large or small, is not
so much a group of people as it is a set of norms, rules, expectations, stereotypes,

roles, attitudes, beliefs, and so forth that typify and serve to define that society. All these elements are essentially "rules"—ways of behaving or judging behavior as appropriate or inappropriate, good or bad, right or wrong. A member in good standing of any social system has learned and internalized them. In this way, one is said to be "socialized" into the society. And the society, at least in terms of its defining elements, is located in only one place: inside the heads of its individual members.

The social context, then, is located both outside the communicative event and inside the heads of the communicators. The social context really does exist in both places when you consider where one looks in order to find the context. Of course, the social norms and rules that each individual carries around are only representative of the larger social context, but cultures rarely write down their norms and beliefs in the form of a constitution and set of bylaws. Each culture relies on each generation to pass on to the next generation those standards. This passing on of the culture to new entrants is the process of socialization that keeps the culture alive and allows changes in cultural traditions and values over the course of several generations. When any two (or more) people are interacting with one another, their communicative relationship is always being influenced by the social as well as the physical context.

THE INFLUENCE OF CONTEXT

To say that the physical and social contexts influence communication occurring within their boundaries is to say little of the nature or direction of that influence. Sometimes the context serves to enhance the relationship—to help it along or to allow the communicative relationship to progress. Sometimes the context inhibits the relationship, keeps it from progressing, and actually functions to destroy the relationship. In other words, the context definitely influences communication, and that influence may be either constructive or destructive to the relationship.

To some extent the context always serves to *constrain* the participants in the communicative event. That is, the context serves to narrow down the number of potential interpretations that are available. For example, when you meet someone at a fraternity or sorority "mixer," you already know a number of things about that person (a college student, member of a Greek organization, similar age group) and about what interests you might have in common (value of education, social enjoyment, classes at the college, different majors, etc.). The constraints thus serve as guidelines to tell us how to act and what behavior is considered appropriate within that context. At times the guidelines serve to enhance development of the relationship; at other times they function to retard or even terminate relational development.

Now the term "constraints" may sound somehow "evil" or "bad." After all, as members of our democratic society, we have come to value freedom and individual choice. The idea of constraints is rather antagonistic to freedom of choice. But think of freedom of choice in the sense that you are at a loss as to what to do or how to act. You look for clues or hints that will provide you with some direction. It's like being lost in a wilderness area. That feeling of freedom of choice is that you are lost. You long for a map of the area that would constrain some of that freedom and allow you to find your way out of your predicament. Constraints that tend to enhance a relationship are like maps that tell you the correct or appropriate thing to do in a given context.

But constraints in the context can function in the interpersonal relationship either constructively or destructively. For example, a typical story line of a romantic novel involves an accidental and unsatisfying encounter as "boy meets girl" for the first time. Boy may collide with girl in a crowded department store, causing her to drop the packages she was carrying. Each is in a hurry to get somewhere and considers the other rude. Later they meet in a different context, perhaps "properly introduced" by a mutual friend at a party, and their love for each other blossoms. The first context was not conducive to continued communication; the other context enhanced it.

Some contextual constraints provide rather clear guidelines for what constitutes appropriate behavior within that context. The physical context of a classroom is a good example. Other contexts allow for fewer constraints and fewer guidelines as to what behavior is appropriate. What do you say to a high-pressure salesperson without appearing rude? This example comes readily to mind because of a recent personal experience. My wife and I consented to a sales presentation of a home-improvement product and quickly realized we had little interest in it. Nevertheless, we sat through *four hours* of the presentation before we finally convinced the salesman that we were definitely not planning to purchase his product. We functioned in this communicative situation under the constraints of a social system that governs "politeness" with strangers. The fundamental constraint, I guess, is that you just don't tell people who are guests in your home to leave. Thus, in order to conform to the constraints of "being polite to guests," we sat through an entire evening of a sales pitch. I am still embarrassed to admit that we made this gross error in judgment, but to this day I resent that salesman for ruining an entire evening for us—and a Friday evening, no less!

Generally speaking, the number and strength of the guidelines for determining appropriate behavior provided by contextual constraints depend on three factors: the participants' previous experience in a similar context, the amount of information the context provides about the other person, and the amount of similarity or difference between participants that is provided by the context. Let's begin with the first factor.

The number of experiences the participants have previously had in similar contexts provides guidelines for what behavior is appropriate. This constraint of past experiences, typically a positive influence, is a natural outcome of trial and error. As you gain experience in similar contexts, you come to learn which behaviors "work" and which do not. When the situation is new to you, you simply try some tactic, any tactic, because, in the absence of previously learned guidelines, you have no other choice. When the tactic doesn't work (error), you try another and then another. Eventually you discover some tactics that work for you and retain them for future reference. Your previous practice gained from trial and error allows you to select from your repertoire of behaviors those actions which have proved to be successful in the past.

Second, some contexts provide the participants with a considerable amount of information about each other. Two students in the same class, for example, know each other as students because of their context, and the conversational topics relevant to the student culture provide a rich source of information. On the other hand, two strangers meeting on a bus have little information about each other's identity from that context. They are likely to talk about the weather, the bus routes, or other highly general topics; more likely they won't talk at all. Have you ever noticed the fascination people in a crowded elevator have for the lighted floor numbers appearing above the elevator doors? These people certainly have little information about one another and really don't interact at all. In fact, there seems to be an unwritten rule that you just don't talk with other people when you ride an elevator. Staring at the numbers provides an excuse not to communicate.

Clearly, then, some contexts provide more information about fellow communicators than others. The extent to which the context allows the participants to recognize each other's similarities is often the extent to which the context serves to enhance the communicative relationship. The physical context of the classroom, you recall, serves to differentiate the students from the instructor and at the same time emphasizes the similarities among the students. Students are more likely to communicate with one another than with the instructor. Two strangers wearing similar occupational clothing (for example, three-piece suits) are more likely to interact on a bus than persons with dissimilar occupational clothing (for example, three-piece suit versus coveralls). A female is more likely to converse with a stranger who is also female, and a male is more likely to converse with another male. The context can never guarantee what will happen after a conversation begins, but without any communication, no relationship is likely to develop.

Some contexts not only provide little information about the similarities of the communicators but actually involve people who are quite different from each other. The context of intercultural communication is an area of great interest for some students and scholars of human communication. This context, in which a member of one culture interacts with a member of a different culture, is one that maximizes the differences between communicative participants and creates special problems for communication. Some cultures are extremely different from each other. The greater the differences between the communicators' cultures, the fewer the number of guidelines for deciding what behaviors are appropriate. When a member of an Oriental culture (for example Japanese) interacts with a member of an Occidental culture (for example, American), the intercultural context involves extreme differences and few similarities. Communication in such a context would be much more difficult than, say, a context involving an American and an Australian.

The context of communication between members of vastly different cultures is really not of major importance to our discussions of interpersonal communication. However, contexts that emphasize differences of the communicators (similar to intercultural communication) are quite significant. In our discussions in succeeding chapters, we will be quite conscious of subcultural differences (communication between members of groups within the same national culture) that affect human communication. Typically, subcultural differences are conceived as having a destructive effect on the relationship and commonly thought of as a communication "gap" between generations, races, statuses, sexes, and so forth. The so-called gap, however, is a contextual influence and not actually part of communication itself. More on that later.

Summary

The context, we must remember, is not actually a part of human communication. Neither the physical context (the setting or environment in which people communicate) nor the social context (the society or cultural membership of the participants) is a part of the relationship between individual communicators. Examples of individuals who have overcome the negative constraints of the context abound. Recall that Romeo and Juliet developed a rather intimate interpersonal relationship despite the negative constraints of the family context—the feud between the Capulets and the Montagues. But these examples do not deny the fact that both types of context, physical and social, may influence the communication that occurs within their boundaries.

The physical context consists of the objects in the setting and other factors external to the participants and available to the senses. That is, elements of the physical context include anything that the communicators can see, hear, smell, touch, and taste. On the other hand, the social context of communication includes the larger societies or cultures to which each participant belongs and that exist within the individuals themselves. As such, the social context is not immediately available to the senses but is internalized, existing within the heads of the communicators in the form of social norms, rules, values, roles, expectations, stereotypes, beliefs, and so on.

The context, both physical and social elements, serves to constrain the actions of the communicators within a given relationship. Constraints function to reduce the number of possible interpretations available to each participant and thus to reduce the communicator's uncertainty about what courses of action are appropriate within that context. These constraints may serve to affect the relationship by exerting either a constructive (enhancing further development) or destructive (inhibiting further development) influence on the communication. Factors of contextual influence that allow the participant to judge the degree of appropriateness of potential communicative behaviors include the amount of previous experience participants have acquired in similar contexts, the amount of information about the other person available in the context, and the degree of similarity or difference among the participants that is available in the context.

The following three chapters of Part 1 discuss elements of the different types of context and precisely how they influence the process of interpersonal communication. Chapter 3 discusses elements of the physical context, and Chapter 4 discusses elements of the social context.

Because this book is limited to the English-speaking culture (typically American) and because language is such a pervasive influence on communication, Chapter 6 is devoted to the context of language. Of course, language is one of the elements of the social context, even though, like elements of the physical context, much of language is available to the senses. We see and hear people use language, and we see and hear nonverbal aspects of language as it functions in human communication. Language remains, however, a product and a major ingredient of the social context. Human communication may be considered as an exchange between persons, not unlike an economic exchange of buying/selling or bartering. Language is thus the "currency" of that exchange. It embodies a specialized form of social meanings within it, even though we are quite unaware of much of this influence of the social context on our interpretations of meaning. The contextual influence of language is so significant that it is deemed worthy of a chapter by itself.

CHAPTER 3

The Physical Context

"Fried fish tonight, dear?" "I thought Harry gave up cigars."

—Comments on their physical context made by arriving guests, from a TV commercial promoting a room deodorizer

In our society we use the term *communication* to refer to a wide variety of phenomena— from people talking with one another to satellite technology to computers linked together in a network. To cover such a variety of applications, we have devised literally hundreds of definitions of "communication." Even though we are concerned only with human communication in interpersonal relationships, the number of such definitions remains large. Perhaps the most general one of which I am aware is that which defines communication as "the adaptive response of an organism to its environment." This definition includes three terms essential to communication: "organism," "adaptive response," and "environment."

Now this definition of communication is not precisely about interpersonal communication. However, it does focus on the topic of this chapter—the physical context of interpersonal communication. In the first two chapters we discussed the fact that the context (both physical and social) may influence the process of communication between two persons who happen to be located in it. But in order for us to understand how the physical context can influence interpersonal communication, we need to understand these three terms—"organism," "adaptive response," and "environment"—more clearly.

This chapter begins with a discussion of the nature of the human organism. After all, we aren't concerned so much with computers talking with one another as we are with people engaged in developing human relationships. Unlike other organisms, though, humans have adaptive responses to their environment that are just a bit more sophisticated than those of, say, rats or guinea pigs. After all, we like to think of ourselves as a "higher" form of animal life. The environment that is our concern in this chapter is the physical context, so our discussions will include a more precise description of the elements that are contained in that environment. The chapter concludes with a discussion of specific functions of the physical context that affect the process of interpersonal communication.

THE HUMAN ORGANISM

Most, if not all, organisms on the face of this planet surely engage in some form of communication (at least according to the general definition of an "adaptive response to its environment"). As humans, we tend to think that we are better at it, though. And in point of fact we are. Some biologists have suggested that one reason for our superior skill in communication is because of our brain—certainly not in its size but in its development. Without delving into a discussion of neurophysiology, about which I admit I know very little, we do know that the human organism is much more adept at a variety of extremely sophisticated maneuvers. Moreover, these skills are important to us when it comes to making adaptive responses to our environment. Although the total number of human cognitive skills is much larger than this, we will discuss only two of them at this point: sensemaking and self-reflection.

Sensemaking

In Chapter 2 we introduced the notion of *sensemaking*. In the chapters that follow, this topic will continue to be discussed. It is an extremely vital part of human communication and, for that matter, of the process of everyday living. Human sensemaking is, simply put, the ability to discover meaning whenever and wherever you are. Another way of saying it is that sensemaking is the ability to make sense out of anything, even nonsense.

As a human being, you absolutely can't stand being confused. What does confusion mean? Basically, it means that you aren't sure what something means. You acquire something through your five senses. That is, you hear something, you see something, you smell something, you touch something, you taste something. Your first reaction is to "make sense" of the things that you acquire through your senses. The two guests in the TV commercial quoted at the beginning of this chapter are certainly exercising their sensemaking ability. Each of them smelled something upon entering the new environment (the living room of a home), made sense of these smells (as frying fish and cigar smoke), and proceeded to comment on the results of that sensemaking.

In the commercial, the hostess immediately went to the store in search of the ideal deodorizing product which, by some strange coincidence, turned out to be the product being advertised. In doing so, she "made sense" of what she heard her guests say and responded on the basis of that sense. A more appropriate response might have been to show these two paragons of social rudeness the front door.

Human beings possess a remarkable ability (perhaps even need) to reduce their uncertainty and confusion by making sense of any environment in which they find themselves. We take in information available to us in the environment, interpret that information in terms of what it means for our own actions in regard to that environment, and adapt our behaviors accordingly. No other creature on this earth possesses such a refined sensemaking skill.

Self-Reflection

We all know that every individual possesses a self—that unique personality which "belongs to" each individual and renders every human being different from every other. Nonhuman organisms may have a unique self-identity, too. But only a human has developed the ability to reflect upon his or her own self and behave accordingly. In one sense, this ability implies that humans possess a broad streak of selfishness. We see the environment not so much as it *is* but in terms of how we can use it for our own selfish interests. We make sense of our environment in terms of what it means for us. If the environment is not conducive to our own needs and desires, we change it. From the first pioneer who cut down trees in the forest to build a log cabin and the first buffalo hunter who killed for sport, this selfish attitude of humans toward their environment has resulted in irrevocable harm to our own surroundings. Even though human sensemaking ability has achieved a remarkable level of development, the human weakness of self-interest sometimes works to our detriment.

On a personal scale, though, the human attributes of sensemaking and self-reflection constitute a normal and taken-for-granted characteristic of day-to-day existence. Think of your first day of high school or college. You wondered not so much about other people or the school but more about how you yourself would fit in. As you heard your instructor expound upon the values and requirements of this course, your first reaction was probably "What is this course going to do for me?" It shouldn't be particularly embarrassing to admit that you have often taken a required course and thought it was a waste of time. You felt that you weren't able to "do anything" with it. You may have chosen your major on the basis of what you could do with it in order to earn a living upon graduation. These thoughts do not make you a bad person; you are merely behaving normally and exercising that remarkable ability possessed by all humans—sensemaking, combined with a healthy dose of selfishness (an integral part of self-reflection).

The same two human attributes are at work whenever the physical context enters into the process of human communication as a potential influence. When the physical context of human interaction is familiar, either because you have been there or in similar places before, you make sense of your environment immediately and without any conscious effort. Your prior experiences involved earlier sensemaking, the residues of which remain in your memory. Upon entering an unfamiliar or new environment, however, you find yourself in the position of making sense of it and adapting to it as a process of learning something new.

This chapter attempts to make clear what we all probably know from our everyday experiences. In fact, much of education is understanding what we already know but don't think about in any direct manner. Some parts of the chapter, however, may involve aspects of our communicative behavior which are less well known to us, at least in terms of how we influence and are influenced by our physical context. But although they may be subtle, they are nonetheless sometimes highly significant influences on ourselves and on our relationships.

ADAPTIVE RESPONSES

During the past few decades the conservationist and environmental movement has added a word new to the vocabulary of most of us—*ecology*. The word itself is often confused with the mere environment: with forests, national parks, air quality, whales, baby seals, eagles, and so forth. But ecology is a more precise field of study in biology and sociology and deals not with the environment (that is, the physical context) alone but with the *relations* between living organisms (most notably, humans) and their environments. And that is the more important issue in this chapter: elements of the physical context do not influence humans so much as humans respond adaptively to their environment. Because humans possess sensemaking and self-reflective abilities, our behavior within an environment is quite different from that of other organisms.

Proactive Responses

One way to describe this difference between humans and nonhumans is to note the difference between *proactive* and *reactive* adaptations to the environment. Humans are proactive and other organisms are reactive. Humans "act toward" their environment; other organisms "react to" their environment. It has been said, for example, that "Cheese is cheese, and that's why mousetraps work." In other words, a mouse sees and smells cheese, recognizes it as food, and proceeds to eat it. A human would also recognize the cheese as food but would see the danger involved in attempting to eat it. The mere presence of some sensory stimulus (for example, some visual image, some audible sound, some recognizable odor) does not "cause" the human, as a "proactive" creature to respond in some way. Humans rarely just *react* to an environmental stimulus. Humans acquire stimuli through their senses, make sense of the stimuli, and then act on the basis of what the stimuli mean to them. Humans do not act as a result of the stimuli; they act toward the stimuli.

An analogy may best explain this difference between a reactive and proactive model of human behavior. Some people have claimed that, theoretically, a chimpanzee can be taught the mechanical skills of operating an automobile and can even learn to stay in the right-hand lane, to stop at red lights, and to go on green lights. But the chimpanzee is, generally speaking, a reactive creature. When the traffic light changes to green, the chimpanzee goes—*re*acting to the "green means go" signal. The human, however, will not go when the light changes to green if the intersection is clogged with a traffic jam. The human is *pro*active and acts on the basis of sensemaking in the form of "If I go, I will smash into those autos in the intersection, and I might hurt myself."

As you read about the elements of the physical context (and of the social context as well), keep in mind that the human is a proactive being. The context, either physical or social, does not "cause" you to act in any certain way. As a human communicator, you are a sensemaking creature engaged in seeking out ways to act appropriately within any given context. You act toward that context and adapt your behaviors to it on the basis of your having made sense of it. The context is not simply your environment but a situation in which you must find your own way. This is the principle of ecology and of proactivity.

Environmental Interactionism

There are fundamentally two ways in which humans can adapt to their environment: determinism and interactionism. These two views of environmental effects correspond roughly to reactive and proactive responses. According to a deterministic explanation, the environment contains numerous stimuli that channel the perceptual responses of humans within that environment in a specific direction. Stated another way, aspects of the physical context influence the behaviors and perceptions of humans, perhaps without their conscious awareness, who are exposed to them.

On the other hand, an interactional view suggests that humans create or control their environment as much as they are influenced by it. In environmental interactionism, the meaning of the physical context is socially created or defined by humans in their actions toward and within that environment. Determinists believe that the meaning of the physical context resides in the factors or stimuli that are available in the environment itself.

It is sometimes difficult to resist the simplicity of the explanation offered by environmental determinism. We can easily find examples from our past experience of how an environment has "determined" our behaviors. Walk into a church, and assess your own feelings of what constitutes appropriate behavior. You speak quietly, if at all, and wouldn't dream of (as an example) running down the aisles or jumping up and down on a pew. In terms of mass communication, many people believe that TV and magazine advertising works on our subconscious and leads us to buy the product because of those hidden appeals.

Whether its influence on humans is deterministic or interactional (as we are arguing here), many people in our society do respect the power of the physical context. A chain of national restaurants recently remodeled its decor and changed from rows of garishly colored plastic-and-chrome booths to individualized booths separated by privacy screens of naturally finished oak. Hanging from the ceilings in the redecorated restaurants is a multitude of leafy plants. The harsh ceiling lights were lowered and softened, with a light positioned over each booth, giving the overall effect of subdued lighting. Overnight, these restaurants changed their image going from plastic artificiality to coziness, intimacy, and cheer. I doubt that the menu changed significantly, but the food somehow seemed to taste better too.

Now advertising agencies may believe in environmental determinism, but environmental interactionism is undoubtedly a more accurate explanation for understanding the proactive adaptive responses of humans to their physical context. Particularly in terms of their communicative behavior, humans typically define their environment on the basis of their activities within it. A friend of mine, an architect, has told me repeatedly that the first thing he wants to find out about a new building project is what people are supposed to be *doing* in it. Then he tries to design a physical context that is conducive to those activities. He doesn't believe that the environment he designs will determine anyone's behaviors, but he fervently believes the environment can serve to assist the activities that serve to define the environment for the actors.

The point of view underlying this chapter, then, is the interactionally based explanation of the environment and behavior. People's actions create the social meaning of their environment; that is, the environment is defined by the people who act toward it and among themselves. If your conversation with "that special someone" is likely to be important and intimate, you search for an environment that is conducive to this interactional purpose. But even if it isn't, you may define the environment as

Figure 3.1 Two Contrasting Restaurant Scenes

being special if a special communicational event took place there. When I was dating the woman who later became my wife, we first kissed in the front seat of my old Dodge. The physical context was a rather busy intersection in a downtown metropolitan area. However, for us, that place was very special and even intimate.

ELEMENTS OF THE PHYSICAL CONTEXT

Generally speaking, three elements make up the physical context that humans define interactionally: design, decoration, and other people. Design features comprise those elements that are "built into" the setting. Elements of the interior design of a room, for instance, include its size, shape, lighting, soundproofing, placement and shape of doors and windows, and ceiling height. The decoration features typically include those elements that can easily be manipulated or changed; they are not permanent. Such features might include the furniture (size, number, color, texture, placement), wall coverings, pictures, window treatments, floor coverings, room accessories, color, and virtually anything that comes under the heading of room furnishings. The physical context also includes other people, in the sense that the mere presence or absence of others, the number of people present, their proximity to one another, the amount of crowding, and so forth are as much a part of the physical context as the inanimate objects.

Various combinations of these three factors of design, decoration, and people make up the physical context which is, in turn, defined by the human interactions. Compare the two pictures in Figure 3–1. Both photographs depict dining places in a public restaurant, but the physical contexts differ considerably. The photo on the left indicates a private and cozy rendezvous for intimate dining and conversation. The lighting is subdued and falls just on this table; the table is well separated from the others; the tablecloth and candle contribute to an ambience for private conversation. The appearance of a waiter would probably seem to be an intrusion on its privacy.

The photograph on the right suggests a dining environment that differs considerably in the three elements of the physical context. The booth doesn't allow for discretionary movement of furniture, the lighting is overly bright, and people sitting in adjacent booths encroach on one another's privacy. The hard plastic tops of the table and benches contribute to this feeling of harshness. Any conversation in such a setting is likely to be much more formal, much less intimate than the interaction of the people at the table in the first photograph.

Now I don't mean to imply that the settings illustrated in Figure 3–1 will "determine" the conversations that take place in them. In fact, other factors (such as the already developed relationship between the communicators) are undoubtedly more important than the physical context (design, decoration, and other people). Further, the two people in the "intimate" setting may actually want some excitement, frivolity, and gregarious fun. They would then find this setting inappropriate for those interactional functions and might find the physical context of the second picture more appropriate. For purposes of interpersonal communication, the idea is to match the physical context with the purpose of the interaction. Two reunited lovers who greet each other in a very intimate and highly personal manner in a crowded airline terminal are undoubtedly behaving inappropriately in this public setting. But in the comparative privacy of their car, parked in a quiet place, the situation is quite different.

The point is not that the physical context "causes" people to behave in a certain way but rather that it may encourage and be well suited to certain actions that people wish to perform. And this is the point made by my architect friend. The designer of a building attempts to discover what the "normal" interactional activities of the occupants are likely to be and then tries to provide a physical setting that is compatible with those activities. Stated from the perspective of the social actors, the couple wanting an intimate and private dining experience would be more likely to choose the physical context that encourages and is compatible with their communicational purpose.

Perceptions of "Friendly" Rooms

One persistent problem that pops up again and again as one attempts to understand more fully the process of interpersonal communication is the frequent difference between what people *do* and what they *perceive*. This problem will come back to haunt us in later chapters as well. In terms of the influence of the physical context on interpersonal communication, though, the difference between perceptions and behaviors is very apparent. Everyone notices the physical context and, through their sensemaking ability, evaluates that context as "good or bad," "friendly or unfriendly." Whether they behave any differently when engaged in interpersonal communication in these rooms, however, is a matter of some dispute. Humans often think that they behave differently when, in fact, they really don't. Apparently the physical context is a highly significant influence on communicators' *perceptions* of what they do but much less significant in influencing their actual behavior when communicating. In this section we'll be discussing how the physical context influences how people perceive their environments.

Two social psychologists, Maslow and Mintz, conducted some research in 1956 by observing people's reactions to "beautiful" and "ugly" rooms. They created rooms that differed in terms of size, color, illumination, furnishings, and accessories, so that the aesthetic surroundings could be classified as beautiful or ugly. They assigned subjects either to a beautiful or an ugly room, and they asked these subjects to rate pictures of people's faces. Their findings indicated that people tended to *perceive* significantly higher levels of "energy" and "well-being" in the faces when assigned to the beautiful room than they did in the same faces when they performed the ratings in the ugly room. Mintz (1956) conducted some follow-up research to determine whether these reactions were short or long term. He observed people's reactions for a period of three weeks and found that ratings performed in the beautiful room continued to be higher for the duration of the study.

More recent research by Kitchens, Herron, and Behnke (1976) had a similar purpose. These communication researchers observed conversations between people placed in rooms that differed in attractiveness in terms of color, furniture, and accessories. They found that people in the more aesthetically pleasant rooms tended to like their conversational partners more than did those in the unattractive rooms. These findings tend to support Maslow and Mintz's inference that some rooms are "friendlier" than others. That is, other things being equal, some physical contexts tend to encourage more positive interpersonal reactions.

What elements of the physical context make some rooms "friendlier" than others? I'm not sure anyone can provide a definitive answer to that question, but some characteristics are probably worthy of note. Color, for example, seems to be one of the more important decorative features. Overly bright or harsh colors would probably not contribute to the friendly atmosphere of a room. The colors of a friendly room would also be coordinated with the colors of the furniture and other room accessories rather than clashing with them in stark contrast. A similar statement could probably be made for texture, in that the glossy finish of some wall coverings or furniture (such as polyvinylchloride—PVC, that hard, shiny plastic) seems less friendly than the rougher or softer textures of satin-finished woods and pile carpets. Again, vivid contrasts of textures, like colors, would probably not characterize a friendly room.

Indirect lighting or modulated lighting is probably another characteristic of a friendly room. Although it was mentioned previously as a design feature, lighting in the form of floor lamps, table lamps, hanging lamps, and candles is also an easily manipulated decorative feature. Other room accessories can add to the friendly atmosphere: pictures on the wall, throw pillows on the couch, floral arrangements on the coffee table, magazines casually strewn on the end table and pleasant window treatments. A friend of mine has a sunken pit in his living room. The focal point of this pit is a freestanding fireplace with a chimney pipe that rises dramatically about 20 feet to the vaulted ceiling. He has no furniture near the pit, but he has strewn the area with a collection of soft pillows of all shapes and sizes. Your first reaction is to want to lie down on the floor and sink into one of those huge overstuffed pillows. His living room seems *very* friendly.

Another characteristic of friendly rooms concerns the spacing and arrangement of potential communicators, as symbolized in the arrangement of furniture. Furniture can be arranged in a manner that maximizes people's opportunities to communicate with one another. Interior designers have come to call such an arrangement "conversational seating." Later in this chapter, we'll say more about how we use space in interpersonal communication.

The point here is that the three elements of the physical context (design, decoration, and people) can be varied to produce an atmosphere that encourages interpersonal attraction and favorable perceptions of other people. In other words, the physical context can be manipulated so that people perceive that they are surrounded by an atmosphere of friendliness—hence, the "friendly room."

Communicative Behavior and "Friendly" Rooms

It's quite clear that people perceive some rooms as friendlier than others. It is equally clear that they perceive their interactions in such rooms to be "friendlier" as well. The question that remains is whether humans' perceptions of their communication is consistent with their actual communicative behavior. A few years ago I was the advisor of a graduate student who developed an interest in how and whether physical contexts influence interpersonal communication. After reading extensively the research evidence associated with this topic (such as the studies discussed above), she discovered that nearly all studies had observed the influence of the physical context on how humans *perceive* their environment and each other, and a few studies attempted to observe some isolated factors often associated with human communication (such as interpersonal attraction and number of messages sent and received). But she found no study that sought to observe the impact of the environment on how humans actually communicate with one another in normal conversation.

Sue Pendell (1976) conducted her own study by placing groups of three individuals in three different rooms that varied in terms of interior design and decoration. The three rooms were virtually identical in size, but they differed in the design feature of shape (rectangular, square, and oval). She then decorated the rooms to provide varying degrees of aesthetic appeal, with bare walls and institutional metal folding chairs at one extreme and pleasant wall coverings and modern, comfortable chairs at the other. In a burst of creativity, she designated the three levels of decoration as "rasty," "mediocre," and "classy." She then directly observed the interactive behaviors, the communication, of these three-person groups as they discussed a subjective problem-solving exercise. After their discussions, she asked them individually whether they noticed their physical context and whether they felt it influenced their conversations.

Pendell found that the communicators definitely "made sense of" both the design and decorative features of the rooms in which they interacted. This result is not particularly surprising. (Have you ever been in an oval room? It really looks strange. And let me assure you that the "rasty" rooms were *really* rasty!) Furthermore, the people generally perceived that the environment did influence their conversations, although they didn't feel that the degree of influence was necessarily great. The surprising result of Pendell's research concerned the actual influence of interior design and decoration on interpersonal communication. In every comparison she made, Pendell was unable to find even the slightest trace of difference in the communication conducted in the different rooms. The people in the oval room interacted about the same way as those in the square or rectangular rooms. People in the classy room communicated in about the same way as those in the rasty room or in any other kind of room.

So what did Pendell conclude? Apparently people notice the design and decoration features of their physical contexts. They may even think that the environmental stimuli influence their interpersonal communication. Despite these perceptions, however, people apparently communicate in a similar manner (at least when they have similar reasons for engaging in communication) regardless of the physical context in which they find themselves.

What, then, do we make of this rather confusing difference between perceptions of the physical context and communicative behaviors? On the one hand, we know that humans have very active sensemaking abilities. They are certainly aware of their physical contexts and may even perceive their own behaviors and reactions to (or judgments of) other people differently on the basis of their environments. But when it comes to the question of whether humans actually communicate differently in different settings, the influence of the environment is apparently minimal.

But don't our perceptions influence our behavior in interpersonal communication? Common sense would tell us that we typically behave on the basis of what we perceive. Certainly what we perceive and how we perceive it must be important to interpersonal communication. And they are. But we need to be reminded once more that commonsense knowledge tends to simplify what is really much more complex. Apparently our perceptions are an influence, but not as strong an influence on how we communicate as we might think. Discussions in virtually every chapter in Part 2 and Part 3 of this book will continue to emphasize this point.

We can make one final observation concerning this discussion, an observation that will appear in more detailed discussion in Part 2. People's perceptions of objects and other people differ considerably. What some people perceive as a "messy" room, for instance, may be seen by others as "natural" or "lived in." Conversely, a "neat" room may also be perceived as "plastic" or "sterile." Now this information probably does not come as a great shock to anyone with normal intelligence and even a minimum of social experience. What may be surprising, and infinitely more important, is the fact that what people *perceive* and what they *do* are often considerably different too. That is, our perceptions are not as closely linked to our behaviors as we might think. Moreover, what we perceive or think we do and what we actually do are often quite different. That is, our perceptions of our behaviors and our actual behaviors are often not closely linked.

COMMUNICATIVE FUNCTIONS OF THE PHYSICAL SETTING

At this point in our discussion, we already suspect that the extent of the physical context's influence on communicative behavior may not be as great as we might have thought. But the more important issue is not *how much* the physical context affects communication but, rather *how* and *in what way* communication functions within a given physical context. In fact, we often make the mistake of attempting to explain what we don't understand by searching for "causes" of what we then consider to be "effects" or outcomes. We can, for instance, change our question from "How much does the physical context affect communication?" to "How do people communicate with each other in regard to certain aspects of their physical context?" In doing so, we switch the emphasis from a cause-effect explanation to an attempt to understand the environmental interaction between physical contexts and human communication.

Recall that humans are proactive creatures and act toward environments in order to create their meanings. That is, you create the meaning of your environment on the basis of your actions within it. For example, family members usually consider the family room as a much more intimate context. They watch TV, have conversations, and relax in that room. The living room is more formal. That's the room in which the family entertains guests. Human beings are proactive and come to understand their physical environment in terms of the actions they perform within it. At this point in our discussion, we need to understand just how humans use their environment—that is, how they function communicatively in regard to their physical context.

The Function of Space

Not too many years ago it was quite fashionable to compare the behavior of other animals with that of humans and, by analogy, to discover alleged insights into our own behavior. Biologist Robert Ardrey (1970) wrote several best-selling books on the topic of animal-human comparisons and reflected the popular interest in, among other things, the concept of "territoriality." According to this principle, animals stake out geographical areas to which they claim ownership. Even household pets will exercise territoriality and challenge any intruders, such as other dogs or cats or humans, who don't "belong." The proliferation of "No Trespassing" signs along the highways demonstrates the human propensity for exercising similar territorial rights and the principle of property ownership.

Territoriality is a principle based on distance. Think of a wild animal surrounded by a series of ever-increasing concentric circles, with the animal at the point of radius or the bullseye of the target. An intruder who enters the outer circle captures the attention of the animal, who becomes wary. The intruder enters the next inner circle, and the animal probably growls a warning. He enters the next circle, and the animal takes flight. Finally, as he gets too close, inside the innermost circle, the animal attacks. Edward T. Hall (1966) adapted the principle of territorial distance to humans and postulated four concentric circles, which he characterized as progressively closer degrees of interpersonal relationship: public distance (12 feet and more), social distance (4 feet to 12 feet), personal distance (1½ feet to 4 feet), and intimate distance (0 to 1½ feet). The assumption is, one might guess, that the person who intruded into the zone of intimate distance but was not an intimate partner would be the object of attack by the human animal.

We must, however, guard against the natural tendency to accept too uncritically the analogy between human and animal behavior. One is easily seduced by such territorial explanations of animals transferred to explanations of human behavior.

We are all aware of our own territorial behaviors in a library, for instance, when we place "markers" (books, backpacks, etc.) of our territory's boundaries on the long table. We apparently do so in order to discourage other library patrons from sitting too close to us. Laboratory research has also shown that when rats are overcrowded in their cages, they develop what has come to be called "behavioral sink"—abnormal and socially disruptive behavioral patterns such as physical aggression, abnormal violence during mating, and destruction of kinship units.

Watchers of human societies are quick to transfer this explanation to human overcrowding in urban tenements because of their high incidence of rapes and violent crimes, family disintegration, drug abuse, and other antisocial behaviors. Certainly overcrowding may be a factor that contributes to urban violence, but many other sociological, psychological, and economic factors also contribute to urban problems. Human behavior, unlike the behavior of other animals, is much more complex and not to be understood by way of an overly simple explanation.

One problem of assigning the "territorial imperative" to humans is that it defines space only in terms of mere distance and then compounds the problem by interpreting distance negatively. The person feels "violated," then, if the nonintimate other enters the zone of intimate distance. But we humans are remarkably adaptive animals. We often experience total strangers within this intimate distance and think little of it. When we go to a movie theater, the person sitting in the next seat (only millimeters away) is likely to be a total stranger, but we don't feel "violated" (although we may "fight" with the stranger over who gets to use the single arm rest). When we enter a crowded elevator, we are often actually touching total strangers; but we don't feel that we need to attack them. Of course, we usually stand perfectly straight and keep our arms close to our bodies, but we "make sense" of the situation and adapt our behaviors accordingly without particularly feeling the negative imperative of territorial distance.

Scholars involved in the study of nonverbal behavior have coined the term "proxemics" to denote the use of space in human interaction. One concept of proxemics, relevant to our present discussion, is "personal space." Personal space is probably the human equivalent of territoriality, but it doesn't function solely as a matter of distance. When humans use space, the most important characteristic is not mere distance (as in territoriality). Rather, personal space is more like a "bubble" around each of us, which we carry around with us as we move. But the bubble analogy is not totally accurate. For one thing, the size of our bubble varies with the situation. It is probably rather large when camping in a wilderness area; we resent the intrusion of any other camper, even one who may be hundreds of yards away. The bubble is very small, virtually nonexistent, in the crowded elevator. Moreover, the bubble is not really round, either, but is much larger directly in front of us and quite small behind us.

In point of fact, the term "proxemics" is probably unfortunate. It implies that the key factor in how space functions in human interaction is proximity—how near you are to another person in terms of distance. But studies have consistently demonstrated that mere distance is not what "personal space" is about and, further, is not particularly significant to interpersonal communication. The more relevant attribute of how humans use their personal space is *accessibility*. A classic social psychological study of married-student housing on a university campus by Festinger, Schachter, and Back (1950) may have been the first clue that accessibility, rather than proximity or distance, was the key to understanding how space functions in human interaction.

These researchers asked residents of housing units to name those neighbors whom they knew best and with whom they had developed friendly relationships. Not surprisingly, they discovered that most friendship choices involved residents in the same or nearby buildings. But unexpectedly, perhaps, friends did not always live in the nearest apartment units. When they looked more closely at the design of the buildings, they discovered that friends consistently shared the same mailbox location or the same set of stairs or other common meeting places. The friends consistently had more interpersonal contact with each other. Even though other people might have lived physically closer by, they were actually less accessible and did not offer as many opportunities for interaction. The conclusion of this research is that people's accessibility to each other, the opportunity for interpersonal communication, is the influential factor of personal space.

Robert Sommer (1969) discovered a similar phenomenon when he observed people's choices of seating arrangements around a rectangular table (see Figure 3-2 on p. 44). He found that people tend to choose different arrangements on the basis of their purpose for interaction. For conversations, people chose to sit diagonally with the other person (A with B or F, D with C or E) or directly across from each other (B with F, C with E). Such seating positions provide maximum accessibility in the sense that the conversational partners are easily within one another's visual fields. Arrangements similar to these would be consistent with "conversational seating," discussed earlier.

When interacting with another individual in cooperative behavior, as when two students study for the same exam, the partners choose to sit side by side. Such an arrangement allows them to be "on the same side," if I may engage in a play on words, but the cooperating member does not "intrude" on the other's field of vision and distract the other's attention from studying. The seating arrangement for coaction (independent and parallel activities, as when two students study for different exams) involves seating choices that are the least "accessible" to interaction. People sitting in positions B and E or in C and F do not intrude on each other's line of sight, nor are they in very close proximity.

On the other hand, you will note that the seats at the ends of the table, even though they are separated by a greater physical distance, are more visually accessible to one another and therefore less preferred. Coactive behaviors involve a seating arrangement with the least amount of mutual accessibility. Of course, unlike conversation, coaction requires a minimum of interaction between the participants. Clearly, the most important factor relevant to personal space is acccessibility, not mere proximity.

How humans use space during interpersonal communication is also influenced by a variety of other factors. Some of these are primarily relevant to the social context but deserve mention here because they also deal with the physical context of space. For example, anthropologists are quick to point out that different cultures use space differently. Italians, for example, are said to stand closer than Americans when they

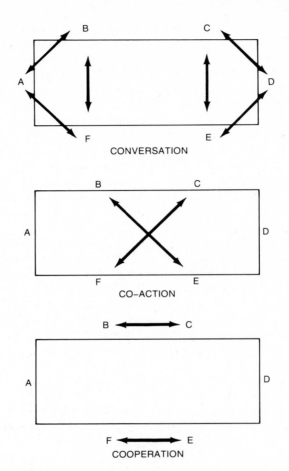

Figure 3-2. Seating Arrangements and Communication Purposes

converse with each other. But subcultural differences among people within our own country also abound. I recall a friend, originally from Louisiana, who always spoke to me at a much closer range than that to which I had become accustomed in the upper Midwest. I always had the feeling that I was leaning over backward whenever I had a conversation with her.

There is also some reason to believe that males differ from females in their use of personal space. Some research evidence (for example, Heshka & Nelson, 1974; Rosegrant & McCroskey, 1975) suggests that females in our culture tend to have a smaller zone of personal space than do males. I urge you to be skeptical, though, of allegations of behavioral differences between males and females in our culture.

The reason typically suggested for behavioral differences between males and females is the existence of sex-role stereotypes in our society. However, these stereotypes are slowly but surely changing as the women's movement influences our cultural myths. Furthermore, most of the research has relied on perceptions of both observers and observed, and the results of those perceptions are apt to be influenced more by expectations, based on the sex-role stereotypes, than by the actual behaviors—another area in which perceptions and behaviors differ. Women, according to our social stereotypes, are more socially oriented than men; therefore, we tend to "perceive" their personal space as smaller. However, no research has established any link between the possession of certain anatomical attributes or hormones and interactive behaviors.

Other factors have also been named as influences on how humans use personal space. The type of relationship itself affects this use of space—friends and lovers tend to stand or sit closer than acquaintances and strangers do. This use of personal space is a good example of how humans proactively use their physical context. They define their physical context in terms of their purpose for interaction. Friends sit closer together because they are friends; they aren't likely to become friends just because they sit closer together.

The point to be gleaned from this discussion of personal space as a function of the physical context is simply this: the actual physical distance separating interactants is a less important factor in human communication than the accessibility of communicators. When the other person is more accessible to you—when he or she is, for example, in your field of vision or sharing the same space—you are likely to have more interpersonal contacts with that person. With greater frequency of interpersonal contact, your opportunity to develop a closer relationship increases.

What is the relative strength of the physical context's influence on interpersonal communication? As you have undoubtedly inferred from the previous discussion, elements of the social context (to be discussed in Chapter 4) and of the physical context sometimes conflict. Sometimes social factors work against the increased opportunity for interaction that is present in the physical context. At times, the social context is so powerful that the physical context's influence on accessibility is minimized. When I first read Sommer's book on personal space and seating choices, for example, I immediately moved my office chair so that any visiting student would sit diagonally across the corner of my desk. As often as not, though, students visiting my office would move the chair to the opposite side of the desk before sitting down. Apparently the instructor-student relationship of the university context is so ingrained that it is a greater influence on the interaction than a simple arrangement of chairs. At least, I don't want to think that I personally intimidate students.

The Function of Expectations

Physical settings also provide clues as to what type of interaction we should expect to take place within each setting. A very familiar example of expectations based on the physical context is the traditional classroom with its rank-and-file student seating and the confrontive, more powerful placement of the instructor. Several years ago my elementary school–age daughter was a student in a class whose teacher removed and stored most of the student desks. She then littered the classroom with tables and chairs, beanbag chairs, pillows, cheery wall decorations, and even a floor lamp or two beside upholstered chairs. What type of teacher-student interaction would you expect takes place in the traditional classroom? Probably a lot of "teacher talk" (lectures) and not much "student talk." The revised classroom context is likely to

The physical setting probably influences these students' expectations of the communication they will have in this setting.
(Tom Turner/Design Conceptions)

give students the expectation of more give-and-take exchanges between teacher and students.

I once overheard several parents complaining about the lack of discipline in this teacher's classes, even though my own daughter insisted that the teacher, whom she liked very much, was really "tough." I have always suspected that the physical context of her classroom was the only evidence that parents had for perceiving this teacher's poor discipline (defined as not enough "lecturing," I guess). Clearly, the expectations of parents are often more attuned to the traditional classroom context.

Actually human expectations and physical contexts probably exert a reciprocal influence on each other. That is, people's prior expectations of appropriate interaction within a particular physical context are probably as much a factor in how they will function in it as are the clues provided by the physical context. Take, for instance, the notion of personal space as it influences humans' accessibility for interpersonal communication. A friend of mine recently confided that he couldn't stand the glazed windows on modern office buildings—those that allow people inside to see out but don't allow people outside to see in (a form of human communication, I suppose). Knowing that others could see him but that he couldn't see them, he felt the urge to push his fist through the window every time he passed by on the sidewalk.

Similarly, when we enter the crowded elevator, we expect to be crowded and don't really resent what would, in other circumstances, be violations of our personal space. In a context with vast quantities of available space, we would probably resent much less formidable intrusions on our private bubbles. The expectations we have as we enter a context are as much a factor of how we function within it as is the way the physical context functions to direct our expectations.

The Function of Uncertainty

Nearly forty years ago, Shannon and Weaver (1949) revolutionized our thinking about information and the way in which humans acquire their meanings. They formulated a mathematical model of communication that has come to be known as "information theory." The idea behind information theory and its application to human interaction offer valuable insights into the nature of human communication. These notions concerning how people communicate with each other in order to reduce uncertainty will also be the subject of discussion in several of the subsequent chapters.

Shannon and Weaver suggested that, probably contrary to common sense, we don't "seek out" information in order to grasp the meaning of something (that is, to achieve certainty) so much as we seek information in order to eliminate the number of potential meanings we might have for it (that is, to reduce uncertainty). Underlying the concept of information theory, then, is the assumption that we already possess a repertoire of potential meanings that are applicable to virtually every context of communication. Our problem, then, is not that we have no idea of what something means but that we have too *many* such ideas. Hence, we need information in order to reduce the number of possible meanings until we have not certainty but a reasonable and manageable amount of uncertainty. In this way, we acquire meaning of who someone is or what someone says through a process of elimination, reducing the number of alternative meanings.

Information theory is often illustrated by way of an analogy—the "pick a card, any card" game. Your task is to discover the identity of a single card in a normal fifty-two-card deck by asking only yes-no questions. You are already aware that only fifty-two possibilities exist, but you also know that asking whether it is the jack of hearts is not a very efficient way to play the game. You would probably prefer to ask "Is it a red suit?" The answer to that question wouldn't identify the card but it *would* cut the number of possibilities in half. You might then ask "Is it a heart?" to reduce your uncertainty further. You continue to ask questions to eliminate alternatives until you know what the card is. In other words, you process information by reducing uncertainty until you know, by process of elimination, the identity of the card.

Now let's apply the notion of "uncertainty reduction" to the process of interpersonal communication. The process of reducing uncertainty underlies much of human communication, at least in the early stages of developing relationships. You begin interacting with another person with some ideas about, for example, the different kinds of people there are in the world. (We will later discuss this set of alternative meanings as "implicit personality theory.") You then search for clues in what the other person says in order to eliminate some of your possible people types. Soon you come to be aware, through a process of elimination, what type is appropriate to the other. For our present discussion, however, we shall limit our discussion of uncertainty reduction to the clues that are available in the physical context.

When you encountered a stranger on the first day of this class, for instance, you already knew a great deal about that person on the basis of this physical context's influence on our expectations. You knew, for example, that the person was an undergraduate student, had some interest in the subject matter of the class (either as relevant to a major or as an elected course to satisfy a requirement), was currently living at or near the school, and so forth. In other words, you reduce your uncertainty about the other person by using the clues that are available in the physical context of the classroom. Furthermore, the physical context allows you a choice of interactional topics appropriate to that context: for example, "What's your major?" "Where's your home town?" "Did you see the game last week?"—all topics associated with the physical context of the school and all seeking to reduce the uncertainty you still have about this person.

Uncertainty reduction is a fruitful way of viewing the process of human communication, at least in its beginning stages. Upon entering any new interaction, the human being feels a need to reduce the amount of uncertainty about the context and the person—to search for information that will reduce the number of possibilities and allow some reasonable basis for attaching meaning to the other person. The first place to look for informational clues is in the physical setting. It provides at least general information about who the other person is and how to behave appropriately in that context. You know, for example, that one kind of dining behavior is appropriate in a fast-food restaurant but that another kind is more appropriate in the fancy French restaurant.

We shall return to the idea of uncertainty reduction in Chapter 8, when we discuss the role of self and the other, the individual level of human communication. We have introduced the topic at this point to suggest that the physical context offers some informational clues that can be used to reduce our uncertainty about how to interact socially. Generally speaking, however, the greater number of informational clues (sometimes called "psychological information") come from yourself and from the other person. Thus, the concept of uncertainty reduction is important in terms of informational clues that are available in the physical context. These will become even more important in Part 2.

THE SOCIAL IMPACT OF PHYSICAL CONTEXTS

The physical context is not just a physical setting with a bunch of visual, oral, and olfactory stimuli floating around waiting to be turned into sensations and perceptions; it is much more than that. It is also a place where human communication takes place and has taken place. "I thought Harry gave up cigars" is certainly an inference about people (specifically Harry) based upon a single olfactory stimulus of the physical setting.

The physical context often contains subtle clues about the social relationship of people within it, too. We have already suggested that the traditional classroom context implies a status or power distinction between instructor and students, and prior experience in other classrooms serves to reinforce that status difference. Walk into a living room with a white carpet and white furniture and you are likely to expect that these parents don't allow their young children to play in this room. It is reserved for entertaining guests. This section discusses other ways in which the physical contexts of communication direct the social expectations of people who interact within them.

As a setting of interpersonal communication, a physical context contains clues about interpersonal relationships that have taken place or will occur within it. The context, for instance, may be someone's "turf"—that is, someone may "own" the setting and consequently have greater power in the relationship that occurs within it, at least in the introductory stages of the communication. A physical context may function to encourge or discourage a developing relationship between people who meet as strangers and engage in interpersonal communication. Or a physical context may include environmental objects or other "residues" that tell people who enter the environment something about the interpersonal relationship of the people who are in that setting. In all cases, the physical context itself may reflect or influence the relationships of people who use that context for interpersonal communication. And this is what is meant by "the social impact of physical contexts."

"Ownership" of the Setting

If you are invited into someone's home for a party or a social engagement, you know who "owns" that setting. The residential setting "belongs to" the host or hostess. You are an outsider invited into the territory of the other person and consequently tend to defer to the other's direction. The host/hostess is entitled to tell you what to eat or whether to eat, when to eat, what to do, when to do it. That is the "right" of the host/hostess. You, as a guest, would be very rude if you did not defer to the owner's directions. Even though guests may appear to be in a position of honor, they feel the need to ask permission to use the phone, tour the home, use the bathroom. Of course, the good host/hostess always accedes to such requests but still has the "power" to do so. The hostess/host–guest relationship creates a clear social distinction in terms of power and status, a social relationship that influences at least the early stages of the interaction.

Defining ownership of the physical context in the above example is easy. But what about the ownership of the setting in a public place, a context that is not the residence of one of the communicators? A scene in a cheap, tawdry spy novel involves a clandestine meeting between the spy chiefs of the United States and the Soviet Union. Naturally, each person distrusts the other and does not wish to allow his counterpart and enemy to have an advantage at this meeting. They have agreed to meet alone (without supporting personnel), in a neutral country (not "owned" by one of their respective countries), and in a public restaurant (clearly no ownership in this public setting). The American quickly discovers that he has been placed in a position of disadvantage as he observes the Russian (through his communicative behavior) usurp "ownership" of the setting.

The Russian, who arrived first (a good tactic), has already ordered a wine that he proceeds to offer to the arriving American (who begins to feel more and more like the Russian's "guest" in the public restaurant). The Russian, apparently a connoisseur of good food, then proceeds to recommend certain items on the menu as being particularly good when prepared by this particular restaurant. He has obviously been there before. The Soviet spy chief has thus gained a social advantage by behaving in a way that lets him claim the ownership role of the public setting.

Keep in mind that the relationship between the physical context and interpersonal communication is interactional, not deterministic. If the setting had determined the behaviors of the participants, the American and the Russian would have been on socially equivalent grounds. But the meaning of the physical context was not just the sensory stimuli present in the restaurant; it was created socially by the people who interacted within its boundaries. The Russian *acted as though* he were the host of the setting. The American, by deferring to the Russian's invitations (he really had little choice without appearing boorish), also *acted as though* he were the guest. The result? The physical context, even though it was a public setting, was defined *through interpersonal communication* to create a difference in status or power between the two men who were peers/equals in all other respects.

To be the "owner" of the setting is to be in a position of greater power. Often sales representatives try to usurp contextual ownership, even though they may be making the sales pitch in the prospect's living room. A sales pitch is certainly interpersonal communication. In the seller-buyer relationship, it is often to the seller's advantage to be in a more powerful social position.

How can a seller attempt to usurp ownership of the potential buyer's living room? One way is to direct where the potential buyers should sit to discuss the product. ("Let's sit at the table here. I can lay out all my materials.") Then the seller takes over the table by covering the available space with visual aids, notebooks, and so on. It's even better if a centerpiece (belonging to the buyer) must be moved in order to make room for the materials (belonging to the seller). One sales technique is to ask the potential buyer for a glass of water, thereby forcing the buyer to "wait on" the seller and play the less powerful role of "servant." A good sales representative will gain "ownership" of a setting in a matter of moments.

Sometimes, however, you may find it to your advantage (depending on the goal or purpose of your communication) not to be in the role of ownership. For instance, hosts and hostesses may own the setting when they invite guests to a party, but they often attempt to shed their ownership role. They allow guests to serve themselves refreshments, give them the run of the house, urge them to act as though they were at home, and generally attempt to share ownership of the setting with the guests. We have all been to parties or dinners in which we felt "at home." They are in direct contrast to other parties at which we felt inhibited, stiff, and unsure of how to behave. The one party may appear to be more formal than the other, but perhaps the most appropriate definition of "informal" is the shared ownership of the setting. The old adage "When in Rome, do as the Romans do" is tantamount to saying that Romans own their setting and have the right to dictate to visitors what they should do. When the owners willingly abdicate the rights associated with ownership, they also abdicate their right to dictate the behavior of outsiders.

Several years ago my daughter went out for the first time with a new young man. When I asked her how she had enjoyed it, she told me it was "weird." Apparently the boy did everything in a very proper manner. He told her where they were going to eat. He opened doors and pulled out chairs for her. He asked her to choose what she'd like from the menu and then proceeded to give the waiter both their orders. He told her what movie they were going to see, and so forth and so forth. Her previous dating experience had apparently been with boys who shared their ownership of the date's physical context. They abdicated their "right" to dictate her behavior, and she apparently preferred that kind of relationship. Thus, she didn't think her date did anything wrong, but she did think he was "weird." To repeat, depending on one's purpose or goal in communication, abdicating ownership may be advantageous. (I don't think she ever went out with that fellow again.)

The Role of the Stranger

What about interpersonal communication situations in which the interactants have had no prior experience in communicating with each other? How might the physical context influence the expectations of strangers when they communicate for the first time? Public settings (restaurants, department stores, shopping malls, transit buses, etc.), we might think, are typically populated with strangers. But if we think that all strangers are alike in all settings, we are surely mistaken.

Strangers are so called because we have had little or no prior acquaintance with them; some strangers, however, remain strangers even after prior acquaintance. I may notice a specific person in a shopping mall and then recognize the same person later in another part of the mall. Even though the prior experience is present in my mind, I continue to consider the stranger as a stranger because the physical context of a shopping mall has directed my expectations regarding my relationship with that person. The stranger remains a stranger, and little opportunity for further communication is available in this setting.

The key to understanding how the physical context influences our expectations of interpersonal communication with strangers is whether the context encourages or discourages future relationships and further interactions. Some public contexts discourage, or at least don't encourage, continued development of relational interaction. The public elevator remains a good example. Even when it is crowded, people don't have the feeling that they know much about their companions. Even though they may converse with one another (usually about how crowded the elevator is), they have little expectation that they will have interactions with one another after they have gotten off the elevator.

The stranger in the elevator or in the shopping mall is more like a part of the physical context, a virtual "nonperson." The stranger has no discernible identity as a specific person and remains a part of the context in your memory even after the elevator ride is over. You may talk about "the person in the elevator" in the same manner as you might discuss the advertisement on the wall of the elevator. The stranger in this context is not much different from any other object in the physical context. Hence, we might identify this setting as defining the expectation of the communicators to regard the stranger *as object*.

Other physical contexts, though, actively encourage the development of social relationships among strangers. The most blatant of such settings is the ever-popular "mixer." The purpose of such a public context is to enable strangers to become acquainted, to engage in small talk, to get to know something about one another. The expectation is that participants in a mixer will have future contacts with one another and that future interaction will be easier because of this prior interactional experience.

High schools, colleges, and universities are notorious for having such get-acquainted parties during the first weeks of the fall term. Fraternities, sororities, and other campus social organizations regularly sponsor parties and mixers. The other person in such a setting is certainly a stranger, but the context defines the stranger not as an object but as an acquaintance. And acquaintances are potentially future friends.

Of course, some chance encounters in stranger-as-object contexts may develop into future friendships. A TV commercial for a breath mint popularizes the myth of boy meets girl in public context, but even this commercial acknowledges the role of typical expectations of such settings. The message is to keep on chewing those little mints because you may need them when you least expect it. The point is that the physical context helps to define the role of the stranger. Whereas some settings discourage continued interaction and thus define the stranger as object, others encourage further interaction and thereby define the stranger as acquaintance.

Social Residues in the Settings

Articles in popular magazines providing advice on "how to decorate your home" typically tell the reader to give your home that "personal touch." Your home, these authors say, should reflect you and your personal tastes. Most of us would probably believe that we can tell a great deal about people as soon as we walk into their homes or apartments. We can tell whether they're neat or messy, whether they're formal or informal—in short, whether we would like to get to know them better or not. People who own physical contexts (typically the home) can modify the physical stimuli of the setting directly by decorating and designing this space to reflect their own individual ideas and tastes—their very identity (see Hayward, 1977).

When we derive expectations and inferences about what people are like from the appearance of their homes, we are not unlike archaeologists who study past civilizations. Because these researchers exist in the present and attempt to understand a society or culture that no longer exists, archaeologists have no choice but to search for physical residues of past cultures, physical objects that have lasted through the ages and function as the "footprints" of the past. The archaeologist digs into the earth and finds tools, pottery, buildings, statues, jewelry, and other physical objects. From these physical residues, the archaeologist makes inferences about actual behaviors of members in a society that is now no more. In the absence of interactive behavior to observe, the archaeologist looks for residues of those behaviors in the form of physical artifacts—not real facts but residues of facts in the form of physical objects.

Artifacts of social relationships also exist in many physical contexts in which interaction has taken place. Clark Olson (1981) studied artifacts of social relationships in the homes of a young married couple, an unmarried couple, and an older married couple. He then generated some intriguing insights into the social residues as well as the nature of some potential differences in these three types of relationships.

Artifacts in the home, Olson discovered, reflect the identities of both individuals and relationships. Prominently displayed photographs, for example, may be the most obvious artifacts, and they may be individual or relational—that is, they may be pictures of one of the individuals or of the couple together as a unit. A displayed trophy is more likely to reflect an individual, but wedding gifts or gifts to "the couple" are often displayed with pride as a reflection of relational identity. Olson suggested that displaying the relational artifacts might reflect the stability or strength of the relationship, the effectiveness of past communication or interaction. Often the artifacts are displayed in a prominent place, such as a fireplace mantle or a wall collection, so that they seem to constitute a "shrine"—a place of honor and reverence.

Olson also discovered that certain sections of homes might contain residues of specific interactional or communicative functions. A kitchen desk with a convenient wall calendar, for instance, was reserved for communication that involved planning activities. In that particular context, the couple compiled grocery lists, talked about their activities for the day, rehashed activities of the past day, and made plans for the weekend. Other areas of the house were reserved for other functions. Each member of one couple had her or his own personal desk which contained the materials "belonging to" that person. That setting was for private functions—reading, studying, meditating—a place of solitude in a physical context whose ownership was otherwise shared.

I once heard a marriage counselor in a radio interview expound on the necessity of never arguing in bed. Her point was that the bedroom was a place for intimate sharing and should not be "defiled" with the blasphemy of arguing. Not only did she appear to recognize the concept and function of artifacts, residues of past interactions in the physical setting, but she also talked about the bedroom in quasi-religious tones—as though it were a place of worship and the marital relationship the focus of reverence. In any case, she clearly recognized the sometimes close connection between the "owned" environment or physical context, the social relationship, and the people within it.

Summary

Because the human being tends to reflect a proactive (acting toward) rather than a reactive (acting in response to) nature, the role of the physical context in human communication is probably not as often deterministic (causing people to behave) as it is interactional (where the meaning of the context is created by human actions). Thus, the physical context may be said to influence and be influenced by the human interactions that take place within it. In this way, the physical context exists as a set of stimuli in the environment as well as a definitional meaning inside the heads of interactants. Both are important to the function of the physical context in human communication.

The physical context comprises three elements: design, decoration, and other people. Design features of the context include those elements that are less resistant to change; the decoration features include elements that are easily manipulated such as movable objects or furnishings; and other people are elements of the physical context to the extent that their presence or absence and their location in reference to the communicators provides another source of stimuli to be interpreted as part of one's definition of the physical context.

The physical setting functions to affect and be affected by human communication to the extent that it provides information about the other person and guidelines as to what constitutes appropriate behavior within that context. Space functions to affect behavior to the extent that it allows greater accessibility and opportunities for interpersonal contacts between communicators. Although the actual influence of the physical context on human communication is probably less than we might think, the context does affect human perceptions relevant to interpersonal attraction and judgments of the other person. Some rooms can be manipulated to encourage a friendly atmosphere. People's expectations upon entering a setting may affect their definition of the setting, and the setting itself may direct one's expectations of the sort of interaction that will take place. People typically search for clues in the physical context in order to reduce their uncertainty or confusion about what to do and how to behave. The process of uncertainty reduction is particularly important during the early stages of communication and relationship development.

The physical context also reflects some elements of the social context or at least provides subtle clues that identify the social relationship among the interactants in the setting. The "owner" of the setting is in a position of greater power or status. When the ownership of the setting is a prior condition of the setting, as when it is the residence of one of the communicators, the host/hostess may abdicate the ownership role in order to minimize social differences. On the other hand, when the context is a public setting, one of the participants may secure a social advantage by acting as though he/she were in the ownership role. Many public settings include the role of social stranger, but strangers differ from one physical context to another. Some settings define the stranger as an "object"; and in others, the stranger is defined as an acquaintance. The difference between physical contexts is based on whether the context encourages or discourages (or does not encourage) further interaction and relational development. Finally, past interactions and relationships within a physical context may leave residues of the nature or stability of that relationship as physical objects (akin to archaeological artifacts) present in the physical context.

CHAPTER 4

The Social Context

Solitude is fine,
but you need someone to tell you
solitude is fine.

—Honoré de Balzac

Every year when our family sits down to Thanksgiving dinner, we know that one food item must be on the table. The turkey, stuffing, sweet potatoes, mashed potatoes, and pumpkin pie are all very nice; but the absolutely mandatory food item is the jellied cranberry sauce that comes in a can. We typically have homemade cranberry relish made from fresh fruit, too; but the jellied cranberries are essential. I'm sure you are familiar with these cranberries. This is the jellied cranberry sauce that, after being removed from the can, retains the exact shape of the can. When our daughters were younger, they delighted in the way the cylindrical glob of red jelly would slide across the serving plate whenever it was passed. One year we sliced the entire glob and arranged the red "hockey pucks" artistically around some salad, and everyone was disappointed. Of course, our family may be a bit strange, but that jiggly red glob has become something of a family tradition on Thanksgiving Day.

At this point you are probably wondering why I am telling you about canned cranberry jelly. The reason is that I want you to visualize this cylindrically shaped red jiggly stuff sitting on a plate. Its shape is an exact sculpture of the can that contained it, but the container is not there. By looking at the jelly, you know precisely the shape and size of the can, even though the can is not there. This is a perfect analogy for the nature of a society or culture—the *social context* of communication or "container" of the communicators.

Too often we think of a social context as only the container, something that exists outside the individual. Each of us, we say, exists within a given culture, as a member of a larger social group. That is true, of course, but it misses the point as to *where* the society is. Priests, ministers, and rabbis are fond of telling their congregations that the church is not the building, not the scriptural writings, not the body of knowledge. None of these is the proper location; the church is inside each member. When the Jews and early Christians were persecuted, their scriptures burned, and their buildings destroyed, their religion continued to flourish. Why? Because their religion was not in the "containers" of the buildings and the books; it was inside the people who supported one another. That can of cranberry jelly illustrates this principle very well. Remove the jelly from the can, and the jelly continues to stand on its own. The cylinder retains its shape because of the interconnections among the molecules—not because it is in a can.

To use "social context" as a singular term, though, is somewhat misleading. Whenever communication takes place, numerous social contexts are present: the relationship of the participants, cultures in which the participants hold a common membership, and additional societies/cultures to which only one of the participants belongs. The influences of all these social contexts are present in any given event of human communication. Some of these contexts influence the communicative event in a beneficial manner; some do not. Which influences are beneficial and which are not? Generally, social contexts emphasizing the similarities of the participants serve to activate the relationship; social contexts emphasizing the differences generally serve to hinder the communication. Thus, in every event of human communication there are both positive and negative influences from the larger social contexts. Those influences are operating at the same time, so that social contexts function both to assist and hinder relational development and the effectiveness of interpersonal communication.

But if so many social contexts are influencing interpersonal communication and those influences are both positive and negative, which influences are the strongest? Which social contexts exert the strongest impact on interpersonal communication? It is a truism that the strongest influence of all is typically the most immediate society, the smallest social context that contains the communicators. The most immediate context, of course, is the relationship created by the participants themselves through their interaction with one another. Recall that Romeo and Juliet's interpersonal relationship ultimately proved to be stronger than the highly potent social contexts of family, that of the warring Capulets and Montagues. That story is fiction, of course, and the strategy employed for solving the relational dilemma (suicide) was certainly more extreme than is typically necessary. Nevertheless, the principle that the closer the social context is to the immediate relationship the greater its influence, holds true even in common and everyday relationships.

This chapter on the social context of interpersonal communication is divided into three basic sections. The first section identifies the various types of social contexts potentially present (within each of the individual communicators) during every act of human communication. The second section recalls that humans are proactive and details how people use the social context for purposes relevant to interpersonal communication. Finally, the third section deals with how social contexts specifically affect people's behavior during the process of interpersonal communication. The perceptive reader will note the absence of any discussion of language—a powerful influence on interpersonal communication and certainly part of a social context. But the influence of language is so significant that it deserves its own discussion in Chapter 5.

TYPES OF SOCIAL CONTEXT

A society or culture is so called because some sizable group of people have something in common. That commonality makes them similar and identifiable as belonging to (that is, members of) a given social community. The commonality that identifies a society, though, is not merely a matter of coincidence. We don't recognize people with red hair, for instance, as a society or culture simply because of this common but coincidental physical feature. Members of a society or culture recognize common ideas, customs, traditions, norms, beliefs, values, role relationships, a sense of belonging. And these identifiable similarities bind people together within a common bond of social membership.

Although there are subtle differences in the way sociologists use the terms *society* and *culture,* our discussions will use them interchangeably. Either term will refer to some recognizable group of people (a social context) who recognize the existence of common bonds (such as customs, traditions, beliefs, values) and, as a result, feel a sense of membership or belonging.

The national society may be one of the most obvious social contexts of communication, along with racial grouping, religious affiliation, and political designation. Because of their size, however, these social contexts are rather far removed from a specific event of interpersonal communication, the principal focus of this book. You will recall that the most influential context of interpersonal communication is the most immediate context, consistent with the principle that the influence of the context is greater as it is closer to the actual communicative event. In this respect, the larger social contexts may be very familiar and even obvious, but their impact on any specific context of interpersonal communication is typically quite small. Our discussions will, instead, focus on those social contexts that influence the interpersonal context most directly.

We will distinguish between two general types of social contexts: *socializing* and *relational.* One socializing context will differ from another on the basis of the kinds of things members learn from belonging to it. The relational contexts focus on the nature of the interpersonal bonds that tie members to each other within the social context. These social contexts overlap each other, of course, in the sense that a particular relational context (such as family) will also socialize its members by teaching them certain customs, traditions, norms, rules, and so on. In that sense, as the following discussion will make clear, the family (a relational context) may also serve the socializing functions of an instructional, innovative, and interpersonal context.

Socializing Contexts

As suggested earlier, a society does not come into existence by coincidence. Societal members do not just wake up one morning and magically possess the norms, values, beliefs, and traditions of a society. They learn them from experienced social members. The norms, values, beliefs, and so on of the society are passed down from one generation to another. The process by which this learning takes place is known as *socialization.* In our large society, the socializing process functions through our social institutions: schools, churches, mass media—and, most important perhaps, the family.

Bernstein (1972, p. 170), a sociolinguist, has classified four social contexts in which the socializing process occurs: regulative, instructional, imaginative or innovative, and interpersonal. Although he discusses these in terms of acquiring language skills, they are relevant to the learning of all aspects of what it means to be a member of a given society. Bernstein also suggests that these socializing contexts occur primarily in the family, as parents teach children about society; but they are just as relevant to schools, mass media, street gangs, and peer groups. In fact, my limited viewing of *Sesame Street* and *The Electric Company,* as my daughters were growing up, convinced me that these children's television programs rather skillfully employed all four socializing functions throughout their tenure on public television.

Regulative Contexts. The regulative context involves the learning of authority relationships and the rules that govern society. Children learn at an early age, for example, not to cross the street before looking both ways and waiting for the light to change, not to sneeze without covering their mouths, to say "please" and "thank you" at appropriate times. Adults learn how to get ahead in their jobs; students learn how to get good grades in a particular course; adolescents learn what to do and what not to do on a date. The regulative context, in short, socializes new members by teaching them rules of conduct, how to behave without violating some social norms—whether the rule or the norm is one that governs the nation-state or a small group of friends.

Instructional Contexts. The instructional context involves learning about the nature of objects and other people. From the adolescent who takes a first sip of beer to the adult who tries to master the intricacies of a personal computer, members of a society continue to learn in instructional contexts throughout their lives. But "instruction" in the taste of beer and operating a personal computer is learning about objects. Socializing with other people is also a lifelong learning activity and more relevant, perhaps, to interpersonal communication.

You can learn about other people in instructional contexts in two different ways. One, people can tell you about other people. Two, you can find out yourself about other people by meeting with them and talking with them. An instructional context continues to function in socializing a member of a culture as long as he or she continues to encounter different kinds of people and to experience a continual variation of people when making new acquaintances. Encountering the same kind of people in a hundred social situations is probably the same instructional context repeated a hundred times. But whenever you encounter a new type of person, you are involved in a new instructional context. Every new social situation constitutes an instructional context in which the individual discovers more social knowledge about the nature of other human beings.

Imaginative or Innovative Contexts. The imaginative context encourages creativity and innovation on the part of the person becoming socialized. Such a context is perhaps the farthest removed from regulative socialization. When one innovates or learns a new and creative behavior, there are no rules for that particular situation. Thus, the individual has few social guidelines indicating what behavior is appropriate. Imaginative contexts are those that are recognized as "exceptions to the rules"; they require spontaneity, innovation, trial-and-error techniques. One function of imaginative socialization is to allow for the development of unique social relationships—special friends and highly individualized role relationships.

In short, people learn from imaginative contexts how to interact with each other without conforming solely to the influence of some larger social context. This is not to say, of course, that rules do not guide the interaction of such personalized relationships. By participating innovatively in a particular interpersonal relationship, the participants learn how to create their own rules for what is appropriate for them. On the other hand, they realize that what is appropriate for that particular interaction is not necessarily appropriate for other social situations.

In other words, virtually every social relationship has rules to determine what is appropriate and what is inappropriate for that relationship. For some relationships, the most important rules can be found in a larger social context. Meet someone at a church social, and you will probably conform to rules appropriate to interpersonal communication in a church. For other relationships, the important rules are created during the process of the interaction. After you get to know someone, you are more likely to be innovative and to do something "different." The imaginative context socializes individuals to learn how to develop their own creative abilities and form unique relationships. Innovative socialization, in essence, encourages individual members of a society to develop their own individual identities.

Interpersonal Contexts. The interpersonal context in Bernstein's list may be somewhat misnamed. In this socializing context, individuals learn to become aware of their own emotions, their inner selves, their innermost feelings, and how to deal with them. The teenager who breaks up with his or her "steady" learns the pangs of adolescent heartbreak. The preadolescent with a crush on that special boy or girl learns the feeling of emotional attachment. Individuals also learn to be sensitive to and aware of the internal states of other people and how to deal with other people's emotions, for instance, as well as their own. How do you respond to the friend whose parents are going through a divorce? What do you say to a person who tells a racist or sexist joke? How do you deal with people who "bare their souls" to you? These are the things that are learned in an interpersonal socializing context.

This type of socializing context as an "interpersonal" context is probably more accurately described as *intra*personal, despite the fact that it nearly always occurs (like other socialization) within a social setting. The emphasis in this context is on becoming aware of and dealing with your own intrapersonal or internalized feelings as well as those of others. This socializing context allows you to learn the nuances of perceiving what is going on inside you and understanding what that means to your own behavior. It also allows you to perceive what is going on inside other people on the basis of what you can observe in their behaviors. Be aware that what you learn in such contexts will influence how you perceive intrapersonal elements in other contexts. And also be aware that your perceptions in interpersonal contexts are also very likely to be wrong. Perceptions, as we have discussed previously, are not the same as behaviors—even though we sometimes think they are.

Socializing contexts offer members of a society the opportunity to learn what it means to belong to a social community. Further, this process of socialization continues throughout life, although the greatest proportion of socialization probably occurs prior to adulthood. But socializing contexts are not really identifiable societies or cultures in which one typically claims membership. Rather, one socializing context

The family is an important context for socialization.
(Michal Heron/Woodfin Camp & Associates)

differs from another on the basis of the sorts of things one learns in that context. Once you learn the rules and customs of a society in a socializing context, you then apply what you have learned in a specific kind of society—a particular kind of social context identified by the nature of the bonds that hold the members of that context together. We are now ready to move our discussion to relational contexts.

Relational Contexts

Throughout your lifetime you participate in an extremely large number of relationships with other people. Moreover, no two of these relationships are exactly alike. Some are closer than others; some are more permanent; some are more pleasing. You will probably have dozens, perhaps hundreds, of different relationships in your lifetime. However, all these relationships fall into a relatively few kinds of relational contexts. That is, the types of connections or bonds that tie you to another person, and thus form an interpersonal relationship, are relatively few in number. The following discussion will include five types of relational contexts or "connections" between participants in interpersonal communication: kinship, friendship, work, social contract, and acquaintanceship.

Kinships. Kinship involves a relational context based on the connections of biological (including adoption) relations. The family is the social context in which much of our cultural socialization takes place. Much of the raising of children involves supplying younger members of the family, at one time or another, with the four socializing contexts discussed earlier. The family, in addition to being an important context for socialization, is typically the longest-lasting relational context as well. People tend to remain in contact with their family members long after they "go out on their own"—virtually for an entire lifetime. When people inform you that they haven't talked with their parents in several years, you are likely to be surprised. Kinship ties are usually much stronger than that.

Furthermore, unlike other relationships, the family regenerates itself with each succeeding generation of children. Many families keep accurate records of their "roots," their family tree, which go back many generations and hundreds of years. I know of no one who has attempted to record "friendship trees" over many generations and hundreds of years. In fact, to attempt to compile such a record would seem ludicrous, but businesses that offer families genealogical research don't seem to lack customers. The family has, perhaps, the greatest stability of all possible relationships.

Friendships. Friendship is also a common social relationship, although the differences among different friendship contexts is enormous. Most people have a variety of friends, but not all friends are alike. In fact, friendships include a vast range of different types of relational contexts. Some people are "really close" friends; some are "good" friends; some are "just" friends. You can talk with some friends about things that bother you, but you wouldn't ask them for advice as to what courses you should take next term. You can talk with other friends about plans for a party this weekend, but you wouldn't think of discussing with them some concern you may have about your health. A friendship context can be an extremely intimate relationship, or it can be a relationship that isn't very close at all.

The single most definitive factor of friendship is, perhaps, that the relationship is based on equality rather than difference. Friendships reflect an absence of status or power differences, at least as friends would consider such differences as being important. Friendship relations involve similarity. Of course, even close friends may be different from each other in many ways, but those differences are not the basis of the friendship. Friends often consider themselves more similar than they may actually be.

Unlike kinship, friendship contexts possess an amazing degree of instability. For one thing, friendships are more voluntary. You choose your friends, but you don't choose your parents. A quarrel between friends can threaten the continuation of a friendship, unlike a quarrel between brothers or sisters. Kinship ties persist regardless of how serious the quarrel was. Furthermore, friendships are unstable as a result of the great social mobility in our society. We Americans tend to move from one city to another and change residences rather frequently throughout our lifetimes. My oldest daughter, for example, lived in six different cities in four different states before she was a teenager. She had friends in each of those cities, but she moved away and the friendships evaporated.

A friendship that remains stable for many years is not common. Friendships tend to last during a certain period of your life, to be replaced by new friendships as you grow older. In this regard, my friendship experiences are rather typical of those of most Americans my age. My closest friend as an infant was a young girl who lived next door, and my closest friend in elementary school was a boy who lived a few blocks away. Today I have no idea where either Kay or Lowell lives or what has happened to them. I recently attended a reunion of my high school graduating class and had the feeling that I didn't really know any of them any more. I still maintain contact with some close friends I had when I was at college, but we are separated by 1,500 miles and rarely see each other any more. As strange as it may seem, the relational context of friendship includes some of the closest and most intimate social ties. But at the same time, it is a highly unstable social relationship.

Work. The relational context that develops when people work together may be considered a matter of coincidence. The workplace is simply the place where people earn the means to support themselves. Members in a relational work context have little choice as to the other people at their place of employment. Other people in the work context just happen to be there, not through any effort or desire on the part of co-workers to select them. Thus, people are thrown together in a work environment to create another important and highly common relational context.

When people live together for eight hours a day, forty hours a week (and their job requirements allow free interaction), they have frequent opportunities to talk with one another. With this frequency of interpersonal contact, the work context may create rather close interpersonal relationships. But a work relationship is not necessarily a friendship; the principal difference is the amount of choice available to the interactants. *You* choose friends; the place of work chooses your work relationships *for* you. Even though you may get along very well with your colleagues at work, those relationships are typically quite different from friendships in that they are limited to the work setting. Of course, colleagues at work may also be friends, but only if and when they expand their relationship beyond the boundaries of the work environment and choose to have frequent interpersonal contacts outside the work setting, as in going out on the town together, having social evenings in each other's homes, or engaging in "play" activities together.

Some of my closest friends, both now and in the past, have also been my colleagues at work. It is not surprising that the frequency of interpersonal contact at work leads to an increased liking, so that work partners maintain interpersonal contacts outside the work setting. In this way, the same people may be members of more than one relational context. Often, of course, people you know at work remain just people you know at work. You may not even like them particularly. And to the extent that you do not voluntarily expand your relationship with them beyond the work setting, the relational context remains only a work context and not friendship.

Social Contracts. The social contract involves a special type of relational context quite different from any of the others. The contractual relationship contains an overt obligation on the part of the members that just isn't present in any other relational context. Husband and wife constitute a socially contracted relationship that goes beyond friendship, kinship, or work context in the kind of obligation it imposes. A wife and husband are "legally married" and, therefore, subject to obligations (such as financial support, communal ownership of property, legal responsibility for actions of children) prescribed by law. The social contract, then, is a relational context that is itself sanctioned by and under the direct influence of a larger social context.

Participants in a relational context of social contract have a connection that is recognized by the larger society or culture. In this respect, the contracted relationship of marriage differs from that of the man and woman who live together as husband and wife. Despite the recent rash of "palimony" suits, members of the nonmarried relational context are under no obligation (at least according to the law) to remain bonded within that relationship. It is a voluntary relational context (similar to a friendship) and hence involves fewer and different kinds of obligations.

Of course, the unmarried couple may act "as though" they were members of a contractual relational context, so that the actual behavior of an unmarried and a married couple may not be very different. Unmarried couples often say, "We *feel* married." The difference, of course, is in the existence of the social contract—not just the "piece of paper" but the recognition and sanction of the relationship by the larger social context. The obligation toward any relationship always exists, to some extent, intrapersonally within each of the members. In other words, they live together long enough to have created an interpersonal socializing context. A social contract involves that intrapersonal obligation, too; but an additional obligation is also present in the social contract. And that obligation comes from the larger social context.

Although marriage is the social-contract relational context that comes most quickly to mind, there are many other contracts in our society. The lawyer-client and the priest-confessor relational contexts share an obligation of confidentiality. Neither the attorney nor the priest is allowed to divulge statements of the client or confessor without express permission. The attorney's obligation is sanctioned by law, the priest's obligation by the doctrines of the church. Both are larger social contexts comprising the social-contract relationship. Other social contracts might include employer and employee, buyer and seller, lender and borrower, landowner and tenant, among others. Although many social contracts invoke the proverbial "piece of paper," others do not. The social contract is not a document at all; it is the identifiable sanctioned influence of some larger social context.

Acquaintanceships. Although we have discussed four highly common and familiar relational contexts involving interpersonal communication, we have not yet addressed the most common (by far) of all social relationships—acquaintanceships. Throughout your lifetime you will have relatively few friends, possibly a somewhat larger number of family members, and an even larger number of work relationships. Add them all together with your social contracts, and you still won't approach the number of acquaintances you will accumulate. Despite the many acquaintances you have and will have in your lifetime, it is difficult to define precisely what "acquaintanceship" means. Begin listing some people you would consider to be acquaintances, and you will have no trouble identifying who they are. On the other hand, you may have greater difficulty in defining precisely what you mean by an "acquaintance," even though you can readily identify people who fit that category.

Let's begin our search for a definition of "acquaintanceship" by asking the experts. Psychologist Stephen Duck (1977) has defined "acquaintanceship" as "the process of getting to know someone in depth from first encounter to established relationships—whether this provokes an increase in liking or not" (p. 15). His definition seems reasonable at first glance, but it assumes something that just isn't true of many (indeed, perhaps most) acquaintanceships. Duck's definition assumes that acquaintanceship is a developmental stage on the way to a closer relationship, a stage that people go through as they develop a friendship.

Certainly no friendship ever begins as friendship; it must start out as acquaintanceship. But many acquaintances remain acquaintances; they never get beyond that point. With some acquaintances, you may eventually develop a close friendship; with others, you keep the relationship at the level of acquaintanceship. In point of fact, most acquaintanceships are not potential or immature friendships. We all have acquaintances who will never be more than acquaintances. And, for the most part, that's the way we want it.

So what do we mean when we say someone is an acquaintance? For one thing, acquaintances tend to see each other and talk with each other rather infrequently. We just don't communicate with our acquaintances very often, at least not compared with our interaction with friends. Consequently, we don't develop our relationship beyond the acquaintanceship level. Naturally there are exceptions to this rule. We may have acquaintances that we see rather frequently (once a week or even every day), but we still don't do any more than exchange greetings and engage in small talk with them. Hence, we don't communicate often with acquaintances. But even when we do, we don't work very hard at our interpersonal communication.

Perhaps the most definitive attribute of acquaintanceship, then, is the lack of depth in these interpersonal encounters, as well as, typically, fewer interpersonal encounters. Interaction with acquaintances tends to remain on a superficial level; it doesn't stray far beyond the "safe" and publicly available information about each other's "self." Friends would probably say that they know a great deal about each other; acquaintances are more likely to say that they don't really know each other very well. Such a statement is similar to saying that your interaction with friends has a different quality than your interaction with acquaintances; your interaction treats the other person (as well as yourself) in greater depth. In this respect, an acquaintanceship is not likely to be used as a socializing interpersonal context. We learn little about our own emotions and beliefs and little of the other person's internalizations.

These, then, are the social contexts, both socializing and relational, embedded in and available to the participants in any given act of interpersonal communication. The interactant brings to the act of interpersonal communication the product of being socialized into a number of larger cultures. Within each interactant, as well, are the influences of other social contexts, other relational contexts that implicitly function to influence the communicative behaviors in some way. And that influence is present to some extent in every act of interpersonal communication.

While you are talking even with a close friend, your other friendships (for example) are present within you, inside your head. You compare this friendship with your other friendships. You use other friendships as a way of guiding your interaction with your immediate partner. You generally communicate under the influence (consciously or subconsciously, explicitly or implicitly) of many other social contexts whenever you engage in interpersonal communication. The precise nature of these influences is the subject of the following discussions.

USING THE SOCIAL CONTEXT

When you encounter a person for the first time, the immediate task you set yourself is to discover just who that person is. One way of doing so is to identify the other as a member of certain social contexts. You interact with each other to discover the other's precise social identity. Work: "What do you do for a living?" or "Do you have a full-time job?" Kinship: "Are you married?" or "Do you have a family?" Acquaintanceship: "Do you know [name of potential acquaintance in common]?" And, of course, there are the usual issues of social identity that come from a larger social context: identity by political affiliation, religious belief, socioeconomic status, club membership, and so on. The social contexts of interpersonal communication provide natural guidelines for your communicative behavior in the "Who are you?" and "Who am I to you?" stage of relational development—in other words, during the early stages of interpersonal communication.

But when you engage in interpersonal communication, there are additional uses you can make of the social context to further the developing relationship. In addition to providing topics for introductory communication, the social context allows participants the opportunity to use it for other purposes, as well. This section discusses three additional uses of the social context that are of primary importance in the early stages of interpersonal communication. Communicators use the social context as a means of comparing or evaluating their present relationships, of providing opportunities for further interpersonal contact, and of offering support when intrapersonal problems arise.

Social Exchange

Social psychologists James Thibaut and Harold Kelley (1959, 1978, 1979) have developed a model for understanding how and why people form relationships with others. Their model, called "social exchange," is based upon perceived "costs" and "rewards," positive and negative values, associated with interacting with another person. On the basis of this "economic" way of looking at relationships, an individual is able to evaluate any specific interpersonal relationship along a scale that ranges from "very good" to "very bad." In addition, the individual uses costs and rewards to rate each interpersonal relationship with other relationships and discover which one is more valuable.

The social exchange model suggests that people treat their interpersonal relationships almost as a stockbroker treats investments. That is, the individual is in the business of "buying and selling" friendships, like buying and selling stocks and bonds, for the purpose of making a personal profit. Social exchange also emphasizes the selfish nature of humans, already discussed, so that people evaluate their friends and acquaintances on the basis of "Who can do the most for me?"—a profit motivation.

According to Thibaut and Kelley, individuals typically compare their immediate relationships with the social context of other relationships (friends with other friends, acquaintances with other acquaintances, etc.). During and after the process of interpersonal communication, each communicator tends to evaluate the worth of that transaction. Whether people make their comparisons on the basis of selfish motives or for other reasons, every relationship is judged *during the interaction* as to its degree of worthiness, and the judgment process is occurring simultaneously in the minds of each participant.

More than once, I have found myself at a social gathering with people whom I didn't know very well. I engaged in idle chatter with someone, but we were both aware that we would probably never see each other after that occasion. Now I'm not very good at doing small talk and quickly run out of things to say. As a result, I soon begin thinking of ways to disengage myself from the conversation and begin surveying the room to see where I might wander next. Often, in situations like this, I notice that my conversational partner's eyes are also wandering, scanning the room for other alternatives, and I realize that we are *both* thinking the same thing about this relationship. If I don't think the other person worthy of more of my time, I have no right to think that the other person is evaluating me any differently. The process of social exchange, judging the relationship against others in the social context, is going on in the minds of both communicators during the process of interpersonal communication.

Opportunity for Interpersonal Contact

Our interpersonal relationships change drastically during the course of our lives. Although these changes are due to a variety of factors, a major influence can be attributed to the social context. During your lifetime your social context undergoes dramatic changes. For the first few years, your social context is restricted to kinship relational contexts. The very small child has very few social contacts outside the boundaries of the immediate family: a few babysitters and some friends of the family. The child's social context expands somewhat with the addition of neighborhood playmates of a similar age, but the social context does not extend far beyond the people who live in the home and immediate neighborhood. When the child enters school, however, the number of people in the social context increases dramatically. High school acquaintances expand the social context even more. In fact, the social context continues to increase throughout life up to a maximum point that occurs some time during adulthood; then there is a continual decrease, so that senior citizens often have social contexts not much larger than those of infants.

The point is simply this. You can use only the social context that is available to you. When your social context offers the opportunity for a variety of contacts and repeated contacts with people, you have variety and closeness in your interpersonal relationships. During adolescence and early adulthood, you probably have the largest social context that you will ever have. But this social context is large not because it contains a greater number of people but because it involves a much higher level of interpersonal accessibility. More people are available for interaction, and the frequency of interpersonal interaction is extremely high. Most important, perhaps, is the fact that your social context during this period encourages a high level of accessibility and an increased frequency of interaction.

Beginning in junior high school and in increasing amounts during high school and college, the social context encourages an extremely large number of interpersonal contacts. Schools hold informal dances and other social events during virtually every week of the school year. Athletic, dramatic, and musical activities attract students for more social interaction. Clubs and social activities flourish in the school context. Social clubs sponsor parties for members. Church youth groups are constantly hosting activities and parties for their members. City and county governments sponsor youth recreational activities during the summer months. Both boys and girls are encouraged to participate in team-based athletic programs.

It is not just that you consider a large number of people to be acquaintances during this period of your life but that the social context gives you the opportunity to have repeated contacts with more people. As a result, the typical young adult probably has a greater number of friends and acquaintances than do people in any other age group. Friendships require time to develop. Hence, you need to have available to you an adequate number of repeated contacts with the same acquaintance in order to have the time to develop a friendship. Social contexts either minimize or maximize the number of opportunities you have for interaction. Furthermore, your social context (and thus your opportunity for increased interpersonal contact) will change as you enter a different phase of your life.

Older people in our society experience a social context almost opposite to that of the young. An older person's social context tends to decrease in size almost as dramatically as the youth's context increases. As people reach retirement age and leave their work environment, they lose the contacts provided by daily work relationships. Their children have typically left home to establish their own homes, so the frequency of kinship contacts has decreased. Friends of older people tend to travel or move to retirement communities in warm climates. Other friends tend, increasingly, to become ill or die. Older people themselves lose mobility through illness or injury and are restricted to their homes, nursing homes, or the homes of their children.

The social isolation of senior citizens in our society is a widely recognized problem and a topic of study by gerontologists (people involved in the study and treatment of problems associated with aging and the aged). The problem is all the worse for the aged because they have already experienced an active social context. Losing something you've already had makes the loss seem that much greater. Further, senior citizens have lost their active social context through no fault of their own. It is an unfortunate but natural result of aging in our society. Gerontologists who treat problems of older people frequently attempt to increase the social activity of their patients—enlarge the opportunity for interpersonal contacts—as a form of therapy.

Support Systems

Support systems, as the term implies, provide social support to the individual. The individual who experiences a problem in some relationship often seeks out someone else, outside that particular relationship, in order to "talk out" problems. Teenagers who have problems with boyfriends or girlfriends often tell their troubles to other friends, typically of the same sex, and look for help. Recently divorced men and women look for assistance from friends, often other divorced men or women, to help them get through this period of stress.

A friendship may provide an important support system.
(Sepp Seitz/Woodfin Camp & Associates)

A support system does not necessarily require a friendship relation, although it often includes this. For some problems, though, the most helpful social support system is not one of friendship. In fact, the social context that provides support in the form of help may be a group of strangers. Parents Without Partners is a formal organization designed to function as a support system for parents whose spouses are gone because of death, divorce, or desertion. Its members all share the problems of single parents raising children alone. Alcoholics Anonymous, perhaps the most familiar formal support system, is made up essentially of strangers. It was founded to assist people who are attempting to recover from the problems associated with alcohol or drug addiction and is made up entirely of people who have or are recovering from problems with alcohol or drugs.

When people look for a social context to function as a support system and provide assistance, the most significant characteristic affecting their choice is not friendship but commonality. That is, are the people in the support system familiar with this problem? Have they gone through it before or are they experiencing the same problem now? Do they know what it's like to have this problem? Friends who don't have this in common are unlikely to be capable of providing the right kind of support, even though they may be willing to do so.

Although there are exceptions to the rule, people tend to use relational contexts that include members of the same sex as their support systems. Women typically serve as confidantes to other women, and men are more likely to be the confidantes of other men. This rule provides one of the most convincing arguments that ours is a sexist society. Members of our society tend to view male-female relationships as "romantic involvements," or sex-based relationships. Our society encourages small boys to play with other boys or risk being called sissies. Society also socializes girls in the same way, and young girls who play with young boys are called tomboys. The opportunity for interpersonal contact provided by social contexts in our society is very sexist. Consequently, as children grow older, women seek out other women and men seek out other men for companionship and friendship not associated with sexual relations or romance. Women, products of our socialization, typically find it difficult to confide in men, and men find it equally difficult to ask women for social support. Our tendency to dismiss half the population of our society as potential members of support systems is undoubtedly an unfortunate commentary on our society, but it is probably true nonetheless.

INFLUENCE OF SOCIAL CONTEXT

This final section discusses more specific ways in which the social context of interpersonal communication actually influences your choice of what communicative behaviors to perform. Keep in mind, though, that social contexts do not "cause" people to behave in a certain way. Rather, you can gain information from the social context in order to know which behaviors are appropriate and which are not. Since you are a proactive individual, the behaviors you actually perform during the process of interpersonal communication are *always* the result of your choosing to perform them. But your choice is influenced by information, some of which comes from the social context. And remember that information functions to restrict the number of behavioral options available to you.

Social Expections

To be a member of a social community is to subscribe to its norms and values. Every member of a society has been, to some extent, socialized to accept normal social beliefs, to value normal social values, to act normally in social roles, and so forth. Society provides its members with rules to guide their conduct and beliefs. The socializing contexts provide a rather large proportion of the individual's cognitive framework, the intrapersonal level of communication. Socialization gives the individual member of society the cognitive background to interpret objects, people, and events. Interpreting the meaning of any event, object, or person is often attributable to the expectations that an individual has acquired through the process of socialization. Our discussion of these social expectations will fall generally into two categories: roles and stereotypes.

Roles. Roles provide guidelines for behavior; or they are what the social context designates as appropriate behavior in specific relationships. A teacher-student relationship, for example, is defined by roles that the social context of the school has created and defined. The instructor is the instructor and the student the student because those are the roles the school context has assigned them. The context of the school provides the interactants with expectations as to the behaviors that are and are not appropriate to the instructor's and student's roles.

Other relational contexts comprise roles that influence the behaviors of the communicators within them. The contracted relationship of husband and wife defines roles designated by the social context of marriage and family. The same is true of the boss-subordinate relationship in the work context. Because of these role designations, the social context influences interpersonal communication by providing the participants with guidelines for what constitutes acceptable and unacceptable behavior during interpersonal interaction.

Andreyeva and Gozman (1981), both social psychologists, provide one example of the contextual influence of roles on interpersonal communication:

> . . . at a certain period of an individual's life the norms of society prescribe that he should fall in love with another person of the opposite sex. But if this does not occur then the individual is exposed to all the pressures felt by someone subject to group influence who violates group norms. Hence, attraction [of one person to the other] is presumed to be not only determined by external influence but also normative in its essence, and the behaviour that accompanies it is, to a great extent, role behaviour. (p. 56)

What are these people trying to say in this paragraph? We "know" from common sense that people "fall in love" or become friends because of some mysterious ability to discover attractive or admirable personal qualities in the other person. But maybe we "fall in love" because our society expects us to do so. Certainly society tends to treat people who reach the age of thirty without ever having been married as having something "wrong" with them. Moreover, our society tends to punish women more than men who fail to fulfill their "proper" roles in society. Unmarried women are called "spinsters" or "old maids," not highly desirable names; whereas men are merely "bachelors," a more neutral term.

During their teenage years, boys and girls are expected to date, to fulfill the roles expected of them at that stage of their lives. A friend of mine, far from his teenage years and recently divorced, once told me about the discomfort he experienced in going out on dates. I then realized that dating after the age of forty can pose real problems, because what is "expected" and socially very "normal" for teenagers may be quite abnormal for people beyond that age. Somehow the roles expected of participants in a dating relationship are probably much more normal and thus more comfortable for teenagers than for mature adults.

Teenagers typically experience numerous romantic relationships during this period of their lives. Society expects them to have numerous social relationships. At least the social context of their peers involves this expectation. It isn't really unusual for a teenager to "go steady" with several people during the course of a school year, although the teenage society tends to look down on a person who goes steady with several people simultaneously. Parents often refer to such normal adolescents as being "boy crazy" or "girl crazy," but this is probably just the normal adult reaction to the cultural norm of youth. Teenagers are just doing what they are supposed to be doing—what their social context expects of them.

According to Andreyeva and Gozman, "Their affection, with the behaviour and feelings accompanying it, is nothing but a conformity reaction, the urge to be in line with popular patterns." Although we may not want to think so, much of our relational behavior is guided by our reliance on the social context to tell us what roles we are expected to and "should" perform. Social contexts serve as valuable frames of reference by providing us with role guidelines. By conforming to them, we know that we are doing the normal thing. During much of our relational life, we are (at the same time) both victims and beneficiaries of the influences of our social context.

Stereotypes. When we hear the word "stereotype," we are filled with all sorts of negative reactions. A stereotype, we tend to believe, is a "wrong" belief that we should do our best to avoid. Stereotypes provide the reasons for sexism, racism, anti-Semitism, and social prejudices of all kinds. As a matter of fact, though, stereotypes are no more likely to be in error than any other belief that has its basis in "common sense." That is, a stereotype is little more than a widespread belief based on common sense. Recall that common sense is only something considered "sensible" because it is consistent with what many people conventionally believe. In other words, many members of a society believe in a stereotype, and that fact of widespread belief is fundamental to the nature of a stereotype.

Like our belief in stereotypes, we believe common sense without exercising any critical judgment toward it; we accept it without evaluating it on the basis of what we believe to be true because of our own trial-and-error experiences. Uncritical acceptance is also a characteristic trait of a stereotype, something we believe to be true because it is conventional—a lot of other people also believe it is true. Like any commonsense belief, a stereotype is a bias or prejudice because we tend to accept it uncritically, without rendering any independent judgment as to its accuracy or truth value.

A stereotype is also a generalization. That is, we attribute some property to an entire class of people or objects. "The English drink tea" is a stereotype of people from Great Britain. The stereotype attributes the "tea-drinking" property to the entire class of "English." When people indiscriminately apply the stereotype to absolutely every member of the class, they often make errors. And it is the indiscriminate application of stereotypes, as well as the fact that some stereotypes (such as racist and sexist stereotypes) are simply false, that gives "stereotype" its well-deserved bad reputation.

Like all commonsense beliefs, a stereotype often has some basis in truth. Otherwise, why would so many people believe it to be true? Adults, as you can tell from my previous examples, often have a stereotypical image of teenage behaviors. Not only are teenagers "boy crazy" and "girl crazy," but they stereotypically use the telephone for recreational purposes with greater frequency than any other single group in our society. I know of no statistics compiled by the telephone company to support this belief, but many adults do subscribe to this stereotype of teenagers. What's more, this stereotype may have some basis in fact. A friend of mine once confided to me that when he called my home and actually heard the telephone ringing, he assumed that no one was home and hung up. He assumed (quite correctly, too) that if one of my daughters had been home, he would have heard a busy signal.

You will notice that in this discussion of stereotypes I have not advised you to guard against their evil influence or to realize that stereotypes are harmful to effective interpersonal communication. In fact, such advice is not always good advice. We cannot deny that stereotypes do exist and that people use them as guidelines for their behavior in interpersonal communication. In other words, social stereotypes (whether they are true or false) do influence the process of interpersonal communication, despite the fact that their influence is sometimes detrimental to effective communication. On the other hand, some stereotypes actually serve to assist the process of interpersonal communication by giving the communicators some notion of what to expect from their interaction with a new acquaintance. Stereotypes, even though they originate in the social context and are the product of socialization, however, actually function at the intrapersonal level of communication. Therefore, they will be discussed in greater detail in Part 2.

Social Rules

Every social context has its own rules. That is, each society has rules that provide its members with guidelines for distinguishing appropriate from inappropriate behaviors, what is permissible and what is not. Social rules operate like the rules of any game. When you learn a game for the first time, you first learn the rules. But there are two kinds of rules for every game. Some rules, called "constitutive rules," are embedded in the game and are typically written down in a rulebook. The constitutive rules of basketball, for instance, specify five members to a team, allow movement of the ball by passing and dribbling, require that the basket be precisely 10 feet above the playing floor, specify 2 points for a field goal, length of playing time, and so on. In addition to allowing certain behaviors, the rules of basketball also prohibit certain behaviors such as personal fouls, possession of the ball beyond the boundary lines of the playing surface, interfering with the flight of the ball in the cone above the basket, and so on.

The second kind of rules are called "regulative rules" and are created during the playing of the game (for example, 1-3-1 zone defenses, give-and-go plays, location of passing lanes, fast-break plays, and the like). Regulative rules are essentially rules for playing the game—the "teamwork" that goes into it.

By way of analogy, social contexts of interpersonal communication also have constitutive rules, even though few social contexts provide a written rulebook. And communicators develop their own regulative rules during the process of "playing the game" of interpersonal communication. The rules that come from the social context, the constitutive rules, are those behavioral guidelines that communicators know as a result of having been socialized into the larger society. Rules created by the participants during the process of interpersonal communication, the regulative rules, are the strategies that communicators actually use, the behaviors they perform when they engage in interpersonal communication.

In Part 3 of this book, on the relationship level of communication, each chapter will include a discussion of those strategies, the regulative rules of interpersonal communication. The following pages will discuss two types of constitutive rules embedded in the social context of interpersonal communication: "taking turns in conversations" and doing "small talk."

Taking Turns in Conversations. In discussing skills of interpersonal communication, we might overlook the fact that all of us have already developed a large repertoire of necessary skills during our lifetime of communicative experience. Unlike learning a totally new activity, such as playing a guitar or keeping a hackysack in the air, every one of us possesses years of experience in the practice of interpersonal communication. We have developed a number of interpersonal skills, of which we are often unaware, and we have honed them to a rather keen edge. For instance, one ability we have already mastered is the skill of taking turns when we engage in interpersonal conversations. With few exceptions, we are all pretty good at conversational turn taking. In other words, we already know these "rules." But it is difficult to explain precisely how we know when to take turns and exactly what we do at such times.

Sociologists Harvey Sacks, Emanuel Schegloff, and Gail Jefferson (1978) observed people during normal conversations and attempted to describe the rules of turn taking. A partial list of their observations, liberally paraphrased, includes the following:

1. Typically only one person talks at a time. Sometimes two people talk at the same time, but such a dialogue is usually brief.
2. Speakers change frequently.
3. Speakers typically change with no gap and no overlap.
4. Speakers follow no particular order when taking turns.
5. The length of turns varies greatly during conversations.
6. Some speakers typically talk more than others, both in length of each turn and in number of turns.
7. What people say during their turns is typically spontaneous and not prepared in advance.
8. A current speaker can select the next speaker by, for example, directing a question at a specific person, looking at a specific person, or dropping the voice to signal end of turn.
9. A speaker often self-selects a turn without waiting for the permission of the previous speaker.
10. When committing an error in turn taking, speakers work to "repair" the damage. For instance, if two speakers talk at the same time, one will stop prematurely, thereby repairing the damage to the conversational flow.

As you were reading this list of what the authors call "systematics for the organization of turn taking for conversation," you were probably thinking, "I already know that." Every item in the list seems very obvious after we read it, and all of them should be obvious. As a matter of fact, a crucial first step in attempting to improve your skill in interpersonal communication is to become aware of what you are doing when you are communicating—in short, to become aware of the obvious.

Despite the fact that turn-taking skills are almost second nature to us, we can all think of some people who are notorious for violating these social rules. These people often interrupt other people (talk out of turn); they may also refuse to yield a turn by talking too long or continuing to talk louder when someone else wants to take a turn (failure to "repair" the conversational damage). What's more, we are often guilty of violating these norms in our own conversational behavior.

You should not belittle the skill you have already acquired in conversational turn taking. Nor should you belittle my persistent attempts to make you aware of what seems all too obvious. Developing a greater sensitivity to and awareness of the important and the obvious, especially when they are typically ignored or assumed, is as much a process of learning as acquiring some new knowledge that is important but previously unknown.

Small Talk. Most people tend to downgrade the significance of what we have come to know as small talk. What do we mean by "small talk?" It is that talk which transpires in conversations, often but not necessarily between new acquaintances and in the very first phase of developing relationships—the getting-to-know-you stage. Small talk is superficial, focuses on a topic of only minor importance, reveals very little of the speaker's inner self, and is guided by the rules of the social context. Because small talk treats only trivial subject matter (such as the weather) in a superficial manner, we typically consider it to be virtually meaningless and without any special purpose except for "killing time" during conversation. To hold such an attitude too strongly, though, is a grievous error in judgment.

The most obvious but not the only function of small talk is to serve as a prelude to a more fully developed relationship. But to get to something "big," one must start with something "small." People who begin a jogging program, for instance, typically begin by running short distances and building up to longer distances. Successful large corporations usually begin as small businesses. Similarly, the most intimate and satisfying relationships begin with small talk.

Small talk thus allows interactants to ease into the relationship in gradual, incremental steps. While doing small talk, communicators discover information about each other and reveal information about themselves. They are able to compare the present relationship with other contexts, assess the potential worth of the present relationship, and decide whether to continue with the relationship and allow it to progress to a level of greater depth. Small talk thus serves as an essential first stage of maturity. Allowed to grow and develop small talk turns into "large talk." Each interactant can use small talk to test the relational waters before plunging headlong into the relationship.

Small talk also serves an important function in maintaining highly developed relationships. Married couples, for example, often engage in what sounds like small talk and use those kinds of conversations to maintain their interpersonal contacts. At the end of each day, husband and wife may talk to each other about what happened to them during their daily activities. Most of that information isn't intrinsically interesting to the other person, but maintaining the relationship is. Therefore, the small talk with its what-I-did-today topics is satisfying to the interactants because it gives them an excuse for interacting, just talking with one another. And keeping up a high level of interpersonal contacts with the relational partner helps the members to maintain their relationship.

Small talk isn't always about the weather, either. It can be relevant to virtually any topic that is superficial. My wife and I, for instance, often use interpersonal argument as a form of small talk. We never argue about important things, but we often argue about trivialities—the more trivial the better. Perhaps we use argument as small talk because we first met as members of a college debate squad; I'm not sure. But we often engage in arguments as conversational recreation, to help pass the time during long trips in the car.

One recent episode remains vivid in my memory. When we were only minutes away from home at the beginning of a fourteen-hour automobile trip, the tape deck and radio in our car simultaneously ceased to function. We were stuck with each other for the entire trip to our destination and back. During one leg of that journey, a distance of about 250 miles, we sustained a wonderful argument (about the relative merits of chain and non-chain restaurants, as I recall) until we stopped for lunch. Of course, the restaurant we entered offered evidence for our argument, and my wife proceeded to advance a relevant point in support of her side. I immediately interrupted her and said, "Don't tell me now! Wait until we get back in the car!" Looking back, I'm not sure what side of the argument I defended. But because the argument functioned as small talk, it doesn't really make any difference.

The rules of small talk are certainly influenced by the social context, which offers a range of suitable topics (weather, sports, current events, television programs, common acquaintances) and rules for dealing with those topics (don't reveal intimate details of your self, maintain a pleasant demeanor, don't stand too close, change topics frequently, don't disagree vehemently). In fact, the term "small talk" itself probably creates a false impression, because it is actually very important to interpersonal communication.

Relationship Models

The concept of the "role model" is a well-established tradition in sociology. Small children are said to look up to professional athletes and emulate their behavioral styles. Muhammad Ali serves as a role model for many boxers and black youth even today, years after his retirement as heavyweight boxing champion of the world. Adolescents emulate rock musicians, although imitating Boy George seems more like a masquerade. Movie and television stars are often selected as role models. When people pattern their individual appearance and behaviors on those of someone else in their social context, they are said to be using that person as a role model. But the social context may also provide interpersonal relationships that serve as models for the interpersonal relationships of others.

If you are a typical member of our society, the relationship you are most likely to use as a model is that of your parents. Statistics show that the children of divorced parents are far more likely to end up divorced themselves, as opposed to children of parents with stable marriages. But as strong as parental relationships are as relational models for the next generation, the most influential of all in our society may be the relationships depicted by the mass media. Popular music, TV, and the movies often emphasize the power of an intense emotional attachment to another person, typically of the opposite sex. They help to establish a societal model of "love" that is far removed from the reality of actual interpersonal relationships.

For over a hundred years, romantic novels have told a similar story: boy meets girl, boy marries girl, boy and girl live happily ever after. Love is said to conquer all. If you love the other person enough, according to this popular myth, all your troubles will be overcome. The unfortunate fact is that this story *is* mythical. Yet people continue to regard it as a norm and attempt to model their own relationships on its virtually unattainable standard.

Relationship modeling works like this. The individual enters a relationship believing in the live-happily-ever-after myth. The individual behaves in the relationship as though this relationship were the same as the mythical relationship. The individual also seeks out relationships that are expected to manifest the model they have seen on TV or at the movies and that is immortalized in popular music. As a result, the individual comes to feel the emotional attachment that the media have associated with the relationship and indirectly with the myth. In other words, if you believe that your relationship with this other person is consistent with the relational model, you come to believe that you must be feeling the emotion that is consistent with such a relationship. In this way, relational modeling tends to influence not only what people *do* but also what they *feel*—emotions as well as behaviors, intrapersonal as well as interpersonal.

Relational modeling often results in disappointment when the participants discover that the "real" relationship is not the same as the "ideal" depicted by the model. When relational problems arise for whatever reason, the participants become disillusioned and the relationship suffers. They may withdraw their commitment to the relationship; they may seek another relationship in their ongoing search for the ideal; they may resent the other person for not living up to the model; or they may seek assistance from a social support system. Whatever the outcome of the "rude awakening," the actual relationship becomes extremely vulnerable and unstable when the interactants discover that it is not like the model.

There are two problems associated with relational modeling. One is the myth that the ideal relationship need only be "attained." The model tends to define the relationship as a "goal." Once the partners have achieved that goal, they supposedly have nothing more to do. Stories may end at the point of "living happily ever after," but the "real" relationship continues. In other words, the relational model typically ignores a fundmental principle of evolutionary development: the inevitability and constancy of change. Relationships ebb and flow, rise and fall, have peaks and valleys. A relationship cannot sustain a honeymoon period for very long. When the honeymoon is over, the problems of *maintaining* the relationship begin. Maintenance is by far the most crucial stage of relational development (as Chapter 14 will show). The relational myth popularized by the mass media creates a problem by ignoring the maintenance stage completely.

The second problem with relational modeling concerns the glorification of suffering in the typical model depicted by the mass media. Movies and popular songs portray sadness and individual suffering in a way that seems beneficial and even rather enjoyable. Many of us enjoy a good cry during movies that portray a lost love, that show the agony of loving someone who doesn't deserve that love and may not even return it. Popular songs, both rock and country, tell tales of unrequited love. "He is a no-good cad, but I love him just the same" goes the story. "She doesn't love me, but my love is strong enough for both of us" is another common theme. These mythical lovers are made stronger ("become better persons") as a result of their painful experience. What the individual who engages in relational modeling doesn't understand is that suffering doesn't feel good. In fact, it isn't fun at all. But the mass media don't tell us about that.

I hasten to add that I am not suggesting that relational modeling should be avoided by interpersonal communicators. Although it often results in ineffective communication and disconfirmed expectations, no quick and easy techniques are available to help you avoid modeling your relationships on mythical ideals. But that isn't really the point. Modeling a relationship on the basis of some mythical ideal is a "normal" contextual influence on the process of interpersonal communication. Increasing your effectiveness as an interpersonal communicator does not mean avoiding doing something that is normal. Rather, you should become aware of and sensitive to these influences of social contexts. You must learn to deal with them because they do, in fact, exist.

One way of dealing with relational modeling is to understand, as fully as possible, the maintenance process of relational development and to work to increase the effectiveness of your communication skills during that stage. We can't deny or ignore the reality of contextual influences on the process of interpersonal communication and pretend that such influences don't or shouldn't exist. We develop our interpersonal skills as we engage in the process of interpersonal communication and behave in a manner appropriate to the recognizable stage of relational development. First comes awareness; then comes practice. Then these two factors (awareness and behaviors) become inseparable so that our interpersonal communication becomes second nature to us. Eventually we won't realize where one (the intrapersonal or the interpersonal) leaves off and the other begins.

Summary

Human beings are social animals. We tend to congregate together within societies and cultures. As a natural consequence of being a member of a social community, we become subject to its influences on our behaviors and beliefs. Socializing contexts teach their new members the rules, roles, values, beliefs, and norms of that society. This passing down of the society's norms and principles from one generation of members to another is called the process of socialization. Socialization takes place in four different contexts: the instructional context, the regulative context, the innovative context, and the interpersonal context.

Relational contexts are identified by the nature of the interpersonal bond that unites the members within a definable relationship. Social contexts, defined by interpersonal ties, include kinship, friendship, work, and contractual relationships as well as acquaintanceships. The boundaries of these contexts often overlap, in the sense that a colleague at work may also be a friend, and a partner in a social contract may also be related by kinship. Generally speaking, the degree of influence that a social context exerts on a given event of interpersonal communication is determined by its closeness to the interpersonal encounter. The most powerful influence is the interpersonal context itself; other contexts decrease in the degree of influence they exert on the interpersonal encounter on the basis of how socially "distant" they are from the participants.

The social context functions to influence interpersonal communication much as does the physical context. Both typically exert their greatest influence on the initial stage of relational development. But the social context, because of its greater variety and susceptibility to change, probably exerts a stronger influence on later stages of relational development.

Participants in interpersonal communication use their social contexts to provide guidelines for how they should behave during interpersonal communication, to provide information about the other person, and to influence the opportunities for interpersonal contact. In addition, the social context functions at the intrapersonal level of interpersonal communication by providing a baseline that allows the individual to compare and evaluate the worth of any particular interpersonal relationship. The social context also functions to increase the opportunities for interpersonal encounters. Because the social context varies as a result of the particular period of one's lifetime, some stages of life provide greater opportunities for interpersonal encounters than do others. The norms and standards used to define appropriate interpersonal behavior, therefore, differ during different stages of life.

Individuals also use their social contexts as support systems when they need help in solving relational problems and validating existing relationships. Contexts that serve as support systems typically include members of the same sex. Social contexts serving as support systems to provide help for individuals with relational problems are not necessarily made up of friends but rather of people who share the same problem.

The social context influences behavior during interpersonal communication by providing a set of general expectations, including rules of conduct, role relationships, and stereotypes. Because one's social context tends to change during the course of a lifetime, the social expectations of rules, roles, and stereotypes also change. People look to the social context to provide them with rules for taking turns in conversations and doing small talk. Members of our society are also susceptible to the social influences popularized by the mass media in terms of idealized relationships, which then serve as models that individuals use to guide their own "real" relationships. Relational modeling affects not only the behaviors but also the feelings and emotions of relational partners. Unfortunately, the mediated model of the ideal relationship tends to ignore the problems associated with the maintenance stage of relational development and to overemphasize the power and significance of the intrapersonally felt emotional attachment.

CHAPTER 5

The Context of Language

Scene 1: Small child is watching the family dog.
 "ROWF!" barks the dog. Dog is let outside.
Scene 2: Small child continues watching. "ROWF!"
 The dog is given food.
Scene 3: "ROWF!" The dog is petted.
Scene 4: Mother: "Junior said his first word today."
 Father: "What was it? Mommy or Daddy?"

> —From a comic strip whose
> identity is no longer in the
> author's memory banks

The story of Helen Keller has always fascinated me. With neither sight nor hearing, two vitally important senses in "normal" communication, she nevertheless learned to read, write, and speak (through sign language, of course). I never miss an opportunity to watch *The Miracle Worker*, a movie based on the stage play dramatizing the early life of Helen Keller and that of her teacher Anne Sullivan, when it appears on TV. The play/movie illustrates the enormous difficulties that were associated with teaching Helen Keller to communicate.

The problem was that Helen had no language, nor did she have any idea of what language was. Anne Sullivan, truly a miracle worker, constantly used sign language to "spell out" names of objects in Helen's hand. Sullivan consistently repeated to the child Helen, "Everything has a name. Every word has a meaning." The climax of the drama was Helen's realization that the finger game was actually a game of words that stood for objects—in the instance of the drama, the first crucial word "water."

The most fundamental function of language is probably the labeling function depicted in *The Miracle Worker*. Words are labels that we attach to persons, objects, and events. Every one of us has a name, a linguistic label used for the purpose of social identification. We also apparently have more things to name than we have names to go around. At least we use the same linguistic label to refer to a number of different objects. To call someone a "turkey", for instance, is not to suggest that he or she possesses large tail feathers and gobbles a lot. And "sucker" generally refers to a person who has nothing in common with a piece of candy on a stick. On the other hand, we appear to "waste" words by having several that refer to the same object. "Couch," "sofa," "divan," and "davenport" all label the same piece of living-room furniture.

I have read that the typical adult American knows the meanings of over half a million words but uses only about 1,500 to 2,000 of them on a daily basis. If these figures are even close to accurate, they suggest that every one of us possesses an amazing repertoire of communicative abilities that we generally take for granted. We all have the capability, as a result of being socialized in our linguistic culture, of knowing and using a large repertoire of the fundamental tools of human communication—words. But some people, we know, are better than others in their use of language. We often refer to their linguistic ability as being "articulate."

At least two factors are involved in "being articulate." One is skill in putting words together and, perhaps, putting a greater variety of words (using a larger proportion of the known vocabulary) together in a greater variety of ways so that they "sound nice." The other factor of being articulate is probably not quite so obvious. Being articulate also involves putting words together in a manner that is appropriate to the social context of the interaction. What may be very articulate in one context may be laughably inappropriate in another.

In this chapter we will discuss social context in terms of how people use the English language. The United States is an English-speaking society. Even though some segments of our nation speak another language, English is our "official" language. But the fact that we all speak English does not imply that every social context in our nation uses English in the same way. In fact, the problems of translating one language into another (for example, Spanish into English) sometimes pale in comparison to the problems of translating one English-speaking social context into another. This "translation" is sometimes more difficult because the communicators are unaware that they are experiencing a translation problem. And even when they are aware, their first tendency is to accuse the other person of using the language incorrectly.

Language has a very close and special connection with the society and its members who use the language. As it is used in social contexts, language takes on the characteristics of the community of people who use it. Actually there are really two English languages: one that is taught in the schools and defined by dictionaries and one that is used during communication. Language, when used, is defined by the social context, or the people who use it. It also serves to help define the social context. This two-way relationship between language and society is known as the *reflexivity* of language and is the topic of discussion in the first section of this chapter.

We shall also discuss in this chapter a concept crucial to human communication—the concept of meaning. As will become increasingly apparent throughout your reading about interpersonal communication, the concept of meaning is highly complex. It is a part of language, a part of the individual communicator's internalized self, and a part of the social relationship and the communicative behaviors during communication. All these different "places" of meaning (places to look for meaning) are important to understanding the process of interpersonal communication. We begin discussing the various "meanings of meaning" in this chapter, as we address the notion of social meaning embedded in language.

LANGUAGE IN USE

First-year college students, some people say, can be classified into one of two types: those who "run scared"and overachieve and those who look for the easy way out and underachieve. When I was a college freshman, one of my roommates was of the latter type. His hometown was a small German community in the Midwest; he spoke only German until he entered the first grade. Even though he was a fourth- or fifth-generation American, his English was heavily accented with Germanic pronunciations. He, of course, immediately enrolled in elementary German, thinking he would have at least one snap course while he became oriented to college life. However, he dropped his German course before midterm because he knew he was failing it miserably. Apparently the German he spoke at home, corrupted by generations of living in America, was quite different from the "pure" German taught in the classroom. My roommate was victimized by thinking that language is language is language.

In the following pages we will be discussing how people modify and, in a very real way, actually "create" their language when they use it for purposes of communication. We will be less concerned with language *as language* than with language *in use*. That is, our discussions will focus on understanding how we use language in the act of interpersonal communication. In order to do that, we will focus on the "rules" of *parole*, regulative rules (remember Chapter 4) created by communicators during the process of interpersonal communication. As we have already noted, this phenomenon, in which people affect language by the act of using it in communication as well as being influenced by the language they are using, is known as "reflexivity."

Langue and *Parole*

Seventy years ago a French linguist by the name of Saussure (1916) distinguished between two forms of language. The words he used to label these two forms (*langue* and *parole*) were in his native French, and they are commonly used by linguists today regardless of their nationality, since English words don't translate well the meanings they have in French. *Langue* refers to the standard grammatical rules of the language that all members of the language-speaking community share. These rules are codified in dictionaries and grammar books, which can then serve as the final arbiters of what is "right" and what is "wrong," what constitutes "proper" and "improper" use of the language. *Parole* refers to the rules created by people who use the language in communication. We can say that *langue* includes the "constitutive rules" of language and *parole* includes the "regulative rules."

Since our major interest is in interpersonal communication, *parole* is more important to us than *langue*. The rules of *parole* reflect the linguistic choices of the people who use the language. Rules of *parole* are constantly changing as changes in usage create new rules. Furthermore, rules of *langue* are standards for the entire community of language users, whereas rules of *parole* are standards for smaller social contexts within the larger community of language users and vary from one subgroup

A competent communicator adapts to the rules of the particular language context.
(Barbara Alper)

to another. Thus, the English language has only one set of *langue* rules but many different sets of *parole* rules.

These two French words are rather ordinary words to linguists but may become cumbersome for our purposes, Hence, we will probably be more comfortable if we can use ordinary English words instead. For the set of invariant rules of grammar, we can just as easily use the term "standard language" or "standard English"; for the set of language rules developed by language users, we will use the term *language-in-use* (hyphenated to indicate its singular meaning). More often than not, I will employ just the term "language" in the remainder of this chapter. Be forewarned that I will be using "language" to refer to "language-in-use."

Linguistic Competence and Performance

The noted psycholinguist Noam Chomsky (1965) once defined two different kinds of competence in regard to language. He referred to the understanding of the grammatical rules and proper use of standard language as *competence*. He reserved the term *performance* to mean the social use of language, including all the revisions and violations of standard rules typical in any given social context.

According to Chomsky, any individual may adapt to a present social context and use the language in a manner appropriate to that context. He called that use of language "performance." Chomsky was suggesting that although language users may be very competent in knowing what constitutes proper use of the language, their actual "performance" in using the language does not necessarily reflect that knowledge. The truly competent communicator is aware of the rules of language-in-use within any given social context and conforms to those rules—which is another way of saying that the competent communicator follows the guidelines provided by the social context to reduce uncertainty. The competent communicator thus knows what linguistic behaviors to perform in order to behave appropriately.

Perhaps an illustration would make this combination of competence and performance more easily understood. A number of years ago I became well acquainted with Ed, a black student from an urban ghetto. We spent quite a bit of time together in different social contexts, and I marvelled at his competence in adapting his language (and accompanying nonverbal behaviors) appropriately to the specific social context in which he found himself. In the classroom he invariably employed standard English, was consistently attentive, and spoke articulately and with serious purpose. In conversations with me, he "lost" some of his articulateness, often spoke in run-on and fragmentary sentences, used common slang, and was generally very casual. When he encountered a black acquaintance, his speech slurred and slowed down, his voice went up a full octave, the words and phrases were grammatically Black English, and even his posture changed. With my family he was Mr. Politeness personified, consistently smiling and gracious—the perfect "guest."

Ed was a truly competent communicator. He entered the social context, developed an understanding of what the rules were in that context, and behaved appropriately. He obviously understood the rules of standard English, but he was competent enough to know when to use them and when not to.

Reflexivity of Language

Not too long ago I watched a movie on television and heard a conversation something like this:

> "Now that's truly awesome!"
> "Where?"
> "I'd say a ten."
> "Hunk city."
> "Oh, get off it! He's nerdsville!"
> "Just cool out, beach breath."

I'll never know why I watched this movie, one of those insipid beach movies depicting the life of revelry and ribaldry among college students who descend on Fort Lauderdale during spring break. This conversation, or one that came close to it, occurred while a group of bikini-clad females were sunning themselves on the beach and observing the passing parade of swimsuit-clad males. Although much of this dialogue reflects the screenwriter's idea of the way members of the youth culture speak, it also reflects some nuances of actual linguistic usage within a particular social context.

Every generation of young people develops its own special language to use for its own special purposes. Since youth is a time for being "boy crazy" or "girl crazy" while still observing the norms of the social context, special language is developed to reflect these norms. Such words as "hunk," "fox," "ten," combined with adjectives like "awesome," are supposedly frequent in youth talk. Middle-aged men and women may be aware of many of these terms, but they don't typically use them in their own conversations. It wouldn't be "appropriate" for them.

The language is embedded in the social context and reflects the meaning created by people in that social context who use that language. Because the social context of youth changes its population very rapidly (a senior high school, for instance, undergoes nearly a 100 percent turnover in just three years), the special language also changes very rapidly. Some years ago "groovy" was the ultimate adjective. Now "awesome" is becoming passé. On the other hand, when I was in high school the most favored adjective was "cool," and that term experienced a brief resurgence of popularity some years later. Perhaps "groovy" will come back, too.

Language-in-use, to repeat, is reflexive. That is, it influences the people who use it and is in turn influenced by these people. As people use language to create special meanings, that language then changes to reflect the additional meanings created by its use. The special meaning of the language also reflects the social context in which it is used. People, through their use of their special-meaning language, exhibit their membership in that social context. In the sense that we can recognize an accent in the speech of another person, we are able to infer that the speaker comes from a particular geographical region of the country. Most of us are able to spot an accent and associate it with, say, the deep South or some other geographical region, such as New Jersey, Long Island, Boston, Maine, or Missouri. Special words and other ways of using the language also identify the social context of the user.

Regional differences do not account for all the "accents" in language, although such accents may be the most common. Other special social contexts with their own accents include Marinspeak, CB-radio talk, coptalk, computerese, Black English, Valley-girl talk, and the ever-popular teentalk. Marinspeak, so called because of its identification with the "hot tub" culture of Marin County in the San Francisco Bay area of California, now has a vocabulary all its own. Some of its special words have filtered into more widespread use, so that the following monologue seems to make sense: "Hey, I know where you're coming from. But don't lay that heavy trip on me, man. I got my own space, like I'm into meditation now. You know where I'm at?" (Translation: I understand you, but don't tell me your troubles. I am aware of my self in relation to social constraints because of my interest in Eastern mysticism. Do you understand me?)

The craze for citizen-band radios, popularized by the succession of *Smoky and the Bandit* movies (which appear finally to have run out of sequels) and trucking songs, gave the society an entire new vocabulary, including "handles" (nicknames), "smokies" (highway patrol), "double nickel" (55 mph speed limit), "hammer" (accelerator), "seat covers" (female drivers), and others. The computer-in-every-home fad has everyone talking about "interface" and "memory banks" in normal conversation. TV's *Hill Street Blues* has given us such descriptive names as "dirtbags" and "hairballs," among other more unprintable references to evildoers. And things don't just "happen" anymore; they always seem to be "going down." Teentalk is filled with expressions such as "Me an," (meaning someone else *and I*), "goes" (for "says," as in "She goes, 'How ya doin'?'"), and the notorious "ya know" (a modulated pause, literally translated as "uh").

Interestingly enough, as the usage of a special language extends beyond the boundaries of the social context and becomes more common in a larger society, it soon disappears from use in the social context that created it. Language, you recall, is said to be reflexive when it serves to identify members of a particular social context and the members of that particular social context identify with it. However, as more language users outside the boundaries of that social context pick up the expressions and use them as their own, the reflexivity of language within its social context becomes less apparent. Consequently, the special language, no longer reflecting its particular social context, dies away through erosion or benign neglect.

Members of some social contexts, however, resist the influence of linguistic reflexivity. Some contexts, for instance, want to believe in the existence of some central social standard for "proper" language use. According to this belief, a body of rules exists (somewhere), and those rules serve as the standard for language usage throughout the entire society. "Standard English" appears to function, for example, as the norm for network radio/TV announcers and newscasters. Network news reporters overwhelmingly speak with little trace of a regional accent (theirs is sometimes called a "general Midwest" accent) and use almost no special linguistic labels or slang. But if "standard English" does exist and the standard is to be followed universally, then the language-in-use within specialized social contexts is "substandard"—that is, language usage that is not up to the level of, or as good as, the standard of "proper" usage.

Within the last few decades the "deficit theory" (referring to "substandard" language-in-use) has been generally rejected, at least by sociolinguists (people involved in the study of the interplay of society and language). Most educators (not including some English teachers, of course) have accepted large, contextually bound languages-in-use as different varieties of English usage—not substandard varieties, just different kinds of English. Black English is now recognized as a type of English-in-use rather than a problem to be overcome (a "deficit" in the literacy education of young urban blacks). Of course, some educational psychologists may continue to look for reasons why school-aged black youths, because of their socially deprived life in urban ghettos, are "verbally deprived" as well (Labov, 1972). But fortunately the number of people who seem to think in terms of "verbal deprivation" gets smaller with each passing year. Most people today tend to accept the fact that our nation (like Germany, Italy, France, China, and most other countries) contains, within its national boundaries, different varieties or sets of standards of language-in-use and that no single standard for determining "right" and "wrong" usage exists.

It is easy to think of examples of specialized language-in-use for different social contexts, particularly when we think of the various large subcultures in our society—such subcultures as those based on race, regionalism, age group, and special occupations. But language is also embedded in every context. Language looks and sounds "different" because of that context. Furthermore, the language sounds different only to a person who is not a member of that social context. To the language users themselves, their language-in-use is not different at all, but quite familiar.

Recall that competent language users often have the knowledge of other standards of usage but don't necessarily perform according to those standards in all social contexts. Two highly articulate, well-educated, skillful public speakers rarely reflect those skills when engaged in "conversation" with friends. Consider the following conversation:

A: Need a ride?
B: Yeah. Gotcher car?
A: Unh-huh. The Chevy. How 'bout My Wife's Place on th' way?
B: I sure could use a draft. Bad day!
A: Yeah. Me, too. 's go.
B: Hot daa-yum! Yer on!

Apparently these two interactants are car-pooling home from work and plan to stop at a tavern on the way and drink beer because their workday has been unusually difficult. Some characteristics typical of conversation, particularly among friends, are quite apparent in this brief dialogue. Note that each person's turn is grammatically "impure" in the sense that neither tends to converse in complete sentences. One of the few complete sentences occurs in the fourth line of dialogue, and it is grammatically incorrect. The "proper" sentence would be "I could *surely* use a draft."

A nonparticipant in this interaction would find it difficult to understand the objective meaning of each turn, but the interactants themselves would have no difficulty at all in interpreting each other's remarks. Apparently they are both familiar, for example, with the fact that "My Wife's Place" is a business establishment that serves beer, rather than the residence of an estranged spouse. Both communicators realize that the ambiguous "How about My Wife's Place on the way?" is an invitation to interrupt their journey homeward in order to stop and drink beer. "Bad day" is certainly ambiguous on the face of it, but the next speaker clearly has understood that the phrase meant "I have experienced an unusually difficult day here at work."

Note also that conversational language-in-use is virtually always "sloppy." The interactants run their words together, fail to articulate all the sounds in each word, use crude versions of real words ("yeah" for "yes," for instance), and mispronounce some words ("damn" ordinarily has only a single syllable).

Sloppy speech patterns, ambiguity of objective meanings, grammatical errors, and sentence fragments are just a few of the characteristics that are typical and "normal" in conversation, the primary act of interpersonal communication. It is not that interactants in conversation aren't competent in the rules of the standard language; in fact, to converse in the manner reflected in the conversation quoted above is to reflect one's competence in performing conversation in that particular social context. These communicators are using language in a conversation and doing what comes naturally. They are actually following the rules and standards of what conversation looks like and sounds like. To be frank, this conversation is a rather close paraphrase of an actual conversation between two people with superb interpersonal and public speaking skills. In fact, they were professors of communication!

SOCIAL MEANING

The concept of meaning (an extraordinarily significant concept in interpersonal communication) has, itself, a number of different meanings. None of the meanings of meaning, of course, is any more "correct" than any of the others. Like many words in the dictionary, "meaning" has several different definitions. One of the principal reasons for the variation in the meaning of meaning is the locus issue: *where* is meaning located? Where does one look to find meaning?

Depending on where you look, you will find different meanings. A dictionary, for example, is only one place to look for meanings and is typically the last place to look to discover the meaning that is important or even relevant to interpersonal communication. The dictionary is generally a source for standard English as accepted by the larger society, not language-in-use in specific social contexts. The model of communication used to guide our discussion in this book specifies three potential "places" where one can find meaning: in the context, in the individual, and in the relationship. In each of these we will find a different meaning of what meaning means in interpersonal communication. Furthermore, every meaning of meaning is "correct."

For the moment let's distinguish two kinds of meaning—one inside the heads of the communicating individuals and the other in the language-in-use during the act of communication. More precisely, these two kinds of meaning can be phrased this way: (1) we "mean something" by what we say and (2) what we say "has some meaning." These two meanings of meaning are basically the difference between "intention" and "context," between locating meaning in the individual and locating it in the language.

We commonly think of meaning as defined by the intentions of the individual. But for those who continue stubbornly to insist that the most important meaning is what people intend their behaviors to mean, I ask you to recall the case of James Watt. For those of us with short memories, Watt was secretary of the interior just a few years ago. He uttered a number of things in public that got him in deep trouble. He referred to the people who attended Beach Boys concerts as an "undesirable element," and his description of the minorities represented on a national commission became classic for a time. Despite his insistence that his *intended* meaning was perfectly honorable, the language itself apparently had its own meanings in a number of differing social contexts. The public outcry resulted in Watt's resignation from his cabinet post.

No one should dispute the existence or importance of intended meanings. Similarly, no one should dispute the existence and importance of social meanings that are embedded in the language-in-use. The following pages are concerned with the locus of meaning in the context of language-in-use. We will treat four dimensions of linguistic meaning: conventionality, indexicality, style switching, and nonverbal elements of language-in-use. Consistent with the reflexivity of language, the first two dimensions are primarily concerned with the influence of the language on the language users; the last two dimensions deal with the influence of the language users on the language-in-use.

Conventionality

The focus of this discussion is on the social meaning created by and embedded in the context of interpersonal communication. Our discussions have consistently emphasized that meaning is created through its use in social interaction. In fact, we can go farther and assert the truism that language has meaning *only* insofar as it becomes "conventional"—in other words, that language is used *commonly* by members of some culture or society, some social context. We have also suggested that the use of identifiable sociolinguistic choices serves to identify the speaker and inform the hearer about the speaker's membership in certain regional or other social contexts. But the hearer can interpret the speaker's language-in-use only to the extent that it can be identified with a specific social context. In other words, the speaker's use of language must be conventional (typical and widespread) to members of a given social context.

To illustrate, a southern accent is recognizable only because that manner of speaking is conventional (common) in the southern United States. When someone uses language "out of context," though, it doesn't "sound right" because it is not consistent with the conventional usage. A recent movie, *Melanie*, tells the story of an illiterate woman from Arkansas who found herself in the alien neon world of Los Angeles. When introduced to a stranger, she replied, "Pleased to make your acquaintance." This ritualistic response, quite conventional in her regional subculture as polite greeting behavior, was the subject of ridicule by her new acquaintance. As a native of Los Angeles, the stranger found Melanie's greeting out of context and therefore humorous. In other words, she "sounded funny" to him.

To illustrate further, a stereotypical character frequently shows up in televised situation comedies ("sitcoms" in TV-talk). The character is the aged man or woman who tries to talk and act like a teenager. She (but sometimes he) uses every word one could possibly associate with the young, sometimes, in fact, Valley-girl talk. Her language is frequently and painfully interspersed with such words as "groovy," "hunk," "awesome," ad nauseum. Television writers probably intend such characters to be "cute," but audiences are too often struck by the out-of-context language to be amused. The language is conventional only when used by younger people. When uttered by people who have collected Social Security checks for over a decade, it is so unconventional as to be unnerving. Where is the humor in that?

Indexicality

Conventional meanings of language, because they are created through frequent and typical use, "belong" only to the people in a given social context. Thus, the language's range of social meaning is limited to that social context whose members use that language conventionally. The larger the social context, the greater the number of people who understand the meaning of the language, what the language says. In order to "translate" the meanings of language properly, then, communicators give "hints" to each other as to which social context (that is, which conventional meaning) is being used. These hints are known as *indexing* the language-in-use.

To index a meaning is to place the language within some specific social context. That social context may be very large (as in the national society) or very small (as in a specific interpersonal relationship). Some people have suggested that music is embedded in a very large social context. Music is sometimes called a "universal language," apparently because an extremely broad range of people understand and appreciate it. Of course, music (as a language-in-use) has its social contexts, too—particular groups of people who like one kind of music but not others (a form of social prejudice and stereotyping). My daughter once brought home a recently purchased album by Sylvia. When I remarked that I hadn't been aware that she liked country music, she became upset and denied that Sylvia's music was "country." Within her teenage social context, one wouldn't be caught dead expressing a liking for country music. Our mass media have even created a sociolinguistic label for records that appeal to more than one social context. When a record is popular on several of the rock, country, and jazz lists of top tunes, we call it a "crossover."

Most social meanings of language, of course, are something less than universal. They are limited to a rather restricted social context and are not conventionally used beyond that context. The verb "to hit" does not have the universal meaning of "to strike with force." Within some social contexts, "to hit" (often accompanied with "on") refers to making improper advances, typically of a male attempting to "pick up" (but not to lift bodily from the floor) a female. To baseball players, however, "to hit" is used with a different specialized meaning.

A particular word may have more than one particularized meaning, depending on which social context is being "indexed." Every one of these meanings is a social convention, at least in some social context. The problem in communication, then, is to use the language in such a way as to allow the hearer to realize which particularized meaning is represented. This process of pinpointing the appropriate context of the language is, as previously noted, called indexing. The linguistic technique that performs the indexing function is called an *indexical expression*. (For anyone interested in reading more about indexing in language, see Garfinkel & Sacks, 1969.)

Indexing is something like putting subscript numbers on sociological symbols (words and expressions) whose social meaning is otherwise ambiguous (too much uncertainty, too many possible interpretations). The speaker employs an indexical expression that essentially informs the hearer, "I am using meaning$_1$, not meaning$_2$." The solution to the indexing problem, reducing uncertainty of meanings, lies with identifying the social context in which "meaning$_1$" is conventional. When I moved to the "intermountain West," as it is called out here, I was amazed what people meant when they used the term, "back East." Shortly after my arrival here, an acquaintance informed me that he was heading "back East" to visit relatives. I was flabbergasted to learn he was traveling to Omaha, Nebraska! When I lived in South Dakota and Minnesota, our indexing of "back East" was, at least, Cleveland. After having been socialized into the Rocky Mountain culture, I have come to the conclusion that "back East" means virtually anything east of the continental divide, although Denver may stretch this definition a little.

A colleague, interested in sociolinguistic questions relevant to interpersonal communication, was once intrigued with ways of indexing notions pertaining to time. What was meant, he wondered, by the phrase "next Wednesday"? When someone used the phrase on a Sunday, he discovered that few people would misunderstand that this expression ("next") indexed the time three days in the future. On a Tuesday, he discovered that most people interpreted the indexical expression to mean "eight days." But on a Monday, the expression that indexed time was quite ambiguous, and its meaning differed according to relatively small social contexts.

We learn to adapt our individual "styles" to many social contexts.
(Michael Weisbrot & Family)

Indexical expressions, then, provide the hearer with a frame of reference to clarify the social meaning of the language-in-use. The expression is meaningful, of course, only when and because its reference is conventional to the members of a particular social context. To recognize the indexical expression as conventional is to be a member of that social context. People who recognize social meanings are typically the people who have helped create the conventions through their social interaction or have become socialized within that context. By developing a history of relationships within a social context, by interacting with other members of that social context, you essentially undergo a process of socialization and learn the social meanings just as you learn the other social meanings of norms, values, beliefs, and so forth. In this case, you become socialized by practicing the language-in-use of that social context and learn their conventions (the socially particularized meanings).

Style Switching

Americans seem to have a cultural need to classify everything, put things in neat pigeonholes in order to understand them. We tend to do the same thing with people— classify them and thereby "understand" who they are. If people were like letters to be mailed, this classifying task would be simple. Every letter has a zip code and only one zip code. Every letter belongs in one and only one pigeonhole. Social contexts, however, are not like zip codes, and people are not like letters. Social contexts overlap, and every single individual in our society belongs to many different social contexts. If we can use the word *style* to refer to the language-in-use of a particular social context, then *style switching* refers to the ability to change our use of language from the conventions of one social context to another.

We are well aware that every one of us belongs to many different social contexts at any given time of life. We belong to contexts of friendship, work, family, acquaintanceship, geography, politics, socioeconomy, school, age, and so on. At the same time, though, we also know that every person has developed a particular style that identifies membership in a particular social context. Your style is, generally speaking, the way you participate in communication. We already have a variety of sociolinguistic labels to describe the communicative style of any person. Such terms range from "warm" to "cold," "formal" to "informal," "aloof" to "friendly," as well as "conversational," "gregarious," "intimate," and many others. Some people, we think, are "easy to get to know"; others seem more "distant."

Occasionally we think of interpersonal style in terms of some internal quality or individual personality quirk. We treat style as personality when we refer to someone as "extroverted" or "introverted," "sociable," "a show-off," or "shy." What we have come to know as personality traits, though, are more likely to be the ways we have learned our language-in-use, the ways we have learned to communicate in a particular social context. Moreover, we have learned to switch our styles when moving from one social context to another.

Some people encounter problems in switching their styles when they enter a different social context. Years ago, when I was teaching high school in the Midwest, a student in a public speaking course suffered from the worst case of stage fright I have ever encountered. She told me she just *couldn't* bring herself to stand up in front of an audience. Before her first speech assignment, I met with her outside class numerous times, went over her speech outline with her, and encouraged her as well as I knew how. When her turn came to speak, she mumbled a few words, burst into tears, and ran out of the classroom. I couldn't understand it. This student was bright, on the honor roll, active in cocurricular activities, and socially quite popular. I devised a special project for the next speech assignment in which each student was assigned to interview and be interviewed by another student on the basis of a situation I handed out. The interview was conducted with the class as audience, and she performed both roles with no problem.

This student continued to experience stage fright (who doesn't?) during the remainder of the semester, but she controlled it without undue difficulty. The following year she even ran for an office in student government, which meant that she would have to deliver a public speech before the entire student body of about 1,500 individuals. Her parents thought I was the greatest teacher in the world. I didn't argue with them.

Some people, including her parents, thought this student had a personality problem. A more reasonable explanation is that she hadn't learned how to switch styles. She had developed a style for one social context (face-to-face) and was familiar (self-confident) when using that style in that context. She had never had the opportunity to develop a style for the public-speaking context and felt "out of context" in that situation. Because she had difficulty switching styles when she entered the new and unfamiliar context, I switched contexts on her. Her interviewing was really a public context (speaker to audience), but it seemed more like an interpersonal context (interviewer to interviewee). The transition from one context to another required no switch in the communicator's style. She apparently handled the transition to "pure" public context on her own without being hampered by any personality "problem" she allegedly possessed—and this was not (alas!) due to some brilliant teaching technique of the instructor.

We typically engage in style switching when we move from one interpersonal social context to another. When we use the term "the individual's language-in-use," we are essentially referring to that person's style of communicating interpersonally. You don't interact in the same way with your family, for instance, as you do with friends. And you interact still differently when you are meeting someone for the first time. You have developed a style that is appropriate (comfortable) for the relational context in which you find yourself.

Switching styles, the individual's language-in-use, is one part of being competent in interpersonal communication. Knowing when to switch styles and what style is appropriate to the context constitutes an essential first step in becoming a more effective communicator. Of course, your competence is also a function of your ability to perform the appropriate style in each social context. Not everyone is equally competent in all interpersonal styles. However, research has shown (LaGaipa, 1981, p. 85) that people who are rich in one relational context (kinship, for instance) are also rich in others. That is, people with close family relationships also, generally speaking, have many close friends and acquaintances. This means that communicators competent in one style (that is, in one social context) tend to be competent in other styles, as well.

Your communicative style, the way you interact with others, is undoubtedly not a single style. You actually have many styles that you use in different social contexts. The members of one social context classify you within a style that may be quite different from the way your fellow members in another context have classified you. A former student provides an excellent example of what appeared to be two different people. She was a marginal student in several classes—bright enough, but so painfully withdrawn (she spoke only when spoken to, her eyes downcast, voice barely above a low murmur) that her classroom performance was far from excellent. She completed a major in communication with a grade point average barely above the minimum. To be frank, my faculty colleagues and I stereotyped her, attributing her behavior and classroom performance to her status as a minority (black) student intimidated by being in a predominantly white culture. Were we wrong!

I subsequently discovered that this student was very active in black organizations on and off campus and politically active in intercampus and community organizations—a capable and highly respected member of those social contexts. I had the opportunity to see her "in action" (after her graduation) during a banquet in a downtown hotel. She was articulate, forceful, energetic, even extroverted. Her style was almost the exact opposite of her classroom behavior as a student. She had switched styles, to be sure, and her style switching was extreme. She also agreed with me that her classroom style was probably inappropriate, but she had never developed an appropriate style for the classroom context.

This student is probably not typical, but her experience does illustrate that competence in interpersonal communication involves both knowing when to switch styles and performing a style appropriate for that context. Although people who are competent in one social context tend to be competent in most interpersonal contexts, most of us don't feel comfortable or confident on every occasion. Competence in interpersonal communication is undoubtedly relevant to all three parts of the communication model—context, self, and relationship. Feeling uncomfortable or lacking confidence in your own communicative behavior is equivalent to locating communicative competence in your self, the intrapersonal level of interpersonal communication. But if the relationship "works" or is competent, then the intrapersonal feeling of incompetence may not be significant.

Nonverbal Elements

You may think it unusual to be discussing nonverbal elements of communication in a chapter on language. Recall, though, that we are discussing language-in-use, and no one can *use* language in a social context without also using the nonverbal behaviors which are conventional within that context. But there is a problem with discussing nonverbal elements of communicative behavior: we know very little about them. Unfortunately, we think we know much more than we actually do.

Our society abounds with commonsense "knowledge" of nonverbal communication. Much of that "knowledge" is included in the large number of "how to" paperback volumes available in nearly every neighborhood bookstore. Such books as *How to Pick Up Girls* and *How to Close the Sale* (actual titles of real books) promise their readers success in achieving their interpersonal goals (from seduction to salesmanship) primarily on the basis of being able to "read" the other's "body language." These books treat the other person as essentially a "victim" of the reader's newly acquired "power." Unfortunately, they promise much more than they can possibly deliver.

"Nonverbal" is a catch-all term that refers to a confusingly large number of potential nonlinguistic behaviors. Dick Crable (1981) identifies some areas of nonverbal behavior and illustrates the fantastic breadth of this area: "kinesics, proxemics, haptics, oculesics, objectics, chronemics, vocalics, environmental factors, or physical appearance" (p. 66). And Crable's list of jargonistic terms denoting nonverbal elements of interpersonal communication is highly incomplete! To understand all nonverbal behaviors as they function in communication is to understand bodily movements and postures (kinesics), use of space (proxemics), touching (haptics), pupil dilation (oculesics), and on and on and on. Rather than discuss each of these separately, our discussions will treat nonverbal elements as part of the social context and its conventions of language-in-use.

In the first place, we are interested in nonverbal behavior only when it is a part of interpersonal communication. In other words, nonverbal *behavior* is not the same thing as nonverbal *communication*. Every time people cross their legs or fold their arms they are not necessarily communicating anything. Nonverbal behaviors are part of interpersonal communication only when they are interpretable within some social context of language-in-use.

There are fundamentally two ways that nonverbal behavior functions in interpersonal communication. Albert Scheflen (1972), a psychiatrist widely read by people interested in communication, referred to these as the *psychological* and the *communicational* viewpoints of nonverbal behavior:

> If the observer focuses on one member of a group and considers only that member's thought or purpose he will see his behavior as an expression [of a psychological state]. But when the observer looks at this behavior in terms of what it "does" in the larger group then a communicational point of view has been adopted. (p. xiii)

Psychologically, nonverbal behaviors are interpreted as expressions of an individual's internal states, such as emotions. Persons feel sad (internal emotion), so they cry (nonverbal behavior). They feel happy, so they smile. In interpersonal communication, then, the communicators interpret each other's nonverbal behaviors as "messages" that one "gives off" to inform the other what he or she is feeling.

Communicationally, the interactants use nonverbal behaviors to organize their interpersonal relationships on the basis of how the nonverbal behaviors of one person "fit together" with the nonverbal behaviors of others. To understand how these behaviors are organized interpersonally is to understand how the interactants integrate or regulate themselves as they create their interpersonal relationship. Scheflen (1965) himself demonstrated how, by observing only the nonverbal behaviors of kinesics, someone could make the interpretation that a close interpersonal relationship was developing or failing to develop. For instance, during their conversation, Alfred leans closer to Betty and smiles. Betty leans closer to Alfred and returns the smile. Alfred puts his arm around Betty. Betty smiles and places her hand in Alfred's. The behaviors of both participants "fit together" to organize a developing, more intimate relationship.

Another way to describe the "psychological" and "communicational" views of nonverbal behavior is to describe them as *intrapersonal* and *interpersonal*. When a communicator uses the other's nonverbal behavior to infer some hidden emotional state, the nonverbal behavior is part of the intrapersonal part of the process of communication. When the behaviors of both people fit together in an organized and meaningful fashion, nonverbal behaviors are functioning within the interpersonal or relational part of the communication process.

The psychological and communicational (that is, intrapersonal and interpersonal) views of nonverbal behavior are quite compatible with each other. Nonverbal behaviors are *both* expressive and relational, psychological and communicational. In other words, the meanings of nonverbal behaviors are actually located in two different places—in the individual (psychological) and the relational (communicational) components of our model of interpersonal communication. Therefore, we will be discussing nonverbal behaviors in both Parts Two and Three of this book. Naturally, we will be using a different viewpoint of what nonverbal behavior "means" in each of these two sections.

But what about specific kinds of nonverbal behavior? Certainly nonverbal elements of language-in-use (for instance, body movements) are embedded in the social context. Let's begin with the term "body *language*." For one thing, this term is misleading. Gestures and bodily postures do not constitute a "language" as such. They are more accurately described as a *paralanguage,* nonverbal behaviors that accompany a language-in-use and are used to interpret the meaning of the verbal behaviors within a particular social context.

In previous discussions, we talked about some characteristics of normal conversation: slurred speech, incomplete sentences, dropping of some sounds and adding others, and unclear articulation, among others. These paralinguistic characteristics of how the language is spoken (*vocalics* if you wish to impress your friends and neighbors with your jargon) include factors associated with the voice, that is, uttering or speaking the language in a certain way: inflection, pitch, rate, volume, phonetics, and articulation, among others. Gestures and body postures (*kinesics,* and one more addition to your vocabulary) are also part of a paralanguage to the extent that they are used *with* language and help the interactants interpret the meaning of what is said, such as a pointing gesture accompanying the vocalizaton "Sit right here."

Paralinguistic features of language-in-use are conventional only within a particular social context. In moving from one social context to another, you change your paralanguage as you change the verbal elements of language-in-use. Cultural anthropologists are fond of describing differences in nonverbal behaviors between one culture and another. For example, the gesture made by placing the thumb between two fingers of a clenched fist is an innocuous move in the adult-child game of "got your nose." But in some Latin American cultures, that same gesture represents a crude homosexual invitation. Although the differences may not be as extreme as in this case, the meaning of a nonverbal behavior in one social context may be quite different from its meaning in another social context, even when both contexts are included within the same language-using society. For example, you may hug a fellow member of a friendship or kinship context as a conventional greeting ritual, but you may get your face slapped if you try the same nonverbal behavior with a new acquaintance.

Like the verbal elements of language-in-use, there are few nonverbal elements of language that are universal in our English-speaking society. We can all grasp an accent in spoken English and recognize that the speaker is not a native-born speaker of our language. Vocalic features of language are certainly not universal. For example, Japanese have trouble saying the *l* sound prevalent in English; when they say *l,* it sounds more like *r* to us. The German accent in English is more guttural than our pronunciation and includes harsher consonant sounds (substituting *ch* for *j* sounds, for example). But these are the obvious examples of a paralinguistic accent.

The use of appropriate vocalic pronunciations of the language and the inappropriate gestures will also be "heard" as an accent in the language. A friend of mine, a native-born Japanese, once confided to me that he experienced enormous difficulty when speaking English, not in terms of the pronunciation of the sounds (his was nearly flawless) but because of the accompanying gestures. He found it particularly difficult to master the "straight from the shoulder" style of American conversation. As a Japanese native, he had learned (become socialized in) the convention of speaking with downcast eyes and arms close to the body. To do otherwise was to be rude, and rules of politeness are very strict in the Japanese culture. Interacting with native-born Americans, he had the problem of appearing insincere and shy, neither of which he actually was. Even though my friend had learned to pronounce the English sounds (vocalics) with a minimum of accent, he still spoke with a distinct paralinguistic accent in his use of gestures that were not conventional within the American social context. That is, he had little vocalic accent, but he had a strong kinesic accent.

The same phenomenon occurs when we move from one social context to another within our English-speaking society. We already know about style switching, in which we change our language-in-use when we enter a different context; but we may or may not be aware that we also change the nonverbal behaviors that accompany our language. Have you noticed how much more you smile (appropriately pronounced "smie-yul") in polite conversations with strangers? Even the body posture and eating behavior are different when you are at, say, a fancy restaurant as opposed to your home or a cafeteria.

Greeting behavior is also different from one social context to another. You are probably accustomed to shaking hands as the conventional nonverbal behavior when you are introduced to a stranger. Shaking hands is appropriate, whether the new acquaintance is a male or a female. In some social contexts, however, that greeting is not as conventionally appropriate. Have you ever noticed on the *Tonight* show how Johnny Carson and Ed McMahon kiss virtually every female who walks out from behind the curtain? When Johnny informs the audience that he has never met the woman he has just kissed, we realize that the kissing was a ritual greeting between strangers, not even casual acquaintances. I have frequently found myself in a social context in which kissing is the convention for greeting the opposite-sex acquaintance, and I have even gone so far as to attempt to adapt my behavior to this social convention. (After all, when in Rome. . . .) Nevertheless, like too many people, I think, this custom remains somewhat uncongenial to me.

Nonverbal behaviors are certainly an important part of interpersonal communication. Precisely how important, though, remains uncertain. It is quite clear that popular belief ("common sense") probably overestimates the significance of nonverbal behaviors within the process of interpersonal communication. Furthermore, we typically claim more understanding of nonverbal communication than we actually possess. Because nonverbal behaviors function intrapersonally and interpersonally, several of the chapters in Parts 2 and 3 will also include further discussions of nonverbal elements of interpersonal communication.

Summary

Language, a fundamental part of the social context of interpersonal communication, is embedded in the social context and varies from one context to another. The same language, such as English, involves two different types of meaning and rules that govern its use: (1) the rules universal in the language and (2) the rules created as the language is used in communication. Language-in-use creates social meanings interpretable by members of the social context as a result of their conventional (highly frequent and typical) use during interaction among members of that social context.

Virtually every social context develops its own social meanings and conventions. Language is said to be reflexive in that the language-in-use reflects the social meanings of the social context in which it is used, and people who use the language reflect their membership in that social context by demonstrating those conventions in their language-in-use. Language-in-use includes indexical expressions that inform the hearer of the social convention and reduce the uncertainty concerning which meaning is contained in what is said. Social meanings are either universal or specialized, depending on their applicability to the social meaning of language-in-use in the social context. Universal meanings, though fewer in number, apply to every social context that includes the use of that language (such as English). More particularized social meanings are limited to the members of that social context in which the language-in-use is conventional.

Individual communicators develop their own individual adaptations of language-in-use and interact within that style. Each individual has the ability to perform many different styles and switches from one to another upon entering a different social context or a new stage in a developing interpersonal relationship. Understanding what style is being performed and when to switch to a new style is a part of being competent in interpersonal communication.

Using language in interpersonal communication involves using nonverbal behaviors that necessarily accompany it. Nonverbal behaviors function in two ways in interpersonal communication. Psychologically, this may be interpreted as external expressions of some internal or emotional state. Communicationally, the nonverbal behaviors of one communicator "fit together" with those of the other to "organize" and define their interpersonal relationship. The vocalic and kinesic behaviors that accompany language are an inseparable part of the social meanings involved in language-in-use. Like verbal behaviors, the nonverbal behaviors that accompany the language—the paralanguage—should also be appropriate to the language-in-use. When inappropriate, the paralinguistic factors are recognized as an accent in the language.

PART 2

The Individual Communicator

CHAPTER **6**

The Nature of the Individual

Happiness isn't something you experience;
it's something you remember.

—Oscar Levant

I recently had the good fortune to run 226 miles of the Colorado River as it winds its way through the Grand Canyon. This trip, which was made in a five-person inflatable oarboat, will remain one of my most vivid memories. If I close my eyes, I can still see the majestic canyon walls—with their technicolor displays of polished white limestone and vivid redwall, shiny black schist, and rugged black lava cones—soaring straight up to the sky and the brownish-red sand-saturated water of the river itself. I can still hear the sounds of the thunderstorms rumbling down the river and echoing off the canyon walls, the fluttering wings of the bats at night, the splash of the oars in the water, and the deep-throated roar of the rapids. Oh, those rapids!

The rapids on the Colorado River are among the few things in this world that truly deserve that overused adjective "awesome." The sound of all that water is enough to win respect from the most intrepid river traveler. The raw power of the sandy water, our eager but reluctant anticipation as we heard the rumble of the rapids ahead of us (before we could see them), the flow of adrenaline as our boat slid down the smooth tongue of water straight into the boiling rapids at the bottom, the sight of a brown 15-foot wall of water crashing straight down on top of our heads, and the oarsman's quite unnecessary shout to "Hang on!"

After we had left the river and climbed to the southern rim of the Grand Canyon, we found ourselves having to backtrack nearly 400 miles by automobile in order to return to our starting place. Only a few hours later, after twelve days on the river, we were seeing the canyon from up on the canyon rim. The contrast was remarkable. From our vantage point, we couldn't even see the river. Instead, we viewed the vast expanse of the canyon, a huge hole in the ground that extended forever in front of us and on either side from horizon to horizon. We saw hiking trails switchbacking down nearly vertical cliffs and leading straight down to the canyon floor from a dizzying height. I was struck with the incredible difference between my two experiences of Grand Canyon National Park.

Looking down on the canyon from the rim, I could see the enormity of this marvelous work of nature. The feeling was one of limitless space and breathtaking size. On the river, I had looked up at the canyon walls flanking both sides of the river and had felt confined, restricted to the water and to the occasional sand beach clinging precariously to the rock walls. From the rim I had the feeling of being a Peeping Tom, looking in on the canyon from my elevated vantage point. All around me were my fellow sightseers, other Peeping Toms with their blow-dried hairdos, wearing clean clothes and eating ice cream cones. Just hours earlier we had been on the river, several thousand feet below, suffering from the oppressive heat and merciless desert sun. Just the day before, any one of us might have done desperate things for an ice cream cone!

We hadn't showered for twelve days. We were wearing the same clothes we had put on days earlier. For twelve days we had brushed our teeth in brown sandy water. In fact, we had joked that our biggest problem, after the fourth day, was trying to stay upwind of one another. I looked at all the "tourists" peering down at the canyon and felt smugly superior to them. They were only looking at a long-range view, a slide projected on a giant screen, I thought. I, on the other hand, had experienced the "real" Grand Canyon. I had braved the rapids and suffered deprivation on the river. They didn't know what the Grand Canyon was "really" like, but I did.

I am telling you about my Grand Canyon adventure at such length for two reasons. One reason, discovered shortly after I returned home, is that people who have run the rapids of the Colorado River through the Grand Canyon seem to have an irrepressible need to tell virtually everyone else about their experience. But the second reason is more relevant to our task at hand. The "inside" and "outside" views or experiences of the Grand Canyon provide an excellent metaphor for how we understand interpersonal communication and human relationships.

As I suggested earlier, my initial reaction to seeing the tourists on the canyon rim was one of utter condescension. On the river, I thought, I had experienced the "real" Grand Canyon. As TV sportscasters like to say, I had known the Grand Canyon "up close and personal." I didn't realize until later that my river experience had not allowed me to see the enormous expanse of the canyon. From the river I had no grasp of what actually made the canyon "grand." A number of rivers are bounded by 300- to 500-foot walls, but they and their canyons would all be insignificant by comparison. From the river I could not see the literally thousands of miles of hiking trails, the variety of geological formations, or the diversity of weather patterns that ranged from one end of the canyon to the other. In other words, I couldn't see the canyon for the river.

Understanding human communication is not much different. Your understanding is based on *your* viewpoint. When you are on the inside looking out (as a passenger on a Colorado River boat or a participant in a relationship), you have only one view of what's going on and what it means—your own isolated view. You may think that your understanding is more "real" because you are actually participating in the relationship, but it certainly can't be any *more* real than the view of the other participant. And that view may be very different from yours. So whose view is more real?

Your view of your own relationship is certainly more detailed and more vibrant, at least to you, just as the other person's view is more detailed and vibrant to her or him. But one person's view can hardly be more "real" than another person's. In fact, each of the views (yours and the other person's) is incomplete and distorted precisely because you are both participants in the relationship and are therefore biased. You are too close to the relationship. The view from the outside looking in (as from the canyon rim or from the vantage point of a nonparticipant in a relationship) is less personal but more complete. The big-picture view enables you to understand just how complex the relationship is, how many different elements it includes, how it resists simple answers that stem from too much knowledge and too little understanding.

What's the difference between knowledge and understanding? One can "know" something very well without "understanding" it at all. One problem of applying what seems like common sense to the phenomena of human communication is that commonsense knowledge too often comes only from the incomplete and distorted view of the insider. Commonsense knowledge is based on the idea that "I know because I've been there." We can certainly "know" the insider's view, but the insider's view too often lacks the broader understanding that comes from the big-picture view of the outside observer. In a sense, this perspective of the relationship might be expressed by saying "I understand because I haven't been there." For a complete understanding, we need to acquire both the insider's and outsider's views of interpersonal communication, seeing both the self and the relationship.

The next two chapters discuss this "insider's" view of human relationships—interpersonal communication as seen from the participant's vantage point. This part of the relationship might be called a "psychological" understanding of human communication. The emphasis in Part Two is on elements that lie *within* the individual communicator, the *intra*personal level of communication. That is, we will be discussing concepts that cannot be observed and for which we must rely on assumptions and inferences, the truth of which we can never hope to prove. Fortunately, though, proof is rarely necessary, because we generally believe in the truth of these assumptions and don't ask for proof. The principal assumption underlying the discussions in the next two chapters is that we have the ability to discover, in a variety of ways, what is going on inside the other person as well as inside ourselves.

In this chapter we will be introducing the discussions in the chapters of Part Two and attempting to explain this psychological understanding of interpersonal communication. We will focus our discussions on the *locus* of a psychological understanding—the *self* of the communicator. Then we will discuss the three levels of self in interpersonal communication. We conclude by discussing how the self of each participant in interpersonal communication can affect the process of communication and the social relationship.

THE SELF—THE PSYCHOLOGICAL LOCUS

We have previously discussed the fact that the human being is a very selfish animal. As humans, we tend to evaluate and use our environment in ways that benefit us. Each of us tends to judge our experiences by the same criterion: "What can it do for me?" It should not be surprising, then, that we tend to judge other people and our relationships with them in a similar manner: "How can this relationship benefit me?" Within the last few months I have heard two people evaluate their marital relationships, one positively and one negatively, but both used the same selfish criterion. One person said something to the effect that "Just being with her makes me feel good. She is always there when I need her." The other said something like "He just didn't let me grow. I need my own space, and he stifled me."

The psychological part of interpersonal communication locates the meaning of the social relationship "within" the individual, in the communicator's self. When you see your relationship from the viewpoint of your own self, you see it with a sense of ownership. That is, we think of other persons and our relationships with them as "belonging" to us. For example, we say *my* wife, *my* boss, *my* friend, *my* classmate, an acquaintance of *mine*. In other words, we typically define relationships and even other people in selfish terms—how they relate *to us*.

In this section we will be dealing with two issues: how to use a psychological view to understand interpersonal communication and how to understand the internal and external self of the individual communicator. When we understand interpersonal communication from the intrapersonal locus of the self, we must keep in mind the fact that this view of the relationship is a "selfish" view. It leads to an understanding of an interpersonal relationship that is not really what goes on *between* the communicators but what goes on *within* the participant. The psychological view of interpersonal communication is *a* view, but not *the* view. As students of interpersonal communication, we need to understand both views—the insider's (self) view and the outsider's (relationship) view.

Using the Psychological Locus

Now don't get me wrong. When I say a psychological understanding of interpersonal communication is selfish, I am not saying that this view is somehow wrong. On the contrary, it is always correct (to the participant, that is). In fact, such selfishness is really quite normal and very natural. But we need to keep in mind that the psychological locus of understanding is not a complete one. You can't see the entire relationship when you are a participant; you see the relationship only in terms of *your* self. Using the psychological locus of interpersonal communication, then, is similar to avoiding problems that arise when we assume that the selfish view of interpersonal communication is the "real" or "most correct" understanding.

The first problem to avoid is the belief that the insider's view of the relationship is a more accurate definition of interpersonal communication. For instance, when we think that the selfish viewpoint is the most important and "real" one, we create a problem for ourselves and drastically limit our own understanding. What the individual thinks, feels, perceives, knows about the relationship or about another person is no more "real" than what a disinterested observer thinks, feels, perceives, and knows about that same relationship. The individual's feeling *seems* more important; it is certainly more vivid and stronger. But it is merely more personal or individualized because it is related to the interests, desires, and goals of that individual.

The second problem concerns how we understand our experiences. Recall Oscar Levant's pithy saying at the opening of this chapter. The individual participant's view of the experience of communication is not the experience itself. It is the

The individuals in a relationship may have very different views of that relationship.
(Lynne Jaeger Weinstein/Woodfin Camp & Associates)

individual's sensemaking of the experience. Remember the model of communication discussed in Chapter 1. The communication or the relationship (the communicational experience) is not the same as the individual's view of it. Alfred and Betty, as individuals, may have quite different views of their relationship with each other, even though they obviously have but one relationship experience. His own view of his relationship with Betty is more important to Alfred; it seems more real to him. But *her* view of her relationship with Alfred is more important, more real to Betty. Yet neither Alfred's nor Betty's selfish understanding of the relationship is the relationship experience itself. It is the individual participant's selfish reaction to the relationship, and their responses occur *after* the experience.

This process through which meaning is derived—responding *after* the experience—also contributes to a third potential problem. Participants' responses are essentially what they remember about the experience, and memories of events can change over a period of time. Once an interaction has occurred, the event itself doesn't change just because the participants have different understandings of it. But what can change is how each actor defines or understands that interactional experience. That memory can change considerably. For example, you may remember with fondness your communication with a friend. But if you break up with this friend, you are likely to change your memories somewhat and think that you were just fooling yourself at the time.

A fourth problem is that of confusing an emotional residue with the relationship. We sometimes mistake one for the other and come to think of a relationship in terms of the emotion felt by one or more of the partners. Take, for example, the case of love. As much as we have glorified the notion of love in literature and song, we still know very little about it. "Love is blind," goes the cliché, because we tend to idealize the loved one. We ignore faults in those we love; we perceive only goodness and fail to see the loved one in an objective light. But this notion of love has little to do with the relationship of love. It is exclusively associated with one person's emotional response to another person—a psychological and self-centered view of love.

Occasionally we distinguish between different kinds of love, such as *eros* and *agape*, which delineate only two different emotions: romantic and sacred love. But even this distinction maintains the psychological locus of the relationship within the self of each communicator. *Eros* emphasizes the concern for gratifying one's own self-interest and desires, and *agape* emphasizes one's feeling of concern and caring for the other. (See Cunningham & Antill, 1981, pp. 30–31.) Neither emphasizes the relationship *between* the communicators, the relationship that the two loving partners create by interacting together.

In summary, a psychological understanding of interpersonal communication is one important part of a thorough understanding. Several problems, however, may arise from the process through which we derive individual or intrapersonal meaning: this view is limited to the individual's responses *after* the communicative experience; one's memory of the experience can change considerably even though the event itself remains unchanged; and, people may confuse the relationship with their emotional response. These responses will most likely become problems when people think that the psychological locus of the communicator's self is the most important or "real" understanding of interpersonal communication. A psychological understanding, however, is incomplete and insufficient by itself. A more thorough understanding includes the external or pragmatic view as well.

The External and Internal Selves

Central to the psychological locus of human communication is the assumption that the individual self is located somewhere within the individual and is not capable of being directly observed. But this assumption also includes the belief that we can observe the self *in*directly by making inferences about the intrapersonal self by looking at that individual's behaviors. In a sense, then, the psychological locus of communication considers the individual to have two selves or, more accurately, two parts of the self—internal and external.

Carrying this assumption further, we know that the external self and the internal self are not equivalent. Basically, we don't trust the external self, probably because we know that the other person can control external behaviors. Consistent with our selfish interest, we don't trust other people nearly as much as we trust ourselves. The other person, we tend to believe, may be trying to fool us, to manipulate us, to hide his or her true self. The "true" self is, we tend to believe, the internal self— the one that is not so clearly under the direct control of the other person.

The psychological task of communication, then, is to decipher cues from the other person in the form of observable behaviors and actions. We must sort through these and discover which are fake and which are genuine. The genuine cues, of course, are those that allow us to discover the "real" self (the internal self) of the other person. At least, this is what most people in our society conventionally believe.

Most psychologists tend to discount the belief that a "real" self is somehow hidden in the dark recesses of an individual's psyche. But they will also agree that a person's actual behavior may or may not accurately reflect that individual's personality. Obviously people sometimes behave insincerely—in ways that are intended to mask feelings or provide a façade. The smile on the face of the beauty pageant contestant or the political candidate always seems fake, as if it were pasted on. The smile, we say, isn't "real;" it's a façade. The glad-handing used-car salesman represents the stereotype of false behaviors masking impure motives. It has become a favorite ploy of political mud slingers to ask of their opponent, "Would you buy a used car from this person?"

Most of us tend to believe in the "lie-detector syndrome," in which nonverbal cues are believed to be more reliable ways of determining whether the person's verbal behaviors are really valid indicators of the internal self. People can lie with words, we tend to think, but their gestures and other nonverbal behaviors don't lie. Our motto seems to be "Don't pay attention to the words; listen to what she or he is *really* saying." In the words of the old song, "Her lips tell me no-no, but there's yes-yes in her eyes." In fact, the lie-detector syndrome may have been used as the excuse for more criminal rapes and sexual assaults than any other defense.

Of course, there is a valid reason why lie-detector tests are rarely admissible in courts of law. The conventional belief in the absolute validity of nonverbal behaviors is simply misplaced. In point of fact, some people can "lie" nonverbally just as well as they can lie verbally. Furthermore, different polygraph (lie-detector) experts will disagree on how to conduct and interpret the results of polygraph tests. In any case, these experts are doing exactly the same thing that we all do in normal conversation. They are making inferences about the internal self on the basis of observable cues offered by the external self.

What precisely is an inference? An inference is itself a psychological process, a reasoning process that involves drawing a conclusion on the basis of incomplete information. To infer is to use some logic, rational or nonrational, in order to "fill in the blanks" of the missing information and arrive at some conclusion. In other words, to make an inference is to jump to a conclusion on the basis of inadequate data. Some inferences require greater distance in the jumps than others, but all call for a psychological leap to a conclusion.

No one can directly observe another person's internal self. But we all make inferences about other people's internal selves on the basis of what we *can* observe. And the only thing that we can observe is the external self—behaviors or actions. As the discussions in Chapter 7 will make abundantly clear, this undeniable truth about inferential understanding of the psychological self also applies to the way you come to understand your own self. In other words, when you understand your own self, you are also making inferences on the basis of incomplete information.

PSYCHOLOGICAL LEVELS OF COMMUNICATION

From the psychological locus of "self," interpersonal communication is a blend of similarities and differences. We will all undoubtedly agree that each individual is unique. No two humans, even identical twins, are exactly alike in terms of their personalities, beliefs, values, likes and dislikes, and so on. The psychological process of one person is not precisely the same as the psychological process of any other. But we will also agree that this individual uniqueness does not prohibit anyone from engaging in an interpersonal relationship, since two individuals can communicate and create a relationship that embodies them both.

The psychological locus of interpersonal communication involves "seeing" the relationship from the view of each of the communicators. And each person's view of the relationship is a selfish view—that is, a view from the person's self. If communication is to take place, though, the views of both communicators must be similar in some respects, even though we know they will also be different in others. This section discusses those similarities and differences that are contained within the psychological locus of interpersonal communication. We will discuss the "sharing" of selfish views and the different levels of selfish views that are shared.

The "Sharing" of Self

The word "communicate" is derived from the Latin infinitive *communicare*, which literally means "to make common." From a psychological locus, then, interpersonal communication involves two or more people whose "selves" or psychological processes have something in common. For Alfred to communicate with Betty, his psychological process must have something in common (that is, be similar to) Betty's psychological process. Figure 6-1 illustrates this overlap or commonality of Alfred's and Betty's psychological processes. When Alfred and Betty communicate, they simultaneously and individually extend their personal "selves" into the act of communicating through their thinking, feeling, perceiving, believing—in short, through their psychological processes. These processes are going on continually while they are engaged in communicating with each other.

The shaded area in Figure 6-1 indicates that portion of Alfred's psychological process that is similar to (or in common with) Betty's simultaneously occurring psychological process. One might speculate that the communication between Alfred and Betty is more "effective" as the amount of this overlap increases. At least the greater amount of overlap does suggest a greater degree of psychological similarity between Alfred and Betty. The greater the overlap, the more things they have in common with each other.

We often use the word "share" to refer to this commonality of communicators. We share our experiences with each other; we share our meanings with each other. "Share" is a highly respected word in the language we use every day to talk about interpersonal communication. However, the word "share," though highly popular, may be somewhat misleading. Alfred and Betty cannot share any psychological process in the sense that they have the same psychological process, a single psychological process. There will always be two different psychological processes going on during their communication, even though one person's thoughts, beliefs, and so on may be similar to the other person's thoughts, beliefs, and so on.

We use the word "share" to refer to Alfred's and Betty's communication, but we use the term in the same sense that we might say they share blue eyes or red hair. There are two pairs of eyes, two heads of hair. To share the same eye color or

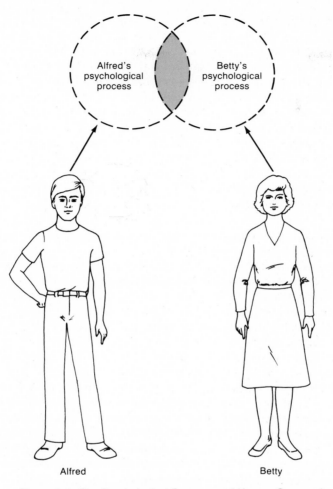

Figure 6-1. The Psychological Processes of Human Communication

hair color is to participate in a coincidence, a characteristic of the two sets of eyes that happens to be common to both. Under no circumstances would we think that Alfred and Betty have the same pair of eyes. In the same sense, we shouldn't think that they could have the same experience or the same meaning or the same emotion, even though they share them.

To share an understanding, then, is not to have the same self (that is, the same understanding) but to have two different individual understandings that have some characteristic in common. That common characteristic is a coincidence of two otherwise different understandings. The coincidence is the extent of overlap of the two understandings, but it is not and can never be a single understanding. Psychological communication is thus a coincidence of different psychological processes and must not be considered to be a single psychological process.

The Level of Sharing

Up to this point we have been discussing each individual's intrapersonal or psychological process as though it were a single process going on inside the individual's head. In point of fact, the psychological process involved in human communication includes several different internal processes going on simultaneously. We might think of these multiple processes as different psychological "levels." At least they are levels in the sense that they include different parts of the self or psychological processes that are "shared" by the participants in interpersonal communication.

Interpersonal communication may include several different participants, each of whom has an individual self (psychological processes). The following discussion will treat only two persons (Alfred and Betty) involved in interpersonal communication. You can extend this discussion to a third person (say, Charlie) simply by adding a third self, a third set of psychological processes.

When you communicate with another person, your intrapersonal process contains a minimum of three different levels. Each of these levels is associated with each of the selves present in the interpersonal setting: your view of yourself; your view of the other, and your view of the other's view of you. (Some people have called these levels "perception," "metaperception," and "metametaperception," although the levels also refer to awareness, as well as perception, of self and other.) Of course, the number of psychological levels can theoretically expand infinitely to include my view of the other's view of my view of the other's view of my view of . . ., ad nauseam. But let's not get too carried away with this infinite regression. We will keep this discussion to the minimum number of three levels.

Figure 6-2 illustrates the three levels of the psychological process associated with two-person communication. As a communicator I can include in my intrapersonal processes only my own view. I can never have any direct knowledge of the other person's psychological process, but I nevertheless make some inferences (that is, I jump to some conclusions) about what is going on inside the other person's head. Thus, I infer my own view about who the other person is, and I also infer what I believe the other person's view is of me. In addition, I also make some inferences about who I think I am. Furthermore, all three of these psychological levels are functioning simultaneously during my communication with the other person, and each of these levels can affect any of the others. For instance, if I view the other person as trustworthy and think that he or she dislikes or distrusts me, I may begin to lower the image I have of myself as a result.

But remember that at least two people are involved in interpersonal communication. At the same time that I am engaging in my own psychological processes with my views of self, other, and other's view of me, the other person is also engaging in parallel psychological processes with the same three levels—the other's view of self, of me, and of my view of the other's self. The result is reminiscent of the hackneyed comedy routine replayed in hundreds of movies and cartoons. In this routine two similarly dressed people face each other through a window or blank space in a wall. To avoid discovery, one of them acts as though the other were looking into a mirror. That person attempts to behave just as the other does and "reflect" the other person's actions.

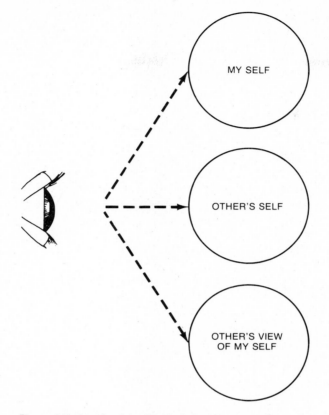

Figure 6-2. Levels of the Psychological Process in
Two–Person Communication

The humor is contained in the fact that the actions are never exact mirror images; they are just slightly out of sync. The mirrored behavior, for instance, is slightly delayed; one person tries to fool the other with sudden and unexpected movements. The behaviors of the two people almost coincide with each other, but they don't quite match. At all times, of course, the audience knows that there is no mirror and that two people are engaging in coincidental and somewhat synchronized actions. This comedy shtick is very similar to the psychological sharing during the normal process of interpersonal communication.

Figure 6-3 portrays this mirror image of the two psychological processes. Alfred tries to mirror his psychological processes with the psychological process he infers is going on in Betty. And Betty is simultaneously attempting to mirror her psychological processes with those of Alfred. The psychological processes of the two individuals are not exactly the same, but each person tries to maintain some degree of overlap or coincidence with the other person at each of the three levels.

Alfred's view of his own self is synchronized to some extent with Betty's view of his self. The reverse is true of Betty's view of her own self and Alfred's view of her. Alfred's view of what Betty thinks of him is synchronized to some extent with

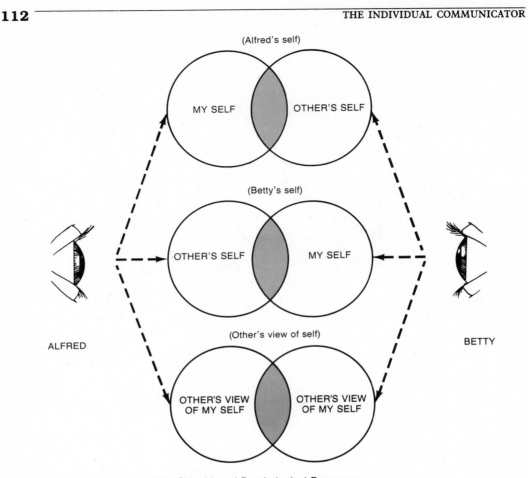

Figure 6-3. Levels of the Coincidental Psychological Processes in Two–Person Communication

Betty's view of what he thinks of her, and vice versa. Each person's views, though somewhat coincidental with those of the other, will always be slightly out of sync with those of the other person, but both will continue to communicate with one another on the basis of the coincidence (the sharing) of their psychological processes. The importance to communication is not that their two psychological processes are indeed similar but that they communicate with each other *as though* they were similar. And because the communicators engage in communication "as though" they shared part of their selves, the psychological processes can affect interpersonal communication and the social relationship.

PSYCHOLOGICAL EFFECTS ON COMMUNICATION

The natural appeal of the importance of psychological processes is so strong that we must constantly remind ourselves that the intrapersonal processes of the individual

Your views of your self and of the other person in a relationship influence and are influenced by your communication with that person.
(Susan Lapides/Design Conceptions)

communicator are not the same thing as the interpersonal relationship. What is going on within the individual is not interpersonal communication; it is psychology. However, the psychological process of each individual communicator can certainly affect interpersonal communication. That is, it can affect the interpersonal relationship.

Because Alfred and Betty hold particular views of self and other, their views may lead them to act toward the other in a certain manner. Thus, the *intra*personal process may affect the way each person behaves in the *inter*personal process. The psychology of communication may affect what the individual does (that is, how the communicator behaves) during communication. In this way, the psychological process can affect communication, the relationship. And that effect can be either positive or negative. That is, it can help the relationship develop or keep it from developing.

But is the person's communicative behavior always consistent with the internalized self? And what if the external behavior is different from the communicator's internal self? Some commonsense beliefs about personal psychology lead us to think of self or personality in terms of the same old dichotomy: what is "genuine" or "real" and what is "false." We often hear about people in terms of their "public image" and then discover that the public image is in sharp contrast with the "private self." And, of course, we immediately think that the private self is more "real" than the public self. (For example, "What is Johnny Carson *really* like?")

To be perfectly frank, no one knows for sure whether there actually is such a thing as a "real" self—and even if it did exist, it wouldn't make any difference to human communication. Now what on earth could we possibly mean by such a blasphemous statement?

To the extent that people's psychological processes can affect how they act and thus their interpersonal relationships, the individual is using some internalized self to guide his or her behavior. But if and when the individual's internalized self directs actions, the communicator is acting on the basis of what he or she knows or believes to be true about the internal self. If the individual's inferred image of self is different from his or her "real" self, the individual would have no way of knowing it. The communicator has no choice but to use the inferred self-image, real or false, to affect behaviors. The individual acts *as though* the inferred self were the real self, whether it is or not. In other words, whether there is such a thing as a real self is simply not relevant to communicative behaviors. The only self that can possibly make any difference at all is the individual's own view of self. Whether the individual's view is accurate or completely false is immaterial. The individual behaves *as though* it were accurate.

Because psychological processes can potentially affect human communication, we cannot ignore them if we want to understand as fully as possible the nature of human relationships. By the same token, we must not think that the psychological processes define the process of human communication. We will consistently treat psychological processes as factors that can affect human communication and social relationships, but they are technically not part of the relationship.

We have already suggested that the psychological process relevant to interpersonal communication functions on three levels: my view of my own self, my view of the other's self, and my view of the other's view of my self. We can also think of these three psychological levels as different kinds of psychological processes. The self-understanding embodied in my view of my own self involves issues of *awareness*. My self-image is essentially a process of how I come to be aware of my own self. Such awareness is not automatic; it involves particular psychological techniques used by all of us on an everyday basis to increase our understanding of who we are.

Chapter 7 discusses issues of self-awareness along with issues associated with the second level of the intrapersonal process—my view of the other's view of my self. To the extent that the other person gets to know or understand who I am, I have given the other person some information about me. To the extent that I come to know or understand the other person, she or he has given similar information to me. This psychological level involves a process commonly known as self-*disclosure*. The self is always hidden from the other person's view in the sense that it is an internal self. But I can reveal portions of my self to the other person (intentionally and unintentionally) through my verbal and nonverbal behaviors. I also make inferences about the other's self on the basis of the verbal and nonverbal behaviors I observe of the other person.

The process of self-disclosure in communication is a bit like being a psychological "flasher." I open my psychological trenchcoat and give the other person a glimpse of my otherwise hidden self. The other person simultaneously does the same and some of these glimpses may be more revealing (more intimate) than others. Each of us makes inferences about the other person's self on the basis of the other's self-disclosing behaviors.

Chapter 8 addresses the psychological level associated with my view of the other. The psychological process involved in this level is that of *perception*. Perception, of course, is a fundamental part of all psychological processes and therefore is discussed in Chapter 7, as well. Chapter 8, however, emphasizes "the other" as an object of perception and discusses how and why people perceive as they do, particularly how they perceive other persons. The remaining two chapters of Part Two, then, discuss the psychological levels that affect interpersonal communication. These chapters discuss them as psychological processes associated with interpersonal relationships: processes of awareness, disclosure, and perception.

One final word before we begin those discussions. When two or more people communicate with one another and thereby establish a social relationship, they unite within a single relationship. There is only one social relationship in the interpersonal setting, but there are also different individual views of that relationship. In fact, there are potentially as many different views of a relationship as there are individuals who are available to view the relationship. Alfred and Betty have only one relationship, but individual persons will differ on how they view Alfred and Betty's relationship. Alfred has one view, Betty has another view, I have a third view, you have a fourth view, and so on.

To view a relationship is to engage in a psychological process that will often seem more "real" than the relationship itself. But always keep in mind that an individual's psychological process can never be anything more than *intra*personal, and an interpersonal relationship is always and inherently *inter*personal. People will sometimes act *as though* their intrapersonal processes actually defined the "real" relationship; and that is why these discussions are important to an understanding of interpersonal communication.

Summary

Looking at interpersonal communication and social relationships from the viewpoint of the individual participants is to locate the understanding of communication within the psychological process. Each individual member of a relationship possesses a personal understanding and meaning of every social relationship in which that person is a member. Because that understanding is so personal and so meaningful to the individual, the psychological understanding is often seen as the "real" meaning of the relationship. In fact, it is not more real so much as it is more vivid. After all, it is consistent with the natural selfish tendency of humans to see their environment in terms of self-fulfillment.

Each individual comes to an understanding of interpersonal relationships on the basis of selfish interests. Consequently, each individual is to some extent unique and will have a view of the relationship that differs somewhat from that of another participant. The individual view is essentially an internal residue or memory of the interpersonal relationship, a personal reaction or response to the experience of the relationship that the individual carries around after the fact. That residual memory often takes the form of an emotion, an individual response to a relationship, which is often mistaken for the experience of the relationship itself.

The intrapersonal or psychological process relevant to interpersonal communication focuses on the self of the individual communicator. Each person has two selves, or a self in two parts: the internal self and the external self. The internal self is not capable of being observed, but the external self (the behaviors or actions) are observable during communication. The psychological task of interpersonal communication, then, is to observe the behaviors of the external self and use those actions as cues to make inferences about the internal self. On the basis of another's behaviors, we make inferences about what that person is like or what that person is thinking or feeling.

To make inferences is to engage in a psychological process by which we come to some conclusion on the basis of inadequate information. The psychological task, then, is also to sort out the valid behavioral cues from the fake cues in order to discover who the other person really is. Conventional belief, not necessarily accurate but often used despite its fallaciousness, suggests that nonverbal behaviors are typically more valid indicators of the internal self than is spoken language.

The psychological processes of individual communicators, though different, do have degrees of overlap or similarity. To the extent that the psychological processes of two communicators overlap, they have something in common with each other. Those psychological processes include three levels relevant to the selves of the communicators: my view of my self, my view of the other's self, and my view of the other's view of my self. All three levels are functioning simultaneously during communication, and all three levels of each person's psychological process are functioning simultaneously with every other communicator's psychological process. The levels may be said to involve three different varieties of psychological processes associated with interpersonal communication: awareness, disclosure, and perception.

CHAPTER 7

The Self

I do my thing, and you do your thing.
I am not in this world to live up to your expectations,
And you are not in this world to live up to mine.
You are you, and I am I,
And if by chance we find each other,
It's beautiful.
If not, it can't be helped.

—A Gestalt Prayer

For decades our society has reflected a massive effort to glorify the individual and the self. The decade of the 1960s was known as the "me generation." The pop psychology of that era emphasized the individual's right to have "peak experiences" and seek "self-actualization." Popular philosopher Ayn Rand wrote about the "virtue of selfishness." Hugh Hefner's "*Playboy* philosophy" extolled the means of self-gratification and a hedonistic life-style. The Staple Singers recorded the highly popular "Respect Yourself," and Mary Travers sang "I Need Me to Be for Me." Even today the aerobics, jogging, and physical-fitness programs are praised for their effectiveness in self-improvement and helping you "to feel good about yourself."

Now just who or what is this inner person (or persons) that we choose to call our "self?" The number of psychological theories for identifying and understanding the nature of one's self is enormous. Since the days of Sigmund Freud, psychologists have created newer and different theories of self and coined the term "personality" to refer to that inner quality that identifies the person's individuality. A more precise definition or identification of self (or one of its counterparts, such as personality) is not particularly important for our purposes. We will have to be satisfied with defining self as that characteristic or, more accurately, group of characteristics that allows an individual human being to be an individual human being.

The human self is that quality which allows every human to be perceived and characterized as an individual who is different, to some extent, from other individuals. It is one of the supreme ironies of psychology that the self, the quality that makes an individual a unique human being, develops through and is probably impossible to attain without social interaction—communication with other human beings. An individual is not born with a self or a personality. At least we have no compelling reason to believe in a genetic explanation for personality. During the course of maturation, the child develops a mature physical body through adolescence and adulthood and a mature self-identity as well. Moreover, the small child becomes increasingly aware of his or her self as physical maturity develops.

Like the physical self, the social and psychological self continues to mature during virtually the entire course of a lifetime. Psychological changes, though, are much more gradual than physical changes after the age of, say thirty. During adolescence, however, the psychosocial self probably undergoes changes as rapid and as profound as the physiological changes taking place in the body. During the period of adolescence, the self is highly vulnerable—more so than during most later periods of life.

Life experiences shape the self of every individual human being. But each person must also be aware of what is happening and what has happened to self. Self-awareness is basically a process of perception that is directed inward. The individual attempts to perceive and thereby understand who he or she is. Guests on the *Johnny Carson Show* and in *TV Guide* interviews often mention having been "in analysis." Besides the fact that having your own analyst must be something of a status symbol in show business, one of the common goals in seeking help from a psychotherapist is to improve self-awareness or self-perception.

This chapter is devoted to your own "analysis," in which you become aware of the various concepts of self and their importance in or relevance to interpersonal communication. Our discussions will include how we humans come to know our "selves" through the psychological processes of perception and awareness. Then we will consider how, why, and when we disclose or reveal these selves to other people.

PERCEPTION OF SELF

Meaning, we tend to believe, is equivalent to perception. That is, we generally believe that our meanings are products of an intrapersonal psychological process. Meanings are in people, we say, not in objects; and we assign meaning to those objects. In this way, one person can have a certain meaning for X, while another person may have a quite different meaning for X. In fact, we often refer to meaning in a sense of "ownership": I "have" a meaning or that is "my" meaning. The psychological process associated with interpretation and assigning meanings to persons and objects is known as *perception*.

And just what is perception? A standard psychological definition might include the following: "Perception is defined as the meaningful interpretation of sensations as representatives of external objects; perception is *apparent* knowledge of what is out there" (Cohen, 1969, p. 6). This definition contains some key elements of perception that are fundamental to any attempt to understand this intrapersonal process.

First, an act of perception requires the presence of some external object to be perceived. In the case of perceiving another person, the external object to be perceived is another human being. In the case of perceiving one's own self, the external object is less evident but nonetheless present. One perceives his or her own self just *as though* the self were another person or an external object. The difference is that perception of self includes more information available for interpretation and is subject to more biases and prejudices than is the perception of some other person or object. Otherwise, the process of self-perception is precisely the same as the perception of any other person.

A second characteristic of this definition is information available for interpretation. The only information that can possibly be available is in the form of sensations—what has been gathered by one or more of the five senses. Thus, I can perceive only what I can see, hear, smell, taste, or feel. Of course, some critic always introduces the case of ESP (extrasensory perception) at times such as these. Some people have demonstrated extrasensory abilities that no one can fully explain. However, most of us don't have those abilities, and our primary interest is in the normal everyday occurrences of interpersonal communication. Hence, our discussion will stick to sensory perception.

A third characteristic of perception evident in the definition concerns the representational nature of sensations. You cannot interpret the meaning of any object directly; you actually interpret the meaning of only the information which you believe "represents" that object. Perception (even perceptions based on direct observations) is never "real" in the sense that one can apprehend the object itself. You can see, smell, hear, taste, feel something; but the only things you have to interpret are the sights, odors, sounds, tastes, and textures that represent that something. You never perceive the object itself. The result is that any knowledge gained from perception (in fact, virtually all psychological knowledge) is never of what something *is* but only what it *appears* to be. And appearances can be deceiving, as we know from mirages, optical illusions, special effects in movies, cases of mistaken identity, and virtually any rerun of *Three's Company*.

Perception can never be more than an "apparent" knowledge of reality. That is, what we perceive is what reality appears to be to us. Naturally, we should never be overly confident of the knowledge we gain from our perceptions. We just never know when we might be the unwitting victims of deceptive appearances. Quite ironically, the knowledge about which we are most positive is precisely the knowledge we do gain from our perceptions. Perceived reality is the most vivid, personal, important, and credible knowledge to nearly all of us nearly all the time. And that is one of the reasons why the process of interpersonal communication and human relationships is so difficult to "understand" yet so simple to "know."

The Nature of Perception

Our discussion of perception has thus far repeatedly emphasized two points: that (1) the knowledge gained from perception is only a reflection of reality and is therefore highly fallible and (2) the knowledge gained from perception is vivid, personal, and thus typically accepted as true, often uncritically. To this point, however, we have not discussed how and why the intrapersonal process of perception works. To understand what is going on when people communicate with each other, we must understand how people come to know about themselves and other people. And because the process of acquiring that knowledge is perception, then we must understand how people perceive themselves and others. How often have we become frustrated because the other person couldn't understand "plain English?" Probably that person couldn't understand what you said because he or she was perceiving something in your words that you did not perceive. As a point of strict fact, English is no more "plain" than any other object of perception. The locus of perception is in the perceiving person, not in the English language.

Perception occurs inside the head of the individual perceiver, not in the object, and is always "apparent" knowledge. Perceived knowledge is always "apparent," even though what is plain to you may not be at all plain to someone else. Furthermore, what is absolutely clear to someone else may be a matter of considerable confusion to you. This paradox of perception, the fallibility yet uncritical acceptance of perceived "facts," is vital to understanding the intrapersonal level of interpersonal communication.

Perception Is Experiential. To interpret the meaning of some person, object, or event is to have some basis on which to make an interpretation. That basis will typically be found in your own past experiences with that person, object, or event or with some similar persons, objects, or events. In the absence of any comparable experience, you will find yourself unable to perceive any meaning. For example, we have all seen movies or TV shows that have depicted some outer-space creature or person from a long-ago past encountering objects familiar to our everyday experience. These objects are not familiar to the alien, who doesn't know what the objects are or what to do with them. How would people from an earlier century perceive a TV set, for example? If they were from colonial America, say Salem, they might perceive TV as witchcraft, a sign of Satan.

Perceiving one's self follows an identical process of drawing from the residues of past experiences. When confronted with a new perceptual experience, you search through your repertoire of past experiences in order to discover the appropriate meanings or responses. If the present experience is absolutely novel and you've never encountered anything like it before, then you experience confusion. You don't know what this experience means.

Perceptions require a basis for interpretation in past experiences. One's perception of self is essentially an interpretation based on the responses to situations in past ordinary experiences, and those previous experiences are contained within the individual's memory. In all cases of perception, your interpreted meaning of a perceived object, person (including your self), or event results from your experiences.

Perception Is Selective. When we perceive something, we tend to take into consideration only certain parts of the person or object we are perceiving. That is, we select only certain characteristics of the perceived object and ignore the others. The result is that we perceive only part of the object and thus tend to make errors in interpretation—errors we might not make if we had considered all the characteristics of the perceived object. But even though selective perception leads to mistakes, it is beneficial in other respects.

For one thing, perception *must* be selective. The capacity of the human brain to process information is quite limited. It is physiologically and psychologically impossible to take into account *all* the information that is accessible to the five senses at any given time. Some information theorists have estimated the capacity of the brain to be approximately seven items of information, plus or minus two, it can process at any one time (see Miller, 1956). Others have suggested that the brain's information-processing capacity is somewhat larger, with an upper limit of fifteen to twenty. Whatever the capacity of the human brain, the number of informational items it can take into account at any given time is certainly and incredibly small. Hence, we have no choice but to be selective when we perceive.

Selectivity in processing information is fundamentally a coping mechanism. Humans have developed rather sophisticated psychological means to cope with their meager information-processing capacity and the mountains of sensory information that are available. Without such a coping mechanism, we would suffer from massive information overload and almost total chaos of meaning that overload entails. The psychological process goes through a sorting or screening process in which we select only the most important items of information gathered from the five senses and ignore the rest. Perceiving selectively, then, is an essential and actually quite beneficial characteristic of human perception. Of course, selective perception also tends to reduce accuracy of perception by not taking into account some potentially important and relevant data.

On what basis do we decide which characteristics of the person or object to select and which characteristics to ignore? For one thing, we perceive what we "want" to perceive on the basis of our internalized attitudes, values, and beliefs. Thus, we are likely to select those characteristics of the perceived object that agree with our attitudes, values, and beliefs and to ignore those characteristics that are irrelevant or opposed to these attitudes and values. In other words, we humans carry around certain experiences or conclusions based on our past experiences. We then use them as criteria for selecting what sensory information is important, relevant, or credible—in short, what information to perceive.

Such intrapersonal phenomena as attitudes, values, and beliefs are important whenever we perceive anything—objects in our environment, other persons, or our selves. When those intrapersonal factors are involved in making interpretations and assigning meaning to sensations, they are called psychological or perceptual "sets." A *set* consists of a network of interconnected attitudes, values, beliefs, and so forth that are based on past experience. The set is a psychological mechanism available for interpreting the information received from the senses and for assigning meanings. The process of selectively applying the set to the sensations and interpreting meaning remains a psychological and intrapersonal process. That is, it takes place within the head of the individual communicator.

Relevant to perceptions of self, selectivity also allows the perceiver to select certain aspects of self to be perceived and to ignore others. Of course, selectivity can also function to deny the existence, importance, or relevance of undesired information. When you realize you have done something you regret or you possess a characteristic you don't particularly like, your first tendency is to deny it or at least downgrade its importance or relevance. In other words, selective perception allows you to protect and defend the image you have of yourself.

Human beings, consistent with the trait of being selfish, have an apparent need to protect their selves. After all, your self is very important to you. When you have

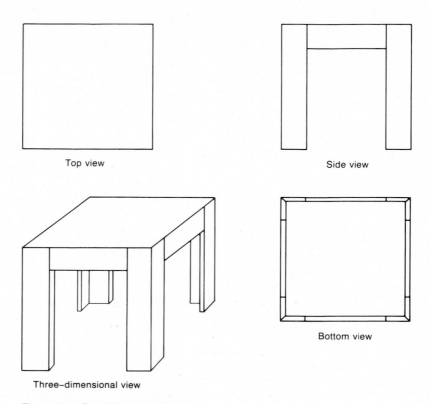

Top view

Side view

Three–dimensional view

Bottom view

Figure 7-1. Four Views of a Table

information that is detrimental to your self-image, you immediately "circle the wagons" and proceed to ward off the "attack." The selectivity inherent in the process of perception allows you to protect your perceived meaning of your own self. When in doubt, perceive what you want to perceive. When it's about your self and it's bad, change your perception to an interpretation that is good. Later discussions will return to the topic of self-protection.

Perception Is Inferential. We have already discussed the fact that the psychological process of perception involves the drawing of conclusions through a logical process of induction. The interpretation that results from perception is, thus, an inference based on incomplete information. In plain English, this means that perceiving meaning involves jumping to a conclusion that is not fully warranted by the available sensory data.

Like selectivity, inferential reasoning is both detrimental and beneficial to the interpretive process. It is beneficial in one way, because acquiring a complete set of details from the five senses is virtually impossible. Take the case of visual perception. You can see an object from only one vantage point at a time. Figure 7-1 shows four drawings depicting four different visual perspectives of a single table. Note that neither the top view nor the bottom view allows the perceiver to see any table legs, and the side view shows only two legs. The perceiver is nonetheless apt to infer the

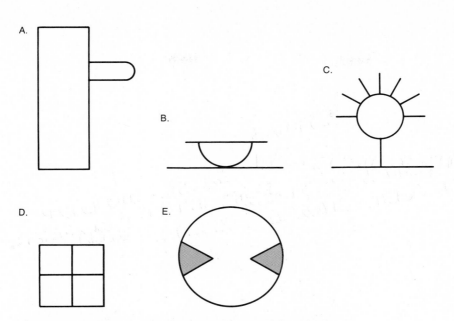

Figure 7-2. Droodles — Case Studies in Perceptual Organization

existence of four table legs. After all, we have all seen enough tables to feel assured that this one will also have four legs.

Visual perception thus allows the interpreter to infer some specific characteristics of the table even though these are not actually visible from any one vantage point. In this sense, at least, the inferential process of perception is necessary and beneficial. It allows the perceiver to interpret a more complete meaning of the object being perceived. Complete information is never possible, so inferences are necessary if one is to draw conclusions from the incomplete information available from the senses.

Perception inevitably involves incomplete information. The perceiver must "fill in the blanks" to complete the picture and provide the missing information. Another way of saying the same thing is to describe perception as a process of "organizing" available information, of placing the known details within a certain organizational scheme that allows you to perceive a more general meaning that goes beyond the mere details. The side view of the table in Figure 7-1 could just as easily have been interpreted as three rectangles, ten lines, the letter "C" lying on its side, or an upside-down "U." The inferential part of the perceptual process is essentially a creative act. When confronted with informational details, you "create" a meaning by organizing those details within some overall meaning in which all the details make sense.

Droodles, whose popularity has unfortunately waned considerably in recent years, provide an excellent example of the creative inferences available in our power of perceptual organization. A droodle is a line drawing that provides minimum information; it is essentially a puzzle. A droodle becomes humorous in the fact that the creative solution to the "what is it?" question is a far-fetched inference. Figure 7-2 shows five droodles, each with its own creative organization of a minimum amount of informational details and a huge inferential leap to an interpreted meaning that is straight out of "left field." Droodle A is identified as a trombone player practicing in a telephone booth (on its side, the droodle is a dead trombone player). B is a fried egg for those who like their eggs sunny side down. C is a spider doing a handstand. D has been described as tic-tac-toe for beginners, but I prefer the interpretation that it is a view of two polar bears eating marshmallows in a snowstorm as seen through a frosted window. One of my favorite droodles is the last one: what you see if you've been thrown down a well by two witches (or if you're inside an empty beer can looking out).

Droodles represent perceptual inferences fostered by a creative imagination that affects the interpretation. When one's own self is the object of perception, the organization of details to make the inference logical is often no less creative than the interpretation of droodles. The human being has the ability to organize details into often very extraordinary interpretations of a self-image. To illustrate, several years ago I talked with an undergraduate student suffering from serious academic problems and in danger of flunking out. Not knowing the student very well, I asked him questions, perused his transcript, and discovered a consistent pattern of details. He had ranked in the lower range of his high school graduating class, his ACT and SAT scores were low, his college GPA was below 2.0, he had changed potential majors three times, and he was not yet a sophomore after four academic quarters.

During our conversation the student informed me that for several summers he had worked as a carpenter, was well paid, and liked his work very much. I was about to launch into my 50-drachma (not worth very much) lecture on why everyone didn't need a college degree and that he could live a happy, fruitful life pursuing his summer job as a full-time profession, but he stopped me short by announcing that he had decided to change his major once again—to communication.

This student had organized all the information about his past experiences and inferred a self-image that was, at best, an interpretation at least as "creative" as those for the droodles in Figure 7-2. According to his perceptions, he had not slept well the night before taking the ACT and, coincidentally enough, the SAT, too. Besides, he told me, those scores weren't valid because he just didn't do too well on standardized tests. The reason for his poor grades in both high school and college was that he just wasn't interested in those classes and performed far below his ability. But now that he had discovered communication and the class he was taking from me, he just "knew" that this major was for him. That, he informed me, was why he was doing so well in my course. I didn't know how to tell him that he was in danger of failing this course, too. We both had the same information but our perceptions of his performance were certainly different. Incidentally, he did pass my course (with a "D," as I recall), and I have not seen him since. He never did become a communication major.

Perception Is Inaccurate.   This student's self-perception was not only a highly creative inference but also probably quite inaccurate. Although this may be an extreme case, every perception we make is to some extent inaccurate. The problems of being influenced by past experiences, selectivity, and inferential leaps render every act of human perception inaccurate. Fortunately, most of the inaccuracies in our perceptions are generally insignificant, so that human communication is not only possible but also pretty effective. On the other hand, the psychological process that produces meaning from sensations leads to a meaning that is, at best, only apparently real. The perceived meaning is several times removed from the reality it allegedly reflects. And the farther perceivers are distanced from the person, event, or object being perceived, the more inaccurate their perceptions are likely to be.

Sometimes the inaccuracy takes the form of overgeneralizing the inference. A short time ago I was babysitting a precocious young girl (about four years old and black) whose mother was attending a meeting in my home. In the middle of our coloring game, she asked me to tell her what color she was. "Aha!" I thought, "Her mother has instilled in her some racial consciousness and pride." Not wanting to appear too stuffy or "adult," I answered her question as though it were a game: "You're purple, aren't you?" "No," she replied, giggling. "Then you must be orange," I said. She giggled some more and shook her head. "I give up. You tell me." I waited for her to tell me she was black. Her response, even though highly accurate, was not what I expected. With a big smile and not just a little pride, she told me, "I'm medium brown!"

Sometimes perceptions are inaccurate when people perceive as the same, things that are only similar—and not necessarily similar in important ways. The case of a mistaken (for example, identity when witnesses to a crime misidentify a suspect) is quite common. Often the similarities include only a general description of height or weight or hair color. When placed side by side, the actual criminal and the wrongly accused suspect often don't look alike at all.

The point is that perceptions are always inaccurate to some extent. We recognize as false only grossly inaccurate perceptions. We typically ignore the common inaccuracies of everyday perceptions. Even though inaccurate perceptions do not always create problems for interpersonal communication, the response "sets" used to perceive other people often lead to inaccurate perceptions of the person who is our communicational partner. The special problems of person perception provide the topic for more extended discussion in Chapter 8.

Perception Is Evaluative. To say that anyone perceives something or someone "objectively" or to use the term "objective perception" is to fool yourself. No perception is ever objective. You interpret on the basis of your past experiences and your own very human selfishness. Hence, all perceptions, no matter how hard you might try to be impartial, are subjective. Perception is an inner, cognitive psychological process. It unavoidably reflects those personal attitudes, values, and beliefs that you use to assign meaning to the object of perception. Perception is not only an intrapersonal process but also a highly personal one. And that inescapable personal involvement in the act of perception renders perception highly subjective.

Steve Duck (1973), a psychologist interested in human relationships, has asserted that "reality cannot be perceived without construal," a process that involves unique and very "personal reasons" for acting in social relationships (p. 136). He goes on to emphasize the "importance of the parallel processes of evaluating what is construed and the inferences from it" (p. 137). Duck makes clear that the inevitable counterpart of subjective interpretation is the process of evaluation. No one perceives just what something "is" without also perceiving how "good or bad" that something is. Rarely if ever is a perceived event, person, or object totally neutral. We tend to

The people you say you know well are usually people you like.
(Alan Carey/The Image Works)

evaluate at the same time as we perceive and as an inseparable part of the perceiving process.

Think back on your own personal experiences. You tend to remember those that had some value for you. And you probably tend to remember more experiences that you valued highly and fewer of those you would like to forget. We rather conveniently tend to forget those experiences that might have neutral value, which is another way of saying that we did not perceive them clearly in the first place. Think of your friends and associates. The ones you really "know" are those you like (a high positive value in your person perception) and those you don't like (negative evaluation). Others, whom you would describe as being neutral toward, are also people you are likely to say that you really don't know very well.

Students (and instructors, too, I might add) rarely take a class without evaluating it in some way. That was "a good course" or "a bad course," you say. When asking another student about a course, your first question is likely to be "Is that a good course?" or "Is the instructor good?" Now think back over all the courses you have taken. The ones that come to mind first are most likely to be the "good" courses and the "bad" courses. The ones you don't remember very well probably don't fall into either category. You evaluate them as neutral, neither good nor bad, and you don't remember them for very long. I still have vivid memories of several dozen courses that I took as an undergraduate. Nearly all of them were exceptionally "good" classroom experiences. Only a very few of them were "bad." The rest of them blur in my memory.

When you perceive your own self, the evaluative part of your perceptual process is extremely important. Generally speaking, most people have a relatively high evaluation of self. That does not mean to suggest that there aren't certain elements of your self that you don't particularly like, but generally your perception of your own self probably reflects a rather positive evaluation. When people tend to have negative self-images, they are likely to have psychological "problems"—a neurosis if the image is only mildly negative and a psychosis if the image is extremely so. A negative evaluation of the self is a psychological reason frequently given for suicides.

But these are extreme examples. People who function relatively normally in life typically evaluate their selves rather positively. Every one of us probably has some mild neurosis, but our basic self-image tends to be rather positive. It is also not surprising that to remain psychologically "normal," we try to protect the positive evaluation we have of our selves.

Elements of Perception

I hope that by this time our discussion has dispelled some of the common myths associated with the nature of human perception. One of those myths concerns the belief that perceived reality is somehow more "real" than actual reality, that it is somehow more "meaningful." Perceived interpretations may be more personal and more crucial to the perceiver's own sense of self, but recall that the perception is only *apparent* knowledge removed several steps from actuality. Interpretations based on perceptions are no less significant because they involve appearances, nor are they more meaningful because they are more personal. In fact, perceptions may be significant precisely because they do involve a personal knowledge closely associated with the human's definition of self.

A second myth is that perception can be likened to the work of a movie camera or giant videotape recorder that one uses to make contact with the world through the senses. But when humans perceive, they don't so much *record* the sights, sounds, and smells of their world as they actively *create* meanings that are not necessarily present in the external environment. Those meanings are often fanciful inferences and reflect the psychological process of the perceiver more than they portray an accurate picture of the world. Furthermore, persons, objects, and events have no inherent value or goodness; the act of perception creates an evaluation and attributes it to those worldly phenomena. The movie camera or videotape recorder has yet to be invented that has the creative power of interpretation, evaluation, inference, and subjectivity present in even the most everyday act of human perception.

What constitutes the act of perception? What goes into human perceiving? What influences perceived meaning? Those questions direct the present discussion. We already know that perception requires a minimum of three ingredients: a perceiving person, an object of perception, and an inferred interpretation or meaning that is the outcome of the perceptual act. The elements specifically involved in human perception, as and when it occurs, provide the topics for discussion in this section.

Sensations and Interpretation. Norwood Russell Hanson (1967), a philosopher of science, made a significant point about the nature of human observation in his philosophical writings. He believed that one can never merely observe and that "pure" observation is not possible. Stated another way, one is incapable of having

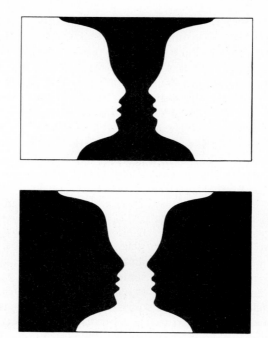

Figure 7-3. The Two–Headed Vase — An Optical Illusion

sensations (that is, seeing, hearing, tasting, smelling, or touching something) without interpreting the meaning of those sensations at the same time. In other words, it is virtually impossible to distinguish between sensation and perception. To illustrate, what happens when you smell a rose? Do you first have a physiological sensation (an odor) and then a psychological perception (the pleasant aroma associated with a rose)? Do you first smell and then later smell a rose? Not likely. You associate your sensation (the smell) with the familiar aroma of a rose (the perceived object) virtually simultaneously.

If perception is truly subjective, then one never just "sees" anything. The perceiver inevitably and unavoidably *sees* it *as* something or other; the perceiver always interprets what is seen. Furthermore, the interpretation will also affect what you do see. Look at the line drawing in Figure 7-3. It is a familiar optical illusion with two equally valid interpretations: one, a fancy symmetrical vase; two, the profiles of two heads facing each other. Note that you can see the vase, and then you can see the two heads. By changing your interpretation, you can make the drawing "snap back and forth" between vase and heads. Your interpretation allows you to see the drawing as vase, then as heads, then as vase, then as heads, and so on. Note further, however, that you cannot see the drawing as *both* heads and vase at the same time. You continue to "see" the same object, but you must see it *as* one meaning or the other—not both.

A number of factors can affect the sensory process. Some people are simply better at using their senses than others. Some people are color blind, for example.

Some people have hearing aids, and others have certain types of hearing loss without wearing hearing aids. I have friends who can't see a thing without their glasses and others who wear glasses just for reading. Some people have told me that my affinity for hot peppers and Mexican food has dulled my own sense of taste. Generally speaking, though, most people function rather well within a normal range of sensory capabilities. The range of their interpretive capabilities, though, is much greater.

Have you ever tried to talk politics with a rabid Republican or Democrat? Religion with a rabid fundamentalist or atheist? The "true believer" has a rather narrow range of interpretations, regardless of the information available to be interpreted. Our internalized beliefs, attitudes, and values affect our perceptions by restricting the number of interpretations we infer from our sensations. Furthermore, the stronger the belief, attitude, or value, the smaller the range of interpretations we have. That is why we tend to find absolutely no good in people or things we dislike intensely and absolutely no fault in people and things for which we have great affection. And when our interpretations have some bearing on how we view our selves, then the number of possible meanings is extremely small. Most of us will normally interpret sensations dealing with self-perceptions in a manner that is consistent with the positive self-image.

Expectations. It is a truism that we tend to hear what we expect to hear and see what we expect to see despite what we *actually* hear and see. Expectations can be a highly potent force in guiding our perceptions, even when all rationality is to the contrary. I can recall when my church's high school youth group gave an annual Halloween party for the junior high group. The highlight of the party was a spook alley in which the "victims" were led into a dark room and treated to a variety of sensations (not including sight) after having been told what to expect. A bowl of cold spaghetti, for example, was described as the intestines of some dead ghoul and cold peeled grapes were eyeballs, among other tactile sensations and expectations appropriate to Halloween. My role in this party was to don a rubber glove and keep my hand immersed in ice water until it was time to shake hands with the "victim." At the moment my hand touched that of the victim, I laughed my legendary fiendish laugh. In all modesty, my part in the spook alley was always the biggest hit.

Now we all know that not even junior-high-age adolescents could possibly believe that spaghetti was intestines, that grapes were eyeballs, or that a cold, wet rubber glove was the hand of the living dead. Nevertheless, we terrified those people for three straight years. Rarely did anyone, boy or girl, fail to be frightened during the trek down spook alley. On the other hand, just because perceptions reflect a logical process of induction, they aren't necessarily rational. Many still weep when they watch a sad movie such as *Brian's Song* (even for the twenty-third time) or are terrified watching a scary one such as *Psycho* (again for the umpteenth time). They expect to have that emotional reaction, and they have it.

Expectations affect perceptions of self just as much as they affect perceptions of an object. You expect that you won't do very well taking a multiple-choice test, and you probably won't. You expect to have a strong emotional attachment to that new girl (or boy) you just met, and you are likely to feel that emotion. In other words, you expect to have your expectations confirmed. When later events fail to confirm

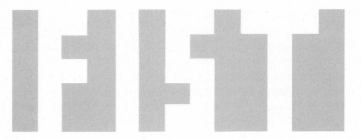

Figure 7-4. Language or Designs — Figure–Ground Relationship in Visual Perception

them, your first reaction is to rationalize this and attribute the result to some unforeseen and uncontrollable circumstance, a quirk of fate. I was once a rabid Minnesota Vikings fan (a source of many frustrations and disconfirmed expectations) and watched them lose a lot of Super Bowls. Why did they lose? Because of some unlucky breaks, some bad officiating, some fluke plays, and a number of other reasons I found at the time. In fact, I don't recall that the Vikings ever lost a Super Bowl simply because the other team was better.

Figure and Ground. You are probably aware of the figure-ground relationship associated with visual perception, even though you may not remember the jargon associated with it. Interpreting the visual image depends on what part of the object is seen as background and what is seen as the figure of interest (the foreground). The illustration in Figure 7-3 is often used to exemplify the figure-ground confusion. If the shaded area represents the background, then A illustrates two profiled faces and B illustrates a vase.

Figure 7-4 illustrates five puzzle pieces, but only because you interpret these five figures as the foreground and the white space as the background. Now "read" the white spaces between the five geometric figures. That is, treat the white space as "figure" and the shaded areas as "ground." Your interpretation should now reveal the word "FIST." As with the two-headed vase, you should be able to reverse figure and ground at will and watch the word appear and disappear, as your perception snaps back and forth between the two interpretations. The key to which perception gives you the meaning is in distinguishing which part of the visual image is the figure of interest to be kept in the foreground and which part of the image recedes into the background.

Figures 7-3 and 7-4 are visual "games." They are simple enough to understand, but they don't seem particularly relevant to self-perception or interpersonal communication. As a game of visual perception, the figure-ground relationship isn't very relevant. But the issue of discriminating between important information (figure) and unimportant information (ground) is highly significant to both self-perception and to interpersonal communication.

Psychologists agree that perception is the fundamental psychological process underlying other cognitive or psychological processes. One psychologist, Jozef Cohen (1969), baldly states, "Numerous higher psychological processes—as learning, memorizing, creating, and discriminating—are a function of the organism's perceptual capabilities" (p. 8). A key to these higher psychological processes lies in the perceptual ability to discriminate between different kinds of information. The perceiver discriminates the good from the bad, the important from the insignificant, the relevant from the irrelevant. Another way of suggesting that perception discriminates between different items of information is to say that perception involves distinguishing information that is "figure" from information that is "background."

When we said perception is selective, we didn't mean only that perception ignores some information. On the contrary, selective perception is also the ability to discriminate between items of information. By selecting some information, the perceiver makes it more significant or more relevant—it is "figure." The perceiver does not necessarily deny or fail to take into account the other information. The perceiver treats that other information as less significant or less relevant—it is "ground."

Comparison. Everyone wants to believe in the truth of his or her own perceptions. The problem arises in how to validate them, how to interpret their truth value. the typical test used to determine whether our perceptions are valid is to compare them with something else. If the perceived meaning is consistent with or similar to the criterion used for comparison, then we typically consider it to be valid. When we encounter a new experience, we check it against our past experiences. If we have encountered similar experiences in the past, we believe in the truth of our perceived interpretation. If the experience is different from other past experiences, the interpretation is likely to be equivalently different.

The human mind craves consistency. Psychologists tell us that, when taken together, our beliefs, attitudes, and values also reflect consistency, because of our need for "cognitive consistency." When we encounter two different values, attitudes or beliefs that don't seem to agree with one another, we are said to experience some cognitive discomfort. We then feel the need to get rid of that inconsistency in order to relieve our psychological discomfort.

One way to maintain consistency in our psychological "set" is to compare our beliefs, attitudes, and values with each other and make sure that they are coherent. The example commonly used to illustrate this need for consistency is that of the smoker who also holds in high esteem the value of good health. Either the smoker quits the nasty habit or rationalizes health by some other means, as by increasing an exercise program or arguing against the medical evidence linking smoking to health problems.

Yet another comparison check on your perceptions is to validate them against those that have the consensus of people in your social context. We engage in social comparison of our own self-perceptions when we compare ourselves with other people. For instance, to check whether you really are as good a student as you think, you compare your grades with those of your classmates. When the grades are posted at the end of each academic term, I constantly hear the same comment from students gathered around the bulletin board: "What did you get?" Why do they care what someone else's grade was unless they want to compare it with their own grades?

We also compare our perceptions with those of a particular social context because we have the desire to be "normal." The values, attitudes, and beliefs that constitute

Figure 7-5. Interpretations Provided by the Context

the widely accepted norms of a society provide a convenient criterion for validating our own perceptions. In this way, a person becomes a "good" and normal member of a social context by conforming, not only behaviorally but also perceptually, to the normal values of that society. Specific means of social comparison in interpersonal communication will be discussed more fully in Chapter 8.

Context. Of all the influences that affect our perceptions, the context may be the most potent. This is not to say that our cognitive system of beliefs, attitudes, and values or our expectations are not important influences. It's just that the context in which we encounter a person, object, or event is so powerful that it is likely to guide our cognitive structures and expectations and thus our perceptions. Figure 7-5 illustrates, with another example from visual perception, just how powerful is the context in determining the interpretation of the sensations. The geometric figure is somewhat ambiguous when seen by itself, that is, when it is isolated from any context. But place that identical figure in a sequence of numbers, and its meaning is clearly "13." In a sequence of letters, its meaning is clearly "B."

Now the illustration in Figure 7–5 did not change; only our interpretation of its meaning changed. This figure is not an optical illusion in the sense that we can make our interpretation snap back and forth between figure and ground and make it "13" or "B" at will. The context surrounding that figure directs our perception and makes an alternative interpretation ludicrous. We find it virtually impossible and nonsensical to read "11, B, 15, 17" or "A, 13, C, D." Either of those sequences, we would insist, just doesn't make sense.

The only issue that remains is what is meant by the "context" of the perceptions. The context that exerts such a powerful impact on perception is the context composed of elements similar to the object of perception. Note that the visual example in Figure 7–5 provides a sequence of similar elements to guide interpretation. When the sequence comprises numbers, we see the figure as a number; when it is letters, we see the figure as another letter. Thus, when we are perceiving a person, the context influencing our perceptions comprises other persons. When we are perceiving an object, the context comprises other similar objects. When it is an event, the context comprises other similar events. In this way, the context always consists of a set of similar phenomena, whether they are persons, objects, events, ideas, numbers, letters, or whatever.

But that is not all there is to context. Once the elements of the context are discernible, perception involves using that context to interpret or discover a "pattern," some organization of the elements in order to create a single unified interpretation. It doesn't require a great deal of perceptual ability to discover the pattern in the visual contexts depicted in Figure 7–5. You can easily continue the sequential string of odd numbers (19, 21, 23, 25, etc.) or alphabetic letters (E, F, G, H, etc.). Context involves perceiving a *pattern* in the set of similar phenomena.

Context and pattern provide crucial components of the pragmatic view that underlies our entire understanding of interpersonal communication. As we shall come to realize, no interpretation of any communicative behavior; verbal or nonverbal, no meaning of any relationship (friend or enemy) is possible without placing it within a context and discovering some pattern in the interaction. The absence of a pattern is equivalent to having no meaning or, at least, to a confusion of too many meanings. Interpreting meanings within their context is a major factor, perhaps the most important single factor, in understanding interpersonal communication and social relationships.

AWARENESS OF SELF

The "Fable of the Poet" is a classic tale in discussions of self-awareness. As the story goes, a poet, throughout his entire life, was constantly victimized by a mysterious veiled figure. The poet gained considerable riches, but the evil figure caused him to lose all his wealth. The poet earned fame through his creative efforts, but the enigmatic figure made it infamy. The figure, whose face was always shrouded by a thick black veil, caused the poet to lose his health and didn't let him sleep at night. It dogged the poet's trail wherever he went and refused to leave him alone.

One day the poet met and fell in love with a beautiful woman. As their relationship grew, the veiled figure seemed to vanish. The poet, freed from his tormentor, was deliriously happy as he made plans for the wedding. Just as the marriage ceremony was about to begin, the doors of the church crashed open and the ghostly figure charged down the aisle shouting, "I forbid this wedding!" Outraged, the poet sprang upon the figure, seized the veil, and ripped it from the face. Horrified, he looked upon his tormentor's face and saw . . . *himself*!

Every fable has a moral, and so does this one. The moral could be phrased in a number of ways, from "You are your own worst enemy" to the Socratic "Know thyself." But perhaps the most important point of the story is the fact that most of us think we know our selves, but we really don't. The first step in self-perception, a big first step, is to become aware of your self—to discover just who and what you are. As a matter of fact, to become aware of your self, *is* self-perception. After all, as you become aware of your self, you are also simultaneously interpreting your self. If the poet had known what we will be discussing in this section, he would have had much less trouble dealing with his veiled figure.

Elements of Self-Awareness

To be aware of self, we must first have some notion of what self is. By "self," we mean simply the identity of the individual. The self identity is the means we use to distinguish any individual from other individuals. This identity separates the individual from the crowd, sets the individual apart from society. In other words, "self" is a term we use to refer to the unique identity of the individual, any individual. When I use the term, I mean nothing more specific or jargonistic than this general definition.

Self-concept. Kuhn and McPartland (1954) have devised a test, as psychologists always seem to like to do, for measuring one's self-perception. Known as the TST (an acronym for Twenty Statements Test), this psychological assessment of self-perception asks for twenty open-ended responses to the single question, "Who am I?" You might even take this test for yourself. After all, it isn't very difficult. Just write "Who am I?" on the top of a sheet of paper and "1" through "20" on the paper underneath the question. Then fill in the blanks. You might begin twenty statements with "I am . . ." and complete the sentence twenty times. I suspect that your first ten statements will be easy; the second ten may be more difficult. You might also discover some things about yourself you may not have known (or been aware of) previously.

So what makes up a person's self-concept? How do you see yourself? Generally speaking, people tend to classify themselves in three ways. If you complete your own TST, you will probably be able to place each of your responses into one of the following three categories: personal attributes or traits, social attributes or traits, and social roles. In other words, you tend to see yourself as possessing certain internalized attributes, certain attributes to describe how you relate to others, and certain role relationships with other people. Some people are likely to perceive their selves more in one area than in another, but these three categories are the basic components of anyone's self-concept.

A personal attribute is a characteristic or trait that you possess, at least in your own perception of self. You may see yourself as having a physical trait (rating yourself as tall or short, male or female, fat or slender, black or white or even "medium brown," plain or pretty or handsome). A personal attribute may also include any ability (noted by such descriptions as dumb or intelligent, verbal or tongue-tied, good with numbers or mathematically stupid, athletic or sedentary, skilled or unskilled, coordinated or clumsy, educated or uneducated, musical or can't carry a tune in a bucket). When I completed my TST, I found it interesting that I included very few personal attributes in my twenty items. My self-concept was oriented more to social relations than to personal introspection. That is, I perceive my self as directed outward more than inward.

A social attribute or trait defines those qualities you think you demonstrate in your relations with other people. Social attributes include such characteristics as friendly or unfriendly, extroverted or introverted, assertive or reserved, outgoing or shy, talkative or reticent, sincere or manipulative, caring or self-conscious. In a way, the social attributes of your self-concept, taken together, may describe the style you use when communicating—at least the communicative style you perceive that you use.

The third component of your self-concept, social roles, involves relationships with other people and in a particular society. When social roles are part of the self-concept, we define our selves in terms of our social relationships with other people. Some social roles in the self-concept identify the self in relationship with a particular person. Several items on my TST involved this type of social role. I don't recall all of my responses, but I know that two of them were "father" and "husband" (or was it "lover?"). Other such roles may include kinship ties (son, daughter, mother, wife) or work relations (teacher, student, carpenter, police officer, bricklayer, business executive, sales representative). Often the self-concept includes simple membership in a social group that is very important to you, a culture whose values are important to your own values and your self-concept, such as Democrat or Republican; Catholic, Protestant, or Jew; American, Hispanic, or Native American; right-to-lifer or freedom of choicer; southerner or northerner; liberal or conservative.

Naturally all aspects of your self-concept are not equally important. Some are more central to what you perceive to be the "core" of your self-concept. Of your twenty responses to the TST, some are more significant to you than others. In other words, elements of your self-concept differ as to their "salience," their significance or prominence in your perception or definition of your self. For example, if I were to respond to the who-am-I query fifty times, I would still not think about writing down my race. I just have no self-identification with Caucasians as Caucasians, probably because I am a member of a racial majority. If I lived in China or Zimbabwe, my racial identification might be much more salient. On the other hand, I would bet a fortune that the mother of my "medium brown" friend would include a racial identification on her TST. The difference between us is not the personal trait itself but its salience in our respective self-concepts. Clearly, what is salient to one person may be quite trivial to another.

The attributes of your self-concept also differ in terms of their *valence*, an indication of how positively or negatively you perceive that attribute. You may perceive yourself as being "fat." Your personal attribute also may have a negative valence. That is, your evaluation of this personal attribute is negative; you hate being fat. You may also perceive yourself as being intelligent, and this personal attribute has a positive valence for you. That is, you like being intelligent. Every attribute you list in your TST responses will have some valence, ranging from extremely positive to neutral to extremely negative and all points in between.

Another characteristic of self-concept attributes involves their stability or likelihood of changing. Some attributes of your self-concept, even highly salient ones, are more likely to change during the normal passage of time than are others. Often role identities, of both high and low salience, change drastically as one gets older and moves into a different phase of life. Your own responses on the TST may have included the role of student or sorority/fraternity member. After graduation, however, these social relationships become progressively less salient and will probably vanish from your list completely in a matter of a few short years.

One's self-concept can change remarkably over a few years, a quality of attributes that is often quite significant. For example, a college friend of mine during our undergraduate days became a highly successful business executive immediately after graduation. He rose in his company to a highly salaried and responsible position within five years of graduation. At that point he resigned and started his own business, which failed miserably after only a single year. I talked with him at that point in his life and was shocked at the change in him. Instead of the brash and gregarious friend who exuded self-confidence (the person I had known and he had been), he was very quiet, horribly confused, and nervous to the point of mental collapse. His self-concept, once very strong, had been shattered. The last time I saw him, though, was the day he flew into Salt Lake City (in his own private plane) on a trip to buy some horses (his hobby) before going to Lake Powell for a few weeks of vacation (on his own luxurious houseboat). He had obviously changed his self-concept along with his fortunes in business. That man is now retired before the age of fifty, living on a very considerable annual income from his two businesses and commuting between his homes and condominiums in three different states.

The stability of any attribute of the self-concept is often difficult to predict. Some catastrophic event or unforeseeable circumstance can alter your life and drastically change your self-concept. But many elements of the self-concept at certain periods of life are obviously unstable and bound to change, just during the normal course of living. For example, certain periods in life are common transition points for revised self-concepts—high school graduation, college graduation, marriage, childbirth, job changes, promotions, and so forth. Thus, some elements of the self-concept change, often quite naturally, and others remain more stable.

Self-esteem. Recall that perception is evaluative, that a perception typically includes a judgment of the object of perception ranging from good to bad. When your own self is the object of your perception, it logically follows that you will also be evaluating your self. The term used to denote one's evaluative perception of self is "self-esteem," an inherent part of your self-concept.

Our previous discussions have suggested that most people generally possess relatively high self-esteem. Now that does not mean to imply that we are all "stuck up" or egotistical just because our self-esteem is high. It means only that the level of self-esteem for a "normal" person living normally is likely to be above a neutral or midpoint rating on the evaluation scale. When a person's own self-esteem is negative, at least *very* negative, that person is probably not very typical and probably in psychological trouble, also.

If you are temporarily "feeling bad" about something, though, that doesn't mean that you have a negative or low self-esteem. Each of us at one time or another has said, "I hate myself when I do things like that." You don't really mean it. Your

Temporarily feeling bad about something that happens does not necessarily affect your self-esteem.
(Sylvia Johnson/Woodfin Camp & Associates)

hatred is directed at your action, not at your self, and it rarely affects your self-concept or self-esteem. The self-esteem, or perceived evaluation of self, is deeper and longer-lasting than a temporary reaction to a specific event or a temporary low point in your life. Your self-esteem is part of the interpretation, the inference, from self-perception and not merely a simple reaction to an event in your life.

Your self-esteem is, however, affected by relatively permanent changes in your life. My friend's self-esteem plummeted because his high expectations for business success were not confirmed; his pattern of past business successes was unbroken until he had his single failure. Because of these past experiences of consistent success, the effect of the lone failure on his self-esteem was even greater than it might have been otherwise. A change in the pattern of past experiences may be an even more important factor affecting self-esteem.

To what extent does your self-esteem affect your behavior, particularly your communicative behavior? The more appropriate question may be "Do people with high self-esteem behave differently than those with low self-esteem?" It may be that because people behave as they do, they have high self-esteem. When your self-esteem is high, you are more likely to have experienced success, perceive yourself as competent or successful, and thus to behave in a self-confident manner. The person with lower self-esteem is, of course, more likely to be the reverse—marked by unsuccessful experiences, a self-perception of incompetence, and unsure of tentative behaviors. Persons with high self-esteem are likely to be more independent; those with lower self-esteem are likely to conform more closely to social norms. Persons with high self-esteem are likely to be more assertive; those with lower self-esteem are likely to be more reticent. At least, people who are assertive, independent, and not easily persuaded have higher self-esteem.

Multiple Selves. Although our discussion has consistently referred to each person's self as though it were a singular identity, we are all undoubtedly aware that none of us possesses only a single self. Each of us has a variety of different self-identities in terms of multiple personal traits, interpersonal attributes, and social roles. As a matter of fact, if you completed a TST for yourself, you indicated up to twenty different selves, all of which describe your unified self-identity.

Some of your selves relate to different social relationships with different people—relationships in which you are a member. They include small interpersonal groups (father-mother-son-daughter, husband-wife, friend-friend) as well as large social cultures (student, American, liberal, conservative). These selves refer to roles you perform in different societies and reflect different aspects of your life, all of which are "true." However, they rarely overlap. That is to say, your many selves do not necessarily represent a conflict between parts of your perceived self. Rather, these multiple selves should be understood as representing a person with diverse activities, interests, and social relationships.

Every time you participate in an interpersonal relationship, you deal with two selves in your self-concept: who you think you are and who you think the other person thinks you are. That is, your perception of your self (your self-concept) in each and every one of your interpersonal relationships includes at least two selves: your own self-concept and the self-concept you perceive others have of you. That means that you have as many selves (in terms of other people's perceptions of you) as there are other persons with whom you communicate.

A third part of your self-concept may seem less "real," but it is no less important. Part of your self-concept involves who you think you are, and another part involves who you would like to be—a kind of "ideal" self. Attempting to narrow the gap between your perceived "real" self and "ideal" self is probably behind most of the current fads relevant to self-improvement. How many of us have ever gone on a diet to get down to our "ideal" weight? We start jogging, join a health spa, take an aerobic class, quit smoking, play tennis or racquetball, read books, take assertiveness training classes, even go to school—all because we want to improve ourselves. The desire for self-improvement is probably an attempt to get our "real" self closer to our "ideal" self.

The "ideal self" part of your multiple selves is also relevant to your self-esteem. To the extent that your perceived "real self" comes closer to your "ideal self," then you probably experience an increase in self-esteem. As people lose weight on their diets, they often experience an increase in self-esteem. When joggers continue to increase their miles or speed, they experience an increase in self-esteem. In other words, the "ideal self" is not so much an outcome of self-improvement as a goal to be strived for but not necessarily attained.

Let me provide an example. I recall, when I was learning to ski, that the progress I made during my first year was enormous. From not being able to stand up on skis, I progressed during that first winter to the point where I believed (quite naively) that I could ski (at least survive) any slope I might choose. Since that time, though, I have made little progress and don't feel any nearer to being my perceived "ideal" skier than I was after that first year. If self-esteem is "feeling good about yourself," then the feeling is greatest during the process of self-improvement, as a result of making progress toward the goal, and not merely a function of the gap (large or small) between the two self-perceptions: who I am ("real" self) and who I want to be ("ideal" self).

Developing Self-Awareness

During the normal process of living and interacting with other people, we all go about developing our self-concept. As long as we continue day-to-day living and interaction, we continue developing this self-concept. The process of "getting in touch with ourselves" is continuous, continuing, inevitable, and unavoidable. Some people, though, are more aware than others of what their self-concept is. Some people are more "in touch with themselves." Thus, if we are to understand fully the intrapersonal level of our relationships and be able to take advantage of it, we need to be aware of our own self-concept and how any changes in it come about. The following discussion approaches the process of self-awareness from three angles: the *reflexive self*, the *social self*, and the *becoming self*.

The Reflexive Self. Visualize yourself looking into a mirror. What do you see? If you answered, "I see myself" or "I see my face," you have not fully grasped the point of reflexivity and what it means for a mirror to "reflect" your image. When you look into the mirror, you see not only yourself but yourself looking back at you. This illustrates the principle of the reflexive self. The self is reflexive to the extent that when you are aware of your self, you are aware that you are aware of yourself. In other words, self-awareness is a two-way street. When you perceive yourself, you perceive that your self is engaging in self-perception. In short, you look at your self looking at your self.

Before this discussion of reflexivity gets too bogged down in word games, let's make the principle of reflexivity really simple. The analogy of hitting a tennis ball or throwing a rubber ball at a wall might help. You direct action toward the wall, and that action is reflected back to you. That is, the ball bounces back to you. Self-perception is like that. You direct action at your self, and that action comes back to you. You are, at one and the same time, both the subject and the object of your actions. Every time you act, you perceive yourself acting. While you are perceiving yourself, you do everything you normally do during an act of perception, including inferring, interpreting, and evaluating. Furthermore, you are able to perceive that you are engaged in perceiving your action. Because you are a human being, a most

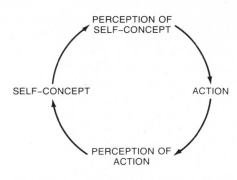

Figure 7-6. The Reflexivity of Self–Concept and Behavior

sophisticated animal, you are able to act and perceive and do both at the same time. That is to say, you are reflexive.

The reflexive process of self-awareness confuses the issue of what "causes" what. Does your self-concept "cause" you to behave in a certain way? Or does your behavior "cause" you to have a certain self-concept? The research we mentioned earlier, that people with high self-esteem tend to be assertive, might lead one to believe that having a high self-esteem "causes" you to act or behave in an assertive manner. Or it may mean that behaving assertively "causes" you to have high self-esteem. But we now know that the self behaves and perceives at the same time—reflexively. Recall that self-reflexivity is a two-way street in which one action (perceiving high self-esteem) reflects back on the action (behaving assertively) in which your self is aware that you are behaving assertively and that your self-esteem is high. Thus, you behave assertively (self as actor) and observe yourself behaving assertively (self as object) at the same time in a two-way cause and effect. Which comes first—high self esteem or assertive action? The answer is "yes."

Now wait just a minute, you are probably saying. Either one or the other is the cause—not both. However, to understand the nature of interpersonal communication, we really need to quit thinking about it in terms of cause-effect relations. It would be nice if we could make human relationships so simple, seeing them as "caused" by certain events, but they are much more complex than that. One of the things that make interpersonal communication so complex is that it is not easily explained in terms of causality. Communication isn't as linear (than is, A causes B, and therefore B is the outcome of A) as we might like to believe.

Figure 7–6 illustrates the reflexivity of self-awareness. Actually this illustration is more accurate than our earlier reference to "two-way street." The fact is that reflexivity is one-way, but the one-way action continues in the same direction until it loops back to the beginning, thus creating a circle. In order to draw the geometric figure of a circle, you typically move your pencil in only one direction, but the pencil continues in that one direction until it returns to the point of origin. Once completed, the circle has no origin—no beginning or end. This cyclical effect is the basis of reflexivity. A cycle has no beginning and no end but is a continuously occurring movement from one point to another. Each element is both the cause and the effect of every other element. I have a self-concept, which I perceive, which leads me to perform some particular action, which I also perceive, which leads me to have a self-concept, which I perceive, which . . . and so on and so on.

For instance, I have self-esteem of which I become aware through perceiving my self-concept introspectively. That perception of my self-concept leads me to assert myself when I interact with another person. I then realize that I have acted assertively, and that perception of my action leads me to believe that I must have high self-esteem, about which I become aware through . . . and so on and so on. Which came first—the high self-esteem or the assertive behavior? The question is precisely the same as the classic chicken-or-egg controversy. In other words, the self (perception and action) is reflexive.

The Social Self. It is one of those ironies of life that the individual human being derives his or her self-concept (and, hence, an identity as a unique individual) by engaging in interaction with others. It is ironic because it is virtually impossible for a person to be an individual without being involved in interpersonal relationships. Jurgen Ruesch has been quoted (see Wilmot, 1980) as saying, "It is well to remember that all the information a person possesses about himself is derived from others. His impression of the impact he had upon others is what makes up the picture of himself" (p. 44). In other words, an individual self perceives and evaluates his or her own actions primarily by perceiving and evaluating the reactions of others, and others' reactions make your own actions much more meaningful. Other people provide a standard by which you can check your own self-concept.

The use of other people as the criterion for judging your own self-concept has been called use of the "social self," a term coined by George Herbert Mead (1913), a sociologist often credited with fathering an approach to social behavior called "symbolic interactionism." Early sociologists also coined the term "looking-glass self" to illustrate how we develop a self-concept through social interaction. As we interact with others, the effect is similar to looking in a mirror. That is, we see reflected back to us, in the behaviors of our fellow interactants, an image of our own selves. The other people behave toward us and, in so doing, provide us with information about our selves. We then use that information to infer, interpret, evaluate our own self-concepts. Hence, communication unavoidably and inevitably results in developing one's self-concept.

To illustrate the looking-glass self, have you ever told a joke and no one laughed? Do that a sufficient number of times, and you begin to wonder about yourself, to lower your evaluation of your self. The looking-glass self also works with students in elementary school. We all know that public schools tend to test their students to death—not just classroom tests, but aptitude tests, IQ tests, and a variety of other standardized tests. These tests then become the basis for pinpointing students with the greatest potential and those who are likely to have academic trouble. The result is often disastrous for the students pegged early in their scholastic careers as "slow learners." These students are told so many times by so many people that they aren't very bright that they begin to *behave* as though they weren't. Students who are told that they are smart also often overachieve in trying to live up to the expectations of others.

Another aspect of developing self-awareness through social interaction is "self-monitoring." When people are sensitive to their own behaviors and those of others during social interaction, they are engaging in self-monitoring. Self-monitoring allows you to become aware of what constitutes appropriate behavior in a social setting. Although self-monitoring typically refers to a sensitivity toward your own behaviors, you can also learn what kinds of behavior are socially appropriate by observing the actions of other people. Whether you are monitoring your own actions (self) or those of another person, you are learning about socially appropriate behavior. The process of perceiving the action is the same; only the person being perceived (self or other) changes.

Self-monitoring is an ability. That is, some people are better at it than others. In fact, psychologists have devised a test to measure how much self-monitoring ability people have. The creator of this test has explained that "The self-monitoring indivdual is one who, out of a concern for social appropriateness, is particularly sensitive to the expression and self-presentation of others in social situations and uses these cues as guidelines for monitoring his own self-presentation" (Snyder, 1974, p. 528).

From research using this test of self-monitoring ability, we can draw several conclusions. One, becoming aware of socially appropriate behavior and adapting it to one's own behavior (the looking-glass self) is an ability possessed by some people to a greater degree than others. Two, self-monitoring ability can be measured, so that people can be distinguished as being high self-monitors, low self-monitors, or average self-monitors (similar to IQ and other psychological abilities). Three, because self-monitoring is an ability, you may be able to improve your own capacity for self-monitoring. You should then be able to develop a clearer perception of your self-concept, along with a greater knowledge of appropriate social interaction. And that ability would make you a more effective participant in interpersonal communication. Your instructor may have some ideas concerning ways to improve your own self-monitoring ability.

The Becoming Self. The self-concept is always subject to change, is constantly developing, is continually being bombarded with new information to be perceived and interpreted. As human beings living in a society and interacting daily with other people, we have large quantities of constantly available information to use in our self-perceptions. Every time we engage in communication, we gain additional information through our looking-glass self and have a continuing check on our current self-concept. That information may, of course, serve to confirm or reinforce our self-concept, or it may tend to disconfirm the self-concept we already have. Whatever effect it may have, the information is always available to us and is constantly affecting our self-concept. In other words, the self-concept never just "is;" it is always in a state of "becoming."

To say that the self is always developing is not to say that our self-concept undergoes radical changes every time we talk with someone new. To the contrary, most individuals have a relatively stable self-concept. In normal day-to-day activities, our perception of self remains rather constant, without significant changes. Several reasons account for this relative stability of the self-concept. For one thing, the nature of perception itself tends to resist massive revisions in our interpretations.

Selectivity, for example, is a powerful force for maintaining present perceptions. We tend to select our interactional partners on the basis of their similarity to us. (Called "social comparison," this subject will be discussed further in Chapter 8.) We tend to select information available from our interactional partners on the basis of whether it reinforces our self-concept and we discount information that disagrees with it. We interpret information from some interactional partners as more valuable than that received from others. That is, we find our self-concepts being confirmed by our friends, and we are likely to believe that the information from our friends is more believable. Therefore, our self-concepts may be in a constant state of becoming and always changing, but that change is typically a very gradual, evolutionary change and not a large-scale modification.

So how does the "becoming self" work? In normal circumstances, we tend to maintain our self-concepts rather easily. Extraordinary circumstances (such as loss of a job, death of a loved one, divorce, etc.), of course, can lead to abrupt and occasionally significant changes in one's self-concept. Such changes, though, are certainly not very common. They involve catastrophic events, crises, that are often the result of changes in the environment beyond our control.

As we said, the "becoming self" is more typically a gradual evolutionary change rather than sudden and drastic changes in one's self-concept. Your self-concept will be constantly becoming something slightly different during the everyday process of living your life. Every life has its ups and downs. Making new friends, getting married, graduating from school, getting a raise in salary—all provide you with boosts in your self-concept; they make you feel good. And moving away from friends, breaking up with that special girl or boy friend, getting a divorce, losing a job, or having an argument with your boss will tend to make you feel bad. Your emotional ups and downs will affect your self-concept as they accumulate over a period of time. These are the normal fluctuations of life, normal fluctuations in your self-concept, and part of your becoming self.

DISCLOSURE OF SELF

When you meet someone for the first time, you engage in talk for the purpose of getting to know that person. Of course, talking also allows the other person to get to know you. In other words, you are "revealing" your self, your individual identity, to your fellow communicator at the same time the other person is "revealing" his or her self to you—what we earlier termed "psychological flashing." The more appropriate term for this getting-to-know-each-other's-self communication is *self-disclosure*, a term first coined by psychologist Sydney Jourard in a book aptly titled *The Transparent Self* (1964). According to Jourard, self-disclosure is "the act of making yourself manifest, showing yourself so others can perceive you" (p. 19).

The fact is that every time you communicate, you are revealing your self, manifesting (making observable through your behaviors) part of your personal identity of self. And you engage in this self-disclosing communication both intentionally and unintentionally. As a communicator, though, you need to be cautious about interpreting every action of the other person as an act of self-disclosure. For one thing, the particular behavior may not be genuine, in the sense that the alleged discloser might be "faking it," behaving in a manner that is not compatible with her or his self-concept. Second, the self-disclosing act is subject to the other person's perception. And we already know that the perceived self is only "apparent" knowledge and may be quite inaccurate.

Although it is probably true that every communicative act may include some self-disclosure, relying on every act to tell you something about the other person's self may be misleading. Therefore, we will adopt a more restricted definition of self-disclosure and use the term to refer only to information that one person tells another about his or her self "which the other person is unlikely to know or to discover from other sources" (Pearce & Sharp, 1973, p. 414).

Self-disclosing communication embodies a real mystique in common mythology concerning communication in our society. Our romantic novels are filled with stories of first meetings between a man and a woman in which they reveal their innermost secrets and consequently fall madly, passionately, and immediately in love. A more objective understanding of self-disclosure reveals a far less formidable impact on interpersonal relationships. Despite an astounding interest and number of studies of self-disclosure in the fields of both psychology and communication (see Chelune, 1979), the fact is that we really don't know nearly as much about it as we think we do. The following discussion attempts to provide a realistic look at our knowledge and understanding of self-disclosing communication and provide a sensible portrayal of its role in interpersonal communication.

Private and Public Knowledge. It stands to reason that the person who knows more about yourself than anyone else is you. It also stands to reason that there are areas about yourself that may be known to others, but not yourself, as well as information that remains private only to you. In other words, all possible knowledge about yourself can be classified into two categories: public knowledge (what other people know) and private knowledge (what only you know). Self-disclosure, then, may be defined as your making public that knowledge which otherwise would be private, known only to you.

Let's be more precise in what we mean by private and public knowledge of self. Joseph Luft (1970), for example, has suggested four different classes of self-knowledge. Luft places his areas within a 2 × 2 matrix and calls it the Johari window—"window" because it represents a four-paned window and "Johari" because it was devised by *Joseph* Luft and *Harry* Ingram (and perhaps because "Johari" sounds more mystical than "Joe-Harry"). Figure 7-7 depicts the Johari window, a representation of public and private knowledge of self.

Each of us has some areas of self that we aren't aware of or prefer not to know about—"unknown area." Naturally, we can't disclose these portions of our self that we aren't aware of. Another area of our private self ("blind area") is a part of our self that we can disclose to others, but probably not intentionally. This area is apparently that part of self-disclosure that leads other people to say that they "know us better than we know ourselves."

The self-disclosure most significant to interpersonal communication is probably the information that is part of your perceived self-concept. When you reveal this

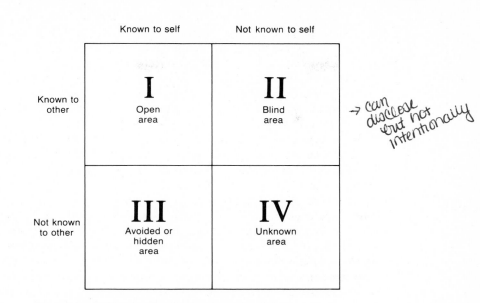

Figure 7-7. Public and Private Knowledge of Self
(The Johari Window)

information to another person through your communicative actions, intentionally or unintentionally, you move it from the "hidden area" to the "open area." This shift is undoubtedly the self-disclosure intended by the widely accepted definition of the term—making known to others information they wouldn't be able to know otherwise.

When we communicate, we make manifest or observable some aspect of our selves. The other person, perceiving this behavior, infers something about us and develops some perception about who we are. And, of course, we do the same perceiving and interpreting when the other person communicates with us. But is that behavior a false or genuine manifestation of the communicator's self? That is the problem faced by the perceiver—to determine whether the apparent self-disclosure is an accurate reflection of the communicator's private self. Does the behavior provide self-disclosing information that is a "false face" or a "blind area?"

For instance, people tell me I am gregarious and extroverted; I tell them I am shy. They say my extroversion is part of my "blind area," unfaced by me but perceived by others. I say that it is a façade and isn't "really" me. Who is correct? That question is unanswerable. More importantly, though, what difference does it make who is correct? Your own self-perception may disagree with the other's perception of your self. It is the potential disagreement of perceptions, not which perceiver is "correct," that is important to interpersonal communication.

The point is simply this. The public and private areas of self-knowledge that are significant to interpersonal communication are the perceived interpretations that each communicator possesses about his or her own self and the self of the other person. Whether they are right or wrong, whether the self disclosure is false or genuine, is simply not important to the process of interpersonal communication. What I perceive is "apparent knowledge" to me; what others perceive is "apparent knowledge" to them. Intrapersonally, the importance of our perceptions to interpersonal communication is whether our perceptions overlap. (You might wish to refer back to Figure 6-3.) Self-disclosure is a part of the psychological process of perception. In interpersonal communication, its significance lies in providing information about private aspects of one's self-concept in order that the communicators' perceptions of each other may coincide or overlap (see Figure 6-3).

Self-Disclosure and Intimacy/Liking. It is only natural to believe that as people disclose their innermost selves to each other, they will probably tend to become more intimate or like each other more. Research has shown some connection between self-disclosure and liking, but that connection is not as straightforward as we might think. Social psychologists Irwin Altman and Dalmas Taylor (1973) have developed a model of interaction they call *social penetration*. Their model provides insight into how self-disclosure is linked with developing intimacy or liking.

According to the concept of "social penetration," the human self can be visualized as similar to an onion, with an inner core surrounded by a layer of self surrounded by another layer surrounded by still another layer, and so on, until the outermost layer is visible to the other person. That outer layer may be considered the "public knowledge of self" visible to other people. Self-disclosure, then (in the sense of the other person's discovering the inner layers of self otherwise hidden from view), is tantamount to peeling away the outer layers of self, "penetrating" the layers to reveal a more private layer of self-knowledge.

Social penetration becomes relevant to interpersonal communication in regard to the topics chosen for conversation. Topics may be said to have two dimensions: breadth and depth. Figure 7-8 illustrates the onionlike self (appearing as a circle but more appropriately as a cross-section of a sphere) and the conversational topics. "Breadth" refers to the number of different topics covered during interpersonal communication; and "depth" refers to a deeper or more personal level of conversation within any given topical area. Naturally, the breadth of topics (the number of topics discussed) is related somewhat to feelings of closeness, in the sense that the more we know about each other in different areas, the more likely we are to perceive that we "know" each other. But depth of topics—penetration to more personal attitudes, beliefs, and values of self—is probably more closely related to feelings of liking or intimacy.

All topics are not alike, in terms of their levels of intimacy. That is, some topics are more likely to be more intimate and private than others. Marriage and family matters, for example, are likely to be perceived as more private than demographic and biographic information about self. Furthermore, some people will disagree on which topics are more personal or private. Several years ago I was advising a graduate student who was interested in the topic of self-disclosure and began observing the interaction of different groups of people and noting the types of topics they discussed. She found that "sex and dating" was a topic rarely discussed by newly acquainted college students, who considered it a "very intimate" topic. However, she also observed a women's consciousness-raising group that discussed the most private details of their sex lives with one another. She concluded that a topic considered

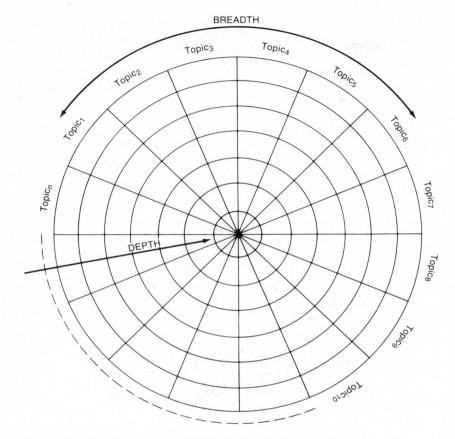

Figure 7-8. Breadth and Depth of Topics in Self–Disclosing Communication

intimate by one group in one situation might be considered very nonintimate by another group in another situation.

The discussion thus far has considered only differences among topics (breadth). Within a topic (depth), however, partners may disclose a deeper level of their private selves to the other. A statement within the topic "marriage and family" could be at a very low level of intimacy (for example, "I am married and have two children") or a rather high level of intimacy (for example, "My husband beat me last night. I don't know what to do. I'm terrified of him, but I can't leave him. Where would I go?"). This latter comment discloses much more *depth*—a layer deep in the private self and far removed from the outermost "public" layer.

Disclosing to another person a deeply penetrating layer of your self typically makes you feel more vulnerable. Self-disclosing communication with depth is risky in most relationships. Your self, especially that innermost core of your private self, is your final refuge of privacy. To disclose a highly personal piece of information about your self is to stand psychologically naked before the other person. Thus,

Partners in a relationship make choices about how much they want to reveal about themselves.
(Joel Gordon)

many people interested in self-disclosure suggest that trust may be as important a factor in the relationship as liking or intimacy. To reveal your private self is to place your trust in the other person. You are, in essence, trusting that other person not to reveal that private information to others, not to hurt you with that information at some later time.

The Norm of Reciprocity. Sociologist Alvin Gouldner (1960) has suggested that one of the most common norms in our society is reciprocity. Reciprocity is the tendency to respond in kind to the other person. He likes you; you like him back. He hits you; you hit him back. In other words, with apologies to the Golden Rule, reciprocity follows the guideline "Do unto others as they do unto you—and do it right away." Reciprocity has also been called the "best documented characteristic of self-disclosing communication" (Pearce & Sharp, 1973, p. 418). In other words, you self-disclose to me, and I will reciprocate by self-disclosing to you, typically at the same "depth" of self-disclosure.

What happens when one person self-discloses and the other person does not reciprocate or does not self-disclose at a similar depth? The respondent would probably be perceived as violating a social norm. That is, the nonreciprocating person was "supposed" to reciprocate but didn't; therefore, that person has violated a social norm. The "wronged" person is likely to react negatively. The tendency to reciprocate is very strong.

The force of a norm is hard to resist. When someone self-discloses to you, you feel a "need" to self-disclose in return. That doesn't mean you always do, but you often feel that you have done something "wrong" when you don't. If you don't like feeling that way, though, you might resent the person who self-disclosed to you. You might say to yourself that you really didn't want to know that much about the other person, and you resent that person for placing you in such a position.

So what is the result of unreciprocated self-disclosure or self-disclosure that is not reciprocated at an equivalent depth? Both persons, the self-discloser and the other person, tend to resent each other—for different reasons, perhaps, but the result is the same. Hence, it may be true that reciprocated self-disclosure tends to bring people closer together. But it may also be true that self-disclosure without reciprocity tends to drive people farther apart. We could easily infer that self-disclosure (even self-disclosure in depth) is not the significant factor related to interpersonal liking or intimacy. Perhaps reciprocity of self-disclosure, particularly reciprocating the depth of self-disclosure, is more important than the amount of self information disclosed.

On the Other Hand . . . . Most of us believe that self-disclosure is effective in developing intimate interpersonal relationships. However, some exceptions to this belief are widely documented. Perhaps the most notable is the phenomenon known as "the stranger on the train"—sometimes called the "bus-rider phenomenon" or "laundering," an apparent reference to the common phrase "washing your dirty linen in public" (Crable, 1981, p. 110). The stranger-on-the-train phenomenon involves the relatively common occurrence where extremely penetrating, personal revelations are made to a brand new acquaintance, even an absolute stranger.

The stranger-on-the-train phenomenon typically occurs *only* when the self-discloser believes that any future communication with the other person is highly unlikely. If the self-discloser were to encounter the stranger at some future date, she or he would be very embarrassed and resent the stranger for being privy to such sensitive information. Without future encounters, however, the self-discloser may actually feel better for having told someone—anyone. The comment of the woman who was beaten by her husband was made to me when I was a Ph.D. student advising undergraduate majors. I had never met the woman prior to that conversation and never saw her again afterward. Whatever the outcome, the stranger-on-the-train phenomenon is certainly self-disclosure involving depth of topic, but equally certain is the fact that it is unrelated to liking or intimacy.

Another exception to the link between self-disclosure and liking involves the timing of the self-disclosure. *When* a person offers personal revelations may be more important than depth of the disclosure or whether it is reciprocated. Disclosing too much too soon to the other person is likely to lead to the other person's withdrawing from the relationship. Any relationship needs to develop at its own pace; attempting to speed up the process through self-disclosure is likely to disrupt that development and lead to a premature and unnecessary breakup.

Self-disclosure occurs most often and at greater depth in relatively early stages of relational growth. People who have already developed highly intimate relationships typically don't disclose themselves to one another very often or at great depth. As a matter of fact, partners in intimate interpersonal relationships often intentionally avoid penetrating self-disclosure as a means of maintaining their intimacy. In conclusion, then, the commonsense belief that self-disclosure and intimacy or liking are directly related is probably not false, but it is undoubtedly overstated.

If we are to understand the nature of interpersonal communication and provide a realistic basis for improving our own communicative practices, we need to adopt a realistic understanding of the role that self-disclosure plays in interpersonal communication. Toward that end, a few hard-headed questions are in order.

1. Is self-disclosure necessary for effective interpersonal communication? Certainly most of us think so. According to one reviewer, "People believe it is appropriate to engage in high amounts of self-disclosure with others whom they like," and "People over-estimate the extent to which they self-disclose to others whom they like" (Bochner, 1982, p. 118). In other words, friends may not exchange much self-disclosing information, but they *believe* they do. Further, people overestimate how much information they actually do disclose.

Some self-disclosure is undoubtedly typical of most effective interpersonal communication. After all, people must certainly tell each other about themselves in order for interpersonal communication to get off the ground. However, because *some* self-disclosure is necessary, it does not follow that *more* self-disclosure is better.

2. Is self-disclosure desirable for effective interpersonal communication? Clearly most of us think so, without qualification. Sometimes, though, self-disclosure (at least in much depth) is quite undesirable. The timing of self-disclosure is probably more important. Often, we are wiser to exercise restraint in disclosing ourselves to others. Therefore, self-disclosure is desirable in some circumstances but undesirable in others.

3. Is self-disclosure important to effective interpersonal communication? Again, most of us think so. And again, we need to qualify the answer. As they achieve a healthy and close relationship, partners will engage in self-disclosure somewhere along the way. They must self-disclose in order to get to know each other, especially get to know each other well. But we have too readily assumed that self-disclosing communication causes (or at least leads to) healthy and close relationships. The effect may be quite the reverse. In other words, it may be more accurate to say that because two partners have a healthy and close relationship, they tend to disclose themselves to one another.

It is now time in our discussion to draw some conclusions about self-disclosure. Bochner (1982) has previously written that "self-disclosure appears to be a highly overrated activity. Perhaps the time has come to lift the fog of ideology surrounding the concept" (p. 121). The following statements about self-disclosure are intended to show that it is important to interpersonal communication. But they are also intended to remove much of the magical quality we often attribute to self-disclosure when we overstate its significance and impact.

1. Self-disclosure is not directly related to intimacy, but relationships developing toward intimacy typically include periods of high self-disclosure.
2. How much people disclose themselves to one another is probably not as important as their incremental increase in self-disclosure at any given time. A sizable increase in self-disclosure probably signifies a growth stage in the relationship. (This topic will be discussed further in Chapter 12.)

3. Self-disclosure is typically reciprocated by the responding person. When it is not reciprocated, self-disclosure often leads to mutual resentment.
4. Greater frequency and depth of self-disclosure are more common in relatively early stages of relational growth and are not typical of highly intimate or well-established relationships.
5. Self-disclosing communication is neither good nor bad in interpersonal communication. Some self-disclosure is typical in developing relationships, but inappropriate or extreme self-disclosure may have a boomerang effect and be perceived as "cheapening" one's feelings.

BEHAVIOR OF SELF

At first glance, the topic of this section seems absurd. The self cannot behave. The self is an intrapersonal psychological part of interpersonal communication. It exists within the individual and comprises beliefs, attitudes, values, cognitions—but not behaviors. But those psychological processes, though they probably can't "cause" us to behave in a certain way (if they did, false roles or unintended behaviors would be virtually impossible), still have implications for understanding how we behave during interpersonal communication.

Psychologist John LaGaipa (1981, p. 75) suggests that the intrapersonal process involved in interpersonal relationships comprises several parts: a *memory* of past experiences and *anticipations* of future experiences. The ability to anticipate what will happen to you can be considered an "implicit psychological resource" which the communicator uses to organize past experiences and provide guidelines for behaving appropriately in the present. As a "resource," these psychological processes do not "make" you behave in a certain way, but they are available to assist you in behaving appropriately. This section discusses several ways in which the psychological processes provide a resource for choosing our behaviors. Sometimes this psychological resource functions to benefit interpersonal communication, and sometimes the resource is detrimental to communication.

Autistic Hostility

Four decades ago Theodore Newcomb (1948) described the problem of "autistic hostility," which occurs in some interpersonal relationships. Autistic hostility begins with some negative first impression. It doesn't matter what led to that first impression. Maybe you didn't like his necktie, maybe she reminded you of someone you didn't like, maybe you just happened to be in a bad mood at the time. The negative impression may be rational or irrational, justified or unjustified. Because you have this negative impression, you avoid further interpersonal contact with that person. Consequently, you never receive any more information about that person, you never get to know any more about that person, and you continue to reinforce your negative impression. How can you do otherwise? You never have the opportunity to receive information to the contrary.

To illustrate, I have a professional acquaintance who, quite irrationally, impressed me negatively when we first met. To this day, my interactions with that person are infrequent, brief, and extremely superficial. This doesn't look good for me. I'm supposed to be an expert in interpersonal communication and should know how to be an effective communicator. I know all about autistic hostility. I've analyzed my relationship with this person and know that it is a classic case of autistic hostility. Others have told me very good things about this person. Yet to this day, our relationship has been victimized by autistic hostility.

Self-Fulfilling Prophecy

If autistic hostility involves a first impression leading to no behavior (that is, little or no further interaction), the self-fulfilling prophecy involves a psychological resource that guides behavior in a certain direction. The self-fulfilling prophecy begins with your anticipation of some future event. Because you expect something will occur, you behave (often unconsciously) in such a way that the anticipated event does in fact occur. For example, you just "know" that you are going to fail that test next week. Hence you think "what good will it do to study for it?" You don't study and, sure enough you fail the test. On the other hand, you might be equally positive that you are going to do well on that test. You study hard, review your notes thoroughly, take the test, and ace it. What made the expectation come true? Your anticipation didn't "cause" it, but it led you to engage in a sequence of behaviors that fulfilled the prophecy.

Self-fulfilling prophecies often affect the outcomes of interpersonal relationships. You "know" that your relationship with that special boy or girl just won't work out. As a result of your expectation, you act disinterested, you see him or her less and less—and sure enough, the relationship doesn't work out. Of course, the anticipation of a great relationship can have just the opposite effect. It leads you to work at making the relationship grow: you become more attentive and helpful, and that sequence of behaviors allows the prophecy to come true.

Self-fulfilling prophecies are present in the larger society as well. In fact, the often discussed "sex-role stereotypes" may be seen as a self-fulfilling prophecy in action. Young girls are often given dolls to play with, told to be clean, and taught to act "feminine." Young boys are given baseball gloves, encouraged to get dirty, and taught to "be a man" and not cry. The traits we come to associate with being masculine and feminine are often the result of trained behaviors throughout the child's growing-up period.

My oldest daughter was a victim of the self-fulfilling prophecy regarding sex-role stereotypes. She had received exceptionally good grades during elementary school, so her mother and I were somewhat surprised when we discovered that her sixth-grade teacher had recommended her for advanced-placement courses in junior-high English but not in mathematics. We asked him why this was so, and he appeared surprised. He responded quite innocently that he wasn't aware that our daughter was interested in math, but he would certainly recommend her. We asked him whether he had asked the same question of the boys he had recommended for advanced mathematics classes. He didn't seem to comprehend why we had asked that question.

Self-fulfilling prophecies are often very difficult to see in operation. Furthermore, we often attribute the results of such prophecies to factors other than the behaviors precipitated by the anticipation of future events. You "blew" the test because you think you're dumb or because the teacher was lousy—not because you didn't study very hard for it. You broke up because she or he wasn't "right" for you—not because you were inattentive. Again, the self-fulfilling prophecy is a matter of perception. Even "apparent" knowledge, whether accurate or false, is still knowledge.

Perceptual Anesthesia

Selective perception underlies the psychological process known as *perceptual anesthesia*. As the term implies, relational partners perceive one another's characteristics selectively; they actively ignore or avoid potentially troublesome areas. Everyone has some characteristic that even their closest friends don't like. Perceptual anesthesia occurs when close friends ignore that undesirable characteristic of the other so that it doesn't affect their relationship. Of course, this anesthesia could be harmful to the relationship if it represented a crucial element that is unduly repressed by the relational partner. The repressed hostility may smolder inside the person and eventually explode. More often, however, the friends ignore a trait that is not particularly serious—only annoying.

Perceptual anesthesia also occurs to *maintain* a close relationship as partners actively avoid potentially disruptive factors. Simply by not taking those factors into account, the relational partners deny their significance. Bochner's (1982) summary of self-disclosure research led to the conclusion that "there is abundant evidence that long-term relationships are maintained by illusions of truth, exaggerations of goodness, and less than full communication" (p. 120). He went on to explain, "When conflict occurs, it is not uncommon for nondistressed [happy and intimate] couples to lie, withhold from, and otherwise deceive each other." He cites research evidence that "found that newlyweds lied to each other to avoid conflicts or reinterpreted their earlier statements so as to deny that any disagreement existed" (p. 121).

You may be shocked that partners in a happy and loving relationship would actually "lie" to each other, but you shouldn't be. Instead, think of it as a matter of priorities. If two things are at stake—telling the truth or maintaining a loving relationship—the truth is apt to come in second best, and well it should. After all, to the couple, their relationship is more important than some blind faith in honesty at all costs.

Perceptual anesthesia, then, is essentially selective perception at work. In this case, though, the perceiver may be intentionally and willfully being selective and ignoring some information that could affect the relationship negatively. Perceptual anesthesia typically functions to protect the relationship and, as often as not, is probably beneficial to maintaining that relationship. We should not think of it in terms of being "good" or "bad," but as a normal part of the intrapersonal level of interpersonal communication.

Self-Protection

Individuals go to great lengths to protect their selves. Some individuals, particularly those with low self-esteem, have rather fragile self-concepts. To avoid psychological harm, they must protect their self-concepts from change and challenge. But even people with strong self-concepts often feel the need to protect them from others.

Self-protection may take several forms. Sociologist Erving Goffman (1971) views protecting self as defending one's "territory" from attack. He describes two perceptual "territories of self" that people commonly protect: "*Information Presence*: The set of facts about himself to which an individual expects to control access while in the presence of others" and "*Conversational Presence*: The right of an individual to exert some control over who can summon him into talk and when he can be summoned . . ." (pp. 39–40).

Goffman's territory of "information presence" is very reminiscent of our earlier discussion of self-disclosure when private knowledge of self is converted into public knowledge, as the self-discloser chooses to do so. The second territory of "conversational presence" refers to other people: the right to choose your partner in a relationship. It is fundamentally the territory of the self that allows the individual the right to choose with whom he or she wants to be involved in a relationship and, when in a relationship, the right of self to choose the time and place of communicating. Goffman's "conversational presence" is self's declaration of the right of privacy, a right to "protect" one's self from any relationship.

One way to protect your self during relational communication is to exercise your right *not* to self-disclose or provide in-depth information about yourself to the other person. Woody Hayes, the late college football coach, is alleged to have said about the forward pass, if you throw a pass, three things can happen to it—and two of them are bad. His football teams at Ohio State University were perennial national powerhouses while flying in the face of most coaching philosophy: they rarely passed the ball. A similar statement could be made about self-disclosing communication: If you self-disclose to someone, that person can respond in any of four ways—and three of them are bad. The respondent may reciprocate your self-disclosure, deny it, ignore it, or reject it. To disclose your self to someone else is to risk your self-concept by placing part of it in the hands of another person. When you feel the risk is too great, you will try to protect it by not self-disclosing.

Another way of protecting yourself in interpersonal communication is to attribute the potential threat to some cause that doesn't affect your self-concept. When something undesirable or threatening occurs in communication, your perceptual ability allows you to attribute the "cause" of that undesirable element to something that does not threaten your self-concept. Psychologist John Harvey and his colleagues (1982) suggest that

> people may sometimes engage in misattributions—probably without much awareness— to dull the experience of self-threatening problems in the relationship. For example, reduction of affectionate contact from a partner can be translated, as "He's been under a lot of pressure lately." We can choose to make the attribution situational ("outside pressures") rather than dispositional ("He has a less affectionate nature") or interpersonal ("He is less affectionate *towards me*"). (p. 113)

One of the key elements in attribution (designating the cause or reason for some occurrence) is to provide a "locus of control" (similar to a cause). We attribute the occurrence to some controlling factor that is either "internal" or "external" to the self. When the partner wasn't as affectionate as formerly, in the example given above, the person attributed the problem to "outside pressures"—that is, to the situation. The person may also protect the self by attributing the problem to the other person, saying that the partner has a "less affectionate nature." Attributing the undesirable occurrence to the other person or the situation ("external" locus) allows us to protect our self-concept. But attributing the occurrence to an "internal" locus ("towards me") is potentially damaging to one's own self-concept. It seems rather obvious that we would, under "normal" circumstances, tend to attribute the locus of relational problems to some factor other than our own self. In doing so, we explain the problem and protect our self-concept and self-esteem.

The self provides a wealth of resources that we can use to evaluate our behavior as appropriate and, reflexively, to interpret the meaning of our behaviors after we've performed them. At the same time, your behavior is a source of information to the other person and provides him or her with information about your self. You may not be intentionally engaging in self-disclosing communication (and thereby manifesting your private self in your behavior), but the other person doesn't know or even care whether you are.

Both of you are perceiving each other throughout your entire conversation. Every time you act or behave during communication (and you are continually behaving during communication), you are "presenting" your self (at least as perceived by the other) for public inspection. Of course, you (as the perceiver of other people's behaviors) also consider every action performed by your partners to be a public display of their selves. As soon as we take the other person into account, all communication is unavoidably and inevitably a presentation of the other person's self. And "the other" is the subject of the next chapter.

Summary

The intrapersonal level of communication concerns the self and the nature of acquiring meaning of self. The psychological process involved in self-meaning is perception, an internalized process of assigning meaning to sensations of objects, persons, or events. Perception, the process by which we acquire all personal knowledge, is experiential, selective, inferential, inaccurate, and evaluative. Perception, though often considered to be valid without qualification, is a subjective portrayal of reality as acquired through the five senses. It is an indirect knowledge gained from interpreting sensations and is, thus, only apparent knowledge.

Perception is affected by internal attitudes, values, and beliefs which, together, comprise past experience. This experience, is, in turn, organized into what is known as a psychological "set," which is used to assign meanings to information received from the senses. Meanings derived from perceptions are also affected by expectations, figure-ground relationships, comparison checks with other bases of knowledge, and the context in which the information appears to our senses.

When one's own self is the object of perception, the task is to become aware of self through the same process of perception used to acquire knowledge of physical and external objects. The identity of one's self is known as the self-concept, a product of self-perception. The way one values, positively or negatively, one's self-concept is known as self-esteem. The self-concept also involves multiple identities, including personal and social traits as well as social roles created in relationships with others. The process of developing an awareness or perception of your own self involves reflexivity, social interaction, and continual evolutionary change.

When one reveals information about one's self to another person, information that person would not be able to acquire otherwise, the process is known as self-disclosure. Self-disclosing communication concerns information that is part of your own private knowledge which you choose, intentionally or unintentionally, to make public to a partner in communication. Self-disclosure has been linked to intimacy or liking and is affected by reciprocity, timing, and breadth/depth of conversational topics. Even though people commonly attribute more significance to self-disclosure and its role in developing relationships, it remains an important element of the intrapersonal level of interpersonal communication.

Elements of the self serve as resources to assist us in determining what behavior is appropriate in a particular social setting. These resources may benefit or harm the development of relationships. Among the ways in which the self and behavior are related are such phenomena as autistic hostility, self-fulfilling prophecy, perceptual anesthesia, and self-protection. All involve the psychological process of perception and its emphasis on inferences, evaluations, and indirect or apparent knowledge.

CHAPTER **8**

The Other

I don't think any woman in power
really has a happy life unless
she's got a large number of women friends . . .
because you sometimes must go and sit down
and let down your hair with someone
you can trust totally.

—Margaret Thatcher

In any two-person communication, then, there are two selves you need to know: yours and the other's. Assuming that you have engaged in a process of self-perception and are now relatively well acquainted with your self, you need know only one more person—the other. Toward that end, this chapter will look at the process of how and why we get to know the other. We will then treat some specific problems involved in perception when the perceived object is another person. Of course, "knowing" the other is only part of the process of interpersonal communication. The other part is actually communicating, behaving toward that other person.

GETTING TO KNOW THE OTHER

Getting to know the other person is not a simple task. It involves the psychological process of perception, of course, and we already know that perception is a highly fallible basis of securing knowledge. That is, perception is inaccurate, selective, subjective, and so forth. Above all, when we perceive another person, we must make inferences on the basis of highly incomplete information. We must base our interpretations on the basis of only the information that is available to our five senses. After all, we can't see, feel, hear, taste, or smell what is going on within the other person. The only sensory information we can obtain from other people is contained in their behaviors or actions (including their physical appearance, clothing, odor, etc.). Hence, when we communicate, we base our perceptions about the other person's self on the communicative behaviors we can observe. Although we seem to look for many types of information from the other, we probably find that three types are most important: the other person's intentions, the other person's internal states, and any similarities between the other person and yourself.

Perceiving the *intentions* of the other person is valuable for several reasons. One, as a means of self-protection, you want to know what the other person wants from you. What are his or her purposes or goals in this conversation? What is she or he after? For instance, in the distant past, a father might ask his daughter's date whether his intentions were "honorable." A second reason to uncover the other's intentions is to be able to evaluate the genuineness or accuracy of the other's observable behavior. An intentional behavior may be genuine or false, and your task is to discriminate between the two. Generally speaking, we probably perceive most behaviors as intentional, but we also use our perceptions to identify precisely what the other's intentions are.

We know that we can't actually observe the *internal states* of the other person, but we continually look for behavioral cues that allow us to infer the other person's attitudes, beliefs, and values. Popular belief suggests that the nonverbal elements of behavior are the most valid reflections of what the person is feeling inside. Whether nonverbal behaviors are more valid than verbal behaviors is open to serious question, but the more important point is that many people believe that they are and look for them in order to perceive the other person's internal states.

The third type of information we seek in the other is some reflection of our own self. That is, we look for any indication of *similarities* to our own self. People who are similar to each other also tend to like each other, at least upon first acquaintance. To meet someone for the first time is to be in a state of perceptual confusion. The other person is unfamiliar; you don't know anything about him or her. You're lost, confused, and maybe just a bit panicky. But when you recognize some similarity in the other person, you feel much better, less confused, and the other no longer seems so strange.

In getting to know the other person, then, you look for information concerning the other's intentions, internal states, and similarities. Now the question is what to do with this information once you have it. The next few pages attempt to answer this question. In interpersonal communication, each communicator needs to know the other in order to accomplish two purposes: uncertainty reduction and social comparison.

Uncertainty Reduction

Whenever you meet someone, especially for the first time, you undoubtedly have a number of questions running through your mind. Just who is this person? What does she or he want of me? What do I mean to him or her? What does she or he mean to me? How should I act with this person? In other words, you enter the communicative situation without a clear idea of what you are supposed to do, who you are supposed to be, or what you are trying to accomplish. Hence, you engage in communication for the purpose of finding answers to some of these questions. From a state of total confusion, you attempt (in the early stages of interaction, at least) to get rid of some of that confusion in order to gain some idea of what types of behaviors are appropriate.

Berger and Calabrese (1975), two communication scholars interested in early stages of communication, call this attempt to discover appropriate communicative behaviors a process of *uncertainty reduction*. The goal of early interaction is to find out about the other person and, on the basis of your perceptions, select from your own available repertoire of potential behaviors those actions that are appropriate. To know how to act is to know who the other person is and who you are in relation to that other. During the early period of interaction, the communicators exchange psychological information. I tell you who I am and you tell me who you are. During this initial period of interpersonal communication, the participants infer self-disclosing information from nearly every behavior of the other person.

Human beings have a need to understand, a need to get rid of ambiguity. They just can't stand being confused. Have you ever been lost? Really lost? Getting lost even in the middle of a city or on a public highway gives you a horrible feeling. Even though you may not be in a life-threatening situation (such as being lost in a forested wilderness or in a desert), the feeling of confusion is enough to create panic. Feeling "lost" in a communicative situation is similarly unpleasant, so people attempt to dispel this feeling as quickly as possible. The process of dispelling that "lost" feeling is called uncertainty reduction.

Because you need to reduce uncertainty about who the other person is, you perceive virtually every act of the other as an instance of self-disclosure. Typically, you attempt to accelerate this process by asking questions. In a context of absolute strangers, the participants typically ask questions seeking answers about the person's background and demographic characteristics: "Where are you from?" "What do you do for a living?" "Do you have a family?"

Some social contexts involve a more specific line of questioning based on the information already available in the context. At a political rally, the conversational topics are likely to involve politics and similarities of political views. When meeting a new employee at work, you are likely to ask questions about the work setting. In other words, in these contexts you aren't merely attempting to get to know the other person but are also trying to get to know the other person *as* a work colleague, *as* a friend, *as* a political ally, *as* a member of a particular relationship suggested by the social setting of your communication.

A note of caution! Don't think of uncertainty reduction as "discovering" the meaning of the other person's self. Discovery may be how we come to understand a foreign language or esoteric mathematics, but uncertainty reduction (virtually the opposite of discovery) is how we typically acquire our everyday meanings, including the meanings of other people, or relationships, and of social events. When you encounter someone, even for the first time, the problem is not that you have no idea about what to expect. Rather, your problem is that you have too many such ideas. In your memories of the past are hundreds, perhaps thousands of social experiences; you've known many people and known about many more people. Your problem is not *what* to expect but *which* of your expectations is more likely to come true. Meaning, then, is not a process of discovery but one of reducing the multitude of potential meanings to a manageable number.

Selecting an appropriate response to the other person is also a matter of uncertainty reduction, not discovery. You already possess a vast repertoire of behaviors. Your problem is to select those that are appropriate to the present situation. You need information to reduce the number of alternative behaviors by eliminating those actions that are inappropriate. In other words, during the early stages of interpersonal communication, you try to reduce the amount of uncertainty you feel about what to do. Meaning is a process of eliminating inappropriate meanings until you feel comfortable with the remaining number of meanings, which you judge to be appropriate. Using a process of elimination, you acquire understanding and meaning through uncertainty reduction. Your perceptual processes, directed toward the other person, will continually be engaged in attempting to reduce your uncertainty about the other person.

Social Comparison

"Social comparison" is the process of comparing your self with other people. According to social psychologist Leon Festinger (1954), people typically experience a need for self-evaluation. It is one thing to know yourself (self-concept), but you also need to know how to value your self (self-esteem). As humans, we need to "feel good" about our selves. Therefore, we engage in a process of evaluating self—our opinions, ideas, accomplishments, self-concepts—through comparing our selves with others. Interpersonal communication provides a prime opportunity for engaging in social comparison.

When we engage in social comparison, we tend to stack the deck in our favor. We rarely compare ourselves with people who are likely to rate higher on our evaluative scale. For example, when we want to compare our intelligence with that of others, we will compare our selves with people who are similar in intelligence. When we want to compare our political beliefs, we tend to compare them with those of people who have similar beliefs. If we are athletic klutzes, we will most likely compare our athletic prowess with that of other klutzes. We compare our socioeconomic status with those of our neighbors who are likely to have a similar status. Social comparison, then, is not so much an attempt to provide an objective evaluation of self as it is an effort to confirm the self-concept we already have. To do otherwise is to risk a loss of self-esteem and increase the risk of psychological problems.

If we compare our selves with people who are similar to us, it stands to reason that we are likely to have interpersonal relationships with people who are also similar to ourselves. When we see that the other person is similar to ourselves in many respects, we also have less uncertainty. We know how to act appropriately because we have acted that way in the past. We feel much more comfortable with people like ourselves. For purposes of social comparison, then, the most important information we need from the other person is self-disclosure that allows us to perceive some similarity.

Keep in mind that the processes of uncertainty reduction and social comparison are limited to the "getting to know you" stage, the early period of interpersonal communication. Continued interaction will lead to reducing the uncertainty you may have and to a clearer idea of how to interact; it will also, very likely, lead to the discovery of similarities. Over time, the processes of uncertainty reduction and social comparison naturally become less important. If you develop a friendship with a particular person, for instance, you will tend to discount the importance of your differences. During early acquaintance, however, uncertainty reduction and social comparison explain much of what goes on as you get to know one another. Your need to assign meaning to your social encounter and to the other person functions through a process of eliminating alternative meanings (uncertainty reduction) and self-evaluation (social comparison).

PERCEIVING THE OTHER

The process of perceiving people (as opposed to inanimate objects) is a special kind of perception, accurately (but not imaginatively) known as "person perception." What is true of all perceptions (experiential, inferential, evaluative, inaccurate, etc.) is also true of person perception, of course. But person perception is unique in that it includes some elements that are not present with other objects of perception. Unlike a mere object, for instance, a person is another thinking, talking, behaving human being, and he or she doesn't sit still waiting to be perceived.

In addition to perceiving the physical characteristics (such as physical attractiveness) of the other person, we try to draw perceptual inferences from the other person's communicative behaviors. Steve Duck (1977, pp. 102–103) suggests that the behavioral cues of the other person are important for three reasons. One, the cue may be pleasant and rewarding in itself. We always like being the recipient of smiles and compliments. Two, the cue provides information that you can then use to form some impressions of that person's inner self—personality, beliefs, attitudes, values, and the like. Three, the cue may provide some implications about the future of the relationship, hints of things to come.

Person perception thus goes beyond processes of uncertainty reduction and social comparison to perceptual inferences about the potential relationship you have or will have with this person. When you engage in person perception, you implicitly ask yourself questions concerning your potential relationship—such as whether you will like the person. At best, your inferences in person perception are guesses about what the other person is like. In other words, we use our perceptual guesses as the principal basis, accurately or inaccurately, for our liking or disliking the other person.

To convert behavioral cues of our communicational partners into inferences concerning their personality and inner self is to engage in a guessing game, a gamble that our inference is correct. And it can never be more than a guessing game; despite the claims made by a number of popular paperback books. To devise a list of "things to do" in order to increase your ability to interpret behavioral cues correctly is like creating a system to beat the odds at Las Vegas. Even though someone may claim to have a sure-fire system to beat the odds, the chances that there is such a system are slim. A guess can be nothing more than a guess. A good guess may be better than a bad guess, but it is still only a guess.

To be an effective communicator is to play the guessing game of person perception with full awareness of what goes into your guesses and that your guesses may not be accurate. Then you will be more apt to revise inaccurate guesses later, when more information is available. After additional interaction, you are able to judge with much more accuracy and confidence what the other person is really like and to revise your earlier perceptions accordingly. Only with additional information that comes with further communication (and not "skill" in making perceptual guesses) can you be relatively sure of your perceptions of the other person.

The purpose of this section is to help you understand what goes into your process of person perception. With that understanding, you are more likely to realize the tentativeness of your person perceptions and that they are likely to be in a state of constant change during continued interaction. The best way to improve your ability in person perception is to realize its inherent fallibility and relative instability. Only in well-established relationships is your perception of the other person likely to reach a point of stability. That isn't necessarily the way it should be; that's the way it is in "real life."

As the perceiver, you control the inferences you make about the other person. To understand the process of person perception, then, is to be aware of what is going on within you when your attention is directed to another person. The following pages will discuss three of these cognitive processes involved in perceiving other people: implicit personality theory, attribution processes, and response sets.

Implicit Personality Theory

Psychologists have identified over two thousand different personality types. Everyone can potentially be classified on every one of those personality scales and rated from high to low in qualities of authoritarianism, Machiavellianism, achievement motivation, self-esteem, assertiveness, intelligence, sociality, and so forth. But testing people's personalities is a long and tedious procedure. You have to devise a test, typically multiple-choice, give people #2 pencils to fill in the circles, forward the answer sheets to a computer for optical scanning, and then wait for the scores to come back. A trained psychologist, with the assistance of a battery of such tests, is able to do a complete personality profile of anyone. We go through a similar testing procedure much more efficiently and quickly whenever we communicate in everyday conversations. Assessing personality types is a natural part of the process of person perception.

We are all amateur psychologists of a sort. We are constantly engaged in psychological measurement and evaluation, even though we are rarely aware that we are doing it. We all carry around with us in our heads an entire set of personality profiles that we use to assess the hidden personalities of people we encounter in social settings. We may not have as many personality types as the well-equipped professional psychologist, but we have a rather long list of personalities in our person-perception "set." Moreover, we don't have to go through the tedious process of machine-scoring tests, either. We simply use our five senses and the other person's behavioral cues. Our psychological assessment may not be as precise as that of the professional psychologist, but it is no less useful to us when we are deciding how to interact with the other person.

This amateur psychologizing is typically known as using *implicit personality theory*, a part of the psychological "set" we use to perceive other persons. Because of our past interactional experiences, we have encountered a variety of different kinds of people or, more accurately, people with different psychological traits. When we interact with people and observe their behavioral cues, we are able to reduce our uncertainty about them by evaluating them according to these traits. With the information from their behaviors, we are able to attribute these personality traits to the other individual and arrive at some perception of who they are.

Just as you have categories of perceived objects that you use to differentiate chairs, tables, trees, and the like, you also have categories of personality traits that you use to differentiate people. Each personality trait is likely to fall somewhere between two extremes on a given scale. We then look for cues in the other person's behaviors so as to assess such traits as warm-cold, friendly-unfriendly, stuckup-humble, sincere-insincere, trustworthy-unreliable, fun-dull, quiet-talkative, shy-assertive, awkward-coordinated, and many more. In fact, you are likely to use the same set of categories in perceiving others that you use in perceiving your self. As you may recall from Chapter 7, those three general classifications were personal attributes, social attributes, and role relationships.

After you have attributed personality traits to the other person, you are in a position to know how to interact. Your first perceptual judgment is likely to be whether you wish to continue interacting with someone having these personality traits. If you like people with these traits, then you will want to foster additional interaction. Your second judgment is to determine what behaviors are appropriate when you are interacting with another person who has such personality traits. You behave differently with shy people, for example, than you do with talkative types. For one thing, you have to spend more time "carrying" the conversation. You are also, with sufficient confidence in your personality assessment, capable of distinguishing behavioral cues that don't fit with the personality ("façades" or "false roles"). With confidence in your assessment, you are able to say, for example, "I know he *seemed* unfriendly, but he isn't *really* like that at all."

Applying implicit personality theory seems amazingly similar to stereotyping. And we all know that stereotyping is bad, don't we? Actually, stereotyping is harmful to interpersonal communication only when we generalize erroneous and prejudiced traits to large groups of people without attempting to assess the individual, or when we use stereotypes as a substitute for attempting to assess the individual person. In the sense that all blacks stereotypically have rhythm (I have a black friend with two left feet who is also a terrible singer) or all professors are absent-minded (perhaps this is a bad example), stereotyping is detrimental to effective interaction in that it short-circuits the process of person perception and interpersonal understanding. It ignores the characteristics of the specific individual in favor of some misplaced and overly generalized characteristic assigned to an entire group of people.

Using implicit personality theory, though, means attempting to understand the specific individual by placing that individual's traits within a scheme of understanding. In essence, it is the opposite of stereotyping. That is, when you stereotype someone, you begin with a general social classification and apply it to an individual human being without knowing anything about that person as a unique individual. When you use implicit personality theory, you begin with the individual and seek to identify him or her as a member of some more general class on the basis of what you know about that person as a unique individual. Uncritical stereotyping is, of course, to be avoided. Implicit personality theory is critical and a highly normal part of the process of person perception.

Attribution Processes

Let's review for a moment. In Chapter 7 we alluded to the intrapersonal process of attributing cause or control of events to someone or something. Typically, we have said, these perceptual processes place the "locus of control" within a person (dispositional) or within the context (situational). As a form of self-protection, we typically see ourselves in situational terms. That is, we attribute our undesirable behaviors to the situation rather than to ourselves, as in "It wasn't my fault; I had no choice under the circumstances." Conversely, we tend to perceive the other person in dispositional terms (see Jones & Nisbett, 1971). That is, when we observe another person's behaviors, we tend to attribute them to some intrapersonal process—something occurring within the person. In this way, we perceive that "She is really stuck up. She passed me in the hall twice today, and she didn't even say hi."

Attribution processes are important to communication for several reasons. For one thing, as human beings we need to construct explanations for why things occur. This apparent need for explanations stems in part from our need to reduce uncertainty. The simplest explanation of all is causal. When we ask, "Why did *I* do such a thing?" we are likely to construct an explanation in terms of the situation—as in "The devil made me do it." And when we ask, "Why did the other person do such a thing?" we typically construct an explanation in terms of the other's intrapersonal processes, that is, in dispositional terms.

In the early stages of interaction, and consistent with implicit personality theory, the behaviors of the other person always seem to be cues that reveal innermost dispositions, intrapersonal feelings, emotions, personality traits, beliefs, attitudes, values. Apparently we know ourselves well enough so that we don't always believe that our own behaviors always reflect our intrapersonal dispositions. But we don't know the other person that well. Therefore, we perceive every behavioral cue as an insight into that person's self.

Emotions are part of those intrapersonal processes we look for in the other's behaviors. We want to know how he or she feels about us, for example. Therefore, the other person's cordial behavior toward you often seems to be perceived as a behavioral cue of liking. On the other hand, we tend to attribute our own emotional displays toward the other person as being caused by the other person—as in "You make me angry" or "You bother me" or even "You bring out the best in me."

Such an attribution is somewhat unusual because, after all, emotions are intrapersonal. We create our emotions internally, and we dissolve them internally. They are part of the relationship only when we attribute them to the other person or to ourselves. Curiously, though, we often think of a relationship in terms of our emotions, at least as we perceive that relationship internally. We might say "We have a loving relationship" or "We love each other." But we need to be aware that the intrapersonal emotion is not the same as the interpersonal relationship. An emotion is your perceptual attribution of an emotion to the other person (or to yourself). A popular song of many decades ago certainly conveyed that notion of attribution. The lyrics went something like "You made me love you. I didn't want to do it."

Second, attribution processes are important to communication in that they

The causes you attribute to another's behavior influence—and are influenced by—the relationship.
(Michael Weisbrot & Family)

accurately depict the reflexive association between psychological states and behaviors. Popular belief has it that our actions always reflect our psychological states. We often think that, because we think or feel something, we act on the basis of that feeling or belief. However (as earlier discussions have revealed), the connection between psychological states and behaviors is more reflexive. We no more act because we believe than we believe because we act. The two, psychological state and action, function together in a cyclical and reflexive loop of influencing and being influenced.

How do our attribution processes depict the reflexivity between psychological states and behaviors? Remember how we attribute cause to our own actions and to actions of others. We see other's behaviors in dispositional terms and our own behaviors in situational terms. Thus, we perceive others on the basis of causal connections between psychological states and behaviors, but we perceive no such causal connection with our own behaviors. In this way, we are likely to respond to others and perceive them on the basis of their behaviors, which we perceptually translate into their personality traits. We may not think that psychological states control our own behaviors, but we tend to think they do for other people, and we behave toward them accordingly.

Third, attribution processes are important to communication because of their reflexive association with the interpersonal relationship, as well. Our attributions will influence the outcome of the relationship (as in wanting to continue interacting), and the developing relationship will also influence our attributional processes. When a relationship is in its early stages and in relationships which are not extremely close (such as acquaintances, "just friends," and the like), you tend to perceive events in either situational (when pertaining to self) and dispositional (when pertaining to other) terms. But in more fully developed relationships or in relationships characterized by genuine liking, you tend to attribute a third cause to the success of your relationship—the relationship itself. In this way, the intrapersonal (attribution) and interpersonal (relationship) levels of communication thus influence each other reflexively.

How does the relationship influence our attribution processes? Let me explain. In the early stages of communication, remember, we tend to attribute situational causes to our own behavior and dispositional causes to the other's behavior. But in more fully developed relationships, such as those of married couples or extremely close friends, a third locus of control emerges. Rather than seeing events caused only by intrapersonal dispositions or situational constraints, relational partners attribute cause or control of events to the relationship itself. It's the relationship that makes friends feel good. The relationship causes them to behave in a certain way. The relationship is the cause of the participants' individual emotions.

Moreover, relational partners tend to perceive events in terms of how they affect their relationship and not just their individual selves. If they perceive events as threats to their relationship, they judge the events to be bad and avoid them. If they perceive the events to be beneficial to the relationship, they judge them to be good and seek them out. In more intimate relationships, the partners tend to define their own selves (both self and other) in terms of their relationship, so that the social relationship itself assumes its own identity—in a way, it assumes its own "self." And that "relational self" or relational identity of the participants is highly significant in maintaining close relationships (see Newman, 1981).

Attributional processes are thus vitally important to interpersonal communication. Furthermore, they are important not only in how they can affect interpersonal communication, but also in how they can indicate the quality of that communication. As long as, and insofar as, the participants continue to perceive themselves situationally and others dispositionally, their communication indicates a "holding back" or tentativeness of relational commitment. Such attributions probably reflect a less intimate relationship or one in the stages of getting started. When participants interpret events and their own self-identities in terms of the relationship as a whole, then the relationship begins to take on its own identity and demonstrates a rather highly developed level of intimate connections between the relational partners—in other words, they like each other.

Response Sets

We already know that we perceive objects by assigning meaning to them on the basis of a psychological "set" formed from our past experiences. We use those organized experiences to judge the present object of perception and, on the basis of its similarity with elements in our set, we assign meaning to the perceived object. In the case of person perception, the psychological set includes a list of personality traits and is known as *implicit personality theory*. Another part of the psychological set, relevant to person perception, includes *response sets*—certain predispositions to respond to the other person in a certain way.

"Response sets" involve making inferential leaps from the other person's behavior to our own behavioral response. Knowing that we will never have sufficient information to know all that we want to know about the other person, we use response sets as inferential shortcuts. I refer to them as shortcuts because they require inordinately huge leaps of inference, in fact, much larger leaps than typical perceptual inferences. Because of this fact, response sets typically involve errors in person perception. The following paragraphs discuss some of the most common response sets used in interpersonal communication.

One common response set that affects the accuracy of person perception is known as the *halo effect*. We perceive a halo effect when we overgeneralize the other's behavior in one situation to other situations about which we know nothing. For example, we notice a colleague who behaves quite irresponsibly at work—he is often late, doesn't get his work done on time, and appears to take no pride in his accomplishments. We then infer that his irresponsibility extends to other areas of his life as well. We assume he is likely to be irresponsible at home—he probably stays away a lot, contributes little free time to his family, and may even cheat on his wife. We might perceive another person as friendly in all our interactions with her. We then assume that she is friendly with other people too and probably has a large social circle. In other words, we use the halo effect and generalize her friendly behavior with us to her interactions with others, but we really have no way of knowing about them.

The problem with perceiving other persons with a halo effect is not simply that it is an inference. All perceptions are inferences. The halo effect is a problem because it is an inference that extends beyonds the bounds of reason. We ignore differences in situations that are likely to affect that person's actions. We fail to take into account the fact that people will behave differently and perform different roles in different situations and with different people. We baselessly assume a consistency of behavior. Thus, the halo effect is an overgeneralized inference based on the false premise that people behave similarly in different situations.

The *leniency effect* is another response set in which we allow our relationships with persons to affect our perceptions of them. We tend to idealize our friends and are lenient in judging them. That is, we tend to judge our friends high (probably too high) on all favorable traits and low (probably too low) on traits that are socially undesirable. In this way, we perceive few faults in our friends and overestimate their positive attributes. We just can't understand why everyone doesn't like them and that they might be less than perfect.

Naturally, the reverse is true of persons with whom we are unfavorably impressed. We tend to judge them too harshly—too low on positive attributes and too high on their negative attributes. Of course, we shouldn't refer to this response set as "leniency." Perhaps, it could be termed a "cruelty effect," although I have never seen that term used by any psychologists.

The point to be gained from this discussion is that person perception, like all perception, is vulnerable to inaccuracies. Person perception, because humans are more complex creatures than inanimate objects, is probably more likely to be in error than are other perceptions. Sometimes person perceptions, accurate or inaccurate, benefit the relationship; sometimes they are detrimental to interpersonal communication. The thing to remember is to be open to additional information and to use it to revise your own person perceptions when that information becomes available to you. On the other hand, such advice is probably superfluous. You will continue to perceive, accurately and inaccurately, despite such advice. Communicative skill does not really develop from making accurate person perceptions. Rather, you develop your communicative skills by developing a keen and accurate awareness of your own perceptual processes and, of course, their limitations.

BEHAVING TOWARD THE OTHER

To be an effective communicator, you want to be able to influence the other person's perceptions of you. You would like the other person to think highly of you, perhaps, or at least to have an impression of you that is consistent with your own purpose in communicating. You may want the other person to see you as a friend, a boss, a sexual partner, an acquaintance, or in any of a number of different social roles. Even though you can't force the other to perceive you in a certain light, you can do something to guide those perceptions. That is to say, you can behave in a manner that fosters the impression you want the other person to have of you. Thus, your communicational task is to provide the other, through your behaviors, with information that the other person can use in perceiving your self—information that is consistent with the perception you want the other to have of you.

You may react negatively to the suggestion that we try to influence other people's perceptions during communication. You might think that you should not try to be so manipulative but should, instead, strive to "be natural," to "be your own self." Such a reaction assumes that your self and the way you present your self are somehow different and even unrelated. However, we already know that we have many different selves and many social roles in many different interpersonal relationships. Furthermore, every one of your selves *is* your "natural" and "real" self. When you are being natural and your own self with members of your family, you wouldn't deny that the way you interact (quite differently) with your friends is also very natural and consistent with your own self.

Keep in mind that you aren't born with a self. You develop it through your social interactions in a constant and changing process of "becoming." In other words, you create your self and your relational role through your communicative behaviors. When you behave differently in different social relationships, you are creating different social roles. In other words, you create different selves in different social relationships. And all of these selves or roles constitute your self, your natural self, even though your behavior and your self in one relationship may be vastly different from your behavior and self in another situation.

I'm sure you have heard the cliché "You are what you eat." (If it were true, I know of people who are Big Macs and others who are pepperoni pizzas. And just think of how many Cokes there are in this world. And I must be a chile verde burrito.) If we reword the saying, though, it is much more sensible: "You are what you *do*." You behave as a friend, and you are a friend. You behave as a lover, and you are a lover. But that doesn't mean you are a friend or a lover with everyone you meet, or that being a lover is not "natural" because you don't behave that way with everyone. Remember that part of your self-concept, a large part of it, is defined in terms of the social attributes you display when behaving with others and in the role relationships you have with others. Therefore, your behaviors with others constitute a very natural part of being your own self.

Of course, some of your behavior might be a façade, a false face, or false role presented to others. When we interact with some people, we sometimes pretend to be someone we are not. But I would hesitate to condemn any role as being "false." Let me illustrate. In a group decision-making class several years ago, a student confided that she simply could not be the leader of her group because she just wasn't a "leader type." She felt that being a leader was not "natural" for her. However, she did behave as a leader in her group and later recognized that she performed that role. She also said that she did so only because she wanted her group to do well and receive a good grade. Throughout the entire term, she insisted that her leadership role was false and wasn't her true self. She attributed a situational locus of control for her behavior and believed that she was the group leader only because the situation demanded it. After having experienced success and rewards from her fellow group members, though, she indicated that she was likely to assume other leadership roles in the future. Apparently her "false role" had become a natural part of her self— but only after she had experienced it.

The reflexivity between behaviors and self-concept is quite strong. After all, you create your self-concept in large part from your social experiences. With new and different social experiences, you tend to create a new and different self-concept. As you proceed to influence other people's perceptions of you through your behaviors, you influence your perceptions of your own self at the same time. Person perceptions influence interpersonal communication, and interpersonal communication reflexively influences person perceptions (both of the other person and of self).

Impression Management

Erving Goffman (1959 & 1963), a sociological theorist, wrote extensively on how every one of us in everyday life engages in "presenting" a self to others. He did not regard such presenting of self as manipulative but, rather, a natural part of social interaction he called *impression management*. Goffman suggested that every time we behave socially with another person, we manage the impressions of that person. Most importantly, we really have no choice but to manage others' impressions of us. By behaving toward another person, we are unavoidably attempting to affect that person's impressions of us. We don't have any choice in the matter: we simply cannot not behave! The only issue in impression management is whether we are aware of *how* we go about managing the impressions of others, not *whether* we do so.

Impression management involves thinking of interpersonal communication as a drama or play. As a participant in communication, you are not only an actor in the drama; you are also the playwright, the author who is writing the script of the real-life drama while engaging in interpersonal communication. When you manage the impressions of the other person in communication, you present your self in two regions of behavior: "front" and "back." "Front" refers to that part of your self that is observable or publicly visible to the other person. Your "front" region of impression management reveals the part of your self that is "onstage." The "back" region refers to your "behind the scenes" behavior, the part of your self that you display when not in the presence (or when you don't know that you are in the presence) of another person.

An example of "front" and "back" may serve to illustrate this difference between "on stage" and "behind the scenes" regions of impression management. Some time ago I walked into the office of a faculty colleague who was engrossed in evaluating some term papers and was clearly distressed by the one he was reading. He scowled through his reading glasses, muttered some epithet (to himself) under his breath, scribbled on the paper, and even scratched himself in a very private place. Although I was standing across the desk from him, no more than 5 feet away, he was apparently not aware of my presence and was behaving in a "behind the scenes" manner. When he looked up and saw me standing there, he immediately behaved with his "front." He removed his reading glasses (the funny ones with only half a lens), smiled broadly, pushed himself away from his desk, and greeted me heartily.

Don't be misled into thinking that my colleague's "onstage" ("front") behavior was a false role and his "behind the scenes" ("back") behavior was more real. He was behaving quite naturally in both instances, but he was in two different situations—one private (at least he thought so) and the other social. In the social setting, the act of communication, he was engaging in impression management; and this behavior was quite natural. In the private setting or "back" region, he was not engaging in impression management. After all, he wasn't aware that anyone was there to have his impressions managed.

Managing impressions, then, is equivalent to interaction behavior. In fact, we could say that all interaction behavior (that is, all communication) is impression management, whether the communicator is aware of that fact or not. The difference between "front" and "back" behaviors, then, is the difference between the two situations of social interaction or private behavior. This means that impression management is behavior directed not so much by your internalized self but by the presence of another person.

My colleague behaved as he did because I was there—not just anybody, but me, my particular self. If a stranger had walked into his office, my colleague would undoubtedly have behaved quite differently. He may have looked expectantly toward the stranger or inquired as to whether he could be of any assistance. He may have stood up and moved to shake the hand of the stranger as a form of introduction. In the case of my presence, a friend and frequent "intruder" into his office, he only shoved his chair back and welcomed me. This "front" was quite familiar to him; I often walked into his office uninvited. He had memories of many previous experiences similar to that one, and he fell easily into that role.

To say that impression management is other-directed rather than self-directed is to say that your interactive behavior focuses on what impression you want the other person to have of you. Often you have some specific goals in mind for a communicative encounter, and you have ample time to prepare your "front" behaviors beforehand.

There is nothing unethical in preparing your impression management. In fact, in many situations you prepare and expect the other person to have prepared for your communicative encounter. When engaging in an employment interview, for example, you attempt to present yourself in the role you think will impress the interviewer most favorably, and the interviewer expects you to have prepared.

During the spring term of each school year, it is quite common for students to come to class dressed to the hilt—three-piece suits and tailored dresses. Beards mysteriously vanish overnight, and short haircuts appear on graduating senior males. Females who have worn sweatshirts and jeans throughout the entire school year suddenly appear in dresses, hose, high heels, and new coiffures. Everyone knows that these seniors are interviewing with prospective employers.

Obviously dress and outward appearance are important elements of impression management, but the most potent influences will always be the interactive behaviors. My instructor in an undergraduate acting class (some years ago) repeatedly stressed the point that more acting is accomplished through *reacting* to others. Impression management could well use that dramatic point as an axiom. When you become aware of your own behaviors and allow the other person to direct them, you begin to judge the appropriateness of your behaviors *as responses to* the other person's behaviors. In impression management, you are less concerned with manipulating the other person and more involved with behaving responsively.

How do you learn to behave responsively with another person? The only rule to follow is to think of your own behaviors, both verbal and nonverbal, as responses or reactions to the other person's behavior. Rather than focusing your attention on how you relate to the topic of conversation or how the topic might relate to you, focus instead on how you relate to the other person and the other person's comment. That ultimately means that you focus on responding to the other's behavior. By being consciously aware that your every action is a response to the other's behavior, you are interacting quite normally and are certainly engaged in managing the other's impressions.

Rhetorical Sensitivity

Rhetorical sensitivity, a concept developed by Rod Hart and Don Burks (1972), two communication scholars, is a quality of perception based on contingencies, otherwise known as the "it all depends" principle. What should you do when communicating with an other? It all depends. How can I get the most out of my social relationship? It all depends. How do I know if that special person likes me? It all depends. Being rhetorically sensitive, in other words, is being sensitive to your self, to the situation, and to the other—especially the other. It means being willing to adapt and being capable of adapting to the other person and to the elements of the social relationship. Rhetorical sensitivity involves perceptual awareness of self, other, and situation. Above all, it involves selecting communicative behavior that adapts to the particular blend of self, other, and situation during your interpersonal communication. In other words, rhetorical sensitivity means adapting to contingencies.

Hart and Burks (1972) are somewhat more specific than glibly saying "it all depends" on contingencies of self, other, and situation and letting it go at that. They highlight five characteristics of what rhetorical sensitivity entails:

> The rhetorically sensitive person . . . (1) tries to accept role-taking as part of the human condition, (2) attempts to avoid stylized behavior, (3) is characteristically willing to undergo the strain of adaptation, (4) seeks to distinguish between all information and information acceptable for communication, and (5) tries to understand that an idea can be rendered in multiform ways. (p. 76)

The following discussion will attempt to phrase these five characteristics a bit more specifically and in more practical terms.

Role Taking. The first characteristic of a rhetorically sensitive communicator is *role taking*. If we take seriously the fact that our self-concept is not a single unitary self but comprises multiple and diverse selves, then we should know that we are different selves with different people. Most importantly, each of these selves is part of the "real" self of each person. All of these selves, taken together, make up the entire self-concept, but rare (if ever) is the situation that calls forth more than one of our selves. That is, we carry around within us an entire repertoire of selves or roles that we can use in any interaction. We then select the appropriate self or role to present in any specific communicative situation. We never have a choice about *whether* to present a certain self or role to another; the only choice is *which* self, from among our vast repertoire, we choose to present in that situation to that person.

Please do not confuse role *taking* with role *playing*. You have probably been involved in some role-playing exercise in some classroom situation in your educational past. In such an exercise, you are given a thumbnail description of a role, a personality, to portray and instructions to "pretend that you are" somebody else. Role playing is a pretense. The role you play is not "you" and is not intended to be part of your self. When role playing, you keep your self separate from the role you are playing, and everyone else is aware of this separation. Role playing is an admittedly false situation and is not relevant to interpersonal communication.

Role taking, on the other hand, is a selection process in which you first perceive the situation and the other person and then select, from your repertoire of roles, the self that you want to present to the other person in this situation. Role taking is normal, natural, typical, and, above all else, an unavoidable part of interpersonal communication. Whereas role playing involves "faking it," role taking is an authentic presentation of self. In role taking you are definitely "being your self." That is, you are being one of your multiple selves.

Stylized Behavior. The second characteristic of rhetorical sensitivity is a caution against *stylized behavior*. Stylizing your behavior is essentially remaining consistent in how you interact with people at different times and in different situations. "Stylization" is just another word for consistency, inflexibility, or monotony. When you avoid stylized behavior, you are inconsistent, flexible, and novel. In short, you "adapt" your behaviors to the person, the relationship, and the situation.

Avoiding stylized behavior means adapting—not communicating in the same manner with the same person all the time. Communication is a process that involves continual evolutionary change. Rhetorically sensitive communicators are aware that the communicative situation changes during the passage of time, and they adapt their interactive behavior to those changes. Just as one naturally adapts behavior when moving from one situation to another (behaving one way with your parents, for example, and another way with your lover), the rhetorically sensitive person also adapts behaviors to changes that occur over time in the same interpersonal relationship. The rhetorically sensitive communicator learns to "go with the flow" and, of course, is able to recognize changes in the flow.

Strain of Adaptation. The third characteristic refers to the *strain of adaptation*. The ability to adapt to changes is central to being rhetorically sensitive, but adaptation is often a real strain. With some friends, for example, you can have fun, but it is quite difficult to have a serious and really intimate discussion with them. The reason for your feeling this way about such friends is that either you or they (or both) find it difficult to adapt behaviors to those two very different kinds of situations. The communicational problems created by autistic hostility and the self-fulfilling prophecy, for example, are essentially problems caused by being unable or unwilling to adapt your perceptions and behaviors to the contingencies of changing situations. It is often easier not to change, to keep your expectations and perceptions constant. Adapting is often the more difficult course of action to take. You risk having your perceptions challenged and even changed.

Let me illustrate. The relationship of a faculty adviser and graduate student is often a very special relationship, but it requires massive adaptations on the part of both relational partners. I have been fortunate to have had relationships with graduate students that have been remarkably satisfying, but they involve interactions vastly different from one another. At times, we were close friends sharing confidences, playing jokes on each other, and insulting each other. At times we were mentor and student, leader and follower, authority and subordinate. When the relationships were successful, we were able to adapt to the changing situations with ease, moving naturally into and out of different roles, occasionally during the same twenty-four-hour period. Sometimes, however, the relationships were not so successful. With some students, I remained only the authority figure. We just couldn't or didn't adapt to a friendship based on equivalence. With other students, I had only a friendship relation, and the adviser-advisee relationship suffered from our inability to adapt to the nonequivalent roles. Adapting behaviors to the changes in the situation within the same interpersonal relationship is often very difficult.

Distinguishing Information. The fourth characteristic of rhetorical sensitivity points out the need to *distinguish the "acceptable" information* from the loads of information available to you in the communicative situation. For example, when perceptual anesthesia is at work, some information is suppressed. Often the relationship benefits from such restraint, too. To be totally honest and candid in a relationship is simply to be following bad advice. The most satisfying and longest-lasting relationships are those in which the partners select the information they include in their interactions with each other, and they select that information on the basis of whether it is appropriate or beneficial to their relationship. They simply ignore or suppress other information.

Multiform Ideas. The final characteristic of rhetorical sensitivity involves the ability to say the same thing in different ways. This final trait of rhetorically sensitive communicators includes virtually all the other four characteristics within it. Rhetorically sensitive communicators select the role self—as well as the information—they wish to present to the other on the basis of its appropriateness to the situation and to the other person. And they also select *how to present* that role and information in the same way—on the basis of its appropriateness to the situation and to the other person. It is simply not enough to know *what* information you want to present; it is equally important to know *how* to present that information. Howard Cosell talks about "telling it like it is"; but information never just "is"—it always exists in some form. And saying it in the appropriate form by adapting it to the communicative situation is part of being a rhetorically sensitive communicator.

Presenting information appropriately is a matter of making the appropriate choice. This final characteristic of rhetorical sensitivity emphasizes the fact that it is not only a choice of *what* information to present but also of *how* to present it appropriately in the situation. Moreover, you cannot avoid making a choice of how to present information during interpersonal communication. Whenever you tell people anything, you must tell them *in some way*. Every communicated message has both form and function—content and expression. And both the content of the message and its form of expression are important. How you say something affects the content of what is said.

For example, you wish to present information to another person at the dinner table in order to achieve your goal of receiving a portion of potatoes. You have various ways at your disposal to present that information. Each one of the following forms of presenting information has the same content as the others, but it differs in the manner of expressing it: (1) "Please pass the potatoes." (2) "Would you pass the potatoes, please?" (3) "When you're not busy, would you pass the potatoes?" (4) "Help yourself to the potatoes and pass them around the table." There are other forms of presenting this information, but I'm sure you get the point.

I am using this example of multiform messages because of a vivid recollection from my childhood. At a fancy Thanksgiving dinner with multitudes of relatives sitting at a long table, I asked (politely, as I recall) my older brother to pass the potatoes. His response was, "Whatsa matter? Your arm broke?" Apparently I did not phrase my request properly or I had overestimated the distance between me and the potatoes. At any rate, when I wanted something from him again, I phrased my request in a manner similar to "Hey! Pass the dressing!" I received it without any hassle.

In developing rhetorical sensitivity, the communicator needs to develop a heightened awareness of the choices that are available: choice of self, choice of information, choice of manner in presenting information. The most important awareness is that these choices are always available even though we may not be aware of the fact that we are making choices. Furthermore, when we communicate, we select from our entire repertoire of roles, information, and ways of presenting information—and, most importantly, *we cannot avoid making these selections (choices)*.

According to Hart and Burks (1972),

Such sensitive awareness is, above all, subject to inscrutable human choices and social probabilities. The rhetorically sensitive person is an undulating, fluctuating entity, always unsure, always guessing, continually weighing. The rhetorically sensitive person deals with the most slippery of intellectual stuff, the values, attitudes, and philosophical predispositions of others. (p. 91)

There are simply no sure-fire formulas for how to become an effective communicator. You can only guess at what is most appropriate and be flexible in adapting to changes and even revising your guesses when they turn out to be bad ones. The thing that really disallows an "easy" solution to effective communicating is that "most slippery of intellectual stuff" which is embodied in the other person.

Attributional Responses

Our discussions of attributional processes have, up to now, treated them only as perceptual processes that locate cause or control of events within a person (dispositional) in the context (situational) or in the relationship. However, attributions may also be evident in the behavior you use to respond to the other's actions. That is, the communicator may respond in a way that clearly attributes some implied meaning to the other person's preceding behavior. For example, consider the following conversational sequence:

"What are we having for dinner tonight?"
"Stop nagging me!"
"I was only asking."

The response to the initial question about dinner clearly attributes a dispositional meaning to that comment. The person is saying, "You are only asking about dinner because you are nagging me to get it ready." The original questioner responds by denying the attribution and is saying, "I wasn't nagging. My question was perfectly innocent, a matter of curiosity."

Often close friends feel they know each other so well that they respond to the other's comments with implied attributions. You may have been involved in a conversation similar to the following:

"You look tired. Did you have a hard day?"
"You don't really want to go out tonight, do you?"
"No, it's not that. But we don't need to go out tonight if you're tired."

The respondent attributes a meaning to the first question by suggesting that it seemed to be an excuse for not carrying through on their original plan to "go out." The response to that comment actually denies that attribution but does leave the door open to not going out—that is, by making the same dispositional attribution ("tired") of the other person.

Both these examples of conversation provide dispositional attributions for the other's behaviors. The attribution, though, could also be situational or relational.

Whatever the attributed locus of control, the attribution (by being expressed or implied in the interactional behaviors) is no longer just part of the psychological or perceptual process; it is now a part of the pragmatic behavioral level of communication.

When the perceptual process of attribution becomes expressed or implied in communicative behaviors, it affects the interactional behaviors of both communicators. For instance, attributing a dispositional locus to the other person places responsibility for the action on that person. The other person now feels compelled to respond. The response may attempt to shift the attributed locus, thereby avoiding the responsibility, or it may attempt to deny it. For example, the above conversation might continue:

> "Do you still want to go out tonight?"
> "You'd rather not go, wouldn't you?"
> "Actually I do, but it's been a really bad day. I'm beat."

The second comment attributes an implied dispositional locus to the first speaker who responds by denying it, saying, "Actually I do." Your dispositional attribution is erroneous, goes this response, but a situational attribution is accurate—the "really bad day." The final comment says, in essence, "I personally want to, but I am a victim of circumstances." or "My spirit is willing, but my flesh is weak."

Any communicative act during a conversation may include an expressed or implied attribution by inferring an underlying meaning to the other's prior behavior. The communicator, in responding to the other person's implied or expressed attribution, has several choices available. The communicator may deny the attribution contained in the other's prior comment by saying, for example, "No, that's not it." The communicator may accept the other person's attribution by saying, for example, "Yeah, I'm really tired." Or the communicator may shift the attributional locus by saying, for example, "I'm just a victim of the situation." In other words, an attribution may be employed as a conversational strategy as well as a perceptual process. And when used as a strategy, attributions affect the entire stream of the conversation.

Interpersonal Confirmation

At the same time as you are attempting to manage the other person's impressions of you, the other person is also trying to manage your impressions. That is, the other person is presenting his or her self to you. As the respondent, you have three options available in reacting to the other's self-representation: you can confirm it, reject it, or disconfirm it. When you respond with *confirmation*, you accept the other person's self-definition as presented. For example, you might respond, "You have an excellent point there. Good idea." When you respond with rejection, you recognize the other person as a person but you deny the self-definition as presented—"You can't possibly mean what you are saying!" *Disconfirmation* goes beyond rejection and denies the other person as a source of the message. When you disconfirm the other person's self-presentation, you may go so far as to ignore the other person's message completely and treat it as though it had never been said.

Confirming responses are obviously preferable to disconfirming responses, at least for happy and healthy relationships. Rejection statements, though, do not disconfirm the other person's self-presentation. In fact, interpersonal rejection involves separating the message from the self-presentation. In denying the message, you accept or take into account the value of the other person's self. We will treat rejection (of ideas—not of self) as a special form of confirmation.

A confirming response is claimed to perform four functions in responding to the other person's self-definition:

1. It expresses recognition of the other's existence.
2. It acknowledges a relationship of affiliation with the other.
3. It expresses awareness of the significance or worth of the other.
4. It accepts or "endorses" the other's self-experience (particularly emotional experience). (Cissna & Sieburg, 1981, p. 259)

A disconfirming response, on the other hand, may be a(n):

1. Indifferent response (denying existence or relation).
2. Impervious response (denying self-experience of the other).
3. Disqualifying response (denying the other's significance). (Cissna & Sieburg, 1981, p. 261)

The following conversation includes an indifferent response:

MAN (to bartender):   Give me a martini. I've had a rough day. Nobody paid any attention to what I said all day long.

   BARTENDER: That's too bad. What'll you have?

An impervious response might include something to the effect of "You don't really mean that; what you're really trying to say is. . . ." The impervious response denies the validity of what the other is saying. A disqualifying response is really a put-down of the other's intelligence, trustworthiness, significance, competence, worth, or whatever. Adults disqualify children when they say, "When you're older and have lived a few more years, you'll think differently."

What makes a comment a disconfirming or confirming response in interpersonal communication? No comment is either confirming or disconfirming until and unless the other person *perceives* the impact it has on his or her self-concept. I may respond with what *I* think is a confirming statement (such as "That's a *good idea*"), but the other person may perceive my statement as condescending or insincere. Whether a response confirms or disconfirms the other's self is ultimately a matter of the other's perception of the response. The above classification system, indicating what constitutes a confirming or disconfirming response, is valid only so long as the other person perceives it as affecting the self-concept.

Some recent research (Smilowitz, 1984) into confirming and disconfirming responses may serve to explain this point more clearly. This study sought to discover whether effective managers in business organizations "confirmed" their subordinates more often than ineffective managers. It seems reasonable to assume, as Smilowitz did, that effective business managers would tend to be more confirming when they interacted with their subordinates. The results of this research, however, were not totally consistent with this assumption. Subordinates of effective managers *perceived* that their managers were somewhat (but not much) more confirming than the subordinates of ineffective managers. But the only differences in the way effective managers actually interacted with their subordinates was in their use of disconfirming responses, which were unexpectedly more frequent (but only slightly) than those of ineffective managers.

So what do the results of this study mean for confirming responses in interpersonal communication? One inference is that what *appears* to be a confirming or disconfirming response and what *functions* as a confirming or disconfirming response in conversations are not necessarily identical. Indeed, some people may perceive an intended confirming response as merely "being polite." Politeness is hardly an act of interpersonal confirmation. In fact, to perceive a statement as "polite" is likely to increase the social distance between the interactants. One is polite to strangers, not friends.

What does the interaction of close friends look like, particularly in light of this discussion of confirming and disconfirming responses? The answer to such a question is likely to differ widely from one set of friends to another. My interactions with close friends, for example, are probably not typical, but they involve a high level of insults and many arguments. I will argue with virtually anybody about virtually anything and don't really care about who's "right." I will insult my friends and do so consistently and frequently. Of course, my friends also argue and insult me in return, also consistently and frequently. To us, such interaction is a symptom of high interpersonal confirmation, but many of our comments appear, on the surface, to be disconfirmations (even disqualifications).

The point is this. An argumentative statement or disagreement may be perceived as a confirming response, even though it may "sound like" it is disconfirming. But to disagree with someone, you must take the other person's opinions seriously and recognize their worth. Otherwise, why bother to argue? It's clearly "easier" to agree, but agreement may imply (or be perceived to imply) that you just don't care enough about the person or the idea to disagree.

It is probably safe to say that interpersonally confirming responses characterize healthy social relationships and effective interpersonal communication. The precise form taken by confirming responses (what they look like), however, is not the same for all situations and all relationships. Statements that seem "obviously" to be confirming or disconfirming are probably typical examples of such responses in early stages of relational development or in acquaintanceships. But when the relational partners know each other well, they may have developed responses that are perceived as confirmation even though an outsider may think otherwise. Part of being rhetorically sensitive is probably recognizing and performing the confirming responses appropriate to the situation and to the other person. In other words, rhetorically sensitive communicators adapt their behaviors to specific interpersonal situations that create their own definition of interpersonal confirmation.

SPECIAL OTHERS

According to psychologist John LaGaipa (1981), people enter relationships in order to achieve one or more of the following goals: identity, affection, expression, socializing, and instrumental aid (p. 77). *Identity* is the feeling of self-worth we enjoy when others provide us with confirming responses. An *affective* relationship is an emotion-based relationship in which you feel loved and needed by the other person. You find an opportunity for *expression* in the kind of relationship Margaret Thatcher talked about—to "let down your hair with someone" and receive emotional support. Many companions and even acquaintances fulfill a relationship based on *sociability*, characterized by conversation, recreation, and common interests. *Instrumental aid*, of course, refers to gaining assistance from other people, either in the form of psychological support (such as sympathy) or economic resources (such as money).

Any one of these goals may be more important than the others because of the demand of the moment. That is, your relationship with a particular person may be more important than others because of some goal you wish to fulfill at the moment. When badly in need of money, for example, you wouldn't be satisfied with receiving only affection or understanding from the other person. A local furnace-repair service once launched an advertising campaign with a slogan that became a local cliché: "When you need me, I'll be there." Obviously, when the furnace doesn't work and it's freezing outside, that kind of instrumental aid is likely to have a very high priority.

The "when you need me, I'll be there" sentiment may express the most important role played by the other person (and by yourself when you are someone else's "other"). When you need to have a particular psychosocial need filled (whether it is for identity, affection, emotional support, companionship, or material assistance), the most important thing is for the other to "be there" to fill that need. The remaining pages of this chapter discuss specific kinds of "other" people who meet our psychosocial needs. Specifically, our discussions address the question: How is the relationship affected when the "other" person is "special" in some way? We'll discuss three kinds of special other people: "significant others," "same-sex others," and "different-sex others."

Significant Others

To any specific person (such as yourself), other people are not all equal. Some people are more important because, among other things, they fulfill many of our psychosocial goals. They give us a sense of personal identity, social and emotional support, affection, companionship, and possibly instrumental aid. These people who fulfill so many of our psychosocial goals are popularly known as *significant others*.

The significant other is, as the name implies, an important person in one's life. A spouse is often chosen as a significant other, and the spouse provides a convenient choice. Husband and wife spend a lot of their time together, live together, go on vacations together, depend on each other, confront common problems together, and are economically tied to each other. Consequently, the spouse is often a significant other who provides many of the partner's psychosocial needs.

That husband and wife are typically significant others is hardly surprising. After all, theirs is a rather stable relationship, typically reflecting an extremely high level of interaction as well as togetherness. But these same factors also create some psychosocial problems.

Although not all married couples are happy and divorce rates continue to be high, the marital relationship is generally a highly stable social system. A marital

One person, a "significant other," may fulfill many of your psychological and social needs.
(Fredrik D. Bodin/Stock, Boston)

relationship is "stable" in the sense that the partners spend a great deal of time together; they have a high rate of interaction exclusively with each other. They aren't separated for lengthy periods of time. Their relationship isn't typically disrupted by normal life changes, such as moving away from each other upon changing jobs. As a result of this stability, marital partners are often available to one another and hence are able to fulfill many of their psychosocial goals for each other (particularly expressive, affective, and sociability goals). That, of course, is the "good news." The bad news is that the same characteristics that make them so stable also create problems in fulfilling the identity needs of one or both.

To fulfill identity goals, one needs some periods of privacy and time for reflection. People need activities that offer opportunities to be alone. A marital relationship, for the same reasons that it is so successful in providing affection, emotional support, and companionship, may function to restrict the personal growth of one or both partners.

It is not uncommon to hear a recently divorced person express continued affection for the former spouse and sadness at the loss of a significant other. Nevertheless, the marriage was felt to be stifling feelings of personal identity. Being "out on your own" is scary for the recently divorced man or woman, but it is also personally fulfilling—at least when that person experiences some personal success (such as finding a new job, receiving a promotion, or discovering that the old self is still attractive to members of the opposite sex).

The goal of instrumental aid is somewhat different from the other psychosocial goals. A significant other is probably not the source of instrumental aid for most people. In fact, a relationship based principally on providing instrumental aid is likely to have a negative influence on the relationship. To rely on others to provide psychological, economic, and material services is to create a relationship based on dependence, so that one of the partners is necessarily subordinate to the other. The subordinate partner may come to resent the one who provides the aid, and the relationship will suffer. An old adage illustrates this phenomenon rather well: "Borrow money from someone and create a friend; loan money to a friend and create an enemy."

Gender

Although our society is slowly coming to acknowledge many of the interpersonal problems caused by sex-role stereotyping, the fact is that whether the other person's sex is the same as or different from yours is likely to affect, for whatever reason, the way you perceive and interact with that person. Certainly, our society has had its consciousness raised concerning such issues as associating certain occupations with gender, using linguistic terms that include implicit references to a gender, giving males higher pay for the same work as that performed by females, and a myriad of other issues. It is rapidly becoming common to see male nurses and airline stewards and female physicians, politicians, and business executives. We still cope with linguistic convolutions using "person" (as in "chairperson" and "salesperson"), but we seem to be getting the idea. However, despite these advances in our awareness of having stereotyped people and social roles on the basis of their sex, we still find ourselves influenced by the gender of the other person when engaging in everyday interpersonal communication.

Precisely how and to what extent the communicator's gender influences inter-personal communication is very unclear. There is some evidence to suggest that men and women communicate differently depending on whether their partner is of the same or the opposite sex. Other evidence suggests just the contrary. This issue will also be considered in Part 3 of this book. Our concern here is the intrapersonal level of interpersonal communication. And when we consider the psychological level of communication, there is simply no dispute. We typically perceive and believe that men and women communicate differently and that their relationships with members of the same sex are vastly different from those with members of the opposite sex.

Same-sex other. Lionel Tiger has argued (rather unconvincingly) in his book *Men in Groups* (1970) that the camaraderie among men is a result of their biological maleness. Therefore, this group relationship that men enjoy is simply unavailable to women. Few people take seriously Tiger's notion of males' social superiority to women, but Tiger does point out two important and unique features of male-male relationships. Relationships of males (1) are based on activities and (2) typically involve groups of three or more.

When men engage in relationships, they are generally *doing* something. They go hunting, fishing, camping, or bowling, or playing ball together. Furthermore, they often engage in these activities not just in pairs but in groups of three or more. Many people believe that this activity-based relationship is a product of the early social experiences of males in team sports. Until very recently, only males played baseball, softball, football, or basketball in school athletic programs and summer recreational leagues. Females were expected to form pep clubs and cheerleading squads. Their athletic activity, if it existed at all, was relegated to individual sports, such as tennis or swimming.

This social experience of team sports remains predominantly a male activity. Today, schools and communities sponsor volleyball, basketball, softball, and track teams for women, but these remain less popular than the equivalent programs for men and they are still not totally accepted by the rest of society. Only within the past few years has the first girl played in the world championships of Little League baseball, but a high school soccer team with a female member was forced to cancel some of its games with other teams whose sponsoring schools refused to play them. The early socialization of males in team sports appears to be a likely explanation for the quality of male-male friendships in later life.

Because male-male relationships tend to occur in larger groups, men often have difficulty in perceiving other individual males as close friends. The result is a perception that males typically don't have close friendships with other males. Not only is this a common perception of society, but men themselves often feel the same way. Studies have shown that divorced males typically experience greater difficulty in coping than do divorced females. For example, males are much more likely to express dissatisfaction with living alone and typically remarry within a few years after a divorce or the death of a spouse. Apparently males perceive that many of their psychosocial goals are fulfilled only with a marital partner and that another male friend just isn't as satisfactory.

Team athletics also may engender in males a feeling that social relationships are competitive, at least with other men. This social competitiveness may affect the male-male relationship in several ways. One, it may be the basis for the "machismo" image that males are supposed to have. A man does not cry or otherwise express or show emotions. A man is always a cool person, a dominating image, the strong, silent type. And, of course, men just don't eat quiche.

A second potential effect of competitiveness in male-male relationships is the perception that males are less likely to self-disclose to other men. Recall that disclosing self to others is risky for the self-discloser; it makes the communicator's self vulnerable to the other. Competitors would resist appearing vulnerable to each other. That is, "Since a main form of winning is exploiting the opponents' weaknesses, men close themselves off from each other so they do not expose any vulnerabilities" (Lewis, 1978, p. 112). Because we often perceive self-disclosure as linked with intimacy and close friendships, we also tend to perceive male relationships as being more superficial and therefore less intimate than female or male-female relationships.

Third, competitive social experiences of males in our society may also make it difficult for men to reveal their "real" feelings to other men. Men seem to use circuitous or roundabout ways to say, "I love you" or even "I like you." Instead of directly expressing their feelings, men will hit each other on the shoulder or understate their sentiments, as in "You're not such a bad guy after all." My wife, among others, has told me that my penchant for insulting behavior with my friends is really symptomatic of a very superficial relationship with other men. I remind her that this is my way of saying "I love you" to men, and doing it in a socially acceptable manner. Besides, my insulting behavior is not discriminatory; I insult female friends, too, with probably the same translation.

Society perceives women's relationships with other women as the opposite of male relationships in many respects. Women have more one-to-one relationships with other women, their relationships contain much more self-disclosure, and they perceive that their friendships with other women are closer or more intimate. Further, women describe their feelings for other women in terms of expressive and affective psychosocial goals (see Booth, 1972). Unlike men, women characterize their close friendships with other women in terms of emotional attachment, love, affection, warmth, intimacy. Consequently, women (together with most of our society) perceive their relationships with other women as more expressive and intimate than relationships among men. Our social stereotypes consider it permissible for women to express their emotions, so they do. Unlike men, women are unrestricted by their sexual stereotypes in forming, expressing, and admitting to close relationships.

Because women self-disclose more to each other, they tend to perceive their relationships as more intimate. Although female-female relationships are not necessarily closer than male-male relationships, they have a different quality and are certainly perceived to be closer. They are more direct, more expressive, and are typically described in emotional or affective terms. The fact that female-female relationships tend to be dyadic (one to one) also leads to greater opportunity for self-disclosure and perceived closeness. Furthermore, female-female relationships tend to be less aggressive and less based on competition than the equivalent male-male relationships.

Women also tend to maintain their friendships with other women much longer than men typically do with each other. Some surveys (see Simon, Crotts, & Mahan, 1970) have shown that many women have maintained what they perceive to be close relationships over several decades. A large proportion of friendships between women begin in elementary or high school and are still in effect when these women are in middle age and beyond. Unlike men, women also report that, even though they have had little or no contact with their friends for years, they continue to regard them as close. Men apparently don't maintain such perceptions after regular contact ceases.

Different-sex Other. When we think of a friendship between a man and a woman, the immediate tendency is to think of sexual involvement and potential marriage. This is the standard, stereotyped view of male-female relationships in our society. Consequently, the views of society place potent restraints on the development of friendships between men and women who aren't married. Some people refer to such cross-sex relationships as "platonic" friendships, differentiating them from "romantic" or "sexual" relationships and thereby reflecting this same societal expectation. If a man and woman are friends, they must be "making it" together. If they aren't, their relationship is "only platonic"—as if something were missing. The natural result of society's view is that both men and women have far fewer friendships and even acquaintanceships with members of the opposite sex than they might otherwise have. Their circle of friends is predominately people of the same sex.

My oldest daughter encountered this societal constraint while she was a high school student. She had several close female friends at that time, but she considered two males to be close friends too. She considered neither of these male friends as a "boyfriend," only a "good friend." She was greatly disappointed when one of them asked her for a date. After that date, she never felt the close friendship again. Actually, dating was the farthest thing from her mind in that relationship; she thought they were "friends."

Society's constraints on male-female relationships change considerably over the normal course of a person's life. During high school, for instance, society allows unmarried males and females much more freedom to have friendships. More specifically, society has no taboo against heterosexual friendships between unmarried partners when the partners are younger than marrying age (whatever age that is). After marriage, however, they are restricted. In other words, neither husband nor wife is expected to have a friendship with a partner of the opposite sex. It just wouldn't "look right" and would probably be considered "cheating" on the spouse. Therefore, outside the marital relationship, married people are restricted to friendships with partners of the same sex. In that way, they need not worry about "what people will say."

Society has probably placed more restrictions on women's friendships with men that on men's friendships with women. For one thing, women have fewer opportunities than men. For instance, the traditional role of housewife severely limits the opportunity of women to meet potential friends. The world of home and children provides women with few chances to meet men with whom they might develop friendships. Furthermore, few social organizations encourage or even allow friendships between the sexes. Such organizations are typically for men only, for women only, or primarily for married couples. In fact, for adult women in our society, the opportunity to have friendships with men virtually requires that they be employed outside the home. But being employed is not enough; they must be employed in positions that are not so exclusively female. Those occupational and professional roles traditionally occupied by women (such as those of nurse, schoolteacher, secretary, or stewardess) are unlikely to foster friendships with men.

One survey (Booth & Hess, 1974) attempted to identify the nature of cross-sex friendships and provides some interesting, but hardly surprising, findings. For both men and women, the survey found, cross-sex friendships are much more common among those who are employed in occupations that include members of the other sex. Moreover, friendships between men and women typically occur only when both men and women have equivalent status at work. A business organization, for example, employing women exclusively as secretaries or typists (men as supervisors, women as subordinates), is not likely to foster cross-sex friendships despite the amount of interaction that might take place.

More cross-sex friendships were reported by people in occupations that required a college education and constituted a professional career for the man and the woman. When both men and women belonged to the same professional or trade association, they were also more likely to develop cross-sex friendships. In many cases, the fact that there are still few women in such occupations or associations has not allowed people the opportunity to develop friendships with people of the opposite sex. Without opportunities for social encounters and interaction, such friendships simply don't have a chance to get started. Clearly, same-sex friendships have far greater opportunities, both in getting started and continuing development, than opposite-sex friendships.

Another constraint involves the unusual view that contemporary society has of the connection between sexual behavior and cross-sex friendship. Society has come to accept the notion that a man and woman can have a sexual relationship without necessarily being very close friends. The increasing societal acceptance and practice of casual sex and one-night stands (for both men and women) are symptoms of such a belief. Oddly enough, though, society does not seem to hold the reverse view—that a man and woman can be close friends without having a sexual relationship.

This kind of "double standard" in society affects the expectations of partners in specific male-female relationships. Individuals find that the possibility of sexual involvement hinders the development of their cross-sex friendships. When confronted with a potential friend of the opposite sex, individuals tend to avoid those who are similar to themselves and choose, instead, opposite-sex friends who are quite dissimilar in terms of age, educational level, and the like. This choice based on difference is quite the opposite of same-sex friendships which, according to social comparison, include people who are similar to each other. It may be that cross-sex friendships develop from a basis of difference in order to avoid the perceived expectation of a sexual relationship.

The Booth and Hess survey results also indicate that women may differ from men in how they practice person perception. The survey found that, although both men and women reported that most of their friends were of the same sex, more men (35 percent) than women (24 percent) reported having friends of the opposite sex. Apparently women tend to use the term "friend" to refer to a person in whom they would confide—as Margaret Thatcher put it, someone with whom they can let down their hair. In other words, women tend to see as "friend" that person who fulfills their expressive psychosocial goals. Men, however, are more apt to use the term "friend" to refer to people with whom they spend leisure time, engage in frequent conversation, are companions—that is, fulfill sociability goals.

We might conclude that the perceptions of men and women may differ considerably. Most importantly, men and women may differ in their perceptions of the nature of friendship itself and how it is perceived. Probably as the result of being socialized differently, women have developed ways of perceiving their social relationships that are different from the ways that men perceive theirs. That is, women seek other persons as friends in order to fulfill their expressive goals, and men seek other persons as friends to fulfill their sociability goals. Whether men and women actually behave differently during interpersonal communication (as a result of their different perceptions), though, is still up in the air. But we will be discussing this topic again in Part 3.

Summary

The psychological process of perceiving the other person during interpersonal communication is called person perception. When the object of perception is another person, the perceptual process is somewhat different than when the perceived object is inanimate. The perceiver of another person attempts to infer the intentions and internal states of the other as well as any similarities with self. The perceptual process of acquiring meaning is to reduce the amount of uncertainty in order to have some idea about who the other person is and what he or she wants.

When perceiving the other, we tend to use other people as a basis for comparing our own values, attitudes, beliefs, and so on in order to evaluate ourselves. This social comparison leads us to select other people who are similar to ourselves, thereby confirming our own selves. We look for clues to the other's self in the behaviors that person exhibits during communication. We consider the behaviors as evidence for inferring the other person's internal states and gain some information about what to expect in future relationships. Much of the process involves applying our own implicit personality theory to the new acquaintance in order to classify that person as similar to the other types of people in our past social experiences.

Person perception also involves attributing factors of cause or control of the behaviors. We often attribute dispositional (intrapersonal) causes to the behaviors of others but situational (controlled by the context) causes to our own behaviors. When relationships attain a more fully developed state, relational partners tend to view events and other persons in terms of how they affect the relationship itself, thereby creating a third locus of attributional control—the relationship as a kind of self.

Certain elements of the psychological set can affect the quality of person perception and increase the chances of making an incorrect perception of the other. Those response sets include the halo effect (overgeneralizing the other's behavior to situations about which we have no information), the leniency effect (overestimating positive traits of friends and underestimating their negative traits), and applying stereotypes. All response sets may affect how we behave toward the other.

The behaviors we perform when communicating with another person are designed to give that person the impression of our selves that we want that person to have. Because each person during communication seeks information about the other person in that person's behavior, every behavior may be perceived as self-disclosing communication. Thus, each person attempts to manage the impressions the other perceives through the behaviors performed during interaction. In impression management, the person selects a role-self to portray, what information to present to the other, and the manner in which to present that information. And every communicator cannot avoid making these three types of choices. The effective communicator, one who is rhetorically sensitive, is aware of making these choices and does so by allowing perceptions of the other person to guide those choices. Communicative behavior thus involves selecting responses to the other person. Specific kinds of responses involve making and responding to attributions implied in the other's behavior and confirming the other person's value as a self.

The other person is often selected for interaction in order to fulfill certain psychosocial goals, including those involving self-identity, affection, expression, sociability, and instrumental aid. Certain people, known as significant others, often fulfill more than one of these goals—particularly affective, expressive, and sociability goals. The sex of the other person also affects the interaction. At least in terms of perceptions, relationships are different when partners are the same sex than when they are of the opposite sex. The question of whether the communicative behaviors of males and females differ remains open, but the perceptions of the quality of male-male and female-female relationships differ significantly.

PART 3

The Relationship

CHAPTER **9**

Introduction: The Nature of Human Relationships

I love you,
Not only for what you are,
But for what I am
When I am with you.
I love you,
Not only for what
You have made of yourself,
But for what you are making of me.

—Roy Croft

We live in a materialistic society. We have become accustomed to measuring an individual's worth or prestige by typically material standards. We measure people's social status by how much money they make, what kind of car they drive, in what kind of home they live, what clothes they wear. We measure the value of an academic major in terms of how much it will increase our earning power after graduation. My wife has told me that when she was a high school student holding a part-time job, she would measure the value of any prospective purchase in terms of how many hours of work it would cost. We spend the better part of our adult lives in a quest for material success and valued material objects. We understand what it means to be rich in material possessions; we are less sure of what it means to be rich in human relationships.

Some societies go so far as to assess the value of a human relationship in socioeconomic terms. In some parts of the world for example, marriages are arranged through a process of economic negotiation. The prospective bridegroom pays the bride's family some negotiated sum in order to compensate them for the loss of their daughter. In other societies in which women are deemed inferior, the bride's parents pay the prospective bridegroom a dowry, ostensibly to have him take her off their hands. In the agricultural society of the American frontier, marriage was closely linked with economics—the need for help on the farm. And large families of sons and daughters resulted from this same need. In India, the caste system forbade marriage or any other form of interpersonal relationship across caste boundaries.

Even today our youth are discouraged from dating or marrying outside the bounds of their own social status, religion, or race. In order to compensate, perhaps, young people create their own caste system to judge the worth of a prospective relational partner. Our high schools abound with their own social strata: who's "cute" and who's not, who's a member of the "in group" and who's not, who's on the basketball or football team and who's not, who's "popular" and who's not. And the male student without an automobile is really a nobody. Generally, though, the ideals of democracy prevail over those of capitalism, so that we are free to form relationships with others as a matter of our own choosing and not as a function of economic negotiation.

To have a relationship and to be able to judge its worth, we are forced to develop a standard of evaluation totally different from our accustomed materialistic criteria. Furthermore, that standard must, to some extent, contradict our typical materialistic standards. Concrete criteria (such as dollars and cents) for assessing a relationship with another person are simply not applicable. So what criteria do we use instead?

Conventional thinking would suggest that we might adopt the standard of emotions. In this way, we would judge a relationship with a certain someone in terms of the degree of our emotional attachment, such as "love," that we feel toward that person. But this standard isn't very satisfactory, either. For one thing, which emotion do we use to judge a relationship? Love is not always appropriate, nor is it easily defined. I recall a line from a popular song of several years ago that went something like "You don't have to *like* someone to *love* someone." Does this mean that a relationship can be evaluated high in "love" but low in "like?" What about emotions such as respect, admiration, anger, resentment, envy, and a host of others? Which has the greatest value?

If emotions are a notoriously unreliable ruler for measuring human relationships (and they are), then we need to find something else to use. But what? Roy Croft's poem, at the opening of this chapter, suggests one alternative. It implies that the relationship between "I" and "you" is "bigger than the both of us." That is, Croft's "I" is different and better for having been a partner in the relationship with "you." And that new definition of self is the basis for the love that his "I" feels toward "you." The key to evaluating our relationships, then, is probably not the emotions we feel toward the other person. Emotions, by themselves, are fickle and contradictory. Rather, the central element is more likely to be the self-concept discussed in Part 2. To the extent that the person is able to define self through the relationship, that relationship (and not just the other person) is valuable.

A major premise of interpersonal communication is this reflexivity between the relationship and the self of each participant. As the following pages will illustrate, the participants do not define their relationship any more than the relationship defines them. We might think of an interpersonal relationship as an economic transaction in which we make a certain investment and then wait to see what return we will receive on our investment. Our actual investment, of course, comprises those communicative behaviors which we contribute to the interaction. And we cannot avoid investing *something*, either. (Remember the axiom, "One cannot not communicate.") The return on our investment (the impact of self's participation in the relationship on self-concept) is the redefinition of our own self-concept, the residue that remains within us as a result of being and having been in that relationship with that particular person.

THE SELF AND THE RELATIONSHIP

Every interpersonal relationship involves a minimum of three parties: one's self, the other, and the relationship. Marriage counselors report that couples often speak of having "O.R. [our relationship] talks," which they describe as "serious discussions about the course of the relationship, as if it were a cohabiting but separate being from either [partner's] identity" (Harvey et al., 1982, p. 120). Of course, "O.R. talks" are not common to many relationships, except close and probably romantic ones. But the fact remains that in every situation of interpersonal communication, "our relationship" does exist as an entity separate from the identity of either partner and is different from either or both.

This sense of the separate identity of relationships allows us to classify other people in terms of the types of relationships we have with them. That is, we tend to group some people as our "friends" and others as our "acquaintances." Even though we recognize a considerable variation among different friends and different acquaintances, we continue to say that "she is one of my friends" or "he is an acquaintance of mine." Generally speaking, we tend to attribute the identity of others in terms of the relationships we have with them. Thus, we identify Jerry as "my friend" rather than as a unique and idiosyncratic human being who is quite different from ourselves or our other friends.

A Model of Self and Relationship

Conventional thinking leads us to think of a relationship as defined by the individual participants. Figure 9-1 (see page 192) portrays this conventional view. But lest we believe that a relationship is nothing more than the overlap of individual personalities, the international symbol of "No way!" is superimposed on the diagram. You will recognize this "overlapping circles" diagram as reminiscent of our earlier discussions of individualistic definitions of communication. The arrows pointing away from Alfred and Betty imply that each communicator extends a self into the relationship, but each also remains rather independent of the other's self and from the relationship itself. The result is that the relationship is nothing more or less than the overlap or coincidence of individual personalities, something they have in common, ostensibly from their own idiosyncratic experiences of the past. This diagram implies further that the "real self" of Alfred and Betty remains independent of their overlap, so that each person remains unaffected by the relationship and by having participated in the relationship. Such an implication is blatantly false.

The fact is that our relationships do affect us and our subsequent relationships. Yesterday's relationships will affect today's relationship. And the relationships we have today will affect those we have tomorrow. Each of us is a different person for having been a partner in an interpersonal relationship, particularly a close one. Any close relationship leaves its mark on the self of each relational partner. And it is that

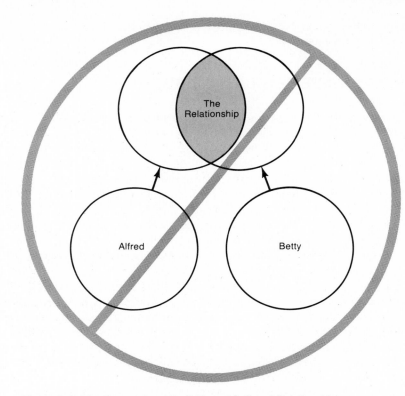

Figure 9-1. The Conventional Definition of Self and Relationship

new and somewhat different self that enters into subsequent relationships. When a close personal friend betrays the confidence of your relationship, you will find it difficult to enter into a trusting relationship in the future. If your previous friendship was very intimate and highly satisfying, you tend to expect a similar level of intimacy and satisfaction in future friendships and feel keen disappointment if they do not live up to your high expectations. In a very real sense, we are not individual selves who enter into relationships; we are relationally mature people who have already loved or hated. Our relationships leave a residue within us, an impact on our selves. And that residue may be the most important personality attribute of our self-concept when we enter into future relationships.

Figure 9-2 is probably a more accurate portrayal of the reflexivity of self and relationship. The first implication evident from this drawing is that "the relationship" has a single identity different and apart from the identity of either Alfred or Betty. Moreover, the relationship is not "controlled' or defined by either Alfred or Betty as the coincidental overlap of independent partners summed together. The relationship is not something that either or both Alfred and Betty "do" but, rather, some additional entity that they are a part of or that they participate in. Furthermore, Alfred and Betty cannot "choose" to remain aloof or separate from the relationship; they have no choice but to participate, at least to some extent. Having thus become

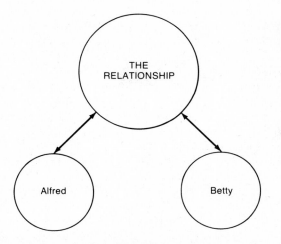

Figure 9-2. A ''Model'' of the Reflexivity of Self and Relationship

a part of the relationship, they are then subject to being affected by it. Hence, the arrows extend from the relationship to Alfred and Betty, the participants.

A number of elements are, of course, missing from the diagram depicted in Figure 9-2. The influences of previous relationships are brought to the present relationship within the selves of Alfred and Betty. Social norms from family, nation, social class, organizational membership, peer group, and so on are also influences on the relationship and reside within the selves of Alfred and Betty.

But the important principle remains. In interpersonal communication, the participation of the relational partners creates a new and different social entity called ''the relationship.'' Further, this relationship does affect the self of each partner who, as a result of being a member of this relationship, redefines his or her self-concept to some extent. And that redefined self may be the most important personality attribute of the individual communicator, at least in the sense that it may have the greatest impact on that person's subsequent relationships.

If you have inferred from this discussion that interpersonal communication involves some element of personal risk, especially a risk of having your self-concept revised, you are absolutely correct. Subsequent chapters in Part 3 will serve to highlight the notion of risk and obligation inherent in interpersonal communication. But don't be alarmed. Virtually everything of any lasting value involves risk. After all, nothing ventured; nothing gained.

The "Law" of Partial Inclusion

Human beings living in a society are constantly torn between what social psychologists like to call the dual interests of "individuation" and "sociation." In plainer terms, every human being is, at the same time, both an individual being with selfish motives and desires and a social being with interpersonal motives and desires. Many of us feel these dual interests during our consistent but generally unsuccessful efforts to participate in the current craze to be physically fit. For purely selfish reasons, we

Everyone wants to maintain an individual identity and, at the same time, participate in a relationship that may redefine that identity.
(Joel Gordon)

want to "get in shape," to lose a few pounds (often more than a few), to be healthy. Yet, I find that I am not motivated to accomplish this essentially individualistic goal through individualistic activities. I have friends who reflect the glow of health, have slender bodies, and have the gaunt look of inveterate runners. They regale me with stories of the joys of running in glorious isolation, communing with nature and self, "being one with self." I've tried jogging and find the isolated activity b-o-o-r-r-r-ring! On the other hand, I will play racquetball, tennis, basketball, or other social games with no urging at all. Apparently my social interests are stronger than my individual interests.

Dual individualistic and social interests are also present in the reflexivity between the participant's self and the relationship. Everyone wants to maintain a self-identity and, at the same time, to participate in a relationship that necessitates the risk of redefining that self-identity. The typical individual, "looking out for number one," looks at the diagram in Figure 9-2 and thinks, "If the relationship is that powerful, why risk being in the relationship in the first place?" Or the response might be, "Figure 9-2 is bunk! I don't change my self-concept so easily, just by having a relationship with someone else. My self-identity is stronger than that." Such responses result from another normal human tendency—to see things in either-or, all-or-nothing terms. But the reflexivity of self and relationship is not a choice between "all" (the relationship is omnipotent) or "nothing" (the relationship is impotent). Central to this reflexivity is what social psychologists call *the law of partial inclusion*.

Simply stated, the law of partial inclusion suggests that the relationship neither demands nor could possibly demand all of the participant's self. Only part of the self of any participant, and typically a rather small part, is included in even the most intimate of interpersonal relationships. Alfred might include more of his self in his relationship with Betty, but he may include much less of his self in his relationship with, say, Charlie.

The economic metaphor used earlier may help to explain this unavoidable law. Every participant contributes to, and thus invests in, the relationship with someone else. Generally speaking, the return on the investment is in proportion to how much is invested. That is, you invest more, and you get more back. Some investments, however, are exceptions to this rule. Some are financial disasters. You may invest your life savings only to discover later that the investment was a mistake. With other investments, you may find a gold mine. You may not contribute much, but you receive a return far in excess of your contribution. But these are exceptions. In nearly all cases, you get out of an investment in proportion to what you put in.

Like financial investments, interpersonal relationships are considerably different in their rates of return. Some relationships have a fairly constant and relatively guaranteed rate of return, usually quite modest, and others require more investment capital but promise a potentially higher return, even though they also represent more of a gamble. Most people will invest only a small amount of their self-identities at first and wait to see their rate of return before increasing their contributions.

The participant in an interpersonal relationship has only one form of currency to invest: behaviors or communicative actions. Committing more of one's self to any relationship, then, involves contributing more behaviors (specifically, more kinds of behaviors) to the relationship. The amount of your self invested in any relationship is thus measured in the number and variety of communicative behaviors you contribute to the relationship. The more behaviors you contribute, the more of your self you invest in that relationship and the greater the impact (rate of return) that relationship will have on your own self-concept. Generally, you contribute more and different kinds of behaviors to a close personal relationship, and you contribute fewer behaviors to a superficial acquaintanceship. On the other hand, your acquaintanceship may develop into a friendship. In that case, you will increase your contributed behaviors during subsequent interaction in the developing relationship.

The point to remember about the law of partial inclusion is that you, the individual, control how much of your self (that is, the kind and variety of behaviors) you contribute to any relationship. You cannot avoid contributing some behaviors, of course, but you can control the number and variety of those behaviors. Moreover, you *must* control the number and variety of your behaviors in the course of the relationship. Whether you are aware of it or not, you will put closure around the kinds of actions you perform in regard to interpersonal communication, whether your relationship is a close friendship or a superficial acquaintanceship. In every relationship you have, there are certain communicative behaviors you commonly use and others that you won't use. During the normal course of interpersonal communication, you have "decided" what your contribution will be in that relationship.

In a nutshell, then, the law of partial inclusion governs all interpersonal relationships. Every interpersonal relationship is definable in terms of the communicative actions contributed by the partners to that relationship. The actions of one partner, in combination with the actions of the other, define the nature of that relationship; all other actions by either or both partners are generally not considered to be relevant to that relationship. In this sense, each individual controls the extent to which her or his self is included in the relationship by putting closure around the types and varieties of behaviors that define participation in that relationship.

Your interpersonal relationships are very different in terms of how much of your self-identity you contribute and to what extent you are therefore affected. But not all your (and your partner's) behaviors are relevant to the relationship. Your relationship is defined by and limited to the behaviors you and your partner use when participating in that relationship. That is, the behaviors that create the *inter*action between you and your relational partner define and limit the interpersonal relationship. Other behaviors that you and your partner are capable of performing (and, indeed, do perform in other relationships) are simply irrelevant to this particular instance.

CHARACTERISTICS OF INTERPERSONAL RELATIONSHIPS

Interpersonal communication and relationships just don't seem to be "real." That is, they involve behaviors and interactions and thus have no material substance. They aren't tangible. The fact is that communication and relationships are not "thinglike." They are indeed intangible in the sense that they comprise events, and events "occur"—that is, they exist only in time. Once an event is over, it's over. It ceases to exist. On the other hand, our attributions of the relationship (such as our emotions or feelings toward the other person) seem to be more "real." But we must keep in mind that those internal and individualized feelings are not the relationship itself but the aftermath of the relationship—the residual effects that remain inside the heads of the participants *after* the interaction with the partner has already created the relationship.

These two elements—the relationship and the effects of the relationship on individuals—must remain separated. We must continue to see the relationship as interpersonal communication and resist the temptation to see the relationship as "thinglike" or having some material substance. The characteristics that serve to define the relationship are created and reflected in the pattern or sequence of communicators' actions toward one another. These actions are not people's internal feelings but rather the external behaviors that occur between people. These actions are events that occur in time and are related to each other in time. Therefore, we will continue to treat interpersonal communication and relationships in terms of their "reality" as events occurring and existing only in time. The remainder of this chapter, then, introduces Part 3 by detailing the five axiomatic characteristics describing all interpersonal relationships.

Relationships Are *Created*

A relationship is not something that just "happens." It is something that results from the communicators' overt acts which create it. Having once been created, a relationship continues to exist with a life of its own, nurtured by the participants and affecting the participants within it. Like any created life, though, a relationship does not stand still. It continues to change, to grow, to develop over the natural course of time. Every relationship is constantly evolving so that it may progress to a new and more intimate stage, or it may regress to a new and less intimate stage. Time cannot and does not stand still. It is constantly in a process of change. Remember the adage often attributed to Confucius: "You can't step in the same river twice." Like flowing rivers, events continue to change normally with the passage of time, and so do relationships.

Relationships Are *Enacted*

The term "enact" is central to the nature of communication and relationships. To enact a relationship is to create the relationship through actions. The components of any relationship are ultimately those actions performed by the participants while communicating within the relationship. Combined, the actions create meaningful patterns of interaction. Alfred can individually create his meaning of Betty, but he can do so only by acting toward Betty. Conversely, Betty's meaning of Alfred results from her having acted toward Alfred. But neither person's definition of the other, though also enacted, is the same as the definition of the relationship as a whole. That relationship results from having been enacted by both Alfred and Betty together. Their relationship is the *inter*action that is created by the particular combination of actions performed by Alfred and Betty in concert.

Relationships Are *Becoming*

To say that relationships are created and enacted is to emphasize the *process* of relating. Any process, by definition, embodies the notion of time and change over time. A relationship, then, is constantly *in process*; it is continually evolving and becoming something different. That process of evolutionary change, applied to interpersonal communication, tells us that we must not think of a relationship as a goal to be attained, a result that comes about when two people get to know each other. A relationship never just *is*; it is constantly changing, constantly moving, constantly becoming something else. To maintain a relationship, then, is to keep changing it.

We may have been indoctrinated, as children, in fairytale folklore concerning the relationship between the beautiful young princess and the handsome young prince who married and "lived happily ever after." As a result of such fairytale tradition—reinforced in novels, movies, and TV shows—we have been led to believe that "falling in love" or "finding that special someone" is all we need to do in order to "live happily ever after." The practical truth of the matter is that maintaining a loving relationship requires a considerable expenditure of energy—energy spent in interpersonal communication. Change is normal and unavoidable. When left alone, relationships atrophy, wither, and die. They need to be revitalized to keep them at the same level of development. In other words, relationships are always in a state of becoming.

Relationships Are *Consequential*

You have probably heard someone say something like the following: "Yes, I'm still seeing him [or her], but it's nothing serious. I don't want to get involved. And he [or she] respects my wishes." Such a comment assumes that the speaker is somehow aloof from and unaffected—that individual persons are somehow separate from the relationships in which they participate. Such a comment is quite consistent, however, with the rather naive view of a relationship depicted in Figure 9-1. But relationships are inherently consequential. Relationships have consequences and affect the people who participate in them, even though they may not want to "get involved."

To behave toward another person is to get involved with that person. Two people acting toward each other create the phenomenon known as *inter*action—the connections between actions and, thus, between the persons who perform those actions. The only way you can avoid getting involved with another person is not to have any communication, to avoid that person like the plague—that is, not to have a relationship at all.

Any and every relationship will have some residual effect on the persons who engage in them. Figure 9-2, with its arrows leading from the single and unitary relationship to the participants, illustrates the consequential principle of relationships. The relationship may not affect Alfred in the same way that it affects Betty, of course. After all, we already know that individual human beings are different from one another and have unique personalities, experiences, perceptions, and so on. But the relationship can, does, and must affect both Alfred and Betty as a consequence of their having been in that relationship. Furthermore, there is nothing that Alfred and Betty can do about it short of not communicating at all.

Relationships Are *Qualitative*

All relationships are different. You, the same person, have many relationships with many different other people. But each of your relationships is different, in some respects, from any of the others. Your relationship with your mother is probably different from that with your father or sister or brother. Yet, all can be described as "kinship" relationships. There are many different people you would call "friends," but some of those relationships are "friendlier" than others. You have different acquaintances, but you feel closer to some than you do to others. In other words, every relationship has a certain quality that makes it different from other relationships.

Naturally, the quality of a relationship is created by the communicative behaviors, the interactions you and the other person perform toward each other. You, together with your relational partner, "enact" a relationship which is, to some extent, unique. The natural result of such interaction is the effect your enacted relationship exerts on your definition of your self. In other words, your interpersonal relationships will unavoidably affect who you are as an individual human being.

Some scholars (Graziano & Musser, 1982, p. 101) have suggested that the quality of interaction can be assessed along three dimensions: *performance, closeness,* and *relevance.* For instance, you may find the performance of the relationship itself very satisfying. That is, you enjoy being with that person. Second, you may experience a feeling of being very close with that special person, but you don't have that feeling with people you don't know well. Finally, you may conclude that some people are simply more relevant to certain areas of your self than are others. Your adviser, for instance, may be very relevant to your educational life but not very relevant to your having fun.

These three criteria are undoubtedly not the only ways to distinguish the quality of a particular relationship, but they do demonstrate that each relationship has a quality that distinguishes it, in terms of its impact on your own definition of self, from your other relationships.

Summary

In Part 3, you will be reading how these five principles of interpersonal relationships are put into practice in creating, enacting, maintaining, and terminating relationships. Throughout these chapters, we will be discussing how "communicating," "interacting," and "relating" are essentially synonymous terms that can be used interchangeably with no significant loss in meaning. The discussion will constantly remind you that "you cannot not communicate," in the sense that all communication comprises behaviors or actions.

In the sense of relating, the discussions will continue to remind you that, paradoxically, you cannot "just" communicate, either. Communication, you will recall, requires a minimum of two persons to make "interpersonal" communication. Thus, you can behave or act toward another person, but your behaviors *by themselves* do not constitute communication. *Communication is the relationship* which you, together with your relational partner or partners, create through your *inter*action. Thus, you do not "communicate" so much as you *engage in* or *become part of* the process of communication.

In one way, the preceding eight chapters have prepared you for the chapters that follow. From our earlier reading we know, for example, that communication takes place in a context that may influence the relationship either positively or negatively. We know, too, that the context includes both physical elements of the environment and, more importantly, social elements of cultures and subcultures to which one or more of the communicators belong. We know that the individual participants possess unique self-identities that they both conceal from and reveal to one another. Each communicator is a perceiving, attributing, rationalizing self who reflexively seeks to assign meaning to the social encounter and to the other person during the process of communication.

In other words, we know from our reading of earlier chapters that communication takes place between two or more thinking, breathing, perceiving people who are affected (particularly in how they define their own self-concepts) by being a part of the relationship process. But between the beginning and end of the interaction is the "stuff" of which the relationship is made, created, enacted, and maintained. And that stuff—the content of the relationship, the practical "doing" of communication, the interaction, the interpersonal behaviors—is the focus of the next five chapters.

The remaining chapters of Part 3 generally follow the five characteristics of interpersonal relationships introduced briefly in this chapter. Chapter 10 discusses the "enacting" of relationships, in which communicative behaviors, because of their "consequential" impact on the participants, become strategies as the individual selves of the partners negotiate their interpersonal relationship. Depending on the nature of the interactional patterns we enact (in cooperation with our partners), that relationship develops a quality that distinguishes it from some relationships and makes it similar to others.

Chapter 11 begins at the beginning of communication. How do we initiate the creative process of developing an interpersonal relationship? What happens during the early stages in the process of interpersonal communication?

The development process of continual change is the major theme of Chapter 12. Why and how do we develop closer relationships with some people and grow farther apart in our relationships with others?

Some relationships, of course, just don't make it. They simply end, sometimes abruptly and sometimes gradually, as the partners (independently or by mutual agreement) decide to terminate their relationship. The creative phase of terminating a relationship is the topic of Chapter 13.

The "becoming" phase of interpersonal relationships is the focus of Chapter 14. In many ways, it is far easier to begin a relationship, to get closer to another person, and even to terminate a once close relationship than to keep a relationship (particularly a close one) going. The strategies involved in maintaining relationships, too often ignored but highly significant nonetheless, conclude Part 3.

The next five chapters are really the "guts" of this book. In order to gain the fullest understanding of and appreciation for how interpersonal communication works and how you can apply the principles of effective communication in the actual process of relating with others, though, the preceding discussion of context and self is a vitally important prerequisite. In order to be practical and apply the principles of interpersonal communication in our day-to-day experiences, however, we must know and understand what we *do* when we actually engage in communication—that is, what we do when we participate in interpersonal relationships.

The practical application of this textbook involves putting the principles of effective interpersonal communication into practice in your communicative behaviors or actions—in short, the "enacting" or "doing" of interpersonal communication. The questions you will be asking of yourself in any communicative situation will be "What do I want out of this relationship?" and "What do I do in order to help me get it?" The answers to those questions should become apparent when you have completed your study of the remaining chapters.

CHAPTER 10

Enacting Relationships: Communicative Strategies and Patterns

Life has no pleasure nobler than that of friendship.
Some people have no enemies, but all their friends hate them.
A friend is someone who knows all about you and likes you just the same.

—"One liners" from unknown
sources

Among the pithy pieces of folk wisdom uttered by the late humorist Will Rogers is the famous statement "I never met a man I didn't like." The most common interpretation of this implies some enviable property of Will Rogers himself, a property that allowed him to see something likable within every other person or which gave him extraordinary skill as a participant in interpersonal communication. Despite these worthy implications of Rogers's statement, we should probably not ignore the possibility that, in uttering these words, Will Rogers was lying through his teeth.

For most of us, communication with others includes the entire range of interpersonal reactions. We rate some people high on our liking scale. We rate others rather low and react to them with supreme indifference. But why? Why do we like some people and not others? Why do we want to get to know some people more than others? Why do we have favorable first impressions of some people, while others "turn us off" immediately? To answer such questions, we must first rephrase the "why" questions and substitute the subtly though significantly different question "How come?"

To ask "why" is to look for the easy cause-effect answer, such as looking for something in the other person (or in us) that causes us to react favorably, unfavorably, or with indifference. A "why" question is probably more appropriate to understanding our reactions to inanimate objects in our environment. We like a movie or a popular song because of something within us that perceives the movie or music as pleasing. We dislike it because of something we perceive as displeasing. In fact, human perceptions probably provide a fairly complete explanation for understanding our reactions to such objects.

When we communicate, though, we do more than merely perceive. We "act toward" the other person and experience the other person's acting toward us. Consequently, it is more accurate to say we *enact* our communication, our relationship. That is, we *create* relationships through our acting toward the other person and that person's acting toward us. Moreover, because actions are events, they take place over a period of time. Our first impressions of the other person may (and often do) change from one moment to the next, as our interaction continues. What seemed important at one time may, during interaction, turn out to be trivial, and vice versa.

Because interpersonal communication is constantly changing, constantly in a process of becoming, we need to rephrase our "why" questions to consider fully the time factor. Hence, understanding the process of enacting relationships requires asking "how come" questions. How does your reaction of liking come about through interaction? How does our relationship develop over time to become what it is right now? How do our relationships with some people come to be pleasant while those with others are unpleasant? Unlike "why" questions, asking "how come" questions forces us to address the issue that we, through our own actions and those of others, are responsible for the relationships we have with others.

The best way to understand how relationships come about is to think of interpersonal communication as a process of negotiation. Each individual communicator possesses individualized motives, wants, desires, interests, and so on. Your individual list of these things is different from every other person's list. Yet very different individuals, communicating with each other, develop an interpersonal bond or relationship that becomes more significant than the differences that separate them.

Interpersonal communication involves a blend of individual differences and interpersonal bonds. Interpersonal communication highlights the independence of individual members while also integrating individual members within a unified relationship. This blend of similarities and differences, of independence and interdependence, that characterizes interpersonal communication is central to the social process of negotiation.

As individual communicators act toward each other, they create the process of negotiating their own individual selves toward the natural goal of achieving some "settlement" or "contract" that unites their independent selves within a relationship. Like negotiation, communication involves individuals functioning to further their own interests. Yet, these same individuals continue to seek elements of commonality with the other, elements that make them similar and on which they can agree.

This chapter describes the process of enacting interpersonal relationships through communication within the framework of a negotiating process. To see interpersonal communication as a process of negotiating differences of individual selves is to focus on the quality of the interaction that inevitably leads to the quality of the settlement or the relationship, the interpersonal bond. Communicative behaviors are not just idle chatter. They are *strategies* we use when acting toward another person. Every time we communicate, we make an offer to the other person, an offer that may affect the quality of the settlement or the relational contract that is the outcome. As in any process of negotiation, interpersonal communicators achieve a settlement *after* a lengthy process of talk. At different stages during their interaction, they come closer to a settlement, move farther away, or make no progress. A settlement or contract defining their relationship, however, is always the outcome of this evolutionary process of interpersonal communication.

All negotiated relationships, of course, do not arrive at the same settlement. Some relationships, like negotiated contracts in general, are more acceptable to the participants than are others. Some contracts enjoy more commitment on the part of the negotiators than do others. The outcome of any particular interpersonal communication, like the outcome of any process of negotiation, is never guaranteed at the beginning. It evolves to some outcome, but the outcome is never final; it is constantly changing. These are the major topics to be discussed in Chapter 10.

QUALITY OF INTERACTION

What is it about the interaction that makes it satisfying to us or that generates our feelings toward the other person? After all, we interact with strangers in generally the same manner, regardless of who the stranger is. We are guided by those conventional norms of our society that tell us how to engage in let's-get-acquainted talk with new people. With some people we seem to hit it off right away; with others, we spend much more time getting acquainted; and with still others, we come quickly (or eventually) to the conclusion that this relationship won't ever "get off the ground." "How come?" we ask ourselves. The answer lies in those characteristics of the *inter*action (not just our actions or the actions of the other person) that identify it as being different from (or similar to) other interaction—in other words, the *quality* of the interaction.

Primary Characteristics

The primary characteristics of the quality of interaction describe interaction in terms of events. Events occur in time and hence are related to each other in time. Events may occur with certain lapses in time between them. Thus, interaction is *discontinuous*. Events may fit together in a logical progression. Thus, interaction is *synchronized*. Events may occur again and again at different times. Thus, interaction is *recurrent*. One event may reflect back on or remind us of an earlier event. Thus, interaction is *reciprocal*. These, then, are the four primary characteristics of interactional quality: discontinuity, synchrony, recurrence, and reciprocity.

Discontinuity. The most obvious characteristic of interactional quality is the fact that it is discontinuous. Even with your closest friends, you do not interact all the time. Hours will go by—days, weeks, months, even years—between the times when you and your relational partner are actually engaged in communicating with one another. During any typical day, even husbands and wives are separated for many hours between periods of interaction. However, the fact that interaction in even the closest and most intimate relationships is discontinuous isn't particularly interesting. What *is* intriguing is that the relationships continue to prosper during the periods of noninteraction, so that when interaction again occurs, the relational partners take up where they left off—often as though nothing had changed or time had not intervened.

A few years ago I experienced a revival of an intermittent and discontinuous relationship. My family was traveling through the Midwest on a vacation trip and were visiting friends and relatives along the way. We had made plans to visit a couple who were close friends during our college days, twenty years in the past. I hadn't laid eyes on either friend for at least ten years. We live 1,500 miles apart and had made contact only through Christmas cards and occasional letters. He had gained at least 20 pounds and sported a full mop of hair (no crew cut), which was entirely gray (not black). He beat me in quantity of weight gain (although not by much), but I exceeded him in amount of hair loss. In nearly every way we were very different.

As we remarked later, our friendship picked up where it had left off over twenty years before. We were laughing, insulting each other, and totally comfortable in our conversation immediately. If we had a "getting reacquainted" period during our interaction, neither of us was aware of it. Our relationship continued as though twenty years of only minimal interpersonal contact had not intervened.

Relationships persist during long periods of noninteraction and absence. Of course, this incident may be somewhat unusual. After all, the typical interpersonal relationship does not involve such a long time lapse between encounters. But every relationship does involve highly discontinuous communication. Periods of hours, days, or weeks intervene between comparatively brief periods of interaction. Then the relationship is reactivated by communication—generally with very little decay in the relationship itself.

Synchrony. A second characteristic of relational quality is the *synchrony* of interpersonal actions. Two people, acting together, create interpersonal communication. They synchronize their actions so that, together, their actions create a recognizable *inter*action. When you interact with a close friend, you always seem to know what to say or how to respond appropriately. And your friend knows what is appropriate in responding to what you say. Together, you and your friend have created a synchronized pattern of actions during your communication.

With even a slight acquaintance, you are also likely to know what response is appropriate because you and an acquaintance also create a synchronized pattern of interaction. But this pattern is one of acquaintanceship rather than friendship. The appropriate response to your friend is often not appropriate in your acquaintanceship interaction. But both types of relationships are synchronized. Your actions "dovetail" (fit together) with the actions of your partner so that, together, they create a unified and identifiable pattern of interaction.

Recurrence. But how do we know how to synchronize our communicative actions with those of our partner? How do we know when an action is "out of sync" with the pattern? The answer is the third characteristic of interactional quality: *recurrence*. All of us have compiled years of experience as interpersonal communicators. By the time you entered kindergarten, you had already been communicating for years. You had known kinships, friendships, acquaintanceships, and a variety of other communicative experiences. At the present stage of your life, you are already a rather sophisticated interpersonal communicator, even though you may not be aware of just how sophisticated you really are.

Your years of communicative experience have allowed you to enact relationships with others, to create synchronized interaction patterns, and to recognize when some action (yours or another's) is "out of sync" with the pattern. You have learned interactional synchrony as a result of the most common of learning modes: sheer repetition. You have participated in so much interpersonal communication, so many interpersonal relationships, that you already know a great deal about what is appropriate and what is not.

You also know, based on your communicative experiences, what criteria to use in order to evaluate interactional synchrony in any relationship. In interaction with a new acquaintance, for example, you know that the criteria for assessing synchrony come from the cultural context—the rules for doing "small talk" in acquaintanceships. In interaction with a close friend, you know that the criteria for assessing interactional synchrony come from your history of past interaction with that friend.

In other words, you can recognize a perfectly appropriate synchronized interaction of acquaintanceship as appropriate to that kind of relationship. But if that same interaction occurred between you and your friend, you would both know that something was wrong. That is, you and your friend would know that your interaction was "out of sync" because you were both using the same criteria to evaluate its synchrony. Those criteria are found in the recurrent, familiar patterns that have characterized your interaction (that relationship) in the past.

The interaction of close friends is so synchronized that other persons, outside that particular relationship, would experience great difficulty in understanding or interpreting the behaviors of either partner, let alone the particular synchrony of their patterns or interactional behavior. Persons outside their relationship are not familiar with the distinctive pattern of synchronized actions because they did not participate in enacting or creating those patterns. On the other hand, the relational partners themselves did create those patterns and hence are very familiar with their own recurring patterns. To outsiders, each partner may appear to be highly sensitive to what the other is feeling inside. In reality, they are just familiar with the synchronized "flow" of their interaction and are thus sensitive to any action that deviates from their own familiar synchronized pattern.

Reciprocity. Earlier we discussed *reciprocity* as a norm of social behavior and a characteristic of self-disclosing communication. But reciprocity is also characteristic of all interaction. You will recall that reciprocity can mean responding to another's action in kind. If Alfred self-discloses to Betty, Betty reciprocates by self-disclosing to Alfred. If Alfred insults Betty, Betty reciprocates by insulting Alfred. But reciprocity involves additional ways in which participants enact or define their relationship with each other.

Generally speaking, reciprocity is the quality of interaction in which each interactant reciprocates the other's definition of their relationship. If Alfred asks a question of Betty, for example, then Alfred is defining his relationship with Betty as one of questioner and answerer. Betty would be reciprocating Alfred's definition of the relationship by providing an answer to Alfred's question. Responding in kind (the "do-unto-others" definition) would suggest that Betty would reciprocate a question by asking another question. But reciprocity, as a quality of interaction, maintains the synchrony of interaction. By responding to Alfred's question with an answer, Betty reciprocates Alfred's definition of the relationship as one of questioner-answerer. In this way, both Alfred and Betty have the same definition of their relationship. Alfred provided the initial definition of their relationship with his question, and Betty reciprocated that definition with an answer.

You might think that this example of a questioner-answerer relationship is rather outdated, given the contemporary cultural tendency to use questions as indirect answers. Consider, for example, the following conversation of Alfred and Betty:

A: Hey, Betty! Want to go get a cuppa coffee?
B: Is the Pope Catholic?
A: Great! How about the cafeteria?
B: Aw, come on! Do submarines have screen doors?
A: Yeah, you're right. Why stay on campus? That pizza place across the street shouldn't be busy this time of day. Want to try there?
B: You wanna lead the way?

This conversation illustrates a high level of synchrony, with Alfred consistently in the role of questioner and Betty consistently providing answers. Even though every one of Betty's answers appears grammatically as a question, both relational partners are clearly aware that inquiries as to the pope's religious preference or a submarine's accessibility function as answers to previous questions and not as serious interrogations requiring answers.

In contrast, the following conversation includes little reciprocity of relational definitions and, consequently, is not highly synchronized:

A: Hey, Betty! Want to go get a cuppa coffee?
B: Why? Are you hungry?
A: Does that mean you don't want to go?
B: Did I say that?
A: Shall we go or not?
B: How long do you want to stay?
A: Did you know that you always answer questions with a question?
B: Do I?

This conversation is going nowhere. Alfred maintains his role as questioner, but Betty resists his relational definition and consistently redefines their relationship with herself in the role of questioner. Alfred appears frustrated at the lack of reciprocity in their conversation and, in his final comment, overtly recognizes that lack of reciprocity by introducing it as a topic of their conversation. His overt attempt to enforce reciprocity doesn't work, though. Betty responds with yet another question.

These, then, are the four *primary* characteristics of interactional quality: *discontinuity, synchrony, recurrence,* and *reciprocity.* Of these four, synchrony is probably the most important to improving your communicative skills. To the degree that the patterns of interpersonal communication are synchronized, your interpersonal relationship is well defined. The lower the level of synchrony, the less clear is the definition of your relationship.

Most definitions of interpersonal relationships focus on the central importance of interaction and these major characteristics of the quality of that interaction. Denzin (1970) provides such a typical definition:

> A relationship exists between two or more people when those people engage in recurrent forms of either symbolic or co-present interaction. . . . For a relationship to exist[,] the parties involved must share the same or similar set of reciprocal definitions about the other. Further, these definitions must extend through time so that the influence of the other does not disappear when he is out of physical, face-to-face presence. . . . It is possible to speak, then, of relationships that are reciprocated and those that are nonreciprocated. Further, there are those that are reciprocated, but unevenly so. (pp. 67–68)

Denzin's final sentence addresses an important fact concerning these characteristics of interactional quality: each is a *variable*. That is, each characteristic is present in all interaction, and it is present to some extent or in some amount. Some interactions are more synchronized than others, for example, but every interaction possesses some level of synchrony that varies from "very low" to "very high." All interactions are discontinuous, but some relationships have more frequent and longer periods of noninteraction than do others. All interactions involve reciprocity, but some relationships have more reciprocity than others. Some interaction patterns are more familiar or more recurrent than others, even in the same relationship.

An analogy may serve to explain more clearly what is meant by a variable, that is, something that varies. Height is a physical characteristic possessed by every human being, and height is a variable of an individual's physical quality. It would be foolish to say of someone that he or she has "no height." Such a statement is, on the face of it, ludicrous. We might say that a person is really short (that is, possesses a low degree of height) or tall (that is, possesses a high degree of height). But we will always recognize that height is a variable of physical characteristics and is present in all human beings. Thus, we should similarly think of the characteristics of interactional quality as variables present in all interaction and in all relationships. But each characteristic will exist in greater or lesser amount in a particular interaction.

Secondary Characteristics

The secondary characteristics of interactional quality include those qualities we typically attribute to the internalized feelings of one or more individuals. These secondary traits characterizing the quality of interaction result directly from the discontinuity, synchrony, recurrence, and reciprocity of interactional quality. A partial list of these secondary characteristics is discussed in the following pages: *intensity*, *intimacy*, *trust*, and *commitment*. When used to characterize a relationship, these traits describe the interpersonal bond created by interaction.

Intensity. The strength or potency of a relationship indicates its degree of *intensity*. To the extent that the interpersonal bond of the relationship (whether friendship or enmity) is strong, that relationship might be said to be very intense. A relationship with high intensity is likely to influence the participants even when one is not in the immediate physical presence of the other.

Intimacy. The degree of closeness between the participants is a gauge of their *intimacy*. We occasionally use this word in our everyday speech and imply a connotation of a purely physical or sexual relationship. "Intimate relations," for instance, is often used as a euphemism for sexual intercourse. We are using "intimacy" here as a much broader term, describing the closeness of the relationship or interpersonal bond. To the extent that a relationship is intimate, the partners experience a very close friendship. A nonintimate relationship (that is, possessing a low level of intimacy) would characterize a casual acquaintanceship or a relationship between people who hardly know each other.

Trust. To the extent that the partners freely engage in high-risk behaviors when interacting with each other, their relationship is characterized by *trust*. Trust exists in the interaction to the extent that the partners mutually risk their selves (that is, their own definitions of self) when they interact with each other. Of course, trust (like every other secondary characteristic of interactional quality) is synchronized or reciprocated to some extent in the interaction. The interpersonal trust may exhibit a high level of reciprocated trust (for example, Alfred trusts Betty to the same extent that Betty trusts Alfred) or a low level of reciprocity (for example, Alfred trusts Betty much more than Betty trusts Alfred).

More importantly, perhaps, interpersonal trust is typically limited to a specific area of interaction or interpersonal behaviors. Alfred may trust Betty to be discreet in maintaining a confidence, so he might tell her a secret (thereby risking his self) and trust her not to blab it to everyone else. On the other hand, Alfred may not trust Betty to catch him if he should fall down, precisely because he knows that Betty does not have the ability (that is, the physical strength) to be worthy of that trust. Within the same relationship, Alfred and Betty may exhibit high trust in some of their interaction patterns and a low level of interpersonal trust in some others.

Commitment. The quality of the interaction that reveals the extent to which the individual includes his or her self in the relationship indicates the participant's *commitment*. As such, a relationship with a high level of commitment is one that is more likely to persist (that is, to last longer) than is another with a lower level of commitment. Relationships with high commitment tend to endure through periods of adversity as well as contentment, through good times and bad, in sickness and in health, despite long periods when there is no interaction.

Relationships with high levels of commitment may not be the most intimate relationships, although they often (perhaps typically) are. Couples who have been married for thirty, forty, or fifty years often remark on the fact that being together is like a habit they can't break. They feel comfortable with each other and have never even considered the alternative of being apart. Such relationships reflect a high level of commitment, even though their interaction may not exhibit much intimacy or intensity. The most appropriate definition of commitment, then, is probably persistence over time—endurance, even though relationships with the highest levels of commitment (that is, identification of self with the relationship) are also likely to be those with correspondingly high levels of intimacy, reciprocity, intensity, and synchrony.

These are some secondary characteristics of the quality of interaction that can be used to describe any and every interpersonal relationship. These characteristics are variables that are present, to some extent, in every interaction. Describing their interaction in terms of these variables defines the interpersonal relationship between the interactants. Two relationships may have some characteristics in common (just as two people may have the same color of hair or eyes), but they will always differ to some extent in one characteristic or another.

When relationships are similar to one another in a variety of these characteristics, we tend to classify those relationships as being of a certain type. For example, relationships with relatively high levels of synchrony, intimacy, reciprocity, commitment, and recurrence are likely to be classified together under a general category of *friendship*. A relationship with relatively low levels of these same characteristics is apt to be classified as *acquaintanceship*. Our discussions later in this chapter will return to the characteristics of interactional quality in clarifying the similarities and differences in different types of interpersonal relationships.

NEGOTIATING INTERPERSONAL RELATIONSHIPS

Nearly all of us are familiar with "negotiation." We have a general idea of what this word means—people sitting down and talking with one another in order to reach some sort of agreement. But negotiation is much more common than we might think. It occurs very frequently in everyday situations. You undoubtedly engage in negotiation yourself. At one time or another, you may have entered into negotiations with your parents to get a higher allowance or to use the family automobile. You may have negotiated with an instructor concerning the grade received on an assignment or in a course. You and your friends negotiate with one another in order to decide what to do on a given night: go to a movie, go to a dance, go to the basketball game, go cruising, and so on. Negotiation is a much more common and routine occurrence than we often think.

A process of negotiation begins with the participants fully aware that they are very different from one another. Negotiation is essentially a process of talking together in order to resolve those differences or reach agreement on some point of commonality. It often involves disagreement, compromise, and argument; but it always involves communication. In fact, all interpersonal communication is, to some extent, a process of negotiation. Two human beings who are different from one another negotiate their individual differences and come to some understanding or settlement that defines their interpersonal relationship.

In formal settings, negotiators represent the interests of some larger body of people, such as the workers or the company, labor or management. Those larger groups have different interests, different desires, different motivations, different goals. When two people engage in interpersonal communication, each person represents his or her own self in negotiating interpersonal relationships. Each communicator has interests, desires, motivations, and goals that are quite different from those of the other. The purpose of the communication process, then, is to arrive at some sort of agreement on areas common to both communicators. That agreement is the interpersonal relationship. It is created neither because of nor despite the differences in goals, motives, interests of the individual selves. Rather, the interpersonal relationship is *in addition to* these individualized differences.

Elements of Negotiating Relationships

The process of creating interpersonal relationships through negotiating individual selves is a unique blend of opposites—opposing forces that are present during communication. Two different individual selves engage in the same activity, talk, in order to reach agreement on things about which they differ at the outset. Each communicator attempts to protect his or her self at the same time he or she is risking self by engaging in the social exchange of communication, by relating with the other person. To understand interpersonal communication is to understand the process of negotiating differences. To understand negotiation is to understand how it blends opposites together into the common interpersonal activity of communication.

Cooperation and Competition

Every time you communicate with another human being, you are engaging in an act that contains elements of both cooperation and competition. You compete with the other person in the sense that you have a self-concept to protect, an image of your self that you wish to maintain. Of course, the other person competes with you at the same time and for the same reason: to protect his or her self-concept. In a very real sense, your self is "competing" with the self of the other person. Your self is quite different from the other person's self, and you (as well as the other person) strive to protect and maintain that self.

While you are competing, you and your communicating partner are cooperating, too. You both speak the same language, you use the same social skills learned in previous encounters, you follow essentially the same cultural rules, you recognize the same social environment, you are both oriented to the same act of social exchange and the topic under discussion, and you follow the rules of taking turns in conversation. Hence, while you are communicating, you are both competing and cooperating with your partner. You both recognize the indisputable fact that you are individually different at the same time that you seek areas of similarity—common interests, experiences, desires, and so on.

During communication, you and your partner are negotiating those differences that separate you. Without necessarily being aware of it, you and your partner are creating something that did not exist when you began interacting. Inevitably, you and your communicating partner will negotiate a settlement, a relationship, that binds you together in some definable and recognizable way. You simply cannot avoid creating that relationship any more than you can avoid communicating.

Your relationship, even a negative or undesirable one, will evolve as you continue the process of interpersonal communication. The precise nature or definition of your interpersonal relationship becomes increasingly clear as you continue your interaction. Whatever the relational settlement that evolves from your negotiation, it will contain elements of both cooperation and competition. In other words, your relationship binds the two of you together into a social unit but maintains the self-identities that make you different.

Commodities and Self

A negotiation process involves the exchange of commodities that one negotiating party possesses and the other desires. When you negotiate with an automobile salesperson, for example, you have a commodity (money) desired by the sales agent and the agent has a commodity (the automobile) desired by you. You compete with each other in the sense that you don't wish to pay more than you can afford and the sales agent doesn't wish to give up too much profit. You then offer your commodity (an amount of money) and the salesperson tells you how much car you can buy for that amount. Each of you offers the commodity you possess in return for some offer of the commodity that the other person possesses. Negotiation, described in this manner, is a series of offers and counteroffers. Each negotiator negotiates by offering some portion of the possessed commodity to the other and expects the other to offer his or her commodity.

Interpersonal communication also involves making offers to the other person in exchange for offers of the other person's desired commodity. The "commodity" each person possesses (and thereby "offers") in interpersonal communication is, of course, the communicator's self. Offering a portion of self, however, should not be confused with disclosing your self to another person. Self-disclosure assumes that you have something to hide from the other person, and that you can reveal your hidden self if you so desire. Self-offering, on the other hand, assumes that your self is a commodity that you possess and may choose to invest in the relationship.

Every time you participate in interpersonal communication, you are making an offer to the other person—an offer of your own self. You value your self as the commodity you have available to invest in the negotiation process, and you value the other person's self as a commodity that you desire. Each time you communicate, you thereby offer that much more of your self to the relationship. And, of course, each time the other person communicates, that person is offering more of his or her self. Like the offers you make when you are negotiating the purchase of an automobile, you have several options you can use to respond to the other person's offer: you can reject it, accept it, ignore it, make a counteroffer, and so on. And, of course, the other person has the same options in responding to your offers.

Risk and Obligations

Interpersonal communication always involves some element of risk. By engaging in interaction, we automatically subject our selves to some obligations and restrict somewhat our own absolute freedom of choice. No longer do we have the right to do anything that we please; we give up some part of that right when we respond to the actions of another person.

Let me illustrate the risks and obligations inherent in the process of interpersonal communication. Some time ago I was riding to campus on a transit bus, and the person sitting next to me initiated a conversation. He said something like "Boy, the bus sure is crowded this morning, isn't it?" Without thinking too much about it, I replied, "Yeah, I guess everybody is going to work at the same time." By responding and entering into the conversation and thus contributing to enacting the relationship, I was "stuck" with continuing the conversation.

Whenever you engage in interpersonal communication, you offer something of your self to the other person.
(Elizabeth M. Wood/Lightwave)

He went on to ask, "Are you going to the university? Most of these people on the bus look like students." I responded that I was indeed on my way to the university and, in subsequent responses, that I was on the faculty of the communication department, that communication certainly was important in today's world, that I didn't know any of his acquaintances in other departments, that the campus surely had changed in the last twenty years, and so on and so on. I also learned that he was an executive in a financial institution, that he was on his way to his downtown office, that he was concerned about some pending legislation affecting banking regulations, that he was a graduate of the university, and so on and so on.

I'm not sure he was aware that his initial question and my response had placed us both in an interactional situation that "obligated" us to continue our interaction. I know that I was not aware of any obligation to participate until I had already become immersed in the conversation. By that time, it was too late for either of us to do much about it until the bus reached my stop and I got off.

The only way either of us could have avoided the obligation of carrying on the conversation would have been to ignore the other person or explicitly state an unwillingness to talk. Such behavior, though, would have entailed being rude, given the rules governing the small talk of new acquaintances in our society. I certainly did not want to risk my own self-concept by engaging in rude behavior, and I suspect that he felt the same constraint. We continued our conversation virtually nonstop until I left the bus.

To my knowledge, I have not seen that person since that day. Our relationship remains a single-encounter acquaintanceship. But during the time of our conversation, we had obligated each other to continue the interaction. Further, we did so just by entering into interaction. Communication itself contains inherent obligations on the part of the participants, even though neither interactant may be aware of it at the time.

Like any negotiation, interpersonal communication inherently gives each participant the "right" to obligate the other person and, of course, to be obligated by the other person. Thus, enacting an interpersonal relationship will always involve some risk on the part of each individual. Knowing that you are in a situation of risk, you tend to be rather tentative—you "test the waters" before plunging headlong into the depths. As in any negotiation, the more you risk of your self, the more you have to gain from the relationship—and the more you have to lose, too.

Unity and Diversity

In all this talk about risks and obligations of self, we sometimes lose sight of the fact that interpersonal communication is really a temporary alliance of very different people who *remain* very different people when they are not communicating or relating with each other. The relationship is the "glue" that holds two individuals together. In other words, every relationship includes two or more individuals who remain unique, even though they are united in the interpersonal relationship.

Within each and every relationship are elements of both unity and diversity, similarities and differences, inclusion and exclusion. Even the closest of friends or the most intimate of lovers are individual people who are quite different from each other. Furthermore, they spend most of their time separated from one another and thus not actually "in relationship." Only a part of each communicator's self is included in any relationship, even the most intimate one. The rest of the self and the rest of the time, each person is quite different from the partner.

When you say, then, that you belong to a social relationship, you are always indicating that the law of partial inclusion is operating. Only part of you belongs to a relationship. Most importantly, maintaining the relationship does not require that you commit more than that part of your self which belongs to it. How much of your self that is will, of course, be up to you. You, the participating individual, decide how much of your self you want to offer to the relationship. You then offer your self, along with the behaviors that you contribute to the relationship and that become patterned with those of your partner.

Communication as a Negotiated Relationship

In creating their relationship, communicators enact a process of negotiating their individual differences (their selves) in order to achieve some common goal (the definition of their relationship). Each of the following characteristics of interpersonal communication is based on viewing the process of enacting relationships as a process of negotiating individual differences.

Interpersonal communication is a blend of cooperation and competition, of commonality and diversity. Every situation of interpersonal communication blends together elements that differentiate the partners from one another (their idiosyncratic personalities) and unify the partners into a single relationship (their interactional pattern). Individuals come together to create interaction. As an individual, each communicator is a unique human being with personal goals, motives, and reasons for entering into a relationship. But these same individuals do have one thing in common: their interaction, their social relationship. Together, individuals create a single outcome: the definition of their relationship. That relationship blends together their own unique and differentiated personalities into a unity—their synchronized interaction patterns, which are theirs and theirs alone. Both the assimilating and the differentiating elements of communication continue to exist throughout their interpersonal relationship.

Interpersonal communication assumes a future agreement on some potential settlement or contract. The title of an old show tune depicts the potential development of any relationship: "This Could Be the Start of Something Big." Who knows what is going to happen in the future when two people interact for the very first time? An appropriate saying, often attributed to Confucius, suggests that "A journey of a thousand miles begins with but a single step." The point is that the eventual outcome of a relationship between any two persons is simply not apparent or predictable from their interaction in early conversations. To be perfectly frank, I can't recall my first interaction with the woman who later became my wife. After twenty-six years of marriage, it probably isn't very important, either.

Every act of interpersonal communication does assume the existence of a potential future, some outcome, some relationship. Some interactions develop into close friendships; many more do not develop beyond the initial meeting. At the time of their first encounter, even the participants have no idea what the relational outcome is likely to be; but the potential for further development is always present, even from the first "Hi, how are you?" greeting. When you begin talking with an automobile sales agent, for example, neither of you knows that the negotiation will conclude with the purchase of an automobile. But the potential for such a contract, settlement, or agreement is present from the very first.

Relationships that persist, that involve commitment (such as close friendships or marriage), never do achieve a "final" stage of development. They are continually negotiated and renegotiated throughout the passing months and years. Just as every individual changes somewhat during the course of a lifetime, so do the relationships in which that individual is a partner. Changes in relationships are a part of the natural process of the evolutionary development of interpersonal communication and require continued negotiation and renegotiation. In other words, relationships are always in a process of becoming, constantly being enacted.

Each participant brings to interpersonal communication a self that is offered as the basic "commodity" to be negotiated through communication. When labor representatives sit down at the bargaining table, they have a "commodity" that they can offer to management representatives—the efforts of their members to produce the services or products of the company. Similarly, management has a "commodity" that it can offer to labor—wages and benefits. Each "side" in the negotiating process has commodities desired by and offered to the other as "bargaining chips." The same principle holds true when individuals negotiate their interpersonal relationships. Each person brings to the situation a "commodity" desired by and offered to the other. In the case of interpersonal communication, that personal commodity is the self of the individual communicator.

In the previous chapter we discussed the law of partial inclusion, which specifies that part of each communicator's self is included in the relationship to the extent that the participant contributes actions to the relational patterns. Furthermore, the relationship neither demands nor desires more than a small portion of the actions of any individual participant. You thus negotiate a relationship with another person by offering certain actions (parts of your self) extended toward the other person. Other persons also "offer" actions or parts of their selves to you.

Together, you and your relational partner create a pattern of interaction that defines your interpersonal relationship. The more actions you offer and that are synchronized with the actions of the other person, the more of your self is included in the relationship and the more likely it is that your relationship reflects a high level of intimacy and intensity. In other words, you risk part of your self every time you act toward the other person during interpersonal communication. In essence, you offer that part of your self to the relationship and obligate that part of your self to the relationship.

Interpersonal communication involves an interactional "settlement" that may or may not incorporate all the offers of each participant's self. Your offering of your self to the relationship in the form of communicative actions does not necessarily mean that you have synchronized your offer into the interactional patterns. The other person has the choice of accepting your offer, rejecting it, ignoring it, or making a counteroffer. You may feel very attracted to the other person and offer a commitment that he or she may not wish to accept. For example, Alfred suggests to Betty that they "go steady" and give up dating other people (an offer incorporating obligation and commitment). Betty likes Alfred, but she also likes dating Charlie and Dave and Eddie. Hence, she makes a counteroffer that they continue dating and think about going steady at some time in the future. The result, in terms of the definition of the relationship, is that Alfred has offered a part of his self (his behaviors), but Betty does not accept his offer. After all, the acceptance of any offer from the other person typically obligates the selves of both partners. When Alfred offered an obligation on his future behavior to forsake dating other people, Betty, by accepting his offer, would also be obligating her own future behavior.

Self-offers, by themselves, do not define the relationship. But the synchronization and reciprocity of self-offers in the pattern of interaction (requiring self-offers of both partners) does define the relationship. In this case, Alfred has self-offered and Betty has also self-offered. Because Betty's self-offer is not congruent with Alfred's, it is more aptly described as a counteroffer. At this point the Alfred-Betty relationship is not well defined because no reciprocity or synchronization is evident. The definition of their relationship will depend on their further interaction and, of course, the recurrence of the reciprocated and synchronized self-offers.

Further, not all offers involve commodities of significant value. That is, not every offer of your self involves a significant part of your self. Your contributions to any conversation may involve topics or interests that do not vitally concern you. Your interactions with friends at work, for example, may be restricted to conversational topics involving your work. You don't discuss topics, such as religion or politics, that you consider important to your self-concept. You don't invite your work partners to your home. You don't offer any part of your self to the relationship that goes beyond the time spent at work. And the other people at work offer no vital parts of self to you.

The result of restricting your self-offers is to limit your interpersonal commu-nication to the work environment. Thus, your relationship does not extend beyond the boundaries of your work context. But your relationship may not demand any greater variety of self offers; any greater degree of commitment may not even be desirable. You and your relational partners may have highly synchronized and reciprocated work-related interaction patterns that are satisfying. The law of partial inclusion functions to provide satisfying relationships, even though your commitment is low.

Negotiated Dimensions of Interpersonal Relationships

Interpersonal communication requires the negotiation of two basic dimensions of a relationship: integration-disintegration and communion-individualism. Figure 10-1 illustrates the intersection of these two dimensions fundamental to interpersonal relationships. The horizontal dimension ("Integration-disintegration") is the dimen-sion of evolutionary development. A relationship that is located to the left of the midpoint on this continuum is one whose interactants are engaging in reciprocal, intense, synchronized interaction. Their interpersonal relationship is growing stronger, at least in the sense that they have integrated their interactive behaviors into a clearly defined pattern of interaction. A relationship located to the right of the midpoint (that is, nearer the "Disintegration" end of the continuum) is one whose participants seem to be growing apart. Their relationship is becoming less reciprocal, less intense, less synchronized. A disintegrating relationship, we could say, is "on the skids."

The vertical dimension (bounded by "Communion" and "Individualism") represents "inclusion of self" in the relationship. A relationship located above the midpoint (nearer the "Communion" end of the continuum) is one whose participants feel closer to one another, more intimate. Crable (1981) uses the term "communion" to refer to "the 'oneness' experienced between two people" (p. 7) and "the almost complete melding of two people into two strong members of a single strong relationship" (p. 291). Crable goes so far as to assert, "Communion is the ultimate

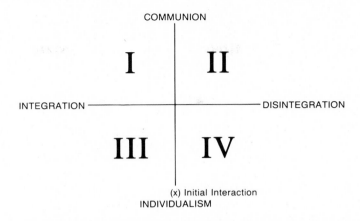

Figure 10-1. Negotiated Dimensions of Interpersonal Relationships

level of human relationship" (p. 7) and describes a relationship located at or very near the top of the "Communion-Individualism" continuum.

"Individualism" characterizes a relationship whose participants retain their highly differentiated identities. They engage in few offers that "risk" their selves; they try not to obligate the other or be obligated by the other during their interaction. Participants in individualized relationships don't change in terms of their own definitions of self very much as a result of having been involved in this communication. They restrict the range of their behaviors; they inhibit their own self-offers during their interaction. They contribute little of their individual selves to the relationship and, as a consequence, they gain (and lose) little for having participated in this relationship.

The individualism-communion dimension denotes, to a large extent, the way the participants themselves define their relationship. If participants ask, "What do *I* get out of this relationship? What does it do for *me*?" then they tend to define their relationship as individualized. If participants define their relationship in terms such as "I am who I am, in part, *because of* this relationship," then they are defining a communal relationship. In other words, participants define their relationship in terms of self (individualism), or they define self in terms of the relationship (communion).

To the extent that the participants in a relationship emphasize their own selves and self-interests, they do not strengthen the relationship. Recall that the elements of the participant's self are those characteristics that make one person different from another. Fundamentally, these characteristics act as a disintegrating influence on the relationship by focusing the participants' attention on things that make them different. Relationships located in quadrants III and IV in Figure 10-1, therefore, are not as strong as the communal relationships of quadrants I and II.

On the other hand, communal relationships also involve more risk of self on the part of the participants. Consequently, when a communal relationship breaks up, the effect is more devastating than when an individualized relationship ends. Generally speaking, communal relationships tend to have more impact on the individual participants; they also tend to be more solid and enduring.

Every one of the relationships in which you participate can be said to fall into one of the four major types represented by the quadrants of Figure 10-1. Type I relationships are highly integrated, communal relationships. Type I relationships include happily married couples, extremely close friends, and tightly knit families or kinships. These relationships would probably be characterized by high levels of reciprocated relational definitions, continuous and frequent interaction, synchrony of interactional patterns, familiar or recurrent interactional patterns, intimacy, commitment, sensitivity, and probably interpersonal trust. If you are fairly typical, you will have very few type I relationships during the course of your lifetime, but you will treasure every one of them. The person who has no type I relationships is poor indeed.

Type II relationships are disintegrating communal relationships and often include relationships that were once rather highly integrated. A couple whose marriage is on the rocks could epitomize a type II relationship, as would friends and relatives whose relationship has been traumatized by some debilitating crisis with which they just couldn't cope. An attorney-acquaintance of mine once told me that his work led him to discover that close families often disintegrated at the time that a wealthy relative died and the will was being probated. Similarly, a friend once told me of losing a friendship because of the unwillingness of the former friend to pay his share of damage to an automobile after a "fender bender" that was his fault. My friend rather cynically confided to me his belief that "The price of friendship is about $50. Above that amount, friendship just doesn't count for much."

Communal relationships more typically disintegrate when their continuity of interaction ceases or abruptly decreases. When close friends separate because one of the partners moves to a different geographical area, they simply have fewer opportunities to interact. Consequently, their relationship begins to disintegrate. Actually, "atrophy" is a more accurate term here than "disintegration." When a broken leg is immobilized in a cast, the leg begins to atrophy from simple lack of use. When the cast is removed, a long period of rehabilitative exercise is needed to return it to its former state. The same is true of interpersonal relationships. Commitment, you will recall, is often a function of persistence or endurance. As interaction tends to be less recurrent and less continuous, it becomes less familiar and thus reflects less commitment, consistent with the adage "Out of sight, out of mind." Hence, type II relationships—communal and disintegrating—often occur when partners in former type I relationships become separated and have little opportunity to communicate. Thus, their relationship atrophies.

Type III relationships are integrated and individualized. They include those relationships that are relatively well defined but not very close. Certain acquaintanceships may include frequent periods of interaction, but they do not develop much "oneness" or unity. Interactants in such relationships are quite content to let the relationship stay at a type III stage of development. Neither partner risks very much or allows self to become highly obligated to the other. Partners may refer to each other as "just friends," but they wouldn't consider their relationship to be any "big deal."

Interpersonal relationships in a work environment often become type III relationships. The partners interact rather frequently—up to eight hours a day and five days a week. But they restrict their communication to that environment, use only conversational topics related to the work environment, and have little interaction outside the workplace. Consequently, their relationships become rather well defined and reflect a high degree of reciprocity, recurrence, continuity, and synchrony. But their interaction also involves little intimacy, commitment, sensitivity, or intensity.

So far, our discussions have included only relationships with positive outcomes. But what about enemies—especially devout and dedicated enemies (type III relationships)? We could characterize such relationships as exhibiting high levels of reciprocity (they hate each other's guts!), intensity (the level of their negative feelings is high), and even synchrony (each person knows how the other will respond). But the relationship of enmity is probably highly discontinuous. People who don't like each other tend to avoid interpersonal contact with each other. (Remember our earlier discussion of autistic hostility?) Consequently, even though a type III relationship is highly integrated, the partners' reciprocated definitions of the relationship are based more on emotional responses than on actual interaction. A type III relationship, perhaps more than any other kind, is quite unlikely to change or evolve to a different type of relationship.

Type IV relationships are disintegrating and individually defined by the participants. Such relationships may be the most common of the four different types represented by the quadrants in Figure 10-1. You have undoubtedly met people at parties, on the bus, in supermarket checkout lines, and other places—people whom you are unlikely to encounter ever again, at least on any regular or expected basis. You probably have (in terms of sheer numbers of people) more casual acquaintances than type I, type II, and type III relationships combined. But type IV relationships probably mean less to you and affect your self-definition far less than any other type of relationship. Your interaction with casual acquaintances is brief and infrequent (low continuity), you learn very little about the other person (low reciprocity), you rarely interact with them (low level of recurrence). Basically, you just don't really care very much about your casual acquaintances (that is, low intensity, low intimacy, low sensitivity, low commitment). Consequently, type IV relationships exert little impact on your life or your self-concept, even though they are large in number.

When you negotiate a relationship "from scratch," you must begin at some point—the point of your first meeting, your initial interaction. That first encounter is not really included within one of the four types of relationships shown in Figure 10-1. "Initial interaction" is characterized by a high level of individual differences, of course, but is neither integrating nor disintegrating in terms of evolutionary development. There is just too much uncertainty, too little information, about the other person to call it a relationship. This point is the "ground zero" of a relationship, the midpoint of the integration-disintegration dimension, and the lowest point on the individualism-communion dimension.

During the process of interpersonal communication, interactants negotiate a relationship that evolves into a certain type. If they expect (or desire) no further interactional encounters, they will immediately and persistently negotiate a type IV relationship and remain casual acquaintances. If they take an immediate dislike to one another, they may negotiate a type III relationship and terminate their interaction, although their mutually unfavorable definition of the relationship will probably persist. If they anticipate that their initial interaction could lead to "something big," they may eventually progress to a type I relationship. But evolution does not happen immediately. In fact, such evolution is a very slow and sometimes painful process.

The love-at-first-sight phenomenon is basically a myth perpetuated by popular music, romantic novels, television dramas, and paperback fiction. "Friendship," according to Mortimer Adler, "is a very taxing and arduous form of leisure activity." What appears in afterthought to have been "smooth sailing all the way" is far more typically a laborious process with many ups and downs. Romantic couples who claim it was love at first sight are most likely to be demonstrating a poor memory than an accurate picture of their initial interaction. Certainly there may be a few exceptions to this "rule," but they are so few as to be unworthy of our attention. Partners may take a liking to one another during that brief period of initial interaction (because of physical attractiveness, for example) and, as a result, will continue and repeat their interactional encounters until they evolve into a type I or type II relationship. Upon reflection, partners in satisfying type I relationships may recall that first feeling of attraction and interpret it as having been "love at first sight."

These four types, defined by the quadrants in Figure 10-1, certainly don't represent the only way to classify interpersonal relationships. They are merely general groupings that enable us to interpret somewhat more precisely what a particular interpersonal relationship means or entails. It is now time to focus on the process of interpersonal communication—what people actually *do* when they communicate with one another.

ISSUES

When two people get together in an act of interpersonal communication, what do they do? Primarily, they talk. When people communicate, what do they talk about? If you answer this question by merely listing topics of conversation (such as the weather, last night's basketball scores, Johnny's new girlfriend, Joan's new car), you are looking at communication only superficially. When they are negotiating what their relationship is going to be, people use such topics in order to discover the answers to questions they consider essential to their eventual "settlement"—the definition of their relationship. Those questions important to negotiating the relationship are known as "issues."

Interpersonal communication is principally talk about specific issues that need to be addressed so that some agreement is possible. In formalized negotiations (such as those between labor and management in a collective bargaining situation), the negotiators begin by trying to discover their points of agreement and disagreement. Each of these points is an issue—a question that, until answered, is a topic to be negotiated or resolved. Some issues are common to virtually every act of interpersonal communication, while others are common to particular stages of the developing relationship. Still other issues are unique to the specific individuals and the relationship they have negotiated. But all interpersonal communication revolves around one or more relational issues.

In the following pages we will discuss two general types of issues that are typical of most interpersonal communication: *informational issues* and *relational issues*. Some of these issues need to be resolved before people can move on to others, and some are typical of particular types of interpersonal relationships. But all involve questions that will guide much of the talk occurring during interpersonal communication.

Informational Issues

Recall that the beginning stages of interpersonal communication involve the need to reduce uncertainty. The situation is new to both participants, and each person is new to the other. The opening stages of such conversations include attempts to reduce uncertainty about the situation and the other person. At such times, certain relational issues are of paramount importance: Who am I? Who is this other person? Do we have anything at all in common? Is it worth my time to continue talking with this person? Will I ever see this person again? Do I want to see this person again? Each of these questions (and many more like them) is an issue that the participants attempt to answer during their initial conversations.

The informational issues peculiar to the beginning stages of interpersonal communication are rather simple. They arise from the newness of the situation and the other person; they arise from a simple lack of information. Hence, communicators find such issues rather easily resolved. All they need to do is acquire information about the other person.

Most of us are fairly skilled at resolving informational issues. We engage in small talk. It is difficult to imagine that the issues addressed by small talk are potentially points of disagreement or conflict. They are simply questions that arise from a state of ignorance—that is, a lack of information. But it takes more than just information to resolve other issues. When their conversation begins to involve issues of each person's self in relation to the other, the communicators find that they need more sophisticated communicative skills. That is, they need more than information to resolve *relational issues*.

Relational Issues

Two relational issues are fundamental to all interpersonal communication: Who am I in relation to you? Who are you in relation to me? Of course, these are the issues as each individual communicator would phrase them intrapersonally. At the interpersonal or relational level, these same issues describe the exchange of talk between the communicators and involve three different classes of issues: (1) "self-as-object," (2) "self-as-other," and (3) "self-as-relational" issues. Although other issues may be important to specific stages of development or specific situations, these three classes of issues are basic to all of interpersonal communication.

Self-as-Object Issues. When interacting about self-as-object issues, neither participant is really taking the other person's experiences, attitudes, or interests into account. Figure 10-2 illustrates a conversation between Alfred and Betty when they are addressing self-as-object issues. Alfred and Betty are engaged in conversation about some topic (denoted as "X" in Figure 10-2, on page 222). Alfred orients his self toward the topic X, and Betty also orients her self toward the common topic X.

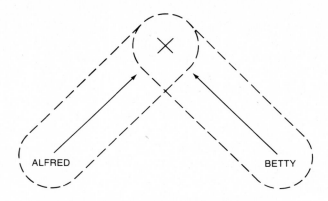

Figure 10-2. Orientation of Interaction Regarding
Self–as–Object Issues

Alfred contributes to the conversation about X only his own personal experiences, attitudes, and interests. Similarly, Betty contributes only her own personal experiences, attitudes, and interests to the conversation about X.

Interpersonal communication addressing self-as-object issues might look something like this:

A: I really had a tough day at work today. Virtually everything seemed to go wrong.

B: My day was pretty normal. I don't know why that is. Some days seem to go pretty fast; others seem to just drag.

A: The first thing that happened was I walked in the door, and the boss was all over me. He wanted to know why I was late. I wasn't late, at least not very late.

B: Yeah, I know what you mean. I remember last week I was just two minutes late, and Jeri wanted to know whether I tied one on the night before.

A: Yeah, really. Then I just couldn't seem to concentrate. I kept looking at the clock all day. It just didn't seem to move.

B: Yeah, I've had days like that, too. Sometimes 5 o'clock just never seems to come.

Self-as-object interaction is essentially conversation in which each communicator defines his or her self in relation to a common topic. Each person takes turns addressing the topic, but rarely do they talk about the other person's comment except as it relates to their own individual experiences. The above conversation is a series of that-same-thing-happened-to-me comments. Neither person attempts to define his or her self in relation to the other. Rather, each person defines his or her self in relation to a common topic. As a result, two individual selves (objects) are related coincidentally to a single topic of conversation. Such conversation means repeatedly taking turns, with each person using the turn to "do his or her own thing."

Have you ever had a joke-telling session with friends? The interaction is very

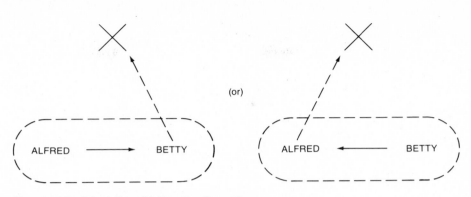

Figure 10-3. Orientation of Interaction Regarding
Self–as–Other Issues

similar. One person tells a joke. the others laugh, and then another person takes a turn telling a joke. You contribute to this conversation as respondent to the other person's joke, but your real contribution is your own joke. So you "wait your turn" to tell it. You have probably often found yourself in such conversations and probably get the feeling that each person is trying to top the others. As a result, you probably begin paying less attention to the others' jokes and spending more effort trying (often desperately) to remember the good jokes that you heard at some time in the distant past.

Self-as-Other Issues. Interaction concerning self-as-other issues takes the form of one person telling the other about his or her experiences and the other person talking about those same experiences. Figure 10-3 illustrates conversation surrounding self-as-other issues. In attempting to resolve self-as-other issues, Alfred orients his self toward some topic and Betty orients her self toward Alfred. (Of course, either Alfred or Betty could be oriented to the other person who is, in turn, oriented to the topic.) The communication addressing self-as-other issues is similar to the interaction of a therapist with a client. The client contributes self experiences and the therapist encourages the client's talk about those experiences. The therapist is a helper, a respondent, a sympathetic listener—but not an active contributor of self experiences.

The following conversation between Alfred and Betty is reminiscent of self-as-other interaction:

A: Boy, this finger hurts! I was playing basketball yesterday, and I jammed my little finger on the ball. It's really sore!

B: Have you tried soaking it in cold water? That's what I always do—to keep it from swelling.

A: Yeah, I did that right away, and I think it helped some. Actually, it didn't hurt too much last night. I mean I didn't have any trouble sleeping. But I woke up this morning, and I could hardly move it.

B: Maybe you bumped it in the night while you were sleeping.

A: I don't think so. But I was sleeping. How do I know if I bumped it?

B: Maybe you ought to see a doctor. You could have broken a bone or something.

A: No, I don't think so. I've jammed fingers lots of times.
B: Still, it can't hurt to see a doctor. You'd probably feel better.
A: Well, maybe you're right.

Both Alfred and Betty are contributing to the same topic—Alfred's jammed finger. But that topic "belongs to" Alfred in the sense that it is his personal or self experience. Betty thus contributes to the topic indirectly. She does not contribute her own experiences concerning jammed fingers; rather, she attempts to provide assistance to Alfred's experience. She is the sympathetic listener, the "therapist" attempting to help Alfred.

Of course, self-as-other interaction doesn't require Betty's contribution to be positive or helpful. She could also be totally unsympathetic and confrontative, as in the following interaction:

A: Boy, this finger hurts! I was playing basketball yesterday, and I jammed my little finger on the ball. It's really sore!
B: Why didn't you soak it in cold water? Any fool knows that's what you do to keep it from swelling.
A: But I did that right away, and I think it helped some. Actually, it didn't hurt too much last night. I mean I didn't have any trouble sleeping. But I woke up this morning, and I could hardly move it.
B: You should have taped it to the next finger. Then you wouldn't have hurt it while you were sleeping.
A: I didn't hurt it while I was sleeping. It just felt worse this morning.
B: How do you know you didn't bump it in the night? You were sound asleep.
A: Well, I don't think I did. I've jammed fingers lots of times. I don't know why this one hurts so much.
B: Oh, don't be such a crybaby. It's just a little finger sprain. You'd think you broke your leg or something.
A: Well, it hurts just the same

This interaction continues to revolve around Alfred's personal experience and Betty's indirect contributions to the topic as she responds to Alfred's experience. The interaction continues to address a self-as-other issue, but Betty's "therapeutic" role has changed. She is no longer sympathetic, no longer helpful. She is unsympathetic and confrontative. But the relational issue being negotiated during this interaction, self as other, remains the same.

Self-as-Relational Issues.   When communicators attempt to negotiate their relationship through self-as-relational issues, their orientation is not to the topic or the other person so much as it is toward the relationship that binds them together. Figure 10-4 illustrates the interaction of Alfred and Betty as they attempt to resolve self-as-relational issues. They continue to be talking about some topic, X, but they are actually addressing it from the viewpoint of their interpersonal relationship. The following interaction reflects Alfred and Betty engaging in interaction addressing a self-as-relational issue:

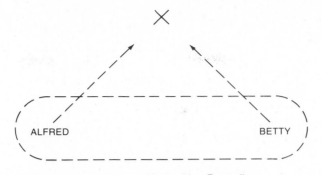

Figure 10-4. Orientation of Interaction Regarding
Self–as–Relational Issues

A: I've been thinking. Maybe we ought to go to sumnmer school next year. I think
    we could get out a lot sooner if we could pick up a few credits during the
    summer.

B: Oh, I don't know. I think we could really have a lot of fun during the summer
    if we didn't have to be hitting the books all the time.

A: Aw, come on! It could be great. We'll still have time to have fun. We could
    play tennis after classes are over; we could swim during the noon hour. And
    we'd still have the weekends.

B: Maybe so, but can we afford it? Tuition and fees are pretty high for just a few
    credits.

A: It's gotta be paid sometime—either during the summer or next spring.

B: Well, it's something to think about, anyway.

Most importantly, self-as-relational interaction assumes that the two selves of
the communicators are interconnected. That is, the self of one relational partner
defines (and is defined by) its relation to the self of the other. During their interaction
revolving around self-as-relational issues, the participants often discuss joint activities—things that both do together. Their conversation includes more than a few
references to "we" and "us."

By contrast, self-as-object interaction may include the same experience (such as
having a tough day at work), but each person's experience is separate from the
other's. The fact that both communicators have the same experience is coincidental.
That is, Alfred had a tough day at work and Betty had a tough day at work. Self-as
object interaction includes two experiences, Alfred's and Betty's. Their interaction
concerns the coincidence that Alfred's experience was similar to Betty's. But in self-
as-relational interaction, only one experience is at issue: the single experience of
Alfred and Betty doing something together.

The issue addressed by the communicators in self-as-relational interaction is the
common orientation of both participants: the relationship, rather than the individual
self of the communicator. Often the relational partners focus their self-as-relational
interaction on a joint experience or activity that involves both communicators, but
they could be talking about any topic that emphasizes their togetherness.

Self-as-relational communication often involves discussion of joint activities.
(Owen Franken/Stock, Boston)

In other words, self-as-relational issues may also involve interaction in which an individual communicator expresses his or her own individual desires or opinions but bases those intrapersonal desires or opinions on criteria derived from the relationship. The following interaction concerns the topic of Alfred's selfish desires, but both participants address Alfred's desire from the viewpoint of their interpersonal relationship:

A: Did I tell you I've got a line on another job? It means I would be making more money, too.

B: That's great.

A: I'm not so sure. It also means that I'll be working every other weekend. We wouldn't be able to see each other much.

B: But still, more money and all. We'll probably survive.

A: I don't wanna just survive. I want to keep seeing you.

B: Well, how late do you work? We can still get together when you're not working.

A: I don't get off until 10 at night. And you're working all day. We'd never see each other.

B: We can still work it out. After all, we'll have all Sunday afternoon to be together.

A: I'm not sure that's enough. I don't think I'll take that job.

B: But it means more money. Just think what we can do with that.

This conversation concerns only Alfred's experience—his new job. But Alfred and Betty discuss his new job *not* in terms of Alfred or Betty individually but in terms of their Alfred-Betty relationship. They continue to talk in "we" terms: *we* will survive, *we* can use the extra money. All the advantages and disadvantages of the new job become topics associated with its effect on their relationship and their relationship's effect on it. The issue addressed in this interaction continues to be self as relational, even though the topic under discussion concerns only the activity or experience of a single communicator rather than one involving both.

If communicators are talking about self-as-relational issues, they must already have negotiated some relationship in the past. Clearly, two people who have just met and are getting acquainted with each other would hardly be engaging in self-as-relational interaction. Only when a relationship has been established somewhat and both parties recognize that some relational settlement has occurred can they address self-as-relational issues.

In summary, self-as-object issues may occur at any time during the developing relationship. New acquaintances seeking areas of common interest will engage in discussions concerning coincidental experiences. Highly developed relationships will also include a fair amount of self-as-object interaction. A husband and wife will typically discuss their experiences when they get together at the end of the day. They will "catch each other up" on what happened to each of them during the day. And those discussions involve taking turns in telling each other what they did since they saw each other last. We already know that interpersonal communication is discontinuous. When friends get together after a period of separation, they will typically engage in "whatcha been doin'?" interaction, which will appear amazingly similar to the interaction of self-as-object issues.

Self-as-other interaction can also occur at virtually any stage of relational development and in virtually any kind of relationship. We often find ourselves needing just to talk with someone. When we feel that need, we often seek out a trusted friend who we know will take on the role of a sympathetic listener. But we will also find ourselves discussing self-as-other issues even with a new acquaintance. To illustrate, I recently met a person who had spent some time in the Middle East during the course of his job as an engineer. Our interaction was almost exclusively devoted to self-as-other issues as he related his experiences and observations about Iran, Saudi Arabia, Israel, Syria, and so on. I found the conversation fascinating. I also discovered a great deal about him, and I suspect that he learned almost nothing about me. After all, I was only an indirect contributor to the central topic, which focused almost exclusively on his experiences.

STRATEGIES

The fundamental unit of interpersonal communication is the *strategy*. Every time you offer your self to the other person during the process of interpersonal communication, you are using a strategy. Why call it a strategy? Because you are always trying to manipulate the other person? Absolutely not! Because interpersonal communication is inherently *consequential*. Every time you offer a comment to a conversation, you potentially affect the negotiated outcome of the interpersonal relationship. Each strategy focuses on one of the issues that must be resolved in order to negotiate the relationship. To the extent that the comment helps to resolve that issue and fits into the pattern of interaction, it is a strategy.

Normally the term "strategy" brings to mind some notion of warfare in which the general adopts a strategy (or tactic) in order to "win" the war (or, at least, the battle). And some strategies in interpersonal communication are similar to that. When we feel that the competing part of communication is greater than the cooperative element, we may be very aware of adopting some strategy to "win" the game of interpersonal communication (such as topping the other person's joke with a funnier one of your own). When we are engaged in an interpersonal situation in which we want to persuade the other person or control the other person's response (such as trying to impress your new acquaintance), we will develop strategies with a high degree of awareness. But probably most often, we communicate with other people strategically, even though we are not aware that our comments (and those of the other person) are strategies.

When you use a strategy during interpersonal communication, you are not always aware that you are using a strategy. You aren't always aware of what portion of your self you have offered to the conversation at the time you offer it. For instance, we often say some things that we later regret having said. We often say some things without thinking about them and later have them come back to haunt us.

At other times, though, we are very aware of what self we are presenting to the other person. In certain situations, we choose our words carefully (that is, are highly aware of what we are saying) in order to get some desired response from the other person. For example, we might want to impress that new acquaintance (you know, the attractive one you'd like to get to know better) with some clever comment in the hope that he or she will respond favorably. The important point is not whether we are aware of what we are saying or doing during communication but that every comment (that is, every self-offer) made during interpersonal communication fits into some pattern and potentially affects the subsequent relationship that is negotiated.

According to at least one psychologist (Mangam, 1981), we are quite unaware of most of the strategies we use in interpersonal communication.

> Much of what is deemed to be "normal" interaction . . . is nonproblematic. Social actors . . . approach interaction already influenced by past social experience and, to a marked extent, their choices (insofar as they are aware of choice at all) are limited, if not determined, by the patterns of behaviour most frequently used by other social actors past and present in what are taken to be similar circumstances. (p. 198)

In other words, we don't negotiate our interpersonal relationships with other people as though we were totally inexperienced. We don't attempt to negotiate relationships anew on each and every social occasion. To a large extent, we are the product of our own past experiences. We know what strategies to use in virtually every interpersonal situation because we've "been there" before. We approach the new communicative situation from our experiences of having been in similar situations in the past. Consequently, we use the strategies that proved successful in the past, and we probably aren't even aware that we are doing so. Only when the situation is new or when some change in the relationship is occurring are we likely to be aware of the strategic choices we are making as we communicate.

Much of what we have come to know as "skill" in interpersonal communication is not really a matter of learning some new techniques or practicing how to be fluent in conversation. Rather, such skill is more likely to involve increasing your awareness of what you are doing while you are engaged in interpersonal communication—that is, being aware that the comments you are making during communication are actually strategic choices. With such increased awareness, you are then able to choose the strategies (your self-offers) that are most appropriate and beneficial to the process of negotiating the relationship you want to have.

The number of potential strategies you could use in any given situation is undoubtedly extremely large. And, of course, the same comment may function as one kind of strategy in one pattern of interaction and a different kind of strategy when it occurs within a different pattern of interaction. It is probably best to think of strategy, then, as an *action* you contribute to the pattern of *interaction*. Therefore, your strategy performs some function because you direct your action toward some relational issue.

In the following pages we shall discuss the various types of strategies in terms of how a particular strategic comment functions within the interaction pattern— whether you direct your strategy toward your self, toward the other person, toward the relationship, toward the situation or context, toward the communicative goal, or toward a specific issue. The following sections discuss each type of strategy and provide some representative examples of each.

Self-Directed Strategies

One class of strategies focuses the topics of the interaction on your own self and your self-offers. The purpose of such a strategy is to inform the other person of a direct connection between your behavior and your self. When you use a self-directed strategy, you are essentially telling the other person how to interpret your self-offer. Most of our strategies do not include an explicit rationale for the behavior. We leave it to the other person to draw some inference about the internal motives or desires that prompt us to behave as we do. On the other hand, we also have the option of telling the other person "how come" we're doing what we're doing. When we choose that option, we are employing a self-directed strategy.

Account Giving. Probably the most common self-directed strategy is giving *accounts*. That is, the communicator strategizes the comment by telling the other person explicitly the reason or reasons for the behavior. In other words, the communicator *accounts for* his or her behavior. Accounts often occur when one of the communicators is accused of committing some offense or error in a previous comment.

When accused of committing some offense, the communicator has several options or strategies to account for the alleged erroneous behavior. One, the offender can provide an account that tells the other person that the alleged offense did not, in fact, occur, such as, "I didn't say that at all." Two, the offender can account for the offensive behavior by attributing the problem to the other person's faulty perception or hearing, as in "I think you misunderstood what I was saying" or "You didn't hear me correctly." Three, the offender can attribute the alleged offense to the situation that forced the improper behavior—"I know that was wrong, but I didn't have any choice." Four, the offender can account for the problem by denying responsibility for the problematic behavior, as in "I didn't mean to say that," "That's not what I intended to say," or "I'm sorry, that was a stupid thing to say." These kinds of accounts attempt to provide excuses or justifications for one's own behavior, particularly when that behavior was erroneous or offensive.

Account giving may also be a strategy to make your intentions or purposes clear to the other person. In other words, you include with your comment the reason (that is, your internal motivation or intention) for making that comment. You will often hear yourself saying something like "I'm just trying to help you" or "I'm saying this only because I really like you." You may also tell the other person how to react to your comment (for example, "You can take it or leave it. That's up to you") or how you will react to his or her response (for example, "You can certainly disagree with me. That won't hurt my feelings").

By using accounts you attempt, in every case, to inform the other person explicitly of the connection between your observable behavior and your unobservable intentions, desires, motivations, attitudes, and so on. Of course, saying what your intentions are does not make your statement truthful. You have probably heard people tell you that they wouldn't be upset if you didn't follow their advice. But then, when you disagreed with their advice, they did become upset. Adapting normally to the benefits of past experience, you probably agreed with their advice the next time, even when you really disagreed. In that case, both of you used strategies that were not truthful, but you succeeded in maintaining your relationship.

Flagging. A second type of self-directed strategy is called *flagging*. If you want the other person to be absolutely clear in interpreting the function of your comment, you can "flag" it by telling the other person what its function is in the interaction pattern. By telling the other person this, you assure yourself that the other will find it difficult to misperceive your comment. Typically, flagging is used to introduce your contribution, as in the following: "This is just an idea off the top of my head." "I'd like to say something in support of that." "I'm going to disagree and explain why I'm disagreeing." "Let me check to see that I've got this straight." "Let me tell you what I think you are saying."

Flagging is a strategy that attempts to avoid the problems that ensue when the other person misperceives how your comment functions during the interaction. By introducing your comment with a flagging strategy, you are informing the other person of what to expect and how to interpret your comment. Because it tries to avoid misperceptions on the other person's part, flagging is often helpful. Of course, a flagging strategy is no guarantee that your statement will not be misperceived, but it should help to shape the other person's reactions.

In choosing a flagging strategy, you should make sure that you are accurate in your interpretation of how your comment will function in the interaction pattern. As Peter Honey (1976) points out, "What is fatal is to flag a piece of behaviour incorrectly." You have probably encountered people who continually flag their behavior with introductory comments such as "I'm not really disagreeing with you. I just want to understand." You just know that this "flag" is incorrect. These people don't want to understand; they want to disagree and use the flag in a transparent attempt to appear open-minded. Soon we come to expect this strategy from these people, and we react in exactly the opposite way the other person intended. We hear the person say, "I'm not really disagreeing with you," and our immediate reaction is "Here comes the disagreement."

Whether it is giving accounts or flagging, the use of a self-directed strategy attempts to make explicit what is otherwise implicit during the process of communication. We give accounts for our behavior and explicitly tell the other person what portion of the hidden self has prompted our behavior. We flag our comments with an explicit description of how our comment functions within the pattern of interaction and try to shape the other person's response to it. By choosing self-directed strategies, we attempt to control, shape, or influence the other person's reactions to our interactive behaviors.

Keep in mind that the self-directed strategy is a type of self-offer that the other person may accept or reject. In attempting to shape the other person's perceptions of your self and your self-offer, you have no assurance that your strategy will do so successfully. Whether your strategy works as you intended it to can only be discovered in the interaction patterns that follow.

Other-Directed Strategies

You may also negotiate your relationship with another person by using an *other-directed strategy* that focuses the interaction on the other person. Other-directed strategies function to "do something to" the other person and may be either competitive or cooperative. Other-directed strategies are often competitive in the sense that you are attempting to control the other person's response, to get the other person to do what you want him or her to do. On the other hand, such strategies may also be cooperative if they function to tell the other person that he or she is important or valued. Other-directed strategies often fall into one of two categories: those designed to gain the other person's compliance and those designed to confirm or disconfirm the other person's self.

Compliance Gaining. The class of strategies known as *compliance gaining* involves an attempt to persuade or manipulate the other person. Using a compliance-gaining strategy implies that you see the interpersonal communication situation as a competitive "game" that you are "playing to win." That is, you want the other person to do something. When you want to persuade the other person toward a particular action or belief, you use a compliance-gaining strategy. When you want to control or manipulate the other person's response, you use a compliance-gaining strategy.

Compliance-gaining strategies implicitly view the other person as an object of your persuasive attempts. Compliance-gaining strategies are, of course, the life blood of advertising agencies. Their task is to get the consumer (the TV viewer, radio listener, or magazine reader) to purchase a given product. In other words, advertisers want the consumer to comply with their purpose in communicating with them. Advertising strategies are inherently directed at the "other person"—the consumer.

Two decades ago, psychologists Marwell and Schmitt (1967) developed a list of potential compliance-gaining strategies. Their list (or some variation of it) remains a relatively complete list of such strategies and continues to be used today by scholars interested in exploring how communicators attempt to manipulate each other during interpersonal communication. The following list is adapted from Marwell and Schmitt's original typology:

1. Promise: "If you comply, I will reward you."
2. Threat: "If you do not comply, I will punish you."
3. Debt: "You should comply because you owe me past favors . . . because of all we have meant to each other."
4. Liking: "I am pleasant and friendly toward you so that you will be in a good frame of mind and will comply."
5. Moral appeal: "You should comply because it is the right thing to do."
6. Self-feeling: "You will feel better about yourself if you comply." (positive) "You will feel worse about yourself if you don't comply." (negative)
7. Altercasting: "If you were a good person, you would comply." (positive) "Only a bad person would not comply." (negative)
8. Altruism: "I really need you to comply, so do it for me . . . do it for someone else, not for yourself."
9. Social esteem: "People will think highly of you if you comply." (positive) "People will think poorly of you if you do not comply." (negative)

Each item on this list of compliance-gaining strategies contains basically one of two strategies—reward or punishment—to persuade others to do what is wanted. Whatever compliance-gaining strategy is chosen, the aim is essentially to reward or punish the other person. The idea is to gain the compliance of other people by saying something like "If you do what I want, you will be rewarded in some positive manner" or "If you fail to do what I want, you will be punished in some negative manner." Most people would probably consider such strategies rather heavy-handed and too blunt to be effective. But it is amazing how many of us are swayed by such appeals, especially when they are used in a subtle way.

Not infrequently, however, people use compliance-gaining strategies in a less-than-subtle manner, and their strategies have a boomerang effect. I recall being "pitched" by an insurance sales agent years ago. His attempts to gain my compliance were not at all subtle and were almost exclusively based on punishments rather than rewards. He asked me the same question countless times. He phrased the question differently each time, but the question always came out sounding like "If you *really* loved your family [moral appeal], you would buy additional life insurance—not for yourself, but for them [altruism]." In my interpretation of his compliance-gaining strategy, the insurance agent was saying, "If you don't buy more life insurance, then you don't really love your family." This strategy boomeranged. I reacted very negatively to it and remembered the name of the insurance company represented by that agent. When I did buy additional life insurance some years later, I made sure that I did not purchase it from that company.

A too obvious attempt to gain the other person's compliance may create a negative reaction. People typically don't like the feeling of being manipulated. They resent not only the persuasive strategy but also the person who attempts to manipulate them. Some advertising agencies have apparently recognized this fact and seem to have discarded many of their traditional "hard sell" strategies. The most successful

TV commercials today are subtle. They appear to persuade consumers by entertaining them. We tend to remember the commercials that are funny, clever, and often better than the program they are interrupting. A strategy for selling the product is effective, of course, only insofar as the consumer remembers the product being advertised in the commercial and actually purchases it. The continuing success of "lite" beer commercials suggests that subtle compliance gaining through entertainment may be a very effective strategy in communicating with a mass audience.

Interpersonal Confirmation/Disconfirmation. A second type of other-directed strategy involves the act of *confirmation*. Such a strategy attempts to tell the other person that his or her self is worthwhile or significant. Like compliance-gaining strategies, confirmation may also appear in a negative form—more appropriately called *disconfirmation*. A disconfirming strategy is the opposite of confirmation; it tells the other person that his or her self is not worthwhile or significant.

The other-directed strategies of confirmation and disconfirmation have not been systematized satisfactorily or consistently demonstrated by researchers. However, a general list of how one might go about confirming or disconfirming others in interpersonal communication has been developed. The following one is derived and adapted (with apologies to the original authors) from the work of communication scholars, Ken Cissna and Evelyn Sieburg (1981):

Confirming Strategies

A. Showing respect
   1. Seriously responding to other's comments
   2. Paying attention when other is speaking

B. Showing involvement
   1. Maintains eye contact
   2. Maintains closeness, leans toward other
   3. Uses personal language, expresses feelings

C. Accepting communication
   1. Dialogue, awaits turn to talk
   2. Makes relevant comments

D. Accepting the other person
   1. Expresses praise or agreement
   2. Uses clear and complete messages
   3. Verbal and nonverbal modes of expression agree

Disconfirming Strategies

A. Showing indifference
   1. Silence, refusal to respond
   2. Attention wanders or engages in unrelated activities

B. Denying involvement
   1. Avoids eye contact
   2. Avoids touch, uses "distancing" behaviors
   3. Uses impersonal language, avoids expressing feelings

C. Rejecting communication
   1. Monologue, interrupts, "talks over" other
   2. Makes irrelevant comments

D. Disqualifying the other person
   1. Expresses insults or name calling
   2. Uses unclear and incomplete messages
   3. Verbal and nonverbal modes are incongruent

Although confirming and disconfirming strategies often appear to be the difference between being rude and being polite, a more appropriate interpretation of these other-directed strategies may be the difference between being cooperative and being competitive. When your orientation toward the other is one of cooperation, you tend to participate in the interaction by confirming the other person both verbally and nonverbally. But when you are competitively oriented toward the other person, you will probably tend to use disconfirming strategies.

Be careful of interpreting cooperative and competitive orientations toward the other person to imply that confirming means agreeing and disconfirming means disagreeing. In fact, quite the opposite is often true. When you disagree, you often confirm the worth of the other person's ideas. When disconfirming others, you would be more likely to ignore their comments and, by so doing, tell them "Your ideas aren't important enough for me to disagree with them."

Cooperation and competition, as used in interpersonal communication, are essentially the relationship of one self to another's self. When you feel that your self is in competition with the other person's, you select strategies that tend to disconfirm the other person's self. In conversation with a persistent and "hard sell" sales agent, you may very well use disconfirming strategies. But if there is no need for your self-concept to compete with the other person's self-concept, you are likely to be more cooperative. In those situations, you use strategies that keep the interaction flowing smoothly. Those strategies are cooperative and tend to confirm the worth of the other person's self concept.

Other-directed strategies generally attempt to "do something to" the other person. You can do something good or you can do something bad. Consequently, other-directed strategies tend to have two sides: reward and punishment, cooperation and competition, confirmation and disconfirmation. Although they may originate from a highly selfish goal, such as getting others to do what you want them to, other-directed strategies are oriented to the other's self and not your own. This class of relational strategies may be the most familiar of all those discussed in this chapter. And other-directed strategies may be the most commonly used when people communicate. We may be more aware of using other-directed strategies than we are when we use strategies of other types.

Despite everything that we know (or think we know) about other-directed strategies, though, they are probably less effective than other types of strategies in the long run. People just aren't manipulated very easily, and they often resent being manipulated. Hence, when others become aware that these strategies are being used on them, the strategies often backfire. Compliance-gaining strategies may boomerang and achieve an effect quite opposite of the one desired.

Relationship-Directed Strategies

A comment that functions directly to define your relationship with the other person is a relationship-directed strategy. Some of these strategies are obvious; others are subtle. Some function to create or initiate change in the relationship; others serve to maintain the existing definition of the relationship. Like all strategies, some relationship-directed strategies are successful; others are complete failures. There are probably hundreds of different kinds of relationship-directed strategies, but our discussions will include only two types: "tie-signs" and "control modes."

Tie-Signs. Sociologist Erving Goffman (1971) coined the term *tie-signs* to refer to objects, acts, events, and expressions that provide evidence of a relational bond that exists between two or more people. Tie-signs may include either or both verbal and nonverbal behaviors and function in several different ways. One, they serve to inform the other participant of how you have defined the relationship. Two, they confirm the existing definition of the relationship for the benefit of both participants. Three, they inform people who are within the social context but outside your relationship of the nature of your relationship.

Tie-signs generally fall into one of three different categories: *rituals, markers,* and *change signals.* A ritual is a set of behaviors or events that have been repeated so often that both partners know the meaning of how it confirms the existence of the relationship. To participate in a ritual tie-sign is to have inside information about what to do. And the only way to acquire that inside information is to have participated in the past interactional experiences that created the ritual. A ritual tie-sign "belongs to" the people who created it. An outsider cannot participate in the ritual without appearing out of place. And the ritual of one relationship will not be the ritual of another except by pure coincidence. A ritual is the direct result of repeated interactional experiences by the people in that relationship who then come to identify the ritual with their relationship.

To illustrate, our family has a number of rituals (as does virtually every family) that often seem peculiar to outsiders. For example, on Christmas morning at our house, Santa Claus comes (even to daughters who have already celebrated their twenty-first birthday). I prepare a big breakfast for everyone, and then we unwrap the presents under the tree. We also unwrap presents one at a time, beginning with the youngest member of the family and taking turns until all the gifts have been opened. On several occasions we have had guests who became frustrated with our family ritual and were visibly impatient at having to wait their turn before they could open their gifts. That ritual belongs to our family and is clearly one of the tie-signs that is identified with family membership.

Tie-sign "markers" are acts or events that lay claim to a territory—in this case, the "territory" of a relationship. When people hold hands in public or walk with their arms around each other, they are telling the world that they have a loving relationship that excludes other people. People often wear similar clothing ("his" and "hers" shirts, for example) that says, "We belong together in this relationship, and you aren't part of it." A tie-sign marker may also take the form of a verbal comment that denotes the relationship (as in "I love you") or pet names for each other (most commonly "dear," "sweetheart," or "honey").

Change signals are tie-signs that function quite differently from rituals and markers. Unlike change signals, rituals and markers are not single acts performed by single persons. They are sequences of acts that members of the relationship create and in which they participate together. It is difficult and rather nonsensical, for example, for one person to hold hands. Rituals and markers involve members of the relationship acting out a "script" that is unwritten, but each member of the "drama" knows his or her part. When one of the members fails to perform his or her role adequately, all members of the relationship know that something is wrong. When that happens, the ritual or marker fails to confirm the relationship and, rather, signals to the participants that some change has occurred or is occurring in the relationship.

A change signal, then, is not necessarily an overt "Dear John" announcement, although such an obvious and direct approach would also signal a change in the relational definition. Change signals are more typically variations in rituals or markers that become meaningful for the participants because the rituals and markers are so familiar, having been repeated so often in the past. If the rituals and markers define and confirm the relational bonds for the participants (and for observers in the social context), then a variation in those rituals and markers signals that some change is taking place in the relationship.

Control Modes. Relationship-directed strategies that implicitly define the relationship in terms of which participant is "in charge" are known as *control modes*. A comment phrased as a command or an imperative (such as "Shut the door") implicitly defines the relationship with the speaker in charge and the listener deferring to the speaker. A comment that contains an imperative or gives instructions is sometimes called a *one-up comment*, also known as *domineering* or *structuring* the flow of the conversation. One-up comments function to restrict the choices of the recipient, who then has the option to defer to the speaker's control with a (you guessed it!) *one-down comment*.

Control-mode strategies seem similar to compliance-gaining strategies, but there is a major difference. Whereas an attempt to gain the compliance of the other person assumes that the speaker has some persuasive or manipulative purpose in mind, control-mode strategies are not manipulative. Control modes seek to define the basis of the relationship in one of two ways: equality or difference. For example, the person who was told to shut the door could easily respond with "Shut it yourself." This interaction reveals a relationship based on equality. Neither party gains or relinquishes the position of control or changes who is in charge in the relationship. This relationship, based on equality, is termed a *symmetrical* relationship. If the person had responded to the above command by actually shutting the door, then the respondent would have deferred to the one-up comment with a one-down comment. The resulting relationship is based on difference (one person in charge and the other person agreeing with the definition). It is therefore called a *complementary* relationship.

But not all control-mode strategies are one-up or one-down strategies. Some comments (indeed, most comments in everyday interaction) define the relationship as one of equivalence—neither person defines self as "in charge" and neither defers to the other's control. Naturally, the use of academic jargon demands that such comments also be given a label. Domineering comments are known as one-up comments, deferring comments are known as one-down comments, and equivalence-defining comments are called (what else?) *one-across comments*.

In most interpersonal relationships, participants move rather easily from symmetrical (neither person in charge) to complementary (one person in charge) interaction and back again. During certain periods of their communication, they may engage in competitive symmetry (one-up comments responding to one-up comments), and at other times they will engage in complementary interaction (one-down comments

Most interpersonal relationships include both complementary
and symmetrical communication.
(Joanne Leonard/Woodfin Camp & Associates)

deferring to one-up comments). Much of the interaction of people in long-term
relationships will probably be equivalent symmetry (one-across comments responding
to one-across comments) in an "I'm OK and you're OK" pattern of communication.
In fact, healthy relationships that maintain themselves over a long period of time
will include frequent changes between symmetrical and complementary interaction
(see Fisher & Drecksel, 1983). But I am getting ahead of myself. This is a topic for
Chapter 14.

Situation-Directed Strategies

Situation-directed strategies are coping strategies that allow the communicator to
define the situation so that he or she no longer feels a victim of circumstances.
Occasionally you may become involved in a communicative situation and feel helpless,
not in control of the situation. The situation may be one that is new to you or not
similar to any communicative situation in your past experience. The situation may
be one in which you feel threatened. You feel that the other person is attempting to
exert control, and you don't want to defer to that control. For whatever reason, you
may find yourself in a situation that requires the use of relational strategies aimed at
defining the situation itself. You would then use coping strategies to regain some
control over the definition of the context, typically a social context.

Coping or situation-directed strategies are comments that make explicit what is
typically a problem of perception. Recall that individual human beings are amazingly

skillful at perceiving what they want to perceive. When the situation is unfavorable, humans cope by perceiving selectively and creatively so as to perceive the situation in a more favorable light. A list of representative coping strategies, then, might include the following:

Reframing: Explicitly redefining the other person's comment so that your comment provides an interpretation that differs from the intended meaning of the other person.

Confronting: Explicitly telling the other person that his or her comment was out of line or inappropriate.

Attributing control: Explicitly telling the other person what prompted his or her comment; may involve disconfirming.

Ignoring: Continuing the interaction as though the other person's comment had never occurred; may involve changing topics.

Being fatalistic: Accepting the situation as beyond your control (as in "It's God's will") and minimizing your own discomfort.

Using humor: Making fun of the other person's comment or explicitly refusing to take the comment seriously.

Countering: Responding to the other person's controlling comment with a controlling comment of equal or greater intensity.

Withdrawing: Terminating the conversation with a comment that explicitly indicates that you are leaving the situation.

Situation-directed strategies are probably less common than other kinds. They occur only at those times when the individual doesn't know what to do. As a result, they rarely occur in relationships that have had some time to develop. They are probably most appropriate in those first encounters with strangers in which you don't feel comfortable. They may also occur with people (for instance, in a work context) who "bug you" but with whom you cannot avoid social encounters. Coping strategies are also frequent in male-female interaction, particularly for females, when the other person is "hitting on" them, making advances, or otherwise forcing unwanted attention on them. In such situations, you have no choice but to cope and then try to avoid similar situations in the future.

Goal-Directed Strategies

To understand how *goal-directed strategies* work in the process of interpersonal communication, we need to have a clear sense of what we mean by the word "goal." Robert Hinde (1979, pp. 25ff) has distinguished between what he calls "ballistic behaviour" and "goal-directed behaviour." Ballistic behavior is like hunting pheasants or shooting down enemy bombers. You have a desired outcome (hitting the target), you aim your weapon, and you fire your gun. The result of ballistic behavior is a hit or a miss, success or failure. Goal-directed behavior is quite different. According to Hinde, "The minimum requirement for behaviour to be regarded as goal-directed is a feedback loop capable of assessing the discrepancy between the present situation and the goal situation, and of initiating appropriate corrections to the current behaviour" (p. 25).

Now what on earth does this mean? And what on earth is a "feedback loop?" A goal-directed strategy is an attempt to adapt to a communicative situation that does not appear to be fulfilling your goals. But if the relationship is to achieve your goal or desired outcome, you need to modify the current pattern of interaction. You won't achieve your goals by merely setting your sights on some desired outcome and "shooting for it." You first need to know what is wrong with the current situation. In other words, you need a feedback loop that first allows you to gain an understanding of the problem in the status quo and then to devise a strategy to correct it.

For example, you have a relationship with a certain person and think that your relationship is not going the way you want. You want to do something about it. What do you do? First, you have to compare the present relationship with the relationship you want. Second, you have to devise some strategy to change the direction of the developing relationship. Goal-directed strategies thus function to *change* the direction of the developing relationship from the status quo. Naturally, if the present relationship is consistent with your goal, you don't need to use a goal-directed strategy.

It is quite impossible to provide a list of goal-directed strategies. Any strategy designed to change the relationship must be adapted to the specific relationship, and no two interpersonal relationships are exactly alike. However, three criteria can help you judge whether a particular goal-directed strategy is likely to be successful. One, is the strategy consistent with your relational goal? Two, is your goal realistic? Three, is your goal challenging?

Basically, the relational goal is a rather clearly defined relationship that you want to develop at some relatively specific time in the future. Furthermore, the goal you set for yourself should be realistic in the sense that the chances of the relationship developing to meet your relational goal are genuinely possible. And, finally, the relational goal you set for yourself should be challenging in the sense that it will require some interactional effort on your part. You are likely to see your relational goal as worthwhile only to the extent that you have to "earn" it. If your relational goal is too easy, you won't find it very satisfying.

When you choose a goal-directed strategy, you generally attempt to raise the level of intensity or intimacy in your relationship. Of course, you could also want to lower the level of intensity or intimacy, but goal-directed strategies that function to deintensify the relationship are typically less challenging. It's easy to lower the intensity or intimacy level of a relationship—just reduce the amount of interaction or stop interacting altogether. It is much more challenging to adopt a goal-directed strategy aimed at intensifying the relationship. But such strategies can be discovered only after a reasonably accurate assessment of the current status of the relationship (the feedback loop) and will vary considerably from one relationship to another.

Issue-Directed Strategies

We shall refer to those comments that relate directly to the information being discussed as *Issue-directed strategies*. These strategies attempt to exert some control over the content of the information or the flow of information being discussed. Specifically, issue-directed strategies function to do something to the issue under consideration during discussion. After all, the issues are the "stuff" that communication is about.

You will recall that an issue is a question or point of discussion about which there is some potential controversy. Communication allows the participants to resolve the issues or come to some agreement on them. Issue-directed strategies address specifically any potential controversy surrounding the question or point being discussed. They contribute or evaluate information and thereby seek to control the information pertinent to the issue. In this way, issue-directed strategies attempt to provide a rational basis for discussion. They seek and provide information concerning the issue while also evaluating the information concerning the issue. They attempt to control the amount and quality of the information that is relevant to conversational topics.

So what can you do with an issue when you contribute to the conversation? The following is a list of issue-directed strategies that attempt to control the relevant information:

Take issue: Express an opinion that supports one side of the issue under discussion. (Example: "I don't think you're being fair to her. She's really a very nice person.")

Challenge the issue: Express an opinion that questions the relevance or significance of the issue. (Example: "I understand where you're coming from, but I can't see why you're so upset. After all, it seems pretty trivial.")

Seek information: Indicate that the issue cannot be resolved without more information; ask the other person if he/she has any additional information. This functions to delay resolution of the issue. (Example: "I'm not sure. Have you heard anything new? Doesn't anybody know any more than we do?")

Provide information: Express additional information concerning the issue under discussion. (Example: "I was talking to her brother yesterday. He said that she was really sick, and nobody knew what was wrong with her.")

Avoid the issue: Delay resolving the issue by changing the topic under discussion. (Example: "I really don't know anything about that: let's talk about something else.")

Seek resolution or compromise: Invite the other person to provide a definitive answer. This may be accompanied by a promise to support the answer. (Example: "You just tell me what to do, and I'll do it.")

Provide resolution or compromise: Suggest a definitive answer to the issue. (Example: "I think we've talked long enough about where we're going to eat. Let's just go to McDonald's and be done with it.")

Combine two (or more) issues: Indicate the similarity of two different issues. Suggest that the issue is part of a broader one. (Example: "You know, all this terrorism sounds just like the 1960s. Remember all the killings that seemed to come all in a row? John Kennedy, Martin Luther King, Robert Kennedy?")

Issue-directed strategies attempt to resolve or seek agreement on issues by dealing with information that may or may not affect the intrapersonal self of one of the communicators. Despite your best intentions, it is not always possible to avoid affecting the self of the other person when you use an issue-directed strategy. Such strategies may appear to be objective in their focus on only the information, but they may also affect the self of one or more of the communicators. For example, what happens when you take issue with an idea advocated by the other person? You disagree not only with the information but also with the person who contributed that information. Hence, any issue-directed strategy may also function as an other-directed or relationship-directed strategy at the same time.

The only way (not just the best way, but the *only* way) to understand how any self-offer or relational strategy works to negotiate interpersonal relationships is to place it within the context of the *inter*action, the sequential pattern of communication involving the exchange of comments from both communicators. Then and *only* then will we be able to understand what is going on in the communication. The remainder of Part 3 focuses on how the strategies contributed by both communicators "fit together" to create some recognizable pattern of negotiated relationship. Our discussions will consistently emphasize *how* the behaviors mean, *how* people negotiate their interpersonal relationships, *how* relationships develop. When we understand the "how come" question, we will have taken a giant step toward becoming more effective and competent communicators.

EVOLUTION OF RELATIONSHIPS

The next four chapters are devoted to different stages in developing relationships: the "getting started" stage, the "growing together/apart" stages, the "let's end it all" stage, and the "keeping it all together" stage. Taken together, these chapters emphasize the evolutionary aspect of relationships. As communication continues, the relationship is constantly changing, constantly in a state of becoming something different from what it was, constantly evolving. Evolutionary change is an inherent and inevitable fact of all relationships, all interpersonal communication. As long as interpersonal communication continues, the relationship is continually undergoing change. More importantly, perhaps, the self-concepts of the individual participants are also continually undergoing change.

Developing interpersonal communication skills involves an awareness of evolutionary change and a repertoire of optional strategies. With awareness and a sensitivity to the change that is occurring in the developing relationship comes the knowledge of what strategy to select in order to keep the relationship developing in the direction you want it to go. But even the most skillful communicator, the person with a heightened sensitivity to the interaction and a variety of strategic choices at his or her disposal, cannot guarantee that every relationship will evolve into a desirable or even satisfactory outcome. One person cannot create an interpersonal relationship; it takes a minimum of two.

The skillful communicator is not necessarily a person whose interpersonal relationships are always satisfactory, even though most of them probably are. It is probably more accurate to think of the skilled communicator as one who is aware of the evolutionary stages of interpersonal relationships and is skilled at knowing when and how to end relationships as well as how to begin them.

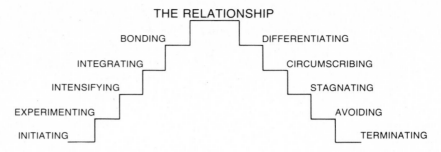

Figure 10-5. Knapp's Stages of "Coming Together" and "Coming Apart"

Stages of Evolving Relationships

Even though no two relationships evolve in exactly the same way, some phases or stages will characterize the evolutionary process of most interpersonal relationships at one time or another. First, two people meet and are initially attracted to each other. They experience a sense of possibility and wonder whether "this could be the start of something big." Next comes what Miriam Rodin (1982) calls the "reconnaissance dance, the set of exploratory moves which allow one to sample the other's company on what might be thought of as trial occasions" (p. 38). These opening moves or "trial occasions" allow each partner to "test the waters" before plunging headlong into the relationship. This testing period may even disconfirm the initial attraction, and one or both partners will decide to get out of the relationship while they can easily do so. After this first stage, the relationship can go either way—get stronger or grow progressively weaker and eventually die out.

Models of Evolutionary Development

One communication scholar, Mark Knapp (1984) has speculated that interpersonal relationships evolve in a parallel fashion. Partners experience a *coming together* evolutionary process parallel to a *coming apart* evolutionary process. Each stage in coming together has its counterpart in coming apart. Figure 10-5 illustrates this parallel development of interpersonal relationships in the form of steps that show how a relationship evolves through stages of *initiating, experimenting, intensifying, integrating,* and *bonding* as it increases in intensity and intimacy. As the relationship deteriorates or comes apart, the evolutionary process is reversed in the parallel stages of *differentiating, circumscribing, stagnating, avoiding,* and *terminating.* Figure 10-5 shows how each "coming together" stage has a parallel stage of development in the "coming apart" process. That is, "initiating" is to the "coming together" process what "terminating" is to the "coming apart" process; "experimenting" is to the "coming together" process what "avoiding" is to the "coming apart" process; and so forth.

Knapp speculated further that each evolutionary stage is characterized by dialogue that represents strategies peculiar to that stage. In fact, the stages may also serve to identify a list of strategies used by participants in the "coming together" and "coming apart" stages. The following table illustrates Knapp's (1984, p. 33) conceptualization of the stages of a developing relationship:

Process	Stage	Representative Dialogue
Coming Together	Initiating	"Hi, how ya doin'?" "Fine. You?"
	Experimenting	"Oh, so you like to ski . . . so do I." "You do?! Great. Where do you go?"
	Intensifying	"I . . . I think I love you." "I love you too."
	Integrating	"I feel so much a part of you." "Yeah, we are like one person. What happens to you happens to me."
	Bonding	"I want to be with you always." "Let's get married."
Coming Apart	Differentiating	"I just don't like big social gatherings." "Sometimes I don't understand you. This is one area where I'm certainly not like you at all."
	Circumscribing	"Did you have a good time on your trip?" "What time will dinner be ready?"
	Stagnating	"What's there to talk about?" "Right. I know what you're going to say and you know what I'm going to say."
	Avoiding	"I'm so busy, I just don't know when I'll be able to see you." "If I'm not around when you try, you'll understand."
	Terminating	"I'm leaving you . . . and don't bother trying to contact me." "Don't worry."

Knapp's model of interaction stages is obviously speculative and, as Knapp admits, "simplifies a complex process." Relationships in real life are certainly not nearly as orderly, and the stages of relational deterioration are not necessarily the reverse of the stages of coming together. Nevertheless, Knapp's model does show how relationships evolve through the passage of time and the continuing experience of interpersonal communication. Knapp's model also emphasizes that any relational stage (or change from one evolutionary stage to another) is identified by the interactional patterns (the dialogue) that the participants create while negotiating their relationships.

Knapp clearly means his stages of relationship development to include both verbal and nonverbal elements of communication, even though he certainly places more emphasis on verbal behaviors—talk. Albert Scheflen (1968), the late psychotherapist, devised another model of relational development based exclusively on nonverbal behaviors. He developed his model on the basis of his experiences and observations of psychotherapists and clients, although it is probably adaptable to any interpersonal relationship. Scheflen uses the metaphor of mixed-sex "courtship" in describing what he calls "quasi-courtship behavior" in interpersonal relationships.

Scheflen's model includes three stages of relational development: *Courtship readiness, positioning for courtship,* and *actions of appeal or invitation.* Scheflen is quick to point out that none of the nonverbal behaviors is meaningful in and of itself. When they come together in this three-stage sequential pattern, however, the nonverbal behaviors provide an insight into how interactants negotiate their relationship in an evolutionary manner. Scheflen's model of relational development can be summarized as follows:

Stage of Development	*Accompanying Nonverbal Behaviors*
Courtship readiness	High muscle tonus (such as a more erect posture, no slumping or sagging) Preening behaviors (Women stroke their hair, rearrange their clothing, pick lint off clothing, etc. Men stroke their hair, readjust ties, pull up socks, button coats, etc.)
Positioning for courtship	Body positioning (Partners turn bodies and heads toward each other, blocking off others.) Body movement (Partners lean toward each other or move chairs closer to each other.)
Actions of appeal or invitation	Invitational actions (Partner holds eye gaze with other, cocks head, exhibits inner wrist or open palm, slow stroking motions of fingers on thigh or wrist, rolling the hip and placing hand on hip.) Reciprocated actions (Partner responds to invitational actions with similar actions.)

Scheflen (1968) stressed that his stages were apparently not limited to interviews with therapist and client: "They [the quasi-courtship behaviors] appeared not only among lovers, but in psychotherapy sessions, business meetings, parties, conferences, and so on. Certainly all of these interactions were not supposed to end in sexual consummation" (p. 184). According to Scheflen, males "court" males, females "court" females, males and females "court" each other without intending any sexual connotation. Courtship is only a metaphor that makes possible a more complete understanding of how people negotiate relationships.

The quasi-courtship metaphor emphasizes that the particular units of nonverbal behavior can be interpreted as meaningful only when they (1) appear within the larger pattern of the three stages and (2) are performed by both participants in the relationship working in concert. At any time during any of the three stages, either partner can cease these quasi-courtship behaviors or even engage in some blocking behavior (such as turning away from the partner, folding arms, leaning away). When one partner fails to participate in the quasi-courtship pattern, the pattern is broken. At that point, any particular nonverbal behavior (such as preening or invitation) becomes simply another behavior that has no particular meaning as quasi-courtship.

Several conclusions about relationship development are to be gleaned from Knapp's and Scheflen's models:

1. Relationships develop and change gradually over time in an evolutionary manner.

2. The stages of a relationship are created and reflected in the pattern or sequence of interaction enacted by the communicators working together.
3. Relationships evolve toward fluctuations in quality of the characteristics of interaction (that is, rising or lowering levels of intensity, intimacy, trust, and commitment), and the change may be in either direction.
4. Skill or competence in interpersonal communication requires awareness of the relational stage and sensitivity to what strategies would be appropriate to that stage.
5. Whatever strategy is used in interpersonal communication is meaningful or effective only when it is seen as part of the pattern or sequence of communication. That is, the meaning or significance of any communicative action or strategy can be determined only when it occurs in the context of interaction patterns enacted by all communicators.

TYPES OF RELATIONSHIPS

The variety of relationships you will have with other people in the course of your life is very large and resists any simple classification. We already know that some relationships are affected by the social context or by the individual personalities of the participants and some relationships seem to be relatively unaffected by those influences. Further, we know that some relationships are significant to us and others are not.

Despite the variation in types of relationships, one element remains constant: all relationships are created, modified, and maintained through the process of interpersonal communication. If the communication is different, then the relationship will be different. Hence, some general classification of relationships is possible, on the basis of the premise that we can perceive some gross differences in their interaction patterns. The remainder of this chapter provides a partial listing of some of those general classes of relationships.

Acquaintanceships

Undoubtedly the most common of all relationships is the acquaintanceship. Perhaps because it is so common, many people (including communication scholars) tend to ignore the relationship of acquaintances and consequently don't know much about it. Steve Duck (1977) has defined acquaintance as "the process of getting to know someone in depth from first encounter to established relationships—whether this provokes an increase in liking or not" (p. 15).

We often tend to think of acquaintanceship as merely a stage we pass through on the way to some more important relationship, such as friendship. Certainly friends start out as acquaintances, but the fact is that most of our acquaintances remain just that—acquaintances. We like some of them, and we probably don't like others. For one reason or another, most of our acquaintances never become friends or anything other than acquaintances. If only because we have so many of them, acquaintanceships are significant.

Friendships

When we think of relationships, friendship is probably the first thing that comes to mind. But the word "friend," as we have already discussed, is used in connection with a variety of vastly different kinds of relationships. All friendships, though, will have some characteristics in common. They are voluntary, even though they may have started when two people were "thrown together." They are generally of higher intensity and intimacy and probably more personal than acquaintanceships. They typically, but not necessarily, include partners who are relatively similar and belong to the same social class. But the term "friendship" is almost a generic term referring to so many relationships (from "just friends" to lovers) that it doesn't describe any relationship very specifically.

Kinships

We have discussed kinship in earlier chapters as a relationship created and influenced by the social context. Unlike friends, whom we choose, we have no choice with regard to our families and relatives. Kinship is simply not a voluntary association of relational partners. Nevertheless, we generally think of families as being relatively close, with above average levels of intensity, intimacy, trust, and commitment. Many families, of course, are exceptions to the rule, but the expectations we have of kinship relations persist.

Romantic Relationships

We often think of the term "relationship" as involving some romantic feelings between a male and female. Certainly "romantic relationship" has received a great deal of publicity, particularly in popular fiction, movies, and TV shows. Romantic relationships almost invariably exhibit a high level of intensity, even when the level of intimacy hits rock bottom. Lovers who break up or marital partners who divorce often harbor very bitter feelings toward their former romantic partners for some time after they have grown apart. But romantic relationships are, perhaps, as different from one another as are friendships. Some romantic partners seem to have a lot in common; others are very different from one another. Some experience frequent arguments; others never disagree. We may tend to idealize romances in the "they lived happily ever after" syndrome, but reality forces us to realize that the maintenance stage of a romantic relationship is perhaps more difficult than that in any other relationship. Moreover, to maintain a romantic relationship is to enact considerable changes in what "romance" means in order to keep the relationship going.

Gender Relationships

The influence of gender on a relationship has already been discussed in an earlier chapter. Scholars tell us that males have found it easier to develop friendships with other males, and females have found it easier to develop friendships with other females. We have probably experienced for ourselves the fact that a male and a female experience great difficulty in being "just friends." Other people expect that a mixed-gender relationship will lead to a romantic relationship, and apparently the relational partners keep that possibility in mind, too. Those expectations seem to be widespread in our society, and that is unfortunate. However, the fact remains that friendships are often limited to same-gender partners, even though romantic partners are often friends, too.

The gender of the partners does influence their interaction. Male friends often engage in interaction that has come to be known as "locker room talk." Such interaction includes aggressive and often crude competition. Nonverbal interaction is also crude and includes a lot of punching and slapping. Female friends are more likely to engage in more intimate nonverbal interaction, such as embracing and touching, as well as more expressive verbal interaction. According to some experts, at least, female friends are more likely to express and reciprocate their emotions and innermost feelings than are male friends. The "macho" image of males fostered in our society probably inhibits males from expressing their emotions and feelings to other males. But maybe this notion of male and female friendships is just a social stereotype that does not really apply to real-life interaction.

Role Relationships

Some relationships are based on roles occupied by the partners in some larger social context. Role relationships (such as teacher and student, parent and child, supervisor and subordinate, colleague and colleague) serve to create a relationship between partners who just happen to belong coincidentally to the same social system. But these same people may also develop a relationship that goes beyond the influence of the larger social context. Some of my best friends are also my colleagues. What began as colleague-colleague work relationships broadened into more personal friendships. I play tennis and racquetball with students who, when we compete, don't seem to be bothered by the fact that I am their instructor (despite my frequent reminders to them that I will be grading their term papers).

Because relationship types overlap so much, the behavior appropriate to the relationship sometimes tends to be confusing. When husbands and wives work in the same office, for example, they interact formally and concentrate on their professional tasks. That must be difficult for them when most of their interaction is much more intimate and romantic. I have often found it confusing to "play teacher" and interact with a student about some new journal article or textbook when I am walking off the tennis court immediately after he or she has trounced me. Most partners in relationships, however, develop ways of dealing with these sources of confusion when moving in and between different types of relationships. Humans are remarkably adaptable creatures who seem to learn from their experiences.

Summary

Participants in interpersonal communication negotiate their relationship with each other as they enact behaviors toward each other. Together, they create interaction patterns that define their relationship. When those patterns are described in terms of their existence as actions or events, the quality of the interaction includes the primary characteristics of discontinuity, synchrony, recurrence, and reciprocity. Secondary characteristics of interaction quality refer to the intrapersonal perceptions of the participants and include intensity, intimacy, trust, and commitment.

When viewed as a process of negotiating relationships, interpersonal communication reflects the following characteristics. It is a blend of cooperation and competition. It assumes a future agreement on some potential settlement or relational contract. Each participant brings to the communicative situation a self, which is the basic commodity to be negotiated. The relationship that is negotiated by interpersonal communication may or may not incorporate all the "offers" of each participant's self.

Through the process of negotiation, participants develop a relationship typically characterized by two dimensions: communion-individualism and integration-disintegration. Thus, four types of relationships are evident. Type I relationships include integrated and communal relationships, such as very close friendships. Type II relationships are disintegrating communal relationships, such as friendships or marital relationships in the process of breaking up. Type III relationships are integrated and individualized, such as actual acquaintanceships. Type IV relationships are disintegrating and individually defined by the participants; an example would be casual acquaintances who very seldom interact.

The process of negotiating interpersonal relationships through communication blends opposite elements together within the pattern of interaction. Those "opposites" that are present during the process of negotiation include cooperation and competition, commodities and self, risk and obligation, and unity and diversity.

All interpersonal communication focuses on certain issues or questions indicating potential points of controversy that need to be resolved through negotiation. Some issues are informational only and require only information from the communicators in order to resolve them. Informational issues are typical of the early interactions of strangers who are highly uncertain about one another and need to acquire informaion in order to reduce their uncertainty. Relational issues concern questions of how each person identifies self with the relationship or the other person; they include self-as-object, self-as-other, and self-as-relational issues.

During the process of interpersonal communication, each person "offers" his or her self to the other person when contributing to the enactment of the interaction patterns. Because every action potentially contributes to the resolution of an issue and the eventual relationship definition, the actions contributed during interpersonal communication are called strategies. Relational strategies include self-directed strategies that attempt to tell the other person the precise connection between the implicit self and the explicit behavior. Giving accounts and flagging are two kinds of self-directed strategies. Other-directed strategies attempt to "do something to" the other person and include compliance gaining and interpersonal confirmation/disconfirmation. A third type of strategy is relationship-directed; it attempts to change or maintain the existing relationship. Relationship-directed strategies include tie-signs and control modes. Situation-directed strategies are coping strategies that allow the individual to define a situation that is threatening or confusing. Goal-directed strategies seek to change the current undesired state of the relationship to an outcome that is more consistent with the individual's goals. These strategies call for a "feedback loop" connecting an assessment of what is wrong with the status quo with the future desired state. Issue-directed strategies attempt to control the quality and evaluation of information contributed to the interaction.

Participants in interpersonal communication negotiate their relationship gradually in a constantly changing pattern of evolutionary development. Models of the various stages in the evolution of interpersonal relationship illustrate the constancy of change, the interpretation of communication actions within the context of the interaction patterns, and the need for awareness of the stages of evolutionary development in order to select appropriate communicative strategies. Types of evolved relationships include acquaintanceships, friendships, kinships, romantic relationships, mixed-gender relationships, and role relationships. However, the variety of different types of interpersonal relationships is very large. Furthermore, no two interpersonal relationships are exactly alike.

CHAPTER 11

Creating Relationships— Initiation, or "Getting Started"

Don't knock the weather. Without it, 90 percent of the people wouldn't be able to start a conversation.

—Anonymous

Despite the fact that friendships are so common, all of us will say we have difficulty in making friends. Meeting new people and making new acquaintances is, for most of us, a stressful experience. Of course, some people always seem to make friends easily and are constantly meeting new people. Salespersons, for example, learn the knack of making conversation with many different kinds of people, but many sales representatives claim to have difficulty in making new friends. Perhaps they repeat the initial stages of relationships so often in the day-to-day activities of their jobs that they treat every person as a "client." Consequently, they have difficulty in moving beyond the early stages of acquaintanceship.

This chapter deals primarily with the "getting acquainted" stage of relationship development. The purpose is to understand what goes on in the process of creating a relationship from scratch. We will discover the things that influence us during this initial stage and what we can do to influence the way in which our new relationship will evolve. Our discussions in this chapter will include managing the first impressions we have of others and they have of us, following the rules of social conduct, making opening moves when initiating conversations, and doing small talk. As in each of the remaining chapters of Part 3, we will conclude with a specific description of the issues and strategies that are normal to and typical of this stage of relational development. The purpose is to recognize the interaction of each evolutionary stage so that we can adapt our interactive behaviors and become more competent communicators.

MANAGING FIRST IMPRESSIONS

It is difficult to overestimate the importance of first impressions on a developing relationship—yet people do it all the time. At least one person has told me that he could tell within one minute (that's sixty seconds) whether a woman he just met would spend the evening (with all the sexual implications) with him. One psychiatrist has claimed that the outcome of any relationship was evident in the first four minutes of interaction. And at least one textbook has asserted that the first *five seconds* of interaction determine the outcome of a relationship.

Such claims are, of course, incredible. The first impressions we have of others (and they have of us) are certainly significant in terms of their potential effect on what will transpire in the interaction. Getting started "on the right foot" is important to any relationship if we expect it to evolve into anything more than a casual meeting. If the first impression is negative, we will probably remove ourselves from the situation and not allow the relationship further opportunities to grow. Whether that time frame is five seconds, five minutes, or five meetings is not important. What *is* important is being able to make appropriate and accurate judgments about the other person and doing all we can to make our first impression on the other person a favorable one.

Your task in the opening moments of conversation with a stranger, then, is twofold. One, you want to make sure your first impression on the other person is favorable. Two, you want to make sure your first impression of the other person is accurate. The first step in managing first impressions, then, is to be aware of what goes into the first impressions you and the other person have of each other. In this section we will be discussing the three most significant influences on our first impressions: expectations, physical attractiveness, and similarity.

Expectations

The expectations we have prior to interacting with the new acquaintance will influence what we are likely to experience in those first moments of interaction. Thus, if you are going to manage your first impressions in interpersonal communication, you need to manage your expectations of that initial encounter. Generally speaking, you have three sets of expectations that influence your first impressions: expectations regarding the situation, the other person, and your goals.

The situation itself will provide us with a set of expectations that influences our social encounters. If we don't want to be there in the first place, we will probably find that nearly everyone we meet "there" confirms our expectations. We already know enough about the process of perception to know that we tend to perceive what we expect to perceive. If we go to the social event with the expectation of enjoying ourselves, then we are likely to encounter people who are enjoyable. The expectations we have regarding the social situation will go a long way toward influencing our impressions of other people in that situation.

We also have a set of expectations concerning other people, an "implicit personality theory," that influences whether we like them or not. We carry around a set of expectations for categorizing people into types that we like and other types that we don't like. In other words, we expect to like some types of people because they are likely to meet our expectations. Specifically, our expectations take the form of criteria or qualities of persons we "like" as well as criteria or qualities that we "dislike." In most cases, our liking criteria stem from the qualities we have perceived in our friends. We tend to like new acquaintances if they are similar to persons we already like. On the other hand, our criteria for disliking someone are not necessarily the opposite of our criteria for liking people. These negative criteria tend to come from a variety of sources and are quite distinct from our criteria for liking.

Psychologist Miriam Rodin (1982) believes that we typically have two sets of criteria (*dislike criteria* and *disregard criteria*) that we use to exclude people from our list of potential friends. Far more people tend to meet our disregard criteria than our dislike criteria. That is, we tend to dislike very few people, but we disregard a whole lot of them. To understand our set of expectations regarding other people, then, our disregard criteria are probably more important than our dislike criteria.

How do we interact with people who meet our criteria of like, dislike, and disregard? If people meet our like criteria, we have a favorable first impression and seek out continued interaction with them. If people meet our dislike criteria, we tend to ignore them and avoid interacting with them. On the other hand, "We don't necessarily ignore people who meet our disregard criteria. In ordinary social situations we may treat them quite courteously, and even interact with them at some length. . . . [But] the interaction is ritual and carried out with glazed attention" (p. 35).

When our first impressions of other people are consistent with our dislike criteria, we never have the opportunity to become friends. More significantly, far more potential friends never have that chance because we disregard them. That is, we tend to carry on conversations with these new acquaintances without ever giving them a chance to become friends. We don't take seriously our interaction with them. We aren't rude to them; on the contrary, we are very courteous. But courtesy is a way of coping with new acquaintances who aren't meaningful to us, whom we disregard. It is just our way of failing to engage them in meaningful interaction. Consequently, our interaction with people who meet our disregard criteria never goes beyond the "getting acquainted" stage.

A third set of expectations will also affect our potential relationship with new acquaintances: the goals we have for the future of this relationship. What kind of relationship are you looking for? Whatever it is, your expectation will influence your first impressions of the other person. For example, a friend once told me that he had joined a country club. He actually didn't like golf very much, but his country club membership, billed as a business expense, was intended to help him make new acquaintances and find new clients for his sales. I asked him whether he had made any new friends among the "upper crust" at the country club, and he replied, "Not at all. They're really stuffy. I wouldn't have anything to do with them if they weren't such good clients."

To this person, every person he met was a potential client. He didn't make any new friends at the country club probably because he didn't expect to make friends. He expected salesman-customer (individualized) relationships, and those were the relationships he developed. Rather surprisingly, he couldn't seem to understand why he didn't develop any friendships (that is, communal relationships). His clients remained clients, and he regretted the fact that they didn't become friends.

Some people continually ask themselves "What can this relationship do for me?" For them, it is likely that relationships will become individualized. They drive freeways, eat in chain restaurants, and stay in chain motels. They get no surprises; they have no unexpected experiences; they play it safe. For persons who expect to gain a set of new experiences and possibly even new definitions of self from new acquaintances, relationships will more likely develop into communal ones. They drive on side roads, look for new and different places to eat and stay, and are open to new and unexpected experiences. They run a greater risk of being disappointed and having unsatisfying social experiences. But they will also, more often, have closer and more satisfying personal relationships. For them, interpersonal communication (and probably life) is pretty risky, but it is not boring.

Physical Attractiveness

Psychological research tells us that we are likely to have a more favorable first impression of persons who are physically attractive than those who are physically ugly. You probably do not find this statement surprising. But don't be too quick to reject it as overly obvious. It does not mean that good-looking people generally have satisfying interpersonal relationships. Nor does it mean that we should have cosmetic surgery if we want to create a favorable first impression on others. In fact, physical attractiveness is not just what you see on a person's outside. It is a set of expectations we have about people and must be understood in the context of what happens in the early stages of interaction.

Some extremely attractive people have publicly stated that their physical assets were actually detrimental to the formation of personal relationships. Actresses or starlets seem continually to be telling interviewers that they are really lonely because people tend either to be intimidated by their beauty or to treat them as sex objects, and not as friends. Most of us don't have that problem. We are condemned to live a life of normalcy—somewhere in the middle between "gorgeous" and "yucky." For the vast majority of people in our society, the influence of physical attractiveness on the beginning stages of interpersonal communication is even more problematic.

In the first place, what is physically attractive to one person may not be to another. For instance, teenage girls will often differ from their fathers on the criteria by which to judge "cute" boys. On more than one occasion, I have been surprised when I actually set eyes on a fellow who had set my teenage daughter's heart aflutter. I often found him quite unattractive (if not downright ugly). But what is cute to one person may meet the disregard criteria of another. Therefore, physical attractiveness certainly does not influence all people (male or female) in the same way.

Perhaps the most important fact concerning our expectations regarding physical attractiveness is that they are often not defined in terms of outward appearance or anatomical features. For instance, when I asked my daughters what they found attractive in a certain boy, they often responded in terms of behaviors and not physical features. They often thought a boy was cute because he was "fun to be around" or he had a "nice smile." And this is the point that is most important in our expectations concerning physical attractiveness and managing first impressions.

Physical attractiveness is not just what you see when you look at someone; it is also the impressions you acquire during the opening moments of interaction. A person who smiles, for example, is often perceived as more attractive than one who remains glum-faced. A person who appears "natural" is often perceived as more attractive than one who appears too formal or "stuck up." Behaviors are often as much a part of attractiveness as are physical features. At the very least, the behaviors of the other person will affect our judgment of that person's physical attractiveness, and our behaviors will affect the other person's judgment of us. Hence, the first moments of interaction are significant in terms of how they influence each communicator's expectations regarding the other's physical attractiveness.

Similarity

Consistent with the saying that "Birds of a feather flock together," we tend to like those people whose interests, attitudes, experiences, and beliefs are similar to our own. In other words, we tend to like people who are most like ourselves. First-time interaction should also be less difficult with people who are similar to us. After all, we should have lots to talk about. And people who are similar to ourselves will tend to reinforce our own beliefs, attitudes, and so forth rather than disagreeing with us. And being agreed with is always preferable to being disagreed with.

On the other hand, similarity and liking are probably reflexive. That is, friends are likely to be similar as much as similar persons are likely to be friends. There are several reasons for this. Friends typically come from the same social class, the same geographical area, the same social groups—precisely because they have more opportunity to get acquainted and become friends. In that case, the fact that friends are similar is merely coincidence. Friends may also be similar because they have frequently interacted in the past. With increased interaction, friends will create their own similarities and have similar outlooks on the world. In such cases, friendship creates a similarity between people rather than being created by their similarity.

So what comes first—the interaction or first impressions? Does the initial period of interaction allow the communicators to discover similarities and, thus, lead to a favorable first impression? Or does initial interaction create a favorable first impression and, thus, lead to perceptions of similarities? Communication scholars Michael Sunnafrank and Gerry Miller (1981) wondered about these questions too. They actually compared the relative influence of attitudinal similarity and initial conversations on strangers' first impressions of each other. Their results were rather interesting.

Sunnafrank and Miller found that, before they interact, people tend to have a more favorable first impression of those who are similar to them. But they also found that even a very few minutes of conversation between dissimilar persons counteracted many of the negative first impressions such people had of each other. In other words, before you talk with them, you will probably expect to like strangers to the extent that you think they are similar to you. However, when you actually talk with strangers who you thought were "different," you discover they aren't so different after all. Consequently, the "getting acquainted" stage may allow the communicators to discover some similarities or things they have in common, but it definitely deemphasizes their differences.

Perhaps the differences between communicators exert less influence on their first impressions of each other than we might think. Perhaps initial interaction reveals similarities that the communicators didn't know about before they started communicating. In either case, we know that, in most situations, strangers know virtually nothing about each other until they actually begin talking. Much of their initial interaction is an attempt to discover things they might have in common. Most importantly, their early interaction will reduce much of their uncertainty about each other and get rid of negative first impressions that were based on simply not knowing anything about the other—that is, uncertainty.

FOLLOWING THE RULES

Discussions in Chapter 4 have indicated that the social context (particularly cultural norms) influences how people behave in interpersonal communication by providing guidelines or rules on what to do and how to behave. That influence is strongest, of course, during the getting-acquainted stage of initial interaction, when uncertainty is at its highest. When you are unsure of what you are supposed to do or what is expected of you, you typically use the standardized conventions of your culture to guide your behavior. In fact, that is often the cardinal rule of much of our behavior: When in doubt, play it safe and follow the rules. This section discusses two sets of those rules: politeness and taking turns.

Politeness

Even as a very small child, you began your education in learning the cultural rules of politeness. Your parents hounded you to say "Please" and "Thank you" at appropriate times, to show respect to others (particularly those older and allegedly wiser), to be pleasant, to avoid bad words, and so forth. In short, you learned manners, the rules of politeness. And if you didn't learn them or didn't practice them at the appropriate times, your parents admonished you to "Mind your manners."

Among cultures or social contexts, there will be some disagreement on the rules guiding each culture's definition of politeness. My Japanese friend, for example, thought that looking directly into the eyes of your partner while speaking was a very rude behavior. My American upbringing taught me that to avoid looking at the other person was rude. "Eye contact" is a consistent point of emphasis in our culture's rules of politeness. I'm sure that, at some time during your formative years, some person in a position of authority told you, "Look at me when I'm speaking to you."

Numerous subcultures also exist within every larger social context, and every one of them has developed its own rules of acceptable behavior. In fact, there are so many subcultures in which interpersonal communication takes place that it would be impossible to list them all. Cultural rules of politeness cover everything from how to speak and what to say to what clothing to wear. A few years ago, for example, Larry Bird (a professional basketball player of some renown) showed up at the annual postseason awards banquet of the National Basketball Association wearing a sportshirt and slacks. Everyone else (males, at least) at the banquet was wearing either a tuxedo or a conservative suit and tie. Bird received his Most Valuable Player award but not without being singled out for his "impolite" choice of attire that, apparently, failed to demonstrate his respect for the occasion. When Larry Bird attended the awards banquet the following year and received his second Most Valuable Player award, he was dressed in a suit and tie.

Being polite in one subculture, though, does not mean that you do the same things you do when you're being polite in another. Hence, following the rules of politeness in our national culture may not be appropriate for demonstrating polite behavior in one of the subcultures. Being polite with your family, for example, may not include the same behaviors as being polite at a fraternity or sorority mixer. Being polite with an instructor may not include the same behaviors as being polite with that gorgeous "fox" or "hunk" you've been dying to meet.

The point to be made here is that the early getting-acquainted interaction with strangers is often a matter of reducing uncertainty by following the rules of some social context and being polite. You know what the rules are from having been acculturated into that social system. The problem of negotiating your interpersonal relationships is rarely one of not knowing the rules of politeness in the early stages. Rather, it is a matter of knowing how and when to get the interaction moving beyond those rules in later stages.

Taking Turns

Interpersonal communication is typically a conversation. Conversation involves the exchange of information in the form of "turns." In this sense, interpersonal communication is similar to playing chess or any board game. You make your move when it is your turn. When it is not your turn, you wait for the other person to move. Taking turns in a conversation is a little like breathing. You know how to do it and do it frequently, but you have a difficult time describing exactly what you do when you do it. But don't worry about it. Recall from our discussions in Chapter 4 that the rules for turn taking have already been written down. In the following paragraphs we will concern ourselves with only two elements of turn taking, however: *turn-allocation techniques* and *repair mechanisms*.

Speakers use turn-allocation techniques in order to "give" their turn specifically to another person. During a conversation involving three or more persons, for instance, every speaker has the option of ending a turn by specifying which person gets the next turn. The speaker then uses a technique to allocate the next turn to a specific person. The most obvious turn-allocation technique is addressing a question to a specific person. A question develops the expectation of "requiring" an answer, and the questioner often selects who should supply the answer.

Any person in the conversation also has the option of taking a turn from another person. Communication scholar Robert Nofsinger (1975) has called this self-selecting turn-allocation technique a *demand ticket*. By using demand tickets, speakers serve notice that they want the next turn. A demand ticket may be in the form of a direct question ("You know what?") or a simple exclamation ("Hey, Al!"). The demand ticket functions similarly to the strategy known as "flagging." It is an explicit statement that tells the other person, "I want to take the next turn." In fact, a demand ticket may explicitly flag the speaker's intention with a statement such as "I'd like to say something to you." By using a demand ticket, the speaker attempts to ensure that the other person makes no error of perception.

Using a demand ticket, though, does not guarantee that the demander actually gets the next turn. Certainly the most common response to "You know what?" is probably "What?" When that exchange occurs, the demand ticket works; the speaker succeeds in getting the next turn. But just because one person "demands" a turn, the other person is not required to relinquish the next turn to the demander. The response to "You know what?" could also be something like "Yeah" or "Not particularly." In other words, the demand ticket is successful as a turn-allocation technique only if and when the other person responds by allowing it to be successful.

The second element of turn taking in conversations is the repair mechanism, which attempts to repair any "damage" done to the conversation when some interactant speaks out of turn (that is, violates one of the rules of turn taking). We are all quite good at taking turns in conversation, but occasionally two or more people speak at once or one person "steps on" another's line. People generally realize when they have violated a turn-taking rule. When they do, they can use any of several repair mechanisms to correct their error. Most commonly, of course, one of the speakers stops prematurely and "gives" the turn to the other person, thereby repairing the damage to the conversation.

Repair mechanisms may also take the form of explicit statements that admit to the rule violation and offer an apology and a remedy. For example, the violator may apologize ("I'm sorry") and remedy the damage ("Go ahead"). The repair mechanism may also give some "account" for the violation, as in "I thought you had finished." The person who violates turn-taking rules (such as interrupting or talking over other speakers' turns) runs the risk of being perceived as rude, boorish, impolite, pushy, and aggressive. To avoid those perceptions (which will certainly create negative first impressions), people often use apologies and remedies as repair mechanisms. By doing so, they may continue to negotiate their relationship with "undamaged" conversation.

MAKING OPENING MOVES

The opening moves in any interpersonal communication situation occur during the first few exchanges of interaction and serve as the "ignition" stage of the relationship. They may not determine what the outcome of the relationship will be, but they will certainly affect whether the relationship will ever get off the ground and have a chance to develop into something more. In this sense, then, the opening moves of "getting acquainted" communication will set the tone for the continued negotiation of the interpersonal relationship.

For the most part, opening moves involve the performance of *rituals*. But do not think of ritual as simply "going through the motions" of insincere and trite behaviors. "Ritual," according to sociologist Erving Goffman (1971), "is a perfunctory, conventionalized act through which an individual portrays his respect and regard for some object of ultimate value to that object of ultimate value or to its stand-in" (p. 62). In the case of interpersonal communication, that "object of ultimate value" includes both the other person, the relationship between them, and the culture in which they both reside. "Ritual," in the sense we use it here, is a celebration of those "objects of value" and is a way of demonstrating respect for them.

When communicators participate in rituals, they are celebrating the value of their culture and the worth of every individual human being who is a member of that culture. In a real sense, to perform a ritual is to confirm the influence of the social context and let both communicators know that this social context is important. Our discussions will consider two varieties of ritual that are important to the early stages of getting-acquainted interaction: *rituals of the situation* and *rituals of greeting*.

Rituals of the Situation

Performing a ritual is simply another way of following the rules. Some rules, such as politeness and turn taking, come from the larger society; others are in the immediate situation. They are the rituals frequently and appropriately used to establish and maintain social contact in that situation. Each situation has its own rituals that are frequently repeated when people enter that situation. When you find yourself in one of these situations, you enact that situation's ritual and let it govern your opening moves. According to Goffman (1971), social contact occurs in one of three different situations: *business, accident,* and *ceremony.*

A business situation "requires" social contact and focuses the conversation on topics that are part of the situation. For example, two people who are colleagues in a work situation need to talk with each other so that they can perform their jobs. When you walk into a store to purchase something, your interaction with the salesperson is a business situation that governs how you behave. You and the salesperson are both aware that the nature of your relationship is "all business." That is, you came into contact in the first place because the situation demanded it. Neither of you has any expectation of further interaction concerning other topics or other areas of interpersonal contact. The result is that you both enact the ritual of seller-buyer interaction.

The second situation involves accidental social contact. You just "happen" to bump into another person because you are both riding on the same bus, standing in the same ticket line, using the same elevator, walking on the same street, or attending the same social occasion. In these situations, social contact may be nothing more than a perfunctory exchange of greetings, or it may lead to further contact at some future time. That is, accidentally meeting someone at a party may be the occasion of your first interpersonal contact, but you may also make plans to continue your relationship before you break off that contact.

Some situations may lead to "accidental" meetings that tend to happen almost regularly. You meet someone at the regular meeting of a club, a social organization, or a church. Because you seem to be "accidentally" meeting the same person again and again, you eventually develop a relationship that extends beyond the limits of the accidental situation. The interaction ritual of the accidental situation may not cause you to maintain interpersonal communication, but its contact allows the relationship to develop into something further.

For example, a former student once told me that he had noticed a fellow student in a class he was taking from me. He apparently found her physically attractive, but his problem was how to make social contact with her. Because of his work schedule, he typically arrived a few minutes late for class and could not select a seat next to her. He frequently waited after class in order to "accidentally" bump into her on the way out the door, but (according to his story) she always seemed to walk out the door while engaged in a conversation with some other student. The day finally arrived, however, when he waited to ask me a question after class, and also waiting to talk with me was the object of his frustrated affections. They talked with me about some common issue related to the class and walked out the door together, continuing to interact between themselves about topics related to the class. The two students began seeing each other regularly after that day, but it wasn't until much later that he told her that their first social contact was no accident. He had planned it all along.

Ceremony is the third type of situation and involves a ritual in which one person supports the other. The ritual is a ceremony in the sense that it accomplishes a particular purpose of interpersonal support. Such situations might frequently occur in relationships that have already established some level of trust or intimacy. For example, one person has a problem and frequently comes to a friend for help. A ceremonial ritual may also involve any person giving assistance to another, even if they were both strangers prior to that time. One person stops to help a stranded motorist, and they establish social contact. One person drops a load of books or packages, and another person performs the ceremonial ritual of helping retrieve the objects. In any case, the ceremony provides a reason for the social contact that places each person in a specific role relationship—the helper and the helpee, the supporter and the supportee. And who knows what will happen when a relationship begins on such a positive note?

Greeting Rituals

The following interaction is a variation of the familiar opening moves that begin a conversation between friends or strangers in our American culture:

A: Hi.
B: Hi.
A: Howya' doin'?
B: Pretty good. How's yourself?
A: Just fine.

No more perfunctory or cliché-ridden interaction ritual appears in our daily lives. Saying "Fine" or making some similar response to "How are you?" is as much a part of our unthinking ritualistic vocabulary as saying "You're welcome" to "Thank you." This is the greeting ritual that frequently constitutes the opening moves in a conversation between two people who bump into each other for the first time or between two friends who have not seen each other for a while. We enact the ritual without thinking about it. It comes easily to all of us.

Communication scholars Paul Krivonos and Mark Knapp (1975) have studied the American greeting ritual and suggest that, despite its perfunctory performance and conventional usage, it performs some highly important functions in our relationships. According to these authors (pp. 117 & 118), the greeting ritual functions in our society: (1) "to mark a transition between a period of absence and a period

Most of us perform greeting rituals without thinking about them.
(Ken Robert Buck/The Picture Cube)

of increased access" (for interactants who have already developed at least an acquaintanceship with each other), (2) "to reveal important information about the state of the relationship between the participants" (although the inquiry into personal health rarely seeks or reveals very important information), and (3) to "serve a maintenance function for interpersonal relationships" (especially the greetings between acquaintances who meet in passing).

When you say, "How are you?" and the other person responds, "Fine," you are telling each other that you have a relational bond that connects—even if that bond is only that you are members of generally the same culture. Of course, some specific subcultures have their own unique greeting rituals (such as the ritual handshake between blacks or fraternity brothers). When you greet each other, both of you expect that more interaction will follow, no matter how brief that interaction. If for no other reason, the greeting ritual is the absolutely first impression either of the interactants has of the other during interaction and is, therefore, important.

Greeting rituals include both verbal and nonverbal components, of course. These elements, when used by both interactants in concert, combine to form the complete ritual. Common greetings typically include such elements as a verbalized recognition of the existence of the other person (such as "Hi" or "How are you?"), a nod of the head typically accompanied by a smile, and some tactile (touching) contact typically of the hands (with all the variety of different handshakes and touching for various cultures). In some cultures, in fact, the tactile contact may include an embrace or a kiss, either on the lips or the cheek. Members of the French culture, for example, typically greet each other with both an embrace and a kiss on both cheeks—men and women alike. Female guests on late-night talk shows frequently greet their male hosts with a kiss, which suggests the existence of some "show business" culture that considers the kiss to be a part of a perfunctory greeting ritual. Many families also use the kiss as part of their greeting ritual. In other cultures or social situations, however, kissing implies a much more intimate relationship.

According to Krivonos and Knapp (1975), the greeting ritual is different for strangers than for pairs who have been previously acquainted. Their observations revealed that previous acquaintances typically greet each other with the following verbal and nonverbal behaviors, in this order: mutual glance, head gesture (such as nodding to the other person), smile, verbal salute (such as "Hi"), a reference to the other person (such as calling the other person by name), a personal inquiry (such as "How are you?"), an external reference (such as "How's the family?"), and a topic initiation ("I've been meaning to speak to you about. . . "). Previously acquainted partners thus use the greeting ritual as a means to move directly into conversation. The ritual is rather complex (that is, contains a variety of different elements), rarely includes any gaps between elements, and is accomplished without much fuss or attention being paid to it.

Strangers generally use a greeting ritual that typically involves the same *types* of behaviors but differs in the *variety* of elements included in the ritual. Strangers tend to enact the following greeting ritual: mutual glance, head gesture, verbal salute, and personal inquiry. As you can see, the greeting ritual for strangers is much less complex and does not always lead smoothly into an extended conversation. Once strangers complete this rather simple exchange of behaviors, they have no rules to guide them in deciding where to go from there.

We rarely rehearse greeting rituals or prepare them in advance. We just naturally "fall into" the ritual because we know it so well. *Sixteen Candles,* one in a series of recent movies that tells the story of adolescent love, contains an episode in which the sixteen-year-old heroine rehearses the greeting she will use when she meets her dream boyfriend for the first time. She practices a variety of greetings in the hallway during a school dance until she decides on the "perfect" opening line. But when the big moment arrives, she becomes flustered and says absolutely nothing. Some time later, when the two adolescents actually do meet for the first time, she has prepared nothing. But they enact their greeting ritual with no problem whatsoever.

The greeting ritual is a convenient and important way to open the interaction, whether the communicators are strangers or good friends. For previous acquaintances, however, the greeting ritual is a natural and smooth way to introduce the conversation. For strangers, the greeting ritual is neither very natural nor sufficient. After the exchange of verbal salutes and personal inquiries, the greeting ritual for strangers concludes. At this point, strangers must be prepared to continue their interaction or slink off in embarrassment. What comes after the greeting ritual in the getting-acquainted stage of interpersonal communication? You guessed it—small talk! Now the conversation starts to get interesting. Or does it?

DOING SMALL TALK

Silence in the middle of a conversation is uncomfortable. It is awkward for both communicators. They have concluded their greeting ritual and are not sure what to expect next. They don't even know whose turn it is to talk. This period of relational discomfort is frequently a part of dialogue in comedy sketches. After an appropriate period of silence to establish the fact that everyone is uncomfortable, the sketch includes some comment that instantly draws laughter. "So . . . ," says one of the characters in a voice that is louder than normal and that draws out the response longer than necessary to enhance the feeling of relational discomfort. Or the comment may be a complete non sequitur, an obviously inappropriate act that introduces a topic without sufficient preparation: "How about them Dodgers?"

Why does the audience invariably laugh when this comedy sketch appears on some televised "sitcom?" The situation isn't particularly funny, and the line itself isn't very funny. Perhaps everyone in the audience has been in a situation just like that one. They are familiar with the awkward feeling of "What do I do now? Why doesn't he speak? Should I say something? What do I say?" At this point, somebody *must* do something. And for the relationship to move to some further stage of negotiation, both people have to do something *together* in the interaction. Fortunately, we have developed a whole repertoire of things to do in such situations. We have even given this "things to do until we can find something better to do" a name. We call it *small talk*.

Misperceptions of Small Talk

Virtually no one likes small talk. Virtually no one likes to do small talk. Virtually no one thinks small talk is important. If it were why do we call it "small" talk? Perhaps we have come to condemn small talk because of some unfortunate but common experiences we've had in the past. Hence, we tend to overgeneralize our experiences as being a problem inherent with small talk. We don't like to do small talk. We think we aren't very good at doing it. So we tell ourselves that it is not important. That is unfortunate.

The first step in improving our skill in doing small talk is to become aware of the misperceptions we may currently have of it. The next several pages will discuss three common reactions that people have to doing small talk. We will treat these objections as problems to be overcome in order that we may improve our interpersonal communication skill and get better at doing small talk.

Objection #1:   "It's all so boring. Just one cliché after another. It's just so superficial. I never get to know the 'real' person."

Response: "Well, what do you expect? You just met the person, for heaven's sake. You want her or him to give you her or his entire autobiography right away? Don't be so impatient. Let things coast for a while. After you get to know each other, things will work out."

Small talk is a "reconnaisance dance" that allows each person to get to know the other. This is a time for gathering information. Judgments about the "real" self of the other person come later. Besides, the only way to make such judgments is to gather information from the other person and give information about your self to that person. Then both of you will have some basis on which to make an informed judgment. Without the opportunity that small talk allows you to gather such information, you will have no basis for establishing any kind of relationship at all.

Objection #2:   "All I ever seem to do is small talk. I meet one person, and just as we're getting to know each other, it's all over. Time to move on to the next person. Then we start all over again."

Response: "You're suffering from the 'cocktail party syndrome.' There are certainly some occasions that virtually force you to have too many and too brief encounters with too many persons. You need, then, to be more discriminating. Select the person or persons you want to spend more time interacting with, and then seek them out again. When the fish are biting, you don't keep all of them, do you? Of course not. You put only the big ones in your creel and throw the little ones back. You ought to be as discriminating with people as you are with trout."

Some situations, like the proverbial cocktail party or "rush" party in fraternities and sororities, include just too many interpersonal contacts and too little time for any of them to develop any depth. This situation may make you feel as helpless as the person who made the objection quoted above. This person is frustrated because the situation seems beyond his or her control. To avoid the feeling of being helpless or not in complete control, you need to develop coping strategies.

Small talk is not the problem here. The problem lies in the excessive demands of the situation. The solution to the problem is to discover strategies to cope with it. The simplest coping strategy is the one provided in the response. Seek out the persons who interest you and initiate another conversation. It should also be easier the second time around. You may also cope with the situation by getting away from the crowd. Suggest to the other person that you continue your conversation in a more secluded place, away from the hustle and bustle of the party. If you are standing, find a place to sit down. When both of you are seated, it is more difficult for other people to interrupt you or for your conversation to be terminated prematurely. Each of these coping strategies is aimed at controlling the situation by providing you with the opportunity to keep the small talk going.

Objection #3:   "Boy, what an ego! All she wanted to talk about was herself. I couldn't get a word in edgewise, even if I had wanted to." (OR) "Boy what a drag! He just wouldn't say anything. I had to do all the talking, and he just stood there like a dummy. I'll bet being married to him is really exciting!"

Response: "I can't believe it! Did you ever consider what the other person was thinking about you? Probably just the opposite! You oughta know that when you're nervous, you tend to either talk a lot or to say nothing. People are different that way. You probably showed how nervous you were by not saying anything (by talking all the time). And she (he) showed how nervous she (he) was by talking too much (by not saying anything). Right now, she's (he's) probably telling a friend about you and saying just the opposite. Now who's the dummy?"

When one person in the interaction carries too big a burden in doing the small talk, the interactants are not demonstrating competence in communicational skills. Both partners should feel that they are contributing equally to the conversation, even though the actual proportion of behaviors will never be exactly equal. The problem in such a situation is undoubtedly that the partners do not feel very comfortable.

You need to employ some communicative strategies that tend to equalize the conversational burden and make both of you feel more comfortable. If you feel you are "carrying" the conversation, strategize your behaviors to encourage the other person to talk more. Ask open-ended questions, ones that require more than a simple yes-no response. Find out what interests the other person. Soon you will have a common area to talk about. If you feel the other person is carrying the conversation, interject some comments that tell about your self. Give the other person the opportunity to get to know you. After all, the other person has already told you about her or his self. Now it's your turn. Take it.

The point to be made here is that small talk is probably more significant than we typically give it credit for being. Small talk is a major part of your interactional life. You will find yourself doing small talk perhaps more than any other kind of interaction. Therefore you really should be good at it.

The way to improve your skills in doing small talk is to practice them. Determine for yourself what the problem is and solve it for yourself by selecting some strategy appropriate to the occasion. You will probably find it amazing just how easy doing small talk is and how significant it is in helping you to negotiate your own interpersonal relationships. At the very least, you'll be invited to more parties. And that can't be all bad!

The Nature of Small Talk

We are all probably familiar with what small talk is like. We can certainly recognize it when we are doing it, and we can recognize it when we observe other people doing it. There are probably four general characteristics of interaction that provide a general description of what we have come to recognize as small talk:

1. "Interviewing interaction"—asking and answering questions.
2. "Safe" topics—removed from self and involving minimal risk.
3. Exchange of demographic information—who you are and where you're from.
4. Variety of different topics—little time spent on each.

Small talk is highly predictable. The exchange of questions and answers, of information about each person's self, is almost a ritual, it is so predictable. But underlying the familiar sequence of interaction is the expectation that something could potentially develop from this conversation. Small talk does more than just kill time until something better comes along. It allows time and opportunity for each partner to size up the other. It keeps the conversation going until the partners discover something that interests them both. Small talk gives communicators an opportunity to "practice" relating with each other. It is the rehearsal for some future performance.

Perhaps the principal function of small talk is to allow the participants to reduce their uncertainty about each other and about the situation. The beginning stages of relationship development are filled with uncertainty. Each person wonders, "Who is this other person? Where are we going? For that matter, who am I to this person? And who is this person to me?" The problem is that neither partner knows much about the other and uses small talk to reduce that uncertainty. Small talk provides the opportunity for the interactional partners to get to know each other and lets them exchange information so that each is able to develop some image of the other's psychological self. Each partner thus gets to know the "real" person of the other.

When we say that each person "interviews" the other in small talk, we mean precisely that. An employer interviews prospective job applicants in order to determine whether to hire them. A communicator interviews prospective relational partners in order to determine whether to include them as eligible friends. In a sense, each person in the getting-acquainted stage of communication is an actor auditioning for a role in an upcoming production called "Our Relationship." Of course, each person is also judging the audition of the other to determine whether to continue with the drama. The extended relationship will come about only if and when each partner accepts the other's audition. Small talk allows the interactants to "try out" for each other before they commit themselves.

While the partners are auditioning each other, they are searching for areas of commonality, some basis on which to build their potential relationship. Two people in a relationship may be very different from each other in many respects. But so what? They will develop their relationship on the basis of what they have in common, not on what makes them different. Hence, small talk serves as a trial-and-error series of conversational topics until the participants find some common ground.

To interpersonal communication, one commonality is worth a hundred differences. Let me illustrate. I have a friendship with a person whom I rarely see these days. We haven't even lived in the same town for fifteen years. Yet, we continue to see each other occasionally and consistently reaffirm our friendship, even after the passage of so much time. I'm not sure what the similarities are that provide the basis for our friendship—we certainly like each other. We both like camping, nature, and dogs. Our differences, however, are far more numerous and serious. We differ on virtually all the important topics of conversation: politics, religion, family life, and choice of professions, to name just a few. But our differences just don't seem very important in the overall scheme of our friendship.

The point is that relational partners will undoubtedly be very different from each other, but those differences are not significant to or even necessarily a part of the relationship. The law of partial inclusion is a powerful influence. Differences between friends become trivial when viewed in the context of the developed relationship. Therefore, small talk may reveal differences between the new acquaintances, but the differences may not be at all important to their relational future. Small talk also provides a search for similarities, and similarities (not differences) serve as the basis for an extended relationship.

During small talk, each interactant attempts to draw some inferences about the "inner self" of the other person. We already know that inferences about a person's self on the basis of that person's behavior are highly prone to error. But that does not prevent us from trying to "psych out" the other person. We are so good (or bad) at perceiving things that we don't need much information in order to make some inferential judgment or perception. Recall that we always use perception to "fill in the blanks" between incomplete information and make judgments even when we don't have sufficient information. This means only that perception tends to be faulty, not that we can't and don't make perceptions on the basis of insufficient information.

Nonverbal behaviors during small talk also reflect the fact that each person is "playing it safe" during this period. You tend to look at the other person's face, particularly when you are in the role of listener, but you generally don't look at the eyes. And only rarely do you and your partner together establish mutual eye contact. That is, during small talk you and your partner will typically look at each other but not into each other's eyes. Locking each other's eye gazes (that is, maintaining eye contact) comes later in the quasi-courtship sequence in the form of reciprocated actions of appeal or invitation.

Small talk must begin somewhere, and it typically begins with areas of conversation that afford minimal risk of self. After all, one doesn't immediately plunge into an unfamiliar swimming hole without first testing the waters. And if the water is frigid, one typically wades in knee deep and allows the body to adjust gradually. There are always some people who dive into freezing water and claim that such practice is better than gradually acclimating the body. But I have always considered them to be foolhardy—high-risk people and perhaps even somewhat abnormal.

Small talk should be allowed to run its course. Communicators will find subjects to talk about that include common interests or self-offers of a more significant nature. Until that happens, the best advice is to remain patient. And if it never happens? Well, not every acquaintanceship is meant to develop into a more extended relationship. Be satisfied with what you have. The greater risk is to accelerate a relationship prematurely or to give up on a relationship too soon. Probably the longest-lasting relationships are the ones that develop gradually over a comparatively long time. "Getting to know you" should be an enjoyable experience in and of itself. So give yourself the necessary time.

Scripts

When we used the term "audition" to refer to how acquaintances function in small talk, we are using the metaphor of the theater. We can extend this dramatic metaphor by referring to small talk as a similar process of enacting dramatic dialogue. Unlike a script prepared by a playwright, though, the scripts involved in the getting-acquainted stage of relationship development are improvised by the social actors even as they speak their lines. As in the improvisation exercises used in acting classes, actors don't prepare their scripts in advance, but are all aware of a common situational premise. Partners then create their own roles as they cooperate in acting out their common premise. The "premise" of initial interaction, of course, is "two strangers meeting for the first time for the purpose of getting acquainted."

A script of initial interaction has several characteristics that guide the acquaintances in making their opening moves. One, a script involves not just the actions of one person but a sequence of actions that are organized meaningfully. Two, a script provides the acquaintances with a set of expectations to guide them in creating their "roles." Three, a script is standardized and generally known to the social actors because they have experienced the same or a similar script in past interactions. Acquaintances do not know precisely what will occur next in the sequence, but they have a general idea of where the interaction is going. Of course, they can use their own comments to influence the future sequence of interaction patterns, but the basic idea of scripting their small talk is to allow each actor to adapt an appropriate response to the behavior of the other person. Scripts deal primarily with generalized experiences, those common to the widest variety of people. Therefore, virtually everyone is qualified, by past experiences, to contribute to the interaction.

Naturally, there are "good" scripts and "bad" ones. A good script allows both social actors to contribute equally from the same set of expectations. A bad script violates expectations and forces one of the participants to adapt to a situation that is out of control. The following hypothetical interaction is typical of a good script and should be familiar to all of us. In fact, good scripts are always familiar. That's what makes them "good":

A: Hi. I don't think I've seen you around here before.
B: No, this is my first time. Do you come here often?
A: Not as often as I'd like. Enjoying yourself?
B: Oh, yeah! That band is really hot!
A: They *are* good, aren't they?

This script takes advantage of the immediate environment to provide a topic for conversation. Both interactants are experiencing the sounds of the music and agree on their judgment. Of course, their script may also be following the rule of politeness, which tells them not to disagree with each other during this early stage of getting acquainted.

The following script is also a good one, but it involves little more than a greeting ritual. Nevertheless, the greetings lead the participants immediately to a point of commonality, which they quickly exploit:

A: Hi. My name is Alfred.
B: Hi. I'm Betty. (They shake hands.) Hello, Alfred.
A: Call me Al. Everybody else does.
B: Okay, Al. Do you live around here?
A: Yup. I went to high school just down the street.
B: You went to Olympus High? I had a lotta friends go there.
A: Really? Who were they? Maybe I know them.

Not all conversations "luck into" a topic of commonality so quickly. Often the script must proceed through the weather and a host of other "safe" topics before the actors find a topic of common interest. The point is not *when* the area of common interest is introduced; it's whether the actors take advantage of it when it does come up. At that point, the actors don't need the script anymore. They can branch out into more creative exploration of their potential relationship.

The following interaction is a "bad" script. It illustrates a creative opening line, but creativity is rarely of value in scripts of getting-acquainted interaction. To be too creative is to violate the set of common expectations. It typically leads to a premature termination of the interaction, and the chance for extended development is lost:

A: Well, how do you like me so far?
B: What?
A: I asked you how you like me so far.
B: But I've never seen you before in my life!
A: Yeah, I know. How'm I doin' so far?
B: How should I know? You're kinda weird.
A: A lotta people feel that way at first, but I grow on you after a while.
B: Yeah, so do warts. Excuse me. There's somebody I need to talk to.

You can just bet that the sudden compulsion to talk to "somebody" is a direct result of the desire to get away from the "weirdo." The actor had the option of attempting to cope with the script by "going along" with what is an obvious violation of the rules for greeting rituals. Actor B might have thought that the "opening move" was clever and could have reciprocated with clever comments such as "I don't think you're doing so hot. But I'm really doing great!" In this way the actor might have coped with the unexpected by using a strategy designed to regain control of the interactive situation. In the script above, however, the actor elected to use a coping strategy designed to withdraw from the situation as quickly as possible. But she couldn't resist taking that "parting shot" and letting "the weirdo" know just how she felt about his deviant behavior. But even after that retort, she continued to adapt to the rules of politeness and terminated the conversation in the ritualized form of asking permission ("Excuse me") to leave.

When interactants are using a script, they are communicating with a common set of expectations. Both communicators know what each is supposed to do. After all, they have played out this script numerous times in the past. But the script is always subject to change, and the wording of each line is not typically prepared beforehand. Each social actor improvises while enacting the script and is prepared to depart from the script at any time during this beginning small talk. When the script is a bad one and violates the expectations of one or more of the social actors (as in the example above), the departure from the script is often an exit line. But small talk that does not bring the relationship to a premature end can lead to continued development.

When Opportunity Knocks . . .

The expectations or social norms that govern "getting acquainted" interaction are both advantageous and disadvantageous to interpersonal communication. They have the advantage of making possible interaction between two highly diverse people in a variety of situations. Small-talk interaction is polite and "safe" in the sense that it is unlikely to threaten anyone's self-concept. The social rules of politeness and use

For a relationship to evolve beyond casual acquaintance, the participants must go beyond safe small talk.
(Richard Kalvar/Magnum)

of scripts make interaction easy, but they also make continued evolution of the relationship difficult. After all, "Nothing ventured, nothing gained." In other words, if the relationship is going to evolve into something other than casual acquaintance, the interaction must move away from rules of politeness and persistent use of low-risk topics.

According to sociologist Suzanne Kurth (1970), "In forming a friendship individuals must 'move' away from what is required to what is clearly voluntary. For this movement to occur, one must make an initial move to indicate that he desires a change in the relationship" (p. 152). Now making that "initial move" from the safety of small-talk interaction is a risky business. Three things can happen, and two of them are bad. One, the other person may not reciprocate your move to a further stage of relational development, and you run the risk of damage to your self-concept. Two, you may develop a relationship that is not satisfying, and you have a more difficult problem of extricating yourself from a developed relationship (the topic of Chapter 13). Three, you may develop a friendship with the person, and you can't have too many friends.

So how do you make that initial move? How do you know that it is the "right" move? How can you make sure that the two "bad things" don't happen? These questions have no sure-fire answers. You simply don't *know* that the move away from small talk is the "right" move. You simply don't *know* that the two bad things won't happen to you. There is no list of "initial-move strategies" that you can memorize and use when the time is right. You have only the option to keep the small talk going until the opportunity comes along to change the direction of the interaction pattern and take advantage of that opportunity. Taking advantage of opportunities also means either making the initial move away from "safe" interaction or responding to your partner's initial move. You cannot change the direction of the relationship alone; only both partners working together can accomplish such a feat.

The interaction during the getting-acquainted stage of relational development is filled with tension. Constantly being polite to each other is not just boring, it is also taxing. You are constantly on guard against making mistakes. In enacting scripts, you are constantly worried about forgetting your lines. In following the rules of society or the situation, you are constantly worried about breaking one. When doing small talk, you are constantly trying to put your best foot forward, to manage the other person's impressions of you. You don't feel at ease with those you don't know very well. Initial moves away from this kind of interaction, then, will invariably involve moves that ease the tension.

A typical opportunity to make an initial move away from the tension-filled interaction occurs when one or both of the partners violates one of the rules governing the situation. An instance of this kind of rule breaking, though, must not appear to be conscious and willful (as in the preceding example of the "bad script"). But accidental rule breaking occurs frequently in polite and stereotyped interaction. The most common violation is probably in the rules of turn taking. Silence is awkward and uncomfortable. Both social actors feel some responsibility to keep the conversation going. Therefore, when a pause occurs in getting-acquainted communication, both will simultaneously be thinking of a comment that fills the gap. And that means that both may simultaneously take the turn, so that both end up speaking at the same time—a violation of turn-taking rules.

When a turn-taking violation occurs, the typical response is to laugh—nervous, not fun-filled laughter. The following hypothetical interaction involves the opportunity to move away from the small talk. It occurs immediately after a period of silence when both partners attempted to speak at the same time. Both partners are aware that they have violated turn-taking rules and attempt to use strategies that repair the damage:

A: I'm sorry. You go ahead.
B: No, it was my fault. You go first.
A: Well . . . [pause] I can't remember what I was going to say. [laughs]
B: [also laughing] Really? Do you have these memory lapses often?
A: No, not usually. But it couldn't have been very important. Now what were you saying?
B: [pause] Now I can't remember what *I* was talking about. [both laughing through the next several comments]
A: Can you believe it? Neither one of us has a memory that's worth a darn.

B: You know, you're right. Come to think of it, I seem to remember that I had this same problem when I was taking my final exams last week.

A: You, too? I'm always suffering from loss of memory, then, too. I think it's called "academic amnesia."

B: [getting serious] You know, it's really fun talking with you.

A: Yeah. Me, too.

Now this conversation seems rather ludicrous. Nothing happens to make the conversation fun except that the partners have released a lot of tension by laughing about their "mistake." Neither partner knows much more about the other person's similarity in attitudes or interests, but they have combined to "break the ice" that inhibited their relational development. Releasing tension, for whatever reason, is a pleasant feeling. And whenever it occurs, the interactants will experience a personal feeling of relief and a joint feeling of being closer together. Releasing tension means that they don't have to be "on guard" anymore; they don't have to be so careful of what they say and do; they don't have to play it so safe anymore. In other words, the interaction is more fun.

The opportunity to make an initial move away from small talk may also occur by identifying some mutual interest or acquaintance as the small talk wanders from topic to topic. The form of the initial move is simply not very important. What is important is being ready to take advantage of any opportunity to make the initial move. That move must be unusual in the sense that it is somehow noticeably different from the interaction that preceded it during small talk. The initial move away from getting-acquainted interaction is out of the ordinary; it is not expected.

Most importantly, both interactants must participate in the change in relational development. One person can make an initial move, but it means nothing unless and until both partners enact the interaction pattern that departs from small talk. If that change in interaction pattern does not occur, then the relationship continues as one of acquaintanceship. If and when it does occur, a potential change in the definition of the relationship occurs.

PATTERNS OF INTERACTION

Often people think of getting acquainted as only a preliminary stage they have to pass through on their way to a more interesting relationship. Hence, we tend to think of those relationships that remain acquaintanceships as somehow "retarded"— relationships arrested in the "normal" process of development and therefore not as "good" as other relationships such as, say, friendships. Such an attitude toward acquaintanceships is undoubtedly mistaken. Throughout your lifetime, you will have far more acquaintanceships than friendships. Even though every acquaintanceship has the potential of developing into a friendship at any time, far more acquaintanceships remain acquaintanceships.

Whether the relationship is a long-term acquaintanceship or a friendship in some early stage, the patterns of interaction that define the relationship are virtually the same. Partners in long-lasting acquaintanceships tend to enact the same communication patterns as partners in the initial stages of a developing friendship. The only difference is that acquaintanceships continue those interaction patterns for longer periods of time and friendships change the patterns to something else.

The research of Katherine Adams (1985) into strategic interaction in interpersonal relationships has remarkably improved our understanding of what people actually do when they communicate within different types of relationships. Most of the discussions in Part 3 of this book, concerning the interaction patterns of different relationships, are drawn from Adams's lengthy study of strategic interaction.

Acquaintances in Adams's study tended to define their relationships in a similar manner:

> "Sue is easy to talk with, but a lot of 'newness still' in the relationship. A real nice person I am enjoying getting to know."
> "I don't know Joe particularly well. We are acquaintances because a context brings us together; otherwise I would not have instigated the relationship on my own."

Partners in acquaintance relationships may feel that the relationship is still "new" and that it could develop into something more. Or they may feel that the acquaintanceship is merely the result of circumstances, such as happening to meet at work as colleagues, and will never develop beyond its present state. Despite the differences in these expectations, though, their definitions of the relationship are quite similar. Most importantly, the interaction patterns of acquaintances are amazingly similar. They generally talk about the same issues in much the same manner, and they generally use the same strategies in accomplishing their interaction.

Relational Issues

Not surprisingly, Adams discovered that acquaintances enacted their relationships by relying heavily on *self-as-object* issues. Each person takes turns telling the other about personal experiences and interests. For example, "I'm really into cameras. I'm constantly taking pictures of interesting things and blowing them up and framing them and things like that." Each person takes turns asking the other about personal experiences and interests but rarely identifies with the other's experiences.

Acquaintances tend to define other people through their own individualized personal experience or relationship. For example, "I have a friend who works for IBM." And each person tends to draw conclusions or generalizations derived from personal experiences. For example, "So as a result, most females don't really establish a career for themselves until they're around thirty." The result is a lot of "I" and "me" (or "you" and "your") talk, but little "we" and "our" talk in reference to the joint relationship of the interactants.

Each acquaintance tends to define his or her self quite independently from the other person or the relationship. Each retains "possession" of his or her self and does not offer much of that self to the relationship. Participants in an acquaintanceship rarely tend to define their selves in terms of the relationship they have with each other. Consequently, each self remains distinct from the other during interaction. Even though the partners may exchange confidences (as in self-disclosure), each person keeps his or her definition of self intact and separated from that of the partner.

The interaction patterns of acquaintances reflect the phenomenon of *parallel selves*. Imagine two parallel lines running side by side into the far distance, much like a pair of railroad tracks. The two rails maintain the same distance from each other, never touching or crossing at any point. The self-offers of acquaintances interacting with each other are similarly parallel. Neither partner typically identifies his or her self with the relationship. Neither partner typically responds to the other person's self-offer as anything but an offer that "belongs to" the other person. Consequently, the interaction continues as a parallel development of each person's self. An interpersonal relationship with which the partners identify themselves is never allowed to develop.

Relational Strategies

Getting-acquainted interaction often includes patterns similar to those of "interviewing." One person serves as the questioner and the other person is the answerer. This pattern of interaction addresses the self-as-object issue by allowing each person to tell the other about personal experiences and opinions. The following hypothetical interaction is typical of this interviewing pattern:

A: Are you a skier, then? It seems like everyone is around here.
B: Yup. I gotta admit I really do enjoy skiing.
A: Cross-country or downhill?
B: I do both actually, but mostly I enjoy downhill. That's really a rush when you're flying downhill in deep powder. There's nothing like it in the whole world.
A: You must be a pretty good skier then.
B: Oh, I don't know about that. I got a lotta friends who are better, but I keep up with them pretty good. Do you ski?
A: Some, but mostly cross-country. It's a lot cheaper, and I like to get outside in the wintertime. Most people I know seem to do nothing but watch TV when there's snow on the ground. I've gotta be doing something, or I get bored stiff.
B: Where do you go? In the touring centers, or do you get off in the back country?
A: I've been to a lot of places, but generally I go on established trails. I'm a little leery of avalanches. How about you? Do you like to break your own trail?

Interviewing allows each partner to tell the other about personal experiences and opinions. Furthermore, each person easily switches roles in this interviewing pattern, from being the interviewer to being the interviewee and back again. The answers tell about personal experiences, and the questions ask for or invite the other person to tell about personal experiences. The result is a pattern in which each person tells the other (whether asked or not) about things that are personal. These exchanges tell each partner a great deal about the other's self while keeping that self separate from the other person and the relationship.

The interaction patterns can also reflect parallel selves when the response to the other's personal experience says, in essence, "Me, too." For example, one person may respond to a personal experience with a comment that says, in essence, "That same thing happened to me:"

A: I just can't stand the dentist chair. I get so tensed up.

B: I know what you mean. I'm always gripping the arms of the chair.

A: The last time I went, the dentist told me, "Ease up. I'm not going to hurt you." Dentists always lie like that.

B: Oh yeah. Whenever he says that, watch out. You know that pain is coming.

A: Isn't that the truth? I remember once the dentist started to drill before the Novocaine started working, and I thought I was gonna go through the ceiling.

B: Oh, that's terrible! I can imagine how that felt. It's bad enough when the stuff wears off and every tooth in your head hurts.

A: He said he was sorry, but that didn't help much. It still hurt.

B: Don't you just hate it when he says he didn't mean to hurt you? I don't think I could ever be a dentist. To be hated by everybody, even little kids.

A: Really. I don't think I would want to look in people's mouths all day, either. Especially when they have halitosis.

This interaction reflects a personal experience that is common to many people. Each person contributes to the interaction by drawing on his or her own individual experience. But the experience is personal to each acquaintance individually rather than one that they shared together. In other words, each of the acquaintances had an individual experience, and the coincidence or similarity of those individualized experiences provides the basis for their interaction. The selves of the acquaintances overlap only because of coincidental experiences. Each partner's personal experience parallels the personal experience of the other, and their interaction continues to reflect a parallel-selves pattern.

Even when acquaintances exchange personal opinions, their interaction continues to reflect the same pattern of parallel selves. To be polite, the respondent feels obligated to agree with the other's opinion, even though agreement may not accurately reflect his or her opinion. The obligation to agree, regardless of what you may really think, is greatest when the other person invites (and implicitly expects) you to agree. The following hypothetical interaction reflects such obligatory agreement of opinions:

A: I just don't understand how we can continue to knuckle under to all these terrorists. Like that thing in Iran and then the airplane hijacking in Lebanon. I think we should just go over there and bomb 'em all to pieces. Don't you think so?

B: We gotta do something, that's for sure.

A: Those guys are just trying to get some publicity, that's all. I think the government oughta tell all those TV guys and journalists that they can't give them any air time. Every time one of these things happen, they just oughta make a big news blackout, right?

B: I admit a lotta those terrorist guys like to get on camera a lot. You're right, they seem to play to the media parading the hostages around, shooting their guns and everything.

A: Yeah, just go over there and drop an atomic bomb or something. I bet we wouldn't have so many hijackings and stuff any more.

B: Well, I don't know about that, but something's gotta be done.

When you engage in "polite" interaction, you feel compelled to abide by the social rules that govern such interaction. One rule that seems implicitly to govern "good manners" is not to disagree too much with the other person. Disagreeing is tantamount to showing disrespect. Consequently, even when the other person states absolutely outrageous opinions (such as "nuking" entire countries), you don't want to run the risk of appearing disrespectful. Rather than saying the obvious "Are you out of your mind?" or "That's the most asinine thing I've ever heard," you bide by the rules and behave as the person in the above interaction does. Although you may not express wholehearted agreement, you don't disagree either.

The rules of politeness obligate you to respond in a manner that avoids rudeness. Acquaintances just don't know each other well enough to disagree very much. And besides, interaction with acquaintances just isn't important enough to spend the effort to disagree. The result is a continuation of the parallel-selves pattern, even though it may not reflect your "real" self.

The obligation to be polite does not mean that you don't ever disagree with your acquaintance-partner. It means that the obligation to avoid disagreeing is so strong that you feel the need to justify or apologize for your disagreeing response. Hence, when you are about to disagree with an acquaintance, you may flag the answer with a precise statement that a disagreement is coming (for example, "You may be right, but . . ." or "I have to disagree with you about that, but . . ."). Your flagging strategy will also tend to minimize the importance of the disagreement. You may also use a strategy that disclaims responsibility for the disagreement by attributing it to some other person or aspect of the situation (for example, "I was reading an editorial in the paper the other day that didn't agree" or "I'm probably wrong, but . . .").

In any case, the acquaintance who wants to disagree still has the freedom to do so. But the obligation of observing the social rules of politeness is so strong that the acquaintance feels the need to phrase the disagreement in such a way as to avoid potentially negative reactions. It is apparently better to ignore the outrageous opinions of others than to let them think you are rude.

Reciprocity has been discussed earlier, particularly in regard to self-disclosing communication. That is, when someone tells you something about his or her self, you are likely to tell that other person something about your self on the same topic and with about the same depth of disclosure. This kind of reciprocity associated with self-disclosing communication involves the tendency to respond "in kind." In-kind reciprocity is essentially analogous to the golden rule—"Do unto others as they do unto you."

Acquaintances tend to reciprocate each other's self-offers in kind. They seem to be saying "You tell me something about your self, and I'll tell you something about my self." You and your acquaintance-partner then take turns telling each other about personal experiences, opinions, interests, and the like. This kind of interaction, typically in terms of self-disclosing communication is another symptom of a parallel-selves pattern. The self-offers that are embodied in in-kind reciprocity do not include a definition of self based on the relationship but, rather, a definition limited to one's personal self-concept. The comments may disclose a little or a lot about one's self-concept, but they offer a definition of self that is quite separate from the relationship.

The pattern reflects the characteristic of two distinctive self-concepts moving through the interaction on parallel tracks—in other words, parallel reciprocity.

In summary, interaction patterns of acquaintances reflect comments that address self-as-object issues. Comments consistently reflect each person's orientation to his or her own self-concept. The result is an interaction of parallel selves, with each person maintaining and, to some extent, protecting his or her individual self-concept. Self-offers consistently refer to personal experiences, interests, and even opinions that belong to the individual. When acquaintances discuss the same experiences, their interaction reflects general but individually distinct experiences that merely happen to coincide with each other. Reciprocity in the interaction, like that of self-disclosing communication, is merely a response in kind, in which acquaintances take turns relating similar experiences or opinions.

The interaction patterns of acquaintances may reflect the interpersonal communication of partners who have just met and will ultimately move into a relationship of greater intensity and intimacy. Or they may reflect a long-term acquaintanceship, in which partners maintain their relational definition for an extended period of time (often for years). At any point in time, though, the interaction patterns of acquaintances or acquaintanceships are subject to change and further development—toward increasing or decreasing communion or toward increasing or decreasing intimacy, intensity, and trust.

As their definition of their relationship evolves to something new and different, the communicators enact different interaction patterns to reflect that new and different definition. In fact, as the participants enact a new and different interaction pattern, they tend to create a new and different definition of the relationship. In other words, "interaction patterns" and "definition of the relationship" are equivalent terms. And those changes of interactional patterns and relational definitions, for better or for worse, are the subject of discussion in the next chapter.

Summary

The initial stage of a developing relationship is commonly known as the "getting acquainted" phase of communication. This interaction may include newly acquainted partners who move through this first stage on their way to friendship or partners who are maintaining a long-term relationship that does not move to a different stage of development. We use the term "acquaintances" to refer to a preliminary stage of relational development and "acquaintanceship" to refer to a long-term relationship of partners who maintain such interaction indefinitely.

Getting-acquainted interaction involves the mutual attempts of each partner to manage the first impressions of the other person. Common influences on first impressions include prior expectations, physical attractiveness, and similarity of the relational partners. The interaction of this first stage typically reflects the rules and norms drawn from some larger society or social situation to which both relational partners belong. The interaction is polite and orderly, and both partners adhere to the rules of turn taking and socially accepted greeting rituals.

The commonly recognized term for getting-acquainted interaction is "small talk." These opening moves in relational development include an exchange of demographic information, conversational topics involving little risk, generalized discussions about situationally prominent interests (such as the weather), and an exchange of interviewer and interviewee roles. Small talk is highly predictable, functions to reduce each partner's uncertainty about the other, and allows the opportunity for the partners to "audition" each other to determine the potential for further development of their relationship.

The polite and stereotyped interaction of small talk often reflects the use of a "script" in which the sequence of actions is meaningfully organized; both partners have a common set of generalized expectations based on being familiar with the pattern because of their previous interactional experiences. Small talk, while making interaction easy, actually inhibits development of the relationship unless the partners depart from their script and precipitate some change. To move away from small talk requires one of the partners to take advantage of some opportunity for change (typically a release of tension) and make an initial move. The departure from small talk also requires an appropriate response that allows both partners to modify the interaction pattern and the definition of the relationship.

Interaction patterns of acquaintances and acquaintanceships reflect discussion of self-as-object issues. Strategies include comments that inform the other person about personal experiences, interests, and opinions as well as prompting or inviting the personal experiences, interests, and opinions of the other person. These interaction patterns place obligations on the communicators to follow the rules of good manners and inhibit disagreement which, when it occurs, is typically flagged with disclaimers or attributions or responsibility away from self.

Patterns of small talk indicate interaction that emphasizes the parallel selves of the interactants. Each partner consistently retains a personal orientation to the conversational topics and avoids a self-offer that incorporates the relationship into his or her definition of self. Reciprocity in small talk reveals a similar parallelism of self-concepts in which each interactant responds in kind to the other's comments, a pattern typical of the reciprocity commonly associated with self-disclosing communication.

CHAPTER 12

Creating Relationships— Integration/Disintegration, or "Ups and Downs"

Love is like a guitar—it's great to play, but there are strings attached.
—Anonymous

Love does not consist in gazing at each other, but in looking outward together in the same direction.

—Antoine de Saint Exupéry

Throughout history poets, novelists, and songwriters have immortalized the phenomenon of love. Yet despite the literally millions of words written on the subject and the availability of numerous dictionaries, no definition of love has ever achieved universal acceptance. Perhaps we are unable to define it satisfactorily because love is not a single thing; it is many things to many people and even different things to the same people at different times. Love is simply too complex to be defined so easily.

Two definitions of love introduce this chapter. The anonymous author seems to be using the "I never promised you a rose garden" approach to defining the concept. Saint-Exupéry defines love on the basis of the interpersonal relationship that unites two people—rather than some emotion felt by one or both partners. As definitions go, this one is probably as good as any and significantly better than most. It emphasizes the fact that love (or any other kind of relationship, for that matter) is what two or more people participate in or join. It is the relational bond that unites two or more people within a relationship and serves to define the selves of the individuals as a result of their being so related.

This chapter is about changes in developing relationships. To enter a new stage of a relationship with another person is to travel into the unknown. You have no guarantee that the relationship will develop into one that you find satisfying, just as you have no guarantee that you won't be hurt by or disappointed in the relationship that develops. In some relationships, you are consciously aware that you and your partner are becoming something more than casual acquaintances. In most relationships, though, you may be quite unaware of any significant relational change until after you have enacted a new definition of that relationship.

Chapter 12 deals with both directions of change—integration and disintegration. Such growth and decline, however, are not necessarily the same things in reverse. That is, the decline of a relationship is not merely a matter of backtracking the road that once led to intimacy. This chapter will discuss the function that emotions play (and don't play) in integrating and disintegrating relationships. We will also discuss the characteristics of both increasing intimacy and declining intimacy, as well as the factors that precipitate the rise and fall of interpersonal relationships. Most importantly, of course, we will discuss the issues and strategies of changes in relationships, the actual communicative behaviors that people use when enacting their relationships. We can never overemphasize that the term "interpersonal relationship" is just another way of saying "interpersonal communication."

THE RISE AND FALL OF INTERPERSONAL RELATIONSHIPS

Probably no two relationships develop in exactly the same way. One highly intimate relationship may have seemed like "love at first sight." Another may have been a slow and gradual process in which each person "sorta grows on" the other. Another relationship may have had a stormy beginning in which intimacy came about despite a "bad start." Similarly, two relationships rarely decline in precisely the same way. One relationship may decline traumatically and dramatically from a state of mutual bliss, while another may reflect a slow and gradual process of drifting apart. Still another relationship may decline after the partners realize that their integration never reached the point that they wanted, so they quit trying and allow their budding relationship to wither and die.

Regardless of the dissimilarities in how relationships develop, one characteristic is overwhelmingly typical of nearly all: they fluctuate back and forth between good times and bad. They have high points and low points. There are many periods of growth and decline. Alan Alda characterized his marital relationship as fluctuating back and forth unpredictably between periods of mutual neglect to "waves" of emotional attachment. Nearly every relationship that develops some noticeable degree of intimacy and involvement (that is, any relationship beyond casual acquaintanceship) will experience its ups and downs. Change is constant in interpersonal relationships. In other words, change is "normal."

Characteristics of Relational Change

One communication scholar, Dick Conville (1983), has speculated that the development of a relationship inherently involves change, that change in one part of the relationship affects the entire relationship. He proposes that there are four typical characteristics of relational change: change is "predictable," change is "unique," change is "oblique to its happening," and change involves "exchange . . . of securities." Whether the change is toward increasing integration (growth) or disintegration (decline), the process of change is similar in these four respects.

To say that change in a relationship is *predictable* is not to suggest that the relational partners are aware of what the outcome of the relational change will be. Nor does predictability, as the word is used here, imply that relational change is irreversible. Once change toward integration or disintegration has begun, a relationship can and frequently does reverse its trend and head in the opposite direction. It may be more appropriate to say that change is *inevitable*. Change *will* occur; that's highly predictable. Furthermore, any change in a relationship also leads to a change in how each partner evaluates and assesses that change.

What happens when two newly married people, for example, experience their "first fight"? That experience will inevitably affect their interaction in future episodes, and it will lead them both to assess their relationship differently. The partners realize that change is occurring or has occurred. After the episode, they know that the honeymoon is over, and their relationship will not be the same as it was before. That single experience may lead to a stronger relationship or a weaker relationship. In either case, both partners will evaluate their relationship differently.

The second characteristic indicates that relational change is *unique*. We already know, however, that relationships develop differently for different people and at different times. That certainly is not news. The point here is that because relational change is unique, no one possesses sure-fire techniques for dealing appropriately with change when it occurs. Hence, every time a change occurs in a relationship, both partners have to struggle with it. It is not enough simply to rely on your past experiences to provide guidelines for how you deal with a particular relational change. Each relationship is unique, so the behaviors that worked in past relationships may be totally inappropriate to the present one. Nearly everyone appears to have a tacit understanding of this fact, too. Although people in the midst of a change in a relationship may seek advice from someone else, they are likely to respond to advice by thinking, "Yeah, but this time is different."

The third characteristic of relational change is that development *is oblique to its happening*. What on earth does Conville mean with such ambiguous and convoluted wording? He is saying only that while people are in the midst of relational development, they often cannot get beyond the immediate situation to see what is happening. In other words, when in the midst of a change in the relationship, the partners may be aware that some change is occurring, but they are so caught up in the immediate details of their relationship that they are unable to do anything about it. Only upon reflection, *after change has occurred*, are they able to understand the nature of the change and how it has affected them personally.

Let's illustrate this notion. Imagine yourself being stuck on a deserted highway with a car that is out of gas. That situation is so significant that nothing else seems important. But you can't do anything about it. Some time later, you may recall being on that road and be able to analyze what you were thinking and feeling at the time. You may even look back on the situation with some amusement or tell the story as an interesting experience. But at the actual time of your disaster, you have no thoughts except how to get yourself out of it.

That understanding comes from retrospection (looking backward) is as true when a relationship is escalating toward intimacy as when it is "on the skids." When two people are in the midst of an integrative change, they are so caught up in the euphoria of the moment that they may not be able to assess what is happening. When the relationship sours, the partners are so caught up in their predicament that all they can think about is how to get out of it. As a matter of fact, about the only way one can understand developmental change of anything (including relationships) is retrospectively. The demands of the immediate situation virtually always take precedence over other factors.

The fourth characteristic of relational change concerns the participants' *exchanging one set of securities for another*. What is a "security"? It's just the opposite of a risk that is inherent in interpersonal communication. Securities, then, are the compensation for the risks in interpersonal communication. Each communicator risks his or her definition of self, among other things. To compensate for that risk, each partner assesses the relationship in terms of some securities that compensate for taking that risk. For example, the potential outcome that "this could be the start of something big" may be sufficient security to warrant taking some risk in extending additional self-offers to the other person.

At any stage of relational development, the partners have established a set of such securities for themselves. For an adolescent couple "going steady," securities involve the availability of the other for the next school dance or weekend date. Each is secure in the knowledge that the "steady" is not dating someone else. However, if the relationship goes through some change (toward either further integration or disintegration), the partners must give up the securities they have established for another set of securities.

That adolescent couple cannot continue going steady indefinitely. At some point they will undergo a change in their relationship toward greater integration or disintegration. They may escalate toward a relational stage of marriage or living together. During the period of change the partners need to decide whether to give up their present securities (guaranteed dates, low cost of living with parents, freedom to go where and do what they please when not with partner) for another set of securities (more time together, independence from parental guidance, sense of permanence in the relationship). The couple may, however, decide to break up. If they do, their transition period also involves greater risk (such as going through the pains of finding a new partner, wondering what your friends think, experiencing a sense of loss) but also carries with it a new set of securities (such as freedom to date anyone, more time for other friends, increased independence).

In the case of either growth or decline, relational partners must assess their relationship in terms of the degree of interpersonal risk and the compensating securities. Furthermore, each partner typically assesses the relational change retrospectively (that is, after the fact), and it always involves a struggle. Relational change is always a time of increased stress, both on the relationship and on the partners individually.

Every interpersonal relationship will involve some change. Even stable relationships undergo periods of individual stress and mutual bliss. Relational change will always involve a struggle—with the relationship, with each other, and with each partner's retrospective evaluations of the relationship. The partners must learn to struggle with relational change by making careful assessments of the risks and securities involved, and they will evaluate relational changes after they have occurred—

that is, retrospectively. The adage that "hindsight is typically 20-20 vision" is appropriate here, as well as the realization that only by taking a retrospective view can relational partners assess their relationship. At least, it is the only way they can assess their relationship with any degree of understanding or accuracy.

Choice and Commitment

The famous American jurist Peter Marshall once said, "In a modern society there is no real freedom from law. There is only freedom in law." On a similar theme is the saying, "If you have a good friend, let him go. If he is a true friend, he will come back to you. If he doesn't, then he was never your friend in the first place." The point of both sayings is the same. Freedom to make choices includes, above all, choosing to place constraints on the choices you make. The most precious choice of all is the choice to commit yourself to something. Without the freedom of choice, of what value is commitment?

Each participant in interpersonal communication continually exercises freedom of choice. Each communicator chooses relational partners, chooses to escalate or deescalate the relationship, chooses to make self-offers to the other person, chooses strategies to enact during communication. The fact that we are usually unaware of making these choices at the time we make them is really unimportant. The process of interpersonal communication is a continual succession of one choice after another. You know you have freedom of choice in a relationship when you choose to commit yourself to that relationship. And there is the paradox. Freedom of choice and commitment (limiting choice) are inextricably interwoven. They are one and the same. To have one is to have the other, and to deny one is to deny both.

The processes of increasing commitment and limiting choice characterize every relationship that is becoming more integrated. Commitment is one of the principal characteristics of intimate, loving, or close relationships. And commitment is inherently a constraint on your freedom of choice—one that is chosen freely. The more committed you are to a relationship, the more constraints you place on yourself, the greater your sense of responsibility, the less actual freedom you enjoy, and the greater the sense of freedom you feel. The truly open relationship is one to which the partners are firmly committed. Commitment necessarily involves reducing your freedom of choice and closing off options that had been available to you.

If increasing commitment characterizes escalating relationships, then what characterizes declining relationships? The obvious answer is "decreasing commitment," but what does that mean? Decreasing commitment may appear to be too much constraint on choice. The relational partners feel "hemmed in" by the relationship, "prisoners" of it. Interestingly enough, the same constraints that lead to *in*creased commitment also lead to *de*creased commitment. How can this be? The answer is that the participants use different attributions for their behaviors.

The difference between increasing and decreasing commitment is the difference between attributing an internal or external locus of control for your constrained actions. When your commitment to a relationship increases, you attribute your behaviors to an internal locus of control—your self. "I know I don't run around as much these days," you say, "but I *want* to stay home more. I'm in love." When your commitment to a relationship decreases, you attribute your behaviors (often the same behaviors) to an external locus of control—the situation or the other person, some cause outside self. "I never get out of the house anymore," you say, "because she (or he) won't let me go. I never have time for myself."

What may have been commitment at one time in your relationship may be understood later, retrospectively of course, as stifling—a loss of personal control or choice. In this sense, then, constraint on your personal freedom of choice characterizes both commitment and lack of commitment, both increasing commitment and decreasing commitment to an interpersonal relationship. The behaviors may be the same, but your attributions of those behaviors differ.

Relational change, toward or away from intimacy, will always involve constraint of choice. Both increasing and decreasing commitment to the relationship are characterized by constraint. In the case of increasing commitment, the communicator attributes commitment to the free choice of self and assesses the relationship as satisfying. In the case of decreasing commitment, the communicator attributes the constraint to the situation or the other person and considers the relationship unsatisfying.

Here again is the blend of the individual and the relational, the self and the relationship, that is necessary to understand the process of interpersonal communication. The relationship affects the individual just as the individual affects the relationship. To understand interpersonal communication is to understand both Parts 2 and 3 of this book and how they fit together to enable us to develop a more complete understanding of interpersonal communication.

THE FUNCTION OF EMOTIONS

Sometimes we use the term "in love" to identify a relationship characterized by the emotion. Unfortunately, we also tend to think that being "in love" may be a delusion and isn't really the emotion of love at all. But "in love" may be a more accurate term than simply "love." It suggests that "love" is something that partners are "in" together rather than something each feels separately. They are equal members "in" a relationship; they participate "in" a relationship rather than just feeling something toward the other person. As a matter of fact, this term more accurately describes membership in a variety of relationships. If we can be "in love," then why can't we be "in like," "in hate," "in acquaintance," "in indifference?" Using the term "in" emphasizes the relationship that includes both the partners and is, to a considerable extent, different from either partner's emotional interpretation of it.

The emotions felt by communicators during and following their interaction are certainly a part of interpersonal communication as much as are the patterns of interactional strategies, the patterns of self-offers. But the emotions felt by the interactants come about as a result of being in the relationship. They may affect the future of the relationship as each interactant assesses it retrospectively and intrapersonally. The following discussion describes the important functions performed by emotions during interpersonal communication but does not consider them to be synonymous with the relationship. Fundamentally, emotions belong to individual communicators as they retrospectively make attributions about the relationship and inferences about the other person.

As Attributions

Humans seem constantly to be in the process of making assessments and evaluations of their experiences. When confronted with some novel experience, we attempt to make sense of it. Perhaps that is the reason underlying the Rorschach inkblot test used by psychologists. We attempt to find some meaning in even a random inkstain. We read the *Peanuts* comic strip and find humor, and not just a little familiarity, in Charlie Brown's attempts to see animal shapes in cloud formations. Human beings are notorious for trying to make sense out of everything they encounter. We just can't stand uncertainty and take every opportunity to reduce it.

A relationship has no emotions. Only individual people have emotions. The behaviors that people perform when engaging in interpersonal communication have no emotions. The people who perform those behaviors have emotions. You can feel some emotion when you communicate, but your feeling can never be part of your behavior. As feelings, your emotions are inevitably internalized and hidden within you. You will naturally experience some feeling, as one of the communicators, about a relationship you have with someone else. And you will naturally project your feeling to the other person and, consequently, to the relationship itself. When you project your feelings outside yourself, you are engaging in attribution; you attribute the cause or locus of control of your internalized feeling to an external source—the other person and the relationship.

When you feel good or at ease interacting with another person, for example, you want to attribute that feeling to the other person and to the relationship. Your attribution thus allows you to see the other person and the relationship in terms of the emotion you are feeling. You are likely to call the other person "friend" and the relationship "friendship." You may even call the other person "lover" and the relationship "love." As sensemaking attributions go, your assessment of the relationship typically occurs after the interaction. That is, you tend to make your attributions retrospectively, after the fact. Those attributions then guide your expectations of what will happen in further interaction.

We are so good at attributing our own emotions and feelings to someone and something else that we think everyone else does it, too. Hence, when you feel some emotion and attribute it to someone else, you often believe that the other person feels the same emotion and attributes it to you. "I love you," for example, is tantamount to saying, "We love each other." Perhaps this is part of the "norm of reciprocity." When we feel some emotion toward another person, we think the other person reciprocates that emotion. When you think someone likes you, you also tend to like him or her in return. If you think someone hates you, you almost automatically hate that person back. Consequently, emotions attributed *to* another person ("I love you") go hand in hand with emotions attributed *from* the other person ("You love me"). Therefore, the emotions we feel ourselves become virtually synonymous with emotions felt by both communicators, and we use them to characterize the interpersonal relationship.

As Inferences

Most of us subscribe to the conventional wisdom that we can tell what a person is thinking or feeling by observing what that person does. We think we can "read" what people are thinking or feeling, for example, by looking closely at their eyes. "The eyes," it is said "are the mirror of the soul." Of course, we also know that some people try to hide their emotions. To the extent that they do so, we consider them good poker players. Some people may fake their emotions so well in their behavior that we may even make errors in our inferences with regard to their internalized emotions.

The point to be gleaned from this discussion is that people do attempt to infer intrapersonal dispositions in the behaviors of other people during interpersonal communication (see Kelley, 1979, pp. 3–6). Whether we can infer emotions from behavior or whether we are correct when we do so is not important. We *think* we can, and therefore we do. To understand the process of interpersonal communication is to understand how, from observing their behaviors, people make inferences about what others are feeling inside.

A recent study of marital relationships (Sillars, Pike, Jones, & Murphy, 1984) provides some insight into the inferential process that participants use when they are engaged in interpersonal communication. The following discussion summarizes the conclusions of their study.

1. *The most immediate information available is the information with the greatest influence on inferences.* The term "immediate" refers to the information that is most readily accessible. You tend to think the information that is available to you is the most important and therefore accurate information. Obviously, the most immediate information about feelings are the statements that actually express feelings (such as the words "I love you"). We know it's easy to fake this behavior, but we still consider it very important information.

2. *Nonverbal behaviors are the primary source of information used to infer the partner's feelings and emotions.* This result is not surprising. Our previous discussions have indicated that we tend to think that people cannot control (and thereby fake) their nonverbal behaviors as easily as their verbal behaviors. We also tend to think that nonverbal behaviors are more likely to reflect emotions and feelings than are verbal behaviors (also, probably, because we think it is easy to lie about our feelings verbally). Perhaps because nonverbal behaviors allow so much room for interpretation, we also like to use them to infer what we want to infer about the other person's emotions.

3. *People infer negative feelings much more easily than positive feelings from nonverbal behaviors.* This finding is more surprising than the others. Apparently we think it's easy to tell from other people's nonverbal behavior that they don't like us, but it's difficult to tell whether they do like us. Perhaps we are more receptive to negative emotions than to positive ones. Perhaps we want to avoid the risk of offering too much of our self, so we infer negative feelings in others. Perhaps we just tend to look on the bad side of things rather than the good. For whatever reason, our inferences (based on observing nonverbal behaviors) about other people's emotions and feelings are more likely to be negative than positive. And we are more likely to

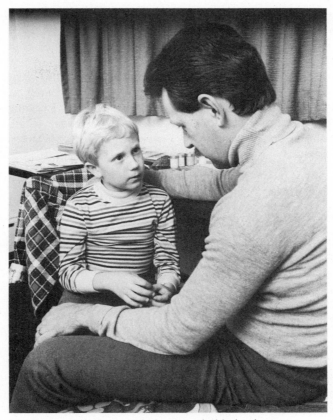

We infer others' feelings primarily from their nonverbal behaviors.
(Michal Heron/Woodfin Camp & Associates)

be more assured of our judgments of other people if the judgment is negative. No wonder people have trouble developing long-time interpersonal relationships!

4. *People strongly overestimate the similarity between their own and their partner's feelings.* The tendency to think that your partner reciprocates your feelings is very strong. You are probably most likely to overestimate your similarity with your partner during periods of relational change, particularly when the change is in the direction of increasing intimacy. After discovering some similarities in the getting-acquainted stage, you tend to think that the two of you are much more similar than you really are. Continued interaction and more development of the relationship will probably reveal more similarity, but it is also likely to reveal more differences. In other words, during that period of excitement when the relationship is escalating, you will probably judge your partner to be more similar to you than she or he actually is.

Emotions and feelings are part of the intrapersonal level of communication and thus are hidden from view. However, the fact that emotions are not observable does not mean that we don't *think* we observe them. Therefore, we use our capacity to make attributions and inferences in order to perceive the emotions of our relational partners. Since we have only the behaviors of our partners to observe, we use those behaviors (both nonverbal and verbal) as the information from which we draw our inferences and our attributions.

The emotions we experience and perceive in others are significant in affecting the development of relationships. Our emotions may exert their greatest impact during periods of evolutionary change in relational development. That is, emotions most strongly affect relational development when the relationship is moving toward or away from a higher level of intimacy and intensity. Consequently, our emotions lead us to expect and think we are experiencing a greater change than is actually occurring.

CHARACTERISTICS OF INTERPERSONAL RELATIONSHIPS

When you are actually involved in interpersonal communication, you are not always aware of what is happening in the interaction. Only after you remove yourself from the interactional event can you reflect back on what happened and make some judgment about your relationship. In other words, despite the influence of prior expectations on your perceptions, you come to understand the meaning of your relationship retrospectively.

One of the most important skills of interpersonal communication involves being aware of what is happening in your relationship—in the patterns of interaction—as quickly as possible. Your immediate awareness of what your interaction means is probably lowest during the periods of evolutionary change in your relationship. But in order to enhance your awareness and interpretation of interaction, you need to know what to look for. Furthermore, you need to be on the lookout for the interactional phenomena that signal when a change in the relationship is occurring. The purpose of this section, then, is to discover what interactional elements to look for and then to see how those elements reflect changes of growth or decline in the relationship.

General Characteristics of Relational Interaction

The number of potential characteristics of the relationship dimension of communication is so large as to defy any listing. The following characteristics include only a few of the potential number of functions performed by communication in defining our interpersonal relationships and have been selected from a longer list (see Burgoon & Hale, 1984). These characteristic functions of communicative behaviors provide a starting point in developing our communicational skills. To understand what communication does is to understand what is going on when we interact with someone else.

Verbal Immediacy. This is a catch-all term that refers to the connection between the interaction and the immediate situation. The more immediate the comment, the more directly that comment refers to the relationship, the other person, or the self of the communicator—in short, the elements of the immediate situation of interpersonal communication. Small talk, for instance, is low in verbal immediacy because it includes topics (such as the weather) far removed from self-interest or the relationship.

Comments expressing greater verbal immediacy often signal a change in the evolutionary development of the relationship. The transitional period of interaction toward either integration or disintegration typically includes an increase in the verbal immediacy of the interaction. Recall the opening comment of the bad script—"How do you like me so far?" It is high in verbal immediacy in that it refers directly to one person's feelings toward the other. It is also not appropriate to the getting-acquainted stage of relationship development precisely because it is too immediate. Later on, though, it may signal an attempt to move the relationship to another stage of development.

Recall the list of secondary characteristics of interaction discussed earlier: *intensity, intimacy, trust,* and *commitment.* We can probably think of a verbally immediate comment as referring quite directly to one or more of those characteristics. For example, each of the following comments is high in immediacy:

> "I had a great time tonight. Let's do it again real soon." (Intensity)
> "Talking with you is great fun. I think I'm beginning to like you." (Intimacy)
> "Whatever you want to do tonight is fine with me. I'm sure I'll enjoy myself whatever you decide." (Trust)
> "You mean more to me than anyone else. I want this to last forever." (Commitment)

Each of these comments signals a transitional period toward increasing integration in the relationship. Of course, comments could also signal a transition toward disintegration and still reflect high immediacy (such as "We may be getting too serious. Maybe we should stop seeing each other for a while").

"Immediate" interaction is so called because it refers directly to the relationship or the self of one of the participants. A comment is immediate to the extent that it evaluates or assesses the relationship or the feeling of one of the partners toward the relationship or the other person. If you put into words what you are feeling toward the other person or the relationship, you are contributing to an increase in the immediacy of the interaction. Of course, immediacy is stronger when both partners contribute to the immediacy and reciprocate the other's feelings at approximately the same level of intensity, intimacy, trust, and commitment.

Formality. In some communicative situations, you feel that you must constantly be on your guard. You feel inhibited and bound by the rules of the situation. These communicative situations—such as talking with someone you don't know particularly well, interviewing for a job with a person who has the power to hire you, interacting with an instructor about some classroom assignment—tend to generate interaction with a high degree of *formality.*

Formal situations make communicators conform to some set of rules restricting the freeedom they have in contributing to the interaction. By contrast, informal situations allow communicators a greater freedom of choice and provide them with some information as to what they might expect from the other person. Furthermore, you and your partner develop some informal interaction patterns that are unique to your particular relationship. In informal situations, you feel comfortable and at ease because you know what behaviors are appropriate. In formal situations, you don't feel comfortable because you don't know what to expect or what is expected of you.

Let me illustrate with a conversation I had with a student several years ago. Prior to this particular conversation, this student and I had established friendly relations and had talked at length about rather personal topics. On this particular day I became aware (for the first time, I think) that he was referring to me as "Dr. Fisher" and "Professor Fisher." Now you must understand that students and faculty colleagues alike call me "Aub" or "Dummy" or "Guy"—anything but some formal name. I asked him why he was suddenly being so formal with me, and he appeared surprised. He informed me that he had never referred to me except by the formal title. Our past interaction had been so informal that I had somehow failed to notice this sign of formality in his address.

The degree of formality in interaction is essentially a choice of what set of rules the relational partners use to govern their interaction. When communicators use rules from their situational context to determine appropriateness of their comments, their interaction is formal. When they develop their own rules to determine the appropriateness of their comments, their interaction is informal.

During periods of transition to a relational stage of greater integration, the interactants begin to develop their own rules to guide their interaction. As they recognize those self-created rules in their interaction, their interaction becomes increasingly less formal—that is, more informal. During transitional periods of disintegration, though, their interaction patterns reveal more formality and less informality. The relational partners begin to feel less comfortable in their interaction with each other, and their interaction becomes increasingly "polite." Interaction that reveals a move away from rules that made their relationship integrated is often a first sign that something is going wrong with their relationship.

Openness. In relationships characterized by openness, the relational partners provide each other with information about their inner selves. Openness is not necessarily the same as self-disclosing communication, although self-disclosure is undoubtedly part of the concept of openness. Specifically, the interaction is open to the extent that the partners tell each other about what is going on within them, often at that moment. In fact, one of the techniques that is often used in group work to increase openness is to flag the comment with a statement of openness, such as "I'd like to tell you what I'm thinking [feeling] at this very moment." A primary characteristic of openness is the expression of feelings.

Some people, we tend to believe, are more open than others. We think that some express their emotions more openly or let their emotions show. In this sense, openness is not so much a characteristic of the interaction as it is a characteristic of the interactant (more accurately, perhaps, of the "style" of the person's communication). Generally speaking, we think of an "open style" of communication more in terms of nonverbal behaviors than of verbalizing feelings. We generally believe that people who cry during sad movies, who laugh uproariously at funny jokes, who become visibly angry at news reports on television, are more open. They let their emotions show. They don't keep their feelings bottled up inside. They express what they feel.

The periods of transition as relationships become more integrated or disintegrated will probably reflect increasing or decreasing openness in the interaction. When the relationship is changing toward being more integrated, the communicators will probably be more open in their interaction. Their information will probably also reflect an increase in the amount of intensity, involvement, or commitment to the relationship. The reverse is probably true of a transitional period of interaction reflecting a change toward relational decline. The communicators will provide each other with less information about their feelings and their interaction will reflect less intensity, involvement, or commitment to the relationship.

The number of characteristics of relational interaction is enormous. To continue this discussion by adding more variables to the list would probably be more confusing than informative. The important point to be gleaned is that you should be able to detect a change in your relationship by watching out for changes in one or more of the characteristics of relational interaction. You improve your skills in interpersonal communication to the extent that you become more aware of and sensitive toward these changes. You will probably first experience a feeling that something is "different" before you are able to pinpoint just what that difference is.

Growth in the Relationship

As your relationship becomes more integrated, you naturally will feel a greater involvement. That is, you begin to define your own self in terms of your relationship. You don't necessarily change your self-concept, but you do add to your definition of self and become a more "well-rounded personality."

As you and your partner involve more of your selves in the relationship, the quality of your interaction will also reflect increases in the secondary characteristics— higher levels of intensity, intimacy, trust, and commitment. As you involve more of your self in the relationship, you also constrain more of your freedom of behavioral choice. For instance, as you spend more time with a person, you choose to spend less time with other persons or by yourself. As you commit more of your self to the relationship, you also restrict your freedom to do other things in the future. In other words, you change your expectations concerning your future behaviors. Growth in a relationship inevitably means more involvement of the self of each partner in the relationship.

The most obvious change in interaction brought about by increased involvement is probably in the frequency of interaction, particularly face-to-face interaction. The number of opportunities to talk with each other increases markedly when partners are in a period of relational growth. You begin to seek each other out, to see each other more often, to find excuses to engage in interaction, to make plans for further interaction before the current interactional event comes to an end.

The variety of your interpersonal communication also increases during periods of relational growth. That is, your interactions occur in different situations and at different times. When two students start "getting serious" about each other, for example, they increase the variety of their interaction. They continue to go on dates, of course, but they soon find occasions to study together, to meet between classes for an exchange of greetings, to have lunch together, to visit each other's homes. The kinds of interaction and the variety of situations involving interaction increase during the transitional period of growth.

During a period of relational growth, the partners begin to resent the inherent discontinuity of their interaction. Before ending their interaction on any given occasion, they make specific plans for when they will see each other again. They don't let the conversation end with a ritualistic "See ya' around." They agree on some time and place for their next meeting before they leave each other's presence. One of them is more likely to part with a comment such as "Let's eat lunch together. How about the south door of the cafeteria, say about noon?" When not in each other's presence, the partners in a growing relationship don't necessarily experience uncontrollable anxiety. But when they do meet, they typically feel relief and some alleviation of anxiety at their reunion. In fact, they may even verbalize that feeling in their greeting remark—"I missed you" or "Miss me?"

Partners during periods of relational growth also begin to use the relationship to define their own self interests, goals, or future behaviors. They may respond to a question such as "What are you going to do this weekend?" with a response similar to "I'm not sure yet. I'll have to check with Betty." When someone says, "I didn't know you liked to hike," an appropriate response might be "I didn't either until I tried it. Betty really likes to get out in the wilds, and I like it too." As involvement increases, the relational partners begin to set goals and make plans as a relational unit. They coordinate their free time so they can spend it together. They make plans for the future on the basis of their being together. As their relational involvement increases, they begin to extend their plans and goals farther into the future.

Another change in the interaction that occurs during periods of relational growth concerns what Mark Knapp (1984, pp. 231–232) calls "language patterns." We have called them strategies or self-offers. Knapp indicates three such language patterns that "change as two people reach for greater intimacy": "absolutism," "repetition," and "tense." Statements containing *absolutism* reflect an extreme definition of the relationship or the situation, such as "I'll always love you" or "I'll never leave you." One of my daughter's boyfriends told me once, in a moment of candor he has undoubtedly forgotten, "She is my one and only. I just can't live without her." He hasn't seen her for years.

Absolute statements do not typically reflect a relationship of high intimacy. Rather, they signal a relationship in a transitional period of integrative growth. Relational partners leave the growth stage and enter a period of high intimacy when their comments reflect "a more rational endorsement of the tentative nature of life and love in general" (Knapp, 1984, p. 231).

The second language pattern, *repetition*, also characterizes the relational interaction during periods of growth. During this "honeymoon" period, the partners are constantly expressing their affection and commitment to each other. They repeat their statements by using a variety of different ways of expressing their affection and commitment as well as repeating the same expressions again and again and again. People in a relationship that is evolving toward more intimacy apparently need to reinforce each other about their commitment. Thus, they repeat such statements more often. Partners in a mature relationship don't seem to need as much reinforcement.

The interaction in the relational growth period includes numerous references to the future, a characteristic of the language pattern of *tense*. Communicators apparently orient themselves to anticipating the future rather than dwelling on what has occurred in the past. But they don't have much past, in the sense that they have just moved from a getting-acquainted stage to a period of increasing intimacy. They don't have much of a history of past interaction to look back on. On the other hand, the future is exciting, unknown, challenging—an uncharted area of great promise and potential. Consequently, their interaction reflects this future orientation: "When will I see you again?" "Isn't it about time we bought some new furniture?" "How about taking a camping trip next summer?"

By constantly orienting their relationship to the future, the partners are led to long-term commitments, even when they may not be aware of it. My own personal experience comfirms this conclusion. I never did ask my wife to marry me. Furthermore, she claims (and I agree) that she didn't ask me to marry her. We did marry, though, and neither of us really knows how that came about. We began making plans of where to go, what job to take, and what to do after we graduated from college. We talked about what we'd do after we were married. We talked about where we would get married and who would marry us. But we apparently forgot to go through the step of asking and deciding to get married. Our interaction at that time was definitely oriented to the future—so much so, in fact, that it apparently affected the present. (Deep down, I really think she asked me to marry her, but Irene refuses to admit to that.)

Decline in the Relationship

To some extent, a relationship in a transition period of disintegration is the reverse of a relationship in a transition period of integration. That is, a declining relationship will probably reflect lower levels of the characteristics of interaction quality. For example, the frequency of interactional events will decrease. More and longer gaps between interactions will occur. Partners will interact with lower levels of intensity, intimacy, trust, and commitment. But a relationship on the skids is also more than just the opposite of interaction patterns that signify growth.

Perhaps a metaphor can best illustrate that relational growth and decline are not the same process. When you start the engine of your automobile, you use the ignition switch. The engine begins turning over electrically, the fuel pump sends gas to the carburetor, the carburetor mixes fuel with air, the valves open to allow the fuel mixture to flow into the cylinder, the spark plug ignites the fuel, and the engine starts running.

But what happens when the engine breaks down? It is not simply the opposite of the starting process. For one thing, the engine is still running. However, the fuel lines may be clogged, so the pump is unable to work properly. The carburetor may be dirty, so that the fuel-air mixture is not OK. The spark plugs may be fouled or out of time, so that the ignition sequence is wrong. In short, the engine continues to run, but it doesn't run properly. The driver will know that something is wrong; but—not being an expert mechanic—won't know what to do about it.

When a relationship begins to decline, in a very real sense it is "breaking down." The partners continue to interact, but their interaction is not smooth—it is "running rough." They are aware that something is wrong, but they aren't sure what to do about it. Two choices are immediately apparent: keep it going until it stops completely, or try to fix it so that it runs more smoothly. Relationships and automobile engines are similar in this respect: you can let them go until they're beyond repair, or you can try to fix them.

Unfortunately, it is far easier to repair automobile engines than to remedy problems in interpersonal relationships. A mechanic can often find the faulty part and replace it with a brand new one, but a relational "mechanic" can't so easily repair a relationship. The process of interpersonal communication must retain the basic elements of the relationship (the selves of the individual communicators) even though they may show signs of wear or damage.

Some relationships also go into decline through no fault of the partners or their interaction. They decline because the situation has changed. For example, one of the partners moves to another city. A friend may get married or start a family and have less time to interact. Any number of contextual changes can account for a significant decrease in the amount of interaction or more frequent and longer gaps between the partners' interactional encounters. Environmental changes can affect a relationship just by not allowing it to grow or continue to flourish. As a result, the relationship declines through atrophy or lack of use.

Unlike periods of relational growth, periods of relational decay often send the partners to searching for something that has caused the relational problem. When a relationship is growing, the partners enjoy feelings of increasing integration. They rarely ask themselves why they have those feelings; they just enjoy them because the feelings themselves are so enjoyable. Relational breakdown is considerably different in this respect. The feelings the partners experience during such periods are not pleasant. In fact, such feelings as depression, self-doubt, anxiety, tension, disappointment, and betrayal are downright unpleasant. The normal response to unpleasant feelings is to get rid of them. And how do we do that? "Something must be making me feel bad," we say to ourselves, "so I need to find out what is causing these feelings and do something about it."

Unfortunately, there is seldom a simple cause for the decline in any relationship. And even when you seem to find a cause of the problem, removing the cause is seldom enough to remedy the problem. It's like trying to put out a forest fire. Knowing what caused the fire (a smoldering campfire, for instance) does not help you to fight the fire that is now raging out of control several miles away. It may help you in your attempts to prevent forest fires in the future, but it won't help you put out the present fire.

To remedy a problem of relational decline is to discover the signs of it in the interaction patterns and do something about them. The solution to a relational problem lies in the patterns of communication, the exchange of self-offers. Whatever caused the problem in the first place is now irrelevant. The solution to the problem, then, is to do something to change the patterns of communication, to modify how the partners exchange their self-offers.

Relational breakdowns do not necessarily lead the partners to decide to terminate their relationship. In fact, most periods of relational decline are just disintegrative "lulls" in long-term relationships. During periods of relational decline, partners may try to reverse the trend and return to a period of relational growth. In that case, the period of decline is temporary and becomes a problem of how the partners can maintain the present definition of their relationship. In periods of relational decline, the partners may also attempt to remedy the problem by establishing a new definition of their relationship. That is, they retrospectively make sense of their relationship and redefine their past interaction to mean something different than they originally thought. After lovers quarrel or experience a lengthy period of decline in their romantic relationship, they may reassess their past interaction and decide that their relationship is not really love after all. They then proceed to redefine and enact their future relationship as "good friends."

Relational decline may occur in the middle of or immediately following a period of relational growth. For example, after the honeymoon, the newly married couple realize that they are entering a new period in their relationship. The future that they have talked about so often has become the present, and they need to define their relationship in light of that present. At one time the future had appeared to be brighter and rosier than the harsh reality of their present situation. For example, newly married couples discover they have financial problems they never encountered prior to marriage. The saying that "two can live as cheaply as one" is definitely not borne out in reality.

"After the honeymoon is over" is a phrase appropriate to any interpersonal relationship after a period of intense relational growth. It is not just for mixed-gender couples who have participated in a wedding ceremony. The posthoneymoon period typically implies some relational decline. To remedy these problems, partners often redefine their relationship. They look backward on their past interaction and make new sense of what it now means from the perspective of their present situation.

Adolescent couples often redefine their dating relationship after a period of relational growth and interpret it as something quite different from what they once thought it was. For instance, the newness of their relationship wears off, and they redefine their "true love" relationship to be only infatuation or a crush. The couple may continue to be good friends, or they may go their separate ways, still in search of the ideal partner. In either case, the experiences they shared in their past relationship haven't changed. But their definition of what those experiences meant does change. That is, they retrospectively paused to look back on their past interaction and made a different sense of those experiences. They solved a problem of relational decline by redefining their past relationship.

Redefining even a highly romantic relationship is not a very difficult thing to do. There are many different kinds of love, including brotherly love, erotic love, or unselfish altruistic love (sometimes designated by the Greek word "agape"), and kinship love. When a person says "I love you" to another, our first reaction is to consider that statement an expression of erotic love. But in retrospectively redefining a relationship, the partner can easily and rationally accept that the expression really referred to a brotherly love instead. Consequently, the relationship once thought to be erotic love turns into close friendship. After redefining their relationship, the partners then change their interaction patterns to reflect their new relational definition.

Because a loving relationship may stem from different reasons, partners may cope with relational decline by attributing their past interactions to a different basis or reason. For instance, partners may retrospectively make sense of their past relationship by attributing it to a sense of gratitude rather than love. "She helped me out at a time when I needed help," he says. Thus, the partners redefine their relationship as one based on gratitude (trying to repay the other person) rather than love. Other bases of loving relationships that provide the partners with options to redefine what love meant in their past interaction include attributing their emotions to physical attraction ("He was absolutely gorgeous, but once I got to know him better, he turned out to be really dumb"), influence of the situation ("After he graduated, we sorta drifted apart—he didn't want to go to school dances and stuff"), overactive glands ("It wasn't really love—just lust"), or misperceptions of the other's feelings ("I thought he really loved me, but he was playing around with someone else on the sly").

Partners feel a need for redefinition only during periods of decline in their relationship. During periods of growth, they enjoy the interaction patterns and perceive no problems that need coping with. But when they feel their relationship begin to sour, partners feel the need to cope with the situation, if for no other reason than that they want to rid themselves of the unpleasant feelings that typically accompany relational breakdown. Most periods of relational decline do not lead to ending the relationship altogether. Rather, they typically lead to the participants reassessing the present state of their relationship and redefining what it was in the past. When redefinition occurs, the interactants once again engage in a process of retrospective sensemaking. They redefine their past interaction patterns by employing different attributions for their previous relationship. These techniques serve to protect each partner's self-concept and to keep the relationship going, typically with new patterns of interaction reflecting the revised definition of the relationship.

COMMON FACTORS IN RELATIONAL GROWTH AND DECLINE

Previous discussions have suggested that the human being is often very selfish. Most of the coping mechanisms discussed above seem to have the single purpose of protecting the communicator's own self-concept. When that is the case, the relationships must be more individualized than communal—type III and type IV relationships rather than type I and type II relationships (see Chapter 10). A partner in a communal relationship is probably not so self-centered and is undoubtedly oriented more toward the other person. It is now time to consider how interpersonal communication works in relationships when the partners express greater concern for the interests or self-concept of the other person.

Some psychologists have suggested that the difference between being self-centered and being other-centered is the difference between an emotion and a sentiment. For example, you can love someone in the sense that you feel a personal attachment to your partner (emotion). Or you can love someone in the sense that you care about your partner and have your partner's best interests at heart (sentiment). In other words, your love can be selfish or unselfish, oriented toward an individualized (type III and type IV) or a communal (type I and type II) relationship. When emotional love characterizes the relationship, you are asking yourself, "What can [does] my partner do for me?" Your relationship is thus rather self-centered and individualized. On the other hand, when sentimental love characterizes the relation-ship, you are asking yourself, "What can [do] I do for my partner?" Then your relationship is more other-centered and communal.

Relational growth, of course, can occur in either a self-centered or an other-centered direction. You probably think that other-centered integration would be more likely to develop into a longer lasting relationship, and you would probably be correct. Such a relationship would definitely include interaction with higher levels of trust and commitment, whereas a selfish orientation could well be more intense and more intimate. But if the relationship doesn't work out and goes into a period of decline (and there are never any guarantees), the self-centered relationship presents far fewer difficulties for the partners in coping with unpleasantness. You will find that redefining a self-directed relationship is much easier than redefining one characterized by trust and commitment. It is always easier to rationalize your own behaviors than those of another person.

Despite the fact that individualized relationships are highly common, our principal concern in the following discussion will be with more communal relationships. Interaction characterizing periods of growth toward or decline from a state of communion involves several important functions that help to create the participants' definitions of their relationship. For the most part, these interactional characteristics are visibly present in the interaction, and all of them reflect the communicator's concern for the partner and for the relationship that binds them together.

Conflict

For some reason, our culture has considered conflict to be rotten and nasty. I can recall my mother telling me, as a small child, "Nobody likes an arguer" and "Try to be 'nice' to people." As I remember it, though, our household was rampant with argument despite her admonitions to her sons. Our society is somewhat two-faced regarding this issue. On the one hand, we are taught to develop a competitive fighting spirit and, as adolescents, encouraged to enter contests ranging from athletics, music, and speechmaking to drills and beauty pageants. At the same time, our culture tells us, "Try to be 'nice' to people. Conflict is bad."

It is an undeniable fact that conflict, particularly conflict in interpersonal communication, is so common as to be normal. It is very likely to occur in any relationship you have. Every interpersonal relationship comprises individual human beings with different personalities, different self-concepts, different ideas, different emotions—a whole range of differences. As you get to know each other, you learn more about your partner's interests, attitudes, beliefs, values, and so on. The more you learn, the more likely you are to discover things that make you different, including things you dislike. You need to deal with the things you dislike, or you will be forever bothered by them. During the period of growth or integrative change, the likelihood of significant conflict interaction is extremely high. The "glue" that bonds different individual selves together within an interpersonal relationship does not and cannot work when individuals deny that they are different. Instead, individuals must create their unified relationship by working through their differences. Despite the presence of similarities, individuals in even the closest and most intimate relationships will continue to be different. Their interaction is bound to include some conflict every now and then.

Conflict can certainly harm an interpersonal relationship in obvious ways. If attraction or liking is associated with similarities or common interests, then it stands to reason that dissimilarities or different interests will inhibit mutual liking. Certainly conflict will reveal differences that can potentially disrupt the relationship. Conflict can also generate negative feelings toward the other person, who then becomes an opponent or "enemy." The disruptive effects of interpersonal conflict on a relationship are obvious and make much common sense. The beneficial effects of conflict, though, are much less obvious.

Conflict can also strengthen a relationship in a variety of ways. According to one definition of friendship, "A friend is someone who likes you and refuses to see all your warts. A true friend is someone who sees all your warts and likes you just the same." Relational partners who ignore the intrapersonal elements that differentiate them run the risk of allowing those differences to smolder and become more damaging at a later stage of relational development. Conflict allows the partners to see both their similarities and their differences and to build a relationship on the basis of a more accurate and complete understanding. Conflict also allows relational partners to develop strategies for coping with adversity. The experience of having successfully met crises in the past serves to make the relational bond stronger in the future. The potentially beneficial effects of conflict on interpersonal relationships are as important as the potentially destructive effects.

Keep in mind that conflict is *inter*personal. That is, conflict requires a minimum of two people and must involve communication. No conflict can have any effect on the relationship unless the basis of the conflict involves both people, who disagree or are somehow differentiated from each other. Furthermore, the conflict can affect the relationship only if and when it appears in the form of argument, disagreement, or some other form of incompatible acts occurring in the pattern of communication. Any other kind of conflict is simply not relevant or significant to interpersonal relationships or communication.

There are basically three ways of dealing with conflict. One, you can *avoid* the source of conflict or ignore it, thereby hoping that it will go away. Two, you can *confront* the conflict and deal with it directly, with argumentative interaction, thereby hoping that it will be settled or resolved. Finally, you can *sublimate* the conflict by incorporating it within some more important or significant area, thereby hoping to lessen its importance.

Avoiding Conflict One typical way of dealing with conflict is to avoid it. By avoiding conflict, though, you don't necessarily pretend that it doesn't exist. Rather, you are saying, in essence, "This problem is trivial, not important. It isn't worth talking about." In other words, you ignore the conflict after judging the source of the conflict to be insignificant. The following interaction illustrates one way of avoiding conflict:

> "Please put your things away. I hate picking up after you."
> "Okay, sure. You wanna go out to eat tonight?"

Avoiding the source of conflict deals with conflict by taking no particularly overt or at least permanent action. It is a passive strategy aimed at trivializing the significance of the problem. You can avoid conflict by changing the topic, yielding or submitting without participating in conflict, or simply by avoiding interaction altogether. The response in the preceding example actually combines the first two tactics—submitting and changing the subject.

A recent survey (Sillars, 1980) has revealed that college roommates reported that they typically use similar passive and indirect strategies for dealing with their conflicts. They didn't necessarily believe that avoidance was the most effective or the most satisfying way of dealing with conflict, but they reported that they did it anyway.

Many conflicts are quite effectively resolved by ignoring them. The only problem lies in making an appropriate assessment of the problem's importance. If the source of the conflict is truly insignificant to the relationship, then ignoring it is a good way of dealing with it. Discussing trivial problems at length serves only to blow them out of proportion. If you recognize trivial problems as trivial, they stay trivial. However, if you treat serious problems as trivial, you run the risk of making them even more serious.

Confronting Conflict. When a problem arises, you can acknowledge its existence and actively attempt to solve it. By confronting the conflict, you remove the source of the problem from the relationship and blame it on something else. Without needing to find fault in your partner or the relationship, you attempt to solve the problem by dealing with that "something else." Let's go back to that earlier problem and see what happens when the partner confronts it:

> "Please put your things away. I hate picking up after you."
> "Yeah, we really could use a bookcase or shelves in this room. That way we could have a place to keep these magazines and books and stuff in a permanent place."

The response implicitly suggests that the problem is the lack of storage space (outside the relationship) and offers a solution to this problem (new bookcase or shelves). Confronting conflict is a way of dealing with it by turning the discussion into a problem-solving session. The discussion then becomes a task for the partners to perform through cooperative (including disagreement) effort.

The typical way to solve a problem cooperatively is first to understand it thoroughly and then to find a solution. The response above suggested a solution but could have just as easily sought or provided information concerning the nature of the problem with a comment such as "Yeah, this is a mess in here. We just don't have enough storage space in this room." Or "Where should we put all this stuff? It can't just lie around on the table and floor and make a mess all the time."

Confronting the source of conflict has the advantage of removing the source of the problem so that it no longer has a direct impact on the relationship. It also seeks to avoid blaming self, partner, or the relationship for the problem. The disadvantage, of course, is that the problem may actually *be* located in the relationship or in the partner. Then the partner's response, defining the problem as something outside the relationship, appears to be saying, "It's not my fault. Don't blame me." In this case, the partner appears to be shirking personal responsibility by finding fault with something else. The effectiveness of managing conflict by confronting it depends on whether the partners use this strategy appropriately in the conflict situation.

Sublimating Conflict. When you attempt to sublimate the conflict, you locate the source of the problem within the context of the relationship and then try to treat the problem indirectly. The typical way to sublimate conflict is to compare its significance with that of the relationship and illustrate that the problem is insignificant by comparison. For example:

> "Please put your things away. I hate picking up after you."
> "Hey, if that's all it takes to make you happy, I'll be glad to pick these things up. We really need to share the chores around the house, anyway."

The response in this interaction attempts to show that picking up these things is "no big deal." The relationship is more important. In fact, picking up the things is part of the larger and more important solution to "share the chores around the house." The partner does not take offense at the request to "put your things away" and suggests, in the context of the relationship, that it's really a trivial problem that can easily be solved.

When attempting to sublimate a conflict, you have the option of defining the source of the problem as located in your self, in the other person, or in both. In fact, a typical sublimation tactic is to share the blame with the other person and offer a tit-for-tat resolution. That is, you suggest that you'll do something "in return for" your partner's also doing some action. Such a sublimation move might appear in a comment such as:

> "I know that you've had a hard day, and I've had a hard day too. I tell you what. I'll be sure to pick these things up if you'll just let me finish reading the paper."

When sublimating a conflict, you have the option of defining the problem or the solution as being in your self, in the other person, or in the relationship. Of course, you also have the option of combining these orientations, as in the "you do something for me and I'll do something for you" response. Sublimating a conflict may appear to be a matter of persuading your partner to do something you want (like the person in our example, who wants the other person to tidy up the house).

One pair of communication researchers (Fitzpatrick & Winke, 1979) found that friends typically attempted to persuade their partners by appealing to their feelings for each other. For example, the person might attempt to manipulate the partner by being especially helpful and pleasant, thereby lowering the partner's defenses, before asking the partner to do something. Or the person might appeal to the partner's affection to get him or her to do something—"If you really loved me, you'd do this for me." Or the person might ask for a discussion based on mutual understanding in order to solve the problem—"Let me tell you how I feel so you can understand my point of view. I'll try to understand where you're coming from, too." In all cases, the strategy is to manage the conflict by sublimating it within the context of the relationship.

In practical terms, people experiencing conflict in their interpersonal communication employ a variety of tactics to manage it. Often the tactics appear as a series of trial-and-error attempts. There's nothing wrong with trial and error. You learn from errors and try something new. The only error in managing conflict is to try something, discover it isn't working, and keep doing it anyway. The following interaction, though hypothetical, is a relatively realistic portrayal of conflict as it actually occurs during interpersonal communication:

A: Please put your things away. I hate picking up after you.

B: Okay, sure. You wanna go out to eat tonight?

A: I really mean it. Clean up your mess.

B: Yeah, we really could use a bookcase or shelves in this room. That way we could have a place to keep these magazines and books and stuff in a permanent place.

A: That's not the problem. You just don't put things away when you're finished with them. They had to come from somewhere, so put them back where they came from.

B: I know that you've had a hard day, and I've had a hard day, too. I tell you what. I'll be sure to pick these things up if you'll just let me finish reading the paper.

A: Listen, if we're going to live in the same house, we both need to do what needs to be done. I've worked hard all day, and I can't come home from work and pick up after you, too.

B: Hey, if that's all it takes to make you happy, I'll be glad to pick these things up. We really need to share the chores around the house, anyway.

A: I'd really appreciate that. I just can't keep doing what I've been doing. I really need some help. And I know that you want to help. It's just that . . .

B: I know, I know. I think we need to sit down and talk about this. You tell me all the things I do that bother you, and I'll do the same. Then we can work things out, divide up the chores, and things like that. In fact, why not do it right now while we're thinking about it?

This interaction includes every kind of conflict management the relational partners have to use. Neither partner continues to harp on the same tactic after discovering that it isn't working. Both partners keep the interaction going with a variety of strategies to manage their conflict. The interaction progresses without bogging down in some stalemate in which both partners make up their minds and obstinately keep doing the same thing over and over.

If conflict is managed successfully, a relationship can endure and may even be strengthened.
(Charles Harbutt/Archive)

The avoidance of a stalemate in conflict interaction is probably the difference between successful conflict management and unsuccessful conflict management. Gottman (1982), for example, found that dissatisfied marital partners tended to respond to the partner's complaint with one of their own in a "So's your old man!" kind of interaction. Ting-Toomey (1983), in another study of marital couples, found that maladjusted pairs tended to confront each other with some complaint, and the typical response was for the partner to defend him- or herself or confront the other back. In other words, unsuccessful conflict management means using a strategy that doesn't work and continuing to use it.

Unsuccessful conflict management reflects interaction that bogs down in repetition of the same pattern. The partners aren't managing their conflict and they aren't resolving their conflict. They stalemate the conflict, line up their defenses, and wait for the other to "give in." The best advice to give any pair of relational partners, whether they are experiencing relational growth or relational decline, is to keep the interaction going. Continue to treat the conflict with every means at your disposal. As long as interaction continues, you have a chance of solving the problem that is the source of the conflict. When interaction stops without solving the problem, then the partners have no opportunity to solve it.

Some conflicts, of course, may never be managed successfully. When they aren't, the conflict may result in the end of the relationship. Sometimes terminating their relationship is the only thing left for the partners to do. Sometimes it is the best alternative, too. More often, however, the partners feel that the relationship is worth saving and strive to manage their conflict interaction. When they manage conflict successfully, their relationship is strengthened.

Supportive and Defensive Climates

Several decades ago Jack Gibb (1961) identified two "climates" of interpersonal communication—supportive and defensive ones. A defensive climate is one in which the partners feel somehow paranoid. They feel threatened by the other person or by the relationship and thus feel the need to defend themselves. A supportive climate is the reverse. Partners don't feel threatened by the other person or by the relationship, don't feel paranoid, and are thus more supportive of each other. It doesn't require genius to figure out that a supportive climate is better than a defensive one.

Many contemporary discussions of problematic relationships have focused on the paranoid feelings of defensiveness. This problem is often located in the perceptions of one of the partners, perceptions that are simply faulty. For instance, one of the reasons given for the contemporary increase in marital problems is the increase of women in the work force. Husbands, according to this argument, feel "threatened" by their wives because of the departure from the sex-roles of traditional marriages (husband as breadwinner, wife as homemaker). The problem is particularly serious, apparently, when the wife's income is equal to or greater than the husband's or if the reputation or status of the wife exceeds that of the husband.

I again feel the compulsion to engage in some self-disclosure. My wife and the past three governors of our state are on a first-name basis. The governors don't know that I exist. Through her work, she is frequently quoted in the daily newspapers and interviewed on local television with her name and title superimposed on the videotape. (I once did a "voice over" for a local TV spot, but no one ever knew about it.) More than a few people refer to me as "Mr. Irene Fisher." A newspaper reporter, preparing a feature story on my wife for one of the local newspapers, asked me during the course of a joint interview, "Irene has certainly become famous. What do you think about that?" I truly didn't understand the question. I guess I was supposed to defend myself against being "threatened" by Irene's being "famous." I did bluster some answer, as I recall, but that question continues to puzzle me. And I remain puzzled by the attitude that led the interviewer to ask the question.

One of the quotations that introduced this chapter indicated that "Love does not consist in gazing at each other, but in looking outward together in the same direction." If love is truly that communal relationship uniting the partners in a relational whole that views the world together, then it is not an individualized relationship in which the selves of the partners are competing with each other in order to win some relational contest.

For the same reason, the argument that the wife *must* have her own career in order to achieve "self-fulfillment" is also fallacious. As a practical matter, a wife should have a career to guard against the financial catastrophe following divorce or the husband's death. But to say that the wife can achieve fulfillment *only* through her own financial independence from her husband is to continue to view the marital relationship as a competition in which the partners bring home their paychecks and compare them to see whose is larger.

Partners in a communal relationship define their relationship so that each has an equivalent standing. That definition may be a breadwinner-homemaker relationship or a dual-career relationship. Relational partners define their relationship for themselves and then they look outward at the world, together, as equal partners in their relationship. The world does not and cannot impose on them the "proper" definition of their relationship.

So what does all this have to do with defensive and supportive climates of interpersonal communication? The point is simply this. The climate of defensiveness or supportiveness is more likely to be an aspect of a person's perceptions than part of the actual interaction. Certainly some relationships are based on one partner's dependence on the other. Such a relationship doesn't seem to be particularly "healthy," since the dependent partner appears to have no personality of her or his own. When a relationship stifles the self-concept of one of the partners, their perceptions may engender a defensive climate that appears in their interaction patterns. When that happens, the relationship is in trouble and needs interaction directed at enacting a new definition of the relationship, beginning with changing the perceptions of one or both of the partners.

It may be better to think of the defensive communication climate as a characteristic of relational decline and the supportive communication climate as a characteristic of relational growth. Certainly the kinds of interaction demonstrated by dissatisfied and maladjusted couples—as discovered by Gottman and Ting-Toomey—reflect a defensive climate rather than a supportive one. Furthermore, a defensive or supportive climate of communication is probably only a temporary period the relationship goes through, rather than a definition of the relationship. The only practical advice is to allow the relationship to evolve without developing a competitive orientation toward your partner. If you think you are competing with your partner, you will never develop a communal relationship—and communal relationships are always the most satisfying.

Idealization

Earlier discussions have implied that a period of relational growth may often include a series of misunderstandings. That is, the partners are so caught up in the joy of the moment that they tend to hear what they want to hear and see what they want to see. The period of relational growth induces very pleasant feelings, and those feelings may lead the partners to idealize the object of their affections. When you idealize your partner, you are really perceiving a fictitious person—an "ideal partner" who doesn't really exist—instead of the "real" person who will always have good points and bad points.

Furthermore, the partner who is idealized tends to behave in a manner consistent with the idealization. That is, he or she constantly tries to live up to the partner's expectations. That doesn't necessarily mean that the partner is "faking" a different personality. The partner is simply portraying only a part of his or her self, the part that is most likely to give the other person the best impression. As a result, though, idealization leads one partner to have an incomplete and, to some extent, false impression of the other.

When "the honeymoon is over," the partners often realize that their relationship has been based on some misunderstandings. She discovers that he is not prince charming after all, and he discovers that his beautiful princess isn't as perfect as he thought. Both realize that their future together is not likely to follow the "happily ever after" scenario unless they can learn to see one another more realistically. The discovery that a partner is not perfect rarely signals the end of a relationship. In fact, idealizing the partner is rather common during periods of relational growth, and most relationships continue to develop after the partners discover their misunderstandings.

Generally speaking, a relationship that evolves through a series of misunderstandings will also evolve out of them, given enough time. As the partners continue to interact with each other, they discover and reveal increasingly more information about each other. The normal process of communication, allowed to continue, will reveal any misunderstandings that have developed from past interaction. The only problem occurs when the partners have committed themselves to their relationship beyond the point of being able to reassess and redefine the basis for their interpersonal relationship. But that makes the problem only more difficult, not impossible, to solve.

Unfortunately, all the secondary characteristics of interaction quality do not develop at the same rate. Intensity and intimacy, for example, typically evolve much more rapidly than trust and commitment. Idealizing a relationship generally implies high intensity and intimacy but not necessarily a corresponding high level of trust or commitment. Partners in an idealized relationship often withhold trust and commitment when they feel the relationship is "moving too fast." Consequently, when they discover their misunderstanding (which resulted from idealizing the other person) they "slack off" on their period of relational growth in order to get to know one another better. When that discovery occurs, the relationship proceeds from a period of rapid growth to a period of decline. But the period of decline typically means only that the level of intensity and intimacy reverts back to where it should have been in the first place—equivalent to the levels of trust and commitment.

In every case, the solution to relational problems created by idealization is continued interaction, continued development. And if the partners decide that their relationship doesn't warrant continued growth, they are still free to redefine their relationship and remain close acquaintances or "just friends."

PATTERNS OF INTERACTION

Whether we communicate with friends or with partners who are fast becoming former friends, the strategies we use are amazingly similar. Our strategies reflect an emphasis on the self, typically the self of the partner. Generally speaking, the interaction of growing and decaying relationships allows the partners to compare their selves with each other. When the relationship is growing, the partners discover or emphasize the similarities of their selves. When the relationship is disintegrating, the differences between their selves become more important.

The important thing to remember is that similarities and differences in the individual selves of the communicators are present throughout the entire relationship. The interaction characterizing escalating relationships emphasizes the partners' similarities while ignoring or suppressing their differences. But those differences are significant in the interaction of partners whose relationship is in a period of decline, while their similarities are less significant. In both relational growth and relational decay, however, the partners use strategies that emphasize self even though the emphasis (on similarities or differences of self) differs.

Relational Issues and Strategies

Kathy Adams (1985) discovered in her investigation of relational interaction that friends tend to concentrate on self-as-other issues in their interaction with each other. They described their relationship with friends in the following manner:

> "We can do anything together, and she is fun and understanding."
> "We have a good warm relationship as friends. When we see each other, we can begin conversing as though we saw each other every day. Loren and I are alike. . . ."
> "Sara is easy to relate to. We hold things in common, and she is fun to be with and do things with."

"Friendship" is a term applied to a variety of different kinds of relationship with different levels of intimacy, intensity, trust, and commitment. Although they described their friendships similarly, these couples undoubtedly differed in characteristics of their interaction quality. Some of the couples may have been "best friends," and others may have been "just friends." In every case, though, they described their relationship in terms of their similarities. Friends tend to emphasize their similarities ("We are alike"), the things they have in common that make the other person easy to relate to.

Friends tend to be oriented to the other person. Hence, the interaction of friends includes many "you" statements, for example:

> "Yeah, but there are things that you need."
> "But you chose to do it alone."
> "Like a con artist. Is that what you're saying?"
> "Oh, I think your place is right here."

The interaction patterns of relationships in both relational growth and relational decline differ on the basis of whether they emphasize similarities or differences of the partners. Partners in friendships experiencing either decline or growth focus on self-as-other issues. Interaction during relational decline will also include many "you" statements, similar to the above comments. But even though the relational issues of their interaction are similar, partners in disintegrating relationships tend to use relational strategies to emphasize their differences. When you communicate with a friend, for example, you attempt to assimilate your self with your partner. When you communicate with a partner who is becoming less of a friend, you tend to differentiate your self from your partner. In both relationships, you interact by comparing your self with the self of your partner. The interaction patterns of relational growth and decline differ when the comparison leads to assimilating or differentiating the partners' selves.

The following interaction illustrates the assimilation of the partner's selves and is typical of the interaction of friends, that is, relationships escalating toward friendship:

A: I don't know whether to take that one or to change to a weight training class. I just don't know.
B: Oh, if I were you, I'd stick with the exercise for fitness.

In this case, Betty is offering "advice" to Alfred. Furthermore, Alfred invited her to give him advice by stating clearly, "I just don't know." Betty's advising response thus functions to assimilate her self with Alfred's self.

Another strategy that can serve to assimilate the selves is "supporting," as in the following interaction:

A: I just took a chance and told him how I felt. I thought he might get mad or somethin' but he was really nice about it.
B: Good for you. You stuck up for your rights.
A: Yeah, I guess so. It was kinda hard at first. You know, I wasn't sure what he'd do. He coulda really fried me.
B: I can imagine how hard it was for you. But you were right, and he was wrong. You gotta stand up for yourself when that happens. I'm proud of you.

In this interaction, Betty provides encouragement and support for Alfred, who has told her about his own experience. By supporting her friend, Betty is assimilating her self with Alfred's self. She expresses an emotion (pride) that she feels as a result of Alfred's action. She tells Alfred that she could experience the same feeling that he did ("I can imagine how hard it was for you").

This assimilating strategy is sometimes called "showing empathy." That is, you tell the other person that your self (emotions, feelings, and so forth) is similar to the other person's self. By offering sympathy, advice, and support, Betty expresses empathy or identifies (expresses similarity) her self with Alfred's self.

The interaction patterns of declining friendships may appear to reflect "advising" or "supporting" strategies. However, the strategies in the context of the interaction pattern function to tell the other person how different their selves are. Note the differentiating strategies in the following excerpt from the interaction of partners whose relationship is on the skids:

A: I don't know what I should do. I could sure use the extra money, but working on weekends? I just wouldn't have any free time. I just don't know.
B: Go ahead, do it. You'd have plenty of time during the week. You got all your evenings free, don't you?
A: That's not the same, though. What can you do during the week? I like weekends to go fishing or camping or. . . .
B: I know what you're thinking. You won't have any time to fool around with the boys. Big deal!

A: No, that's not it. I just. . . .

B: Come on. I know you too well. I can read you like a book. You just wanna pal around with your buddies.

A: Well, that may be part of it. But I wouldn't have any weekends at all if I work all this overtime. I do a lotta things on weekends.

B: Now you're just feeling sorry for yourself. Money is too important to you. I know how you think. You'll do it.

This interaction includes comments from Betty that only *appear* to offer advice and support to Alfred. But her comments don't show the similarities between the partners' selves. In fact, they actually differentiate her self from Alfred's. Betty attributes selfish motives to Alfred, and Alfred resists her telling him what he is feeling inside. Betty is not dissuaded, however, and continues to focus her comments on Alfred's feelings. When she makes these comments, Betty implicitly distances her self from Alfred's. After all, Betty doesn't want to "pal around" with Alfred's buddies. By telling Alfred what his feelings are, Betty demonstrates a difference in their selves and functions to emphasize something that makes their selves different rather than something they have in common.

Betty's comments also exhibit a strategy that appears to be "showing empathy" but actually functions quite differently. Note that several of her comments express what Alfred's feelings or emotions are: "I know what you're thinking," "I can read you like a book," and "I know you too well." But these strategies don't "identify" Betty's self with Alfred's self. Rather, they merely express Betty's claim that she "knows" Alfred's self. This strategy is also known as "mind reading"—telling the other person what is going on within him or her. Betty tells Alfred what he is thinking, what he is feeling, what his motives are. And Alfred reacts to Betty's mind reading in a very typical manner. He says, in essence, "You don't know what I'm thinking. Don't tell me what I feel."

The normal response to people who tell you "they know you better than you know yourself" is to deny their mind-reading ability. You generally resent such comments, particularly when they tell you that your motives or feelings are less than perfect and particularly when they are correct. Nothing is more annoying than to hear someone tell you about feelings or motives that you do in fact have but don't want other people to know about. As long as we delude ourselves that others aren't aware, we won't feel guilty about what we're feeling or thinking. As soon as we are forced to admit something uncomplimentary about ourselves, we feel guilty or embarrassed. Our typical reaction is to resent the person who made us feel that way.

In each of the interaction samples above, the partners address self-as-other issues. Alfred tells Betty about an experience or topic that is personal to him. Betty then orients to Alfred and, through Alfred, indirectly toward his personal experience. The partners also change roles so that they take turns presenting the personal experience. That is, Alfred presents his experience to Betty and thus becomes the "other" for Betty's orientation. Later on in their interaction, Betty will introduce some personal topic and become the "other" toward which Alfred orients his responsive strategies. Whether their relationship is growing or declining, the partners will focus their interaction on self-as-other issues. The principal difference between the growing and declining relationships is that in the latter the strategies in the interactional patterns emphasize the partners' differences whereas in the former their similarities are stressed.

Secret Tests

To a large extent, people in a changing relationship (either integrating or disintegrating) experience some uncertainty about the current state of their relationship. Each partner may wonder, "How well are we doing? Is our relationship getting anywhere? Does my partner think, like I do, that we're having trouble?" To reduce their uncertainty about the relationship, partners devise strategies to gain some information about its status. Of course, you can't directly ask your partner about the relationship nearly as easily as you can ask her or him about information regarding self. Hence, you devise strategies that indirectly seek information about the relationship by concealing the true motive behind the strategy. Communication scholars Leslie Baxter and Bill Wilmot (1984) call such strategies *secret tests*.

The purpose of a secret test is to acquire information about the relationship, just as small-talk strategy seeks to acquire information about the other person's self. The most obvious test, of course, would be to ask the other person how she or he felt about you. Although many people in Baxter and Wilmot's survey of male-female relationships reported that they used direct-questioning strategies, any information acquired from direct questions is probably suspect. That is, if you were really uncertain about your partner's feelings toward you, would you unquestioningly accept the truth of the answer to your question, "How do you really feel about me?" Strategies perceived to be most effective are probably those that secretly gain information about the relationship without your partner's knowledge.

A variety of "secret tests" are available to the person who wants to learn more about the current state of the relationship. The one that is most frequently used is called the *endurance test*. This strategy consists of drastically reducing the rewards for the other partner in the relationship or increasing the costs for remaining in the relationship. For example, a physical separation (not seeing each other for some period of time) tests the relationship's endurance. Does "absence make the heart grow fonder?" Or when you're "out of sight," are you also "out of mind?" Another endurance test is to ask your partner to be inconvenienced in some way, such as doing something for you that he or she would not normally or willingly do. A third type of endurance test would involve being rude toward your partner in order to determine whether he or she will sustain the relationship even after seeing your "worst side." Endurance tests all aim at discovering whether the relationship will endure after facing problems. If the partner is still around after you have used an endurance test, then you assume that your relationship is strong.

A second frequently used secret test is called a *triangle test*. This type of strategy, more likely to be used in male-female relationships, involves the use of a third party and places your partner in a situation in which his or her fidelity or jealousy is tested. Is your partner jealous when you see someone else, even if it's not a real date? Is your partner "true" to your relationship by choosing you over someone else? The earlier interaction excerpt involving Betty's mind-reading strategy may also reflect a secret test of the relationship. Betty accuses Alfred of wanting weekends free to have fun with his buddies. Betty may be secretly testing the relationship by implicitly saying, "Who is more important to you—me or your buddies?" When Alfred does not immediately respond by affirming his relationship with Betty, Betty may be thinking that he just failed her triangle test.

Another secret test uses "indirect suggestion." For instance, you make some statement about the nature of the relationship but phrase it in such a way as to imply that you aren't really serious. For example, you might phrase your statement as though you were joking or just kidding around: "When we're married, you can get a great job and support me for the rest of my life. I think I'd like being a person of leisure." Or you can drop some hint about the state of the relationship and wait for your partner's response: "Boy, this party is really stuffy. I think I really prefer being alone with someone I really like than being in a crowd of strangers."

Joking or hinting is a strategy that indirectly asks the partner to respond with some statement that indicates the nature of the relationship. By taking the joke seriously or even extending the joke, the partner is telling you that the relationship is "on track" and still escalating. By taking the hint and leaving the party with you, the partner is saying that your relationship is in good shape. But if the partner ignores the hint, you may have cause for worry.

Baxter and Wilmot (1984) also discovered that women differ from men in their use of secret tests. For example, women reported testing their relationships more frequently than men. This result may indicate either of two different explanations. One, the social relationships of women may be different from those of men. Our sex-role stereotypes lead us to believe that women are more socially oriented and thus may be more "relationally attuned" than are men. On the other hand, the survey also revealed that women and men both reported that their partners (of the opposite sex) used about the same number of secret tests. Therefore, a second explanation is that women may not use any more strategies to assess their relationships than men do, but they *think* that they do.

The problem that continues to plague our understanding of how women and men communicate is the potential and probable difference between what we *perceive* we do and what we actually *do*. Our perceptions, as earlier discussions have emphasized, are influenced by cultural stereotypes and socialized sex roles. The extent to which our actual behaviors, particularly communicative behaviors, are susceptible to those same cultural influences remains problematic.

Accounts

Strategies that provide an excuse or justification for one's own actions are, as you may recall, termed *accounts*. During the early stages of getting-acquainted communication, communicators frequently use accounts to interpret and justify their actions. But the principal issue for interaction in the early stages is "self as object." When the relationship is in a stage of growth or decay, the prominent issue of interaction is "self as other." During these transitional stages in relational development, partners orient their strategies toward the other person. Thus, when partners use accounts in periods of relational growth or decay, they are attempting to interpret or justify one another's actions.

During a period of relational growth, you "account" for the relationship by idealizing your partner and, indirectly, the relationship. A time of relational growth, you recall, is like a honeymoon in which the partners are caught up in the joy of the moment. The future looks bright, and the present is enjoyable. This is a period of idealizing reality, so that you also tend to idealize your partner. That is, you overemphasize your partner's good points and ignore (or fail to perceive) your partner's faults. As the intensity and intimacy of the interaction increases, you idealize the partner and the relationship more and more. You interpret your past interaction as a reflection of true affection, intimacy, and commitment.

During periods of relational decay, you also tend to idealize your partner and the relationship, but you use a "negative ideal." You see your partner as a cad who never really liked you. You think your relationship was never really "true" friendship or intimacy. You continued to fool yourself that it was, until your partner showed his or her "true colors." In other words, account giving during periods of relational decline typically redefines your past interaction by laying the blame for your relational problems on the other person—the perfect target for blame.

Accounts of past interaction during these transitional periods (either growth or decay) in relational development are like the "folklore" of your relationship. You and your partner essentially create your own history after you have lived it. As you look back on your history of past interaction from the perspective of the present, you remember certain events (perhaps that special date or that first argument) as having greater significance than they had at the time they happened. In other words, the significance of past events results from your having attributed significance to them through retrospective sensemaking.

During periods of relational integration and disintegration, accounts are essentially idealized perceptions or interpretations of the other person's behavior and the relationship. But they also appear in the interaction as strategies, particularly during the period of relational escalation. Expressions of affection (such as "I love you") and verbalized descriptions of the other person (such as "You are really a good friend") occur much more frequently during periods of relational growth than at any other time during relational development. For obvious reasons, it is more important for the relational partners to assure each other of their feelings during the honeymoon period. But repeating anything too much or too often leads to a loss of significance and a decrease in value.

Nonverbal Behaviors

Several years ago my wife and I were invited to the home of one of her acquaintances. We spent the evening eating dinner and making conversation. The next day our hostess remarked to Irene (I'm her husband) that we must have a good marriage. When Irene asked her what she meant by that, our hostess replied, "Well, you always seemed to be touching each other." My first reaction was to feel embarrassed. After all, I didn't want to "paw" my wife in public.

That incident sensitized me to be more aware of how we touched each other when we were with other people. I discovered that we didn't paw each other so much as we just casually touched each other's arms or hands or shoulders. I also noticed adolescent couples in public with their arms around each other, walking side by side with their hands in each other's hip pockets, and so forth. Both forms of touching are probably signs of affection, but they also seem different somehow. In one case, touching seems to be a sign of casual intimacy; in the other, it seems to be more a sign of possessiveness.

We tend to have an active perception when we interpret another person's nonverbal behaviors as having particular meaning. In fact, our perception often borders on imagination. We "read into" nonverbal behaviors the meanings we want to find, so that we often perceive meanings that are not intended, not necessary, and (too often) not accurate. The result is that nonverbal behaviors probably influence the *intra*personal level of communication more than the *inter*personal level—that is, the actual interaction.

Some generalizations about nonverbal behaviors in developing relationships are possible and transparently obvious. For example, intimate couples (particularly in the honeymoon stage) are more likely to sit closer together and touch each other more than strangers. Couples during a period of relational decline will be more likely to sit farther apart and touch each other less frequently than they did in the past.

There is undoubtedly a wide variation from one interpersonal relationship to another in terms of how the partners use nonverbal behaviors. Each set of communicators develops its own pattern of nonverbal behaviors during their growth-stage interaction. Consequently, to say that we can interpret certain nonverbal behaviors to "mean" some definition of quality of interaction (such as intensity, intimacy, trust, or commitment) is probably to fool ourselves. One couple may nonverbally display their friendship quite differently from two other friends. Our purpose here is to establish a clearer understanding of how people go about incorporating nonverbal behaviors in their interaction patterns.

Immediacy characterizes nonverbal behaviors as well as it characterizes verbal communication. For example, the behavioral postures in "quasi-courtship behavior" establish nonverbal immediacy in which the partners align themselves as "open" to each other. Other nonverbal indicators of immediacy might include prolonged eye gaze, smiling, nodding, and, of course, touching. However, because the meaning of any nonverbal behavior is subject to how it is perceived, it is impossible to say with accuracy what nonverbal behaviors are typically associated with interaction during periods of increasing intimacy.

The key to understanding immediacy as a sign of relational growth (and declining immediacy as a sign of relational decay) is to interpret nonverbal behaviors within some pattern of interaction. Specifically, that pattern is one in which the communicators seem to be at ease in behaving toward the other and in reciprocating the other person's behavior. Smiling is a good example of nonverbal immediacy that does not always reflect a greater degree of intimacy. New acquaintances smile at each other much more frequently than do intimate couples. Intimate couples don't constantly feel the need to be on their best behavior, as do people who are trying to make a good first impression. Furthermore, all smiles are not the same. The smile of the beauty pageant contestant seems to be "pasted on," but a friend's smile seems warm and inviting. One reason for the apparent insincerity of Miss America's smile is that she always seems to be smiling. Too much smiling is probably as good a sign of low nonverbal immediacy as too little.

Silence is a nonverbal behavior that is given too little credit for its value in interpreting relational development. Think back to some of your own interactions with brand new acquaintances. You were doing small talk, and suddenly there was a period of silence. The feeling you have at such moments is devastating. You feel a compulsion to fill the gap created by silence. Silence is uncomfortable, and you rack your brain to think of something to say to fill the silence—anything! With friends, though, you don't feel uncomfortable when silence occurs. In fact, silence is often a characteristic of a close relationship. When both partners can be interacting with each other silently, they have a rather well-developed relationship. On the other hand, silence becomes a sign of relational decay when the partners no longer feel comfortable when it occurs. "We never seem to talk to each other any more" is a complaint often uttered by people in a decaying relationship.

The point to be made by all this discussion is that interpersonal relationships tend to develop their own patterns of nonverbal behaviors as well as how they should be interpreted. Verbal strategies form a pattern of communication, and so do nonverbal strategies. Both verbal and nonverbal patterns are interpretable by the partners as defining their relationship. During periods in which the partners are growing closer together, they are establishing those patterns (both verbal and nonverbal) that define their interpersonal relationship. During periods in which their relationship seems to be going downhill, they change these interaction patterns, so that the patterns that served to define their intimacy later define the problems in their relationship.

The key to interpreting the meaning of interaction patterns is *change*. When the partners create their own unique relationship with its own unique patterns of interaction, they see those interaction patterns as definitions of their relationship. But when the patterns are repeated too often, the partners get bored with them, with their relationship, and with each other. The breakup of relationships is more frequently the fault of the partners' failure to continue growing and changing. Development means change. The absence of change means more than just a lack of development; it means sliding backward.

We began this discussion of nonverbal behaviors with touching. Experts, who must always make up new labels for everything, call this area of nonverbal behavior *haptics*. We will end this discussion by returning to the function of touching in interpersonal communication. Communication scholars Stanley Jones and Elaine Yarbrough (1985) inform us that the phenomenon of interpersonal touching is very ambiguous, even more so than has been believed. Precisely what touching means in interpersonal communication is extraordinarily difficult to interpret. We can interpret a touch (even the same kind of touch) as a sign of affection, support, dominance, appreciation, aggression, inclusion, confidentiality, attention getting, greeting, or a variety of other things—including accident.

Despite the ambiguity involved in interpreting what touching means, the nonverbal behavior of touching someone is often quite powerful, since actual physical contact commands attention in and of itself. You just can't remain aloof from someone who touches you. To touch someone is to be involved with that someone. Of course, the nature of the involvement may not be what you intended. And when a stranger touches you, you may feel that your "personal space" is being violated and resent the touching—but you can't ignore it. Moreover, even when you touch or are touched by someone accidentally (as in a crowded elevator, for example), you can't ignore it (even though people in a crowded elevator work hard at trying to ignore it). At the very least, you can ignore touching only with considerable difficulty.

Jones and Yarbrough (1985) also discovered that "Contextual factors are critical to the meanings of touch" (p. 50). By "contextual factors" they mean the definition of the relationship, the stage of relational development, the verbal behaviors in which nonverbal behaviors are typically embedded, the pattern of both verbal and nonverbal interaction. In short, the meaning of touch (or any other nonverbal behavior, for that matter) will vary considerably from one communicative situation to another, from one interpersonal relationship to another, from one conversation to another.

This is one of the reasons, perhaps the primary reason, why it is essential to be wary of reading too much meaning into the other person's nonverbal behaviors. You simply cannot interpret any particular nonverbal behavior as having a specific meaning unless you can observe that behavior in the context of the relationship and the interaction pattern. And even then, competent communicators will always try to check the accuracy of their interpretations of nonverbal behaviors with some other information, typically verbal behaviors—talk. In the absence of some information that confirms their interpreted meaning of the nonverbal behavior, they run the risk of drawing some potential conclusion about the relationship that is misleading and possibly very wrong.

There is no doubt that nonverbal behaviors are important to the relational partners during transitional periods of increasing and decreasing relational integration. The problem arises in interpreting their meanings accurately and precisely. The following guidelines are good rules of thumb when dealing with nonverbal behaviors:

1. Never interpret the meaning of any single nonverbal behavior. Always attempt to see that behavior within the context of your present relationship state and the pattern of interaction.
2. Avoid reading too much into the other person's nonverbal behavior. Keep any interpreted meaning of the behavior tentative, and seek confirmation of your tentative interpretation in other behaviors, particularly verbal behaviors. They are less ambiguous.
3. Remember that the other person is also interpreting your nonverbal behavior and may not be nearly as skilled as you are. Avoid the other person's mistakes by being careful about your own interpretations.
4. Always keep in mind that nonverbal behaviors are no more important in communication than verbal behaviors. In fact, because they are so difficult to interpret unambiguously, nonverbal behaviors are probably less important. In all cases, the most important indicator of the relationship is the *pattern* of the behaviors (both verbal and nonverbal)—that is, their sequence in the "give and take" of interaction.

Summary

As people continue to interact with one another, they begin to create their interpersonal relationship. Continued interaction means continued development of their interaction toward a state of increased integration or a state of disintegration. Although relational growth and decay are different stages in the evolutionary process of relational development, they do have many characteristics in common. The difference of interaction in an integrative and a disintegrative relationship is usually more in the pattern or sequence of interaction than in specific behaviors exhibited by the partners. For example, interaction serves to constrain the choices of both partners in the relationship, but the partners in escalating relationships welcome these constraints; those in deescalating relationships consider them confining.

The emotions of relational partners will change during periods of relational change—both integration and disintegration. These internalized emotions are often mistaken for the definition of the relationship. In reality, the emotion is an inference that a partner makes about the relationship in order to make sense of it after the interaction has created it (and, of course, during the interaction). An emotion may also be an attribution of the relationship in the sense that "If I feel this way, it must be love." In any case, however, the emotion is not the relationship but the reaction, either attribution or inference, of the individual relational partner to the communication and serves to make sense of the communication in terms of some feeling toward the other person.

Interaction comprises a number of different characteristics during periods of relational growth and decay. Among these components are relational control, verbal immediacy, formality, and openness. A change in the relationship, toward integration or disintegration, involves a change in one or more of the components of the interaction. The partners in the relationship define their relationship with each other by looking backward (retrospective) on their interaction and making sense of it in terms of their relationship. When the interaction is in the process of changing, then, their definition of the relationship through retrospective sensemaking is also in a process of change.

The growth and declining stages of relational development are often characterized by a combination of factors working together in the interaction patterns of the relational partners. These factors include interpersonal conflict, defensiveness, idealization, and redundancy. The issues addressed by the interactants during these transitional periods of relational development focus on the other person, that is, self-as-other issues.

Interactional strategies include giving accounts, doing secret tests, and providing support and advice to the other. During a period of relational growth, a strategy that offers advice or support to the other person will express empathy to the partner. During a period of relational decay, though, that strategy may appear as "mind reading," which is typically resented by the other partner.

Nonverbal behaviors also function importantly in the interaction during these transitional periods of relational development. However, the meanings of nonverbal behaviors are ambiguous and must be interpreted within the context of the relationship and the interaction patterns.

CHAPTER 13

Creating Relationships— Termination, or "How Can I Leave Thee? Let Me Count the Ways."

It ain't over till it's over.

—Yogi Berra

But when it's over, it's over.

—Joe Garagiola

If at first you don't succeed, try, try again.
Then quit. There's no sense being a damn fool about it.

—W. C. Fields

The end of a relationship is often a traumatic experience. When marital partners divorce, for example, the entire family often feels the impact for years. Their entire lives change and must be reconstituted with different relationships. When good friends separate, they often experience great depression. When I was in the fifth grade, my best friend moved to another town. Although he was only 24 miles away, it seemed like another planet. I was devastated and cried for days. As time passed, however, my feelings and the memory of the relationship dimmed. I have seen him only once since high school graduation, and that was years ago. I doubt that I would recognize him if I were to meet him today.

Because of the trauma associated with dissolving close relationships, we sometimes forget that we end far more of our relationships with not even a twinge of regret. In fact, the most common relational terminations occur immediately after a greeting ritual and a little small talk. We meet a new acquaintance, talk for a few moments, and terminate this brief relationship. Often we never see that person again, and we think nothing of it. Ending brief "new acquaintance" relationships also requires very little skill and is not of significant interest to us. After all, how much skill in interpersonal communication is needed to say "Goodbye" or "So long" or "Take care" or "See ya 'round" or "Have a nice day?"

Our concern in this chapter will be with relationships that terminate after having gone through a relatively extended period of evolutionary development. Ending a relationship that has achieved a relatively high level of integration (such as a friendship) does indeed require skill and relational strategies of interpersonal communication. We will leave the rituals involved in taking leave of new acquaintances to your own resources.

A few words about ending relationships is in order before we begin our discussions in earnest. First, we must not assume that we should always keep close relationships from terminating. When partners are involved in a destructive relationship, they should end it. All close relationships are not necessarily desirable or beneficial to the partners. Not all marriages, for example, should be saved. Some turn out to be terrible mistakes and aren't worth saving.

The noted playwright Henrik Ibsen detailed the story of a wife's leaving her husband in *A Doll's House*, a theme that was scandalous in the late nineteenth century. Some historians of drama have suggested that the negative reactions to this play prompted Ibsen to write *Ghosts* shortly afterward. In this "sequel," Ibsen portrayed the story of a similar wife who remained in her suffocating marriage, and tragedy was the result. Ibsen was aware, long before his time, that some interpersonal relationships are harmful in a variety of ways. They may stifle the potential growth of one of the partners or be destructive in a variety of ways. When such relationships end, the aftermath is a period of welcome freedom, renewed promise of a better future, and a better relational life (often for both partners).

Second, relationships do not always terminate in a neat, orderly manner. The breakup of some relationships is often painful, totally unpredictable, and disorderly. The aftermath of relational termination is often a period of confusion for the partners. They feel a gap in their lives, an empty hole left by the departure of the partner. How the partners attempt to fill that void is often unpredictable, out of character, psychologically unfulfilling, and even harmful.

It is probably safe to say that, just as no two relationships evolve in precisely the same way, no two relationships will terminate in precisely the same way. Every relationship is idiosyncratic and unique to some extent. The elements that make the relationship unique are important in determining the effectiveness and relevance of relational strategies used by the partners to terminate their relationships.

Third, a relationship often terminates despite the fact that one (and sometimes both) of the partners don't want it to end. This may happen because of circumstances beyond the control of the participants. For example, I didn't want my grade-school friendship to end, but I couldn't do anything about the fact that his father found a better-paying job in another town. At other times, a relationship may end because one or both of the partners consider termination to be better than keeping the relationship. New parents, for example, frequently discover that the arrival of their child forces them to terminate or drastically reduce the significance of other interpersonal relationships. In such cases, they choose the option of spending more time with family relationships and less time in casual, friendly relationships.

Work relationships are among those that often terminate for reasons other than the desires of the partners. On several occasions in my life, I have had to terminate relationships with some really good friends, people with whom I was working. When I graduated from college, I left some good friends at the television station where I

A relationship that ends continues to exist only in the memories of the participants.
(Joel Gordon)

was working. When I returned to graduate school to pursue my Ph.D., I left people whom I liked very much. As I write this chapter, my daughter is thinking about completing her senior year in college within a matter of months. She will be leaving an extremely close relationship with her roommate of four years. She is not looking forward to the end of that relationship, but she realizes that it will happen.

Our discussions in this chapter will attempt to make some sense of the "how" and "how come" of terminated relationships. Our discussions will include a few general models that provide a framework for some typical patterns of relational termination. We will also be discussing the intrapersonal, contextual, and interpersonal factors associated with the end of close relationships and, often, the decision by the partners to terminate their relationship. The chapter will conclude with the now familiar discussion of relational and communication strategies that have been associated with the final stage of developing relationships.

MODELS OF RELATIONAL TERMINATION

Recall that the relationship itself has an identity separate from the identities of the individual human beings who participate in it. We tend to think of the relationship as having a life of its own. Therefore, when a relationship is ending, we think of it as "dying." The metaphor of dying is often an appropriate way to visualize how relationships end. They may die suddenly or they may waste away to nothing over an extended period of time. Their death may cause great sorrow among the survivors. The "lifetime" of a relationship will continue to exist in the memories of the survivors. We can go on with this metaphor, but I think you've got the point.

Several scholars have attempted to picture the process involved in terminating relationships within the metaphor of death. These models of relational termination are not actual descriptions of the process of relational termination, though. They are more like scenarios or hypothetical frameworks that we can use to understand some of the different ways that relationships might end. Not every terminated relationship will approximate one of these models, but most will probably reflect the characteristics of one of them.

Passing Away

"Passing away" is a term used by Mark Knapp (1984, pp. 253–256) to describe one model of relational termination. This type of relational termination is a long, slow, and gradual erosion of the relationship. Over a period of time (even years), the relationship loses its vitality. The partners continue in their relationship, but one day they look back on it and discover it isn't as good as it used to be. As in all retrospective sensemaking, the individuals may not realize during the period of its erosion that the relationship was in the process of passing away. But sooner or later, they look back and realize the state of the relationship is not what it once was.

What causes people to grow apart from each other? What went wrong in the relationship? Why aren't things the way they used to be? Unfortunately, these questions have no simple answers. As a matter of fact, they may not even be the appropriate questions to ask. The problems in a relationship involved in passing away are unlikely to be found in some event or incident that "caused" the downward trend. The problems are generally to be found in the partners' lack of skills or efforts to maintain their relationship after it had evolved through a period of integration. They just didn't keep it going after it had its great start. In other words, the problems in a relationship that passes away are often not what the partners did, but what they failed to do.

When a relationship passes away, the partners have failed to deal with the ups and downs of their relational development. Every relationship, during its period of evolution, will go through periods of bliss and stress. Partners will find themselves happy at times and unhappy at others. In order to sustain the good times and get through the bad times, the partners develop rules or interactional patterns to manage the problems that threaten their relational bond. To the extent that they manage these problems (such as conflict) successfully, they develop a history of success and strengthen their relationship. However, the partners in some relationships become paranoid about stressful times (the "down" periods) in their relationship and don't want them to return. In fact, they will do anything to ensure that they don't return. And that may lead to entering the "passing away" process of relational termination.

One pair of friends, for instance, may have been distressed with some critical incident in their relationship. They may have had an argument that left them with feelings of depression. They may have gone through a period of stress, such as the loss of a job. By itself, the down period of their relationship is unimportant. But one or both of the partners may have disliked that period so much that they never want it (or something like it) to happen again. Hence, they develop rules to avoid the circumstances they associate with the bad times. If the distasteful experience in the past involved interpersonal conflict, for example, they tend to avoid those circumstances that might lead to arguments.

In essence, partners in relationships that are passing away cope with their problems by avoiding them—actually by failing to cope with them. Or they ignore problems when they arise and let them fester and continue to exist without being resolved. The result is that the very interactions that let their relationship evolve into a more highly integrated state are not allowed to continue. By avoiding problems, they think they won't have any more of them. But avoidance also means they won't have the experience of being strengthened by successfully solving problems. Soon their relationship becomes dull and boring. Nothing exciting ever happens, and their relationship begins to pass away. It doesn't die immediately; it just fades.

A relationship may also pass away when one or both of the partners avoid discussing something that is bothering them. For instance, you may resent the fact that your roommate doesn't pick up dirty clothes, or doesn't help with washing dishes or cleaning the apartment. But you're afraid that your roommate will "take it the wrong way" if you voice your resentment. So you keep quiet. Furthermore, you tend to watch yourself (perhaps unconsciously) when you engage in conversation for fear that you will say something displeasing. The result is that you are likely to lower your trust and commitment to the relationship, and the relationship will lose some of its intensity and intimacy. Your roommate, not knowing what is wrong, also follows your lead and responds in the same reserved manner. Soon both of you realize that your friendship has lost its "zing" and decide to live somewhere else.

Looking back on what "caused" the passing-away stage, though, you would probably think that not helping to wash the dishes was pretty trivial stuff—certainly not important enough to cause you to break up. And you are correct. That incident is trivial by itself. But continually avoiding problems is not trivial. Avoidance soon becomes the strategy that is always used to deal with (or fail to deal with) the bad times in the relationship. The ultimate reason for your breakup is likely to be the pattern of avoidance, a pattern that is difficult to see even for one skilled in retrospective sensemaking. More importantly, you can't do anything about it after the relationship ends. The trick is not to develop the habit of avoidance in the first place.

The relationship that most commonly ends through passing away is the one in which friends are separated from each other for long periods of time. Discontinuity of interaction, you will recall, is a primary characteristic of relationships, but too much discontinuity can destroy the healthiest relationship. For instance, your best friend moves away, not necessarily far away, and your day-to-day interactions become less frequent. Soon your friendship deteriorates simply because you aren't able to continue frequent interaction. Take another common example. A married couple is separated from each other because of the demands of a job that requires travel or army service or some other circumstances that enforce prolonged absence and reduced continuity of interaction. Through no fault of their own, the husband and wife grow apart. Their relationship just passes away.

A typical suggestion for avoiding such an end to a relationship is to advise the partners to remind each other frequently of their affection for each other. But keep in mind that passing away is a process that involves a gradual loss of intensity, intimacy, trust, and commitment over a long period of time. Relationships that pass away are often those that become dull and boring to the partners. Constant repetition of the same things (even "good" things) will also become dull and boring. To tell your partner constantly and repeatedly, "I love you" is to make the words dull and boring, without much meaning.

Partners in long-term, intimate relationships develop different ways of saying "I love you" without necessarily uttering those words. They help each other with menial tasks. They show concern (often just talking or listening with interest) about the things that interest the other. They surprise each other with spontaneous displays of affection. But even surprises get boring after a while if they are constantly repeated. The partners who don't let their relationship pass away are partners who create a variety of ways to show the intensity, intimacy, trust, and commitment in their relationship. The key word is *variety* in displaying their affection, not merely displays of affection by themselves.

Sudden Death

Psychologist Steve Duck (1982) has described one model of terminating relationships as "sudden death." Relationships terminate in sudden death when one partner becomes aware of some "new, surprising, and significant negatively charged information about a partner" (p. 7). The most obvious "negatively charged information" that immediately comes to mind is unfaithfulness—the discovery by one of the relational partners that the other is having an affair with someone else. The unfaithful act of the partner is typically viewed as a serious betrayal of the intimacy, trust, and commitment in the relationship. The third person is also viewed as violating the relationship and is often considered to be just as "guilty" as the philandering partner. Unfaithfulness not only betrays the relationship but also violates the taboos of society.

Of course, negative information does not necessarily involve the intervention of a third party in the relationship. One person may discover, for instance, that the partner is revealing confidential information to other people. Especially in highly intimate relationships, what goes on in the relationship is private to the partners. Partners consider that other people on the outside have no business knowing the innermost details of their relationship. Furthermore, relational partners know a great deal about each other because of the high degree of self-disclosing communication during the growth stages of their development. One person self-discloses to a partner with the expectation that such information is only for that partner's ears. To discover that the partner has told someone else is to believe that the partner has violated the trust inherent in the relationship.

But infidelity does not always lead to divorce, and betrayal of a confidence does not always result in the end of a relationship. In other words, the mere discovery of negative information about the partner does not necessarily result in sudden death of the relationship. In fact, many relationships continue to exist after such discovery.

The question then becomes "How come?" How is it that some relationships die and others don't?

Negative information by itself cannot "cause" the sudden death of a relationship. The relational partners must "allow" the information to end the relationship. If they feel that their relationship is stronger or more important than the information, then they continue. But even when sudden death does not occur, the relationship is not the same as it was. The relationship evolves into a new definition. It may have less intensity, intimacy, trust, and commitment; but more likely it will have a different kind of intensity, intimacy, trust, and commitment. In some cases, the relationship may be even stronger.

Even the "sudden death" model of relationship termination emphasizes the fact that relationships seldom completely die. They often continue, but in a redefined state. Former marital partners often remain friends after a divorce. Some divorced couples say that they are even better friends with their former spouses after the divorce. Friends who were once close often continue to interact, but they have redefined their relationship as one of "just friends."

One final comment about the "sudden death" model of terminated relationships. Negative information about the partner is often used by one or more of the partners as an excuse to justify breakup after the fact. Persons accused of infidelity often claim that they were not unfaithful until long after the relationship had suffered from severe breakdown. They claim that their unfaithfulness was not really a violation of the relationship as much as it was a symptom of a relationship that had already ended for them. In their view, the relationship had already terminated before the act of unfaithfulness. In other words, the negative information about the partner is often seen as the cause of relational termination even though the relationship was already passing away.

Precisely what makes one relationship terminate and another continue is a matter of what the relational partners *do* when they are going through this stage. They may have little choice about whether the relationship terminates; they may continue to interact within a redefined relationship; or they may consciously decide to end it all. The termination of a relationship is an act of creating the end of the relationship through interpersonal communication. (Note the title of this chapter—*"Creating Relationships—Termination."*) In all cases relational termination is observable and interpretable as a process of interpersonal communication. Communication *is* the relationship, and termination is part of the process in the evolutionary development of many relationships. Thus, termination of relationships is part of the process of interpersonal communication.

Pre-Existing Doom

Occasionally relationships terminate because the individuals are just not compatible. That is, for some reason the relationship appears to have developed beyond its optimum level. Although these instances of relational termination are not necessarily frequent, you probably know people who just "weren't meant for each other." Sooner or later, these couples discovered their mistake and dissolved their relationship—sometimes as friends and sometimes as enemies.

A relationship often has a way of "snowballing" beyond its normal rate of evolutionary development. The partners may have thought it was love at first sight, only to discover that they were nearsighted. In fact, that metaphor is not necessarily humorous. People may be attracted to each other for some superficial reason (such as physical attractiveness) and, in putting their best foot forward, behave differently in each other's presence than they would normally. As a result, the relationship is fine as long as they are in each other's presence. Over time, though, as they continue to interact and relax together, they discover things about each other that they don't particularly like. Partners in such relationships tend to attribute their emotions (such as love) to the relationship, only to discover, eventually, that their feelings are not the same as the relationship.

This model of relational termination goes by the label of "pre-existing doom" (Duck, 1982, p. 5). That is, the relationship contains elements (typically within one or both of the partners and not easily observable) that threaten the relationship. As long as these elements continue to be hidden, the relationship will continue to develop. As soon as they are exposed, however, the relationship will probably terminate.

Recall the earlier discussion of perceptual anesthesia in Chapter 7. We perceive certain elements of another person's character, beliefs, attitudes, and the like. But we may fail to perceive (through selective perception) elements that are quite dissimilar with our selves or that we find distasteful. As long as those elements are never brought to the forefront of our perception, as long as we are not aware of those distasteful or dissimilar elements in the other person, they will not affect our interpersonal relationship. But when we do become aware of them, the relationship is in danger of ending.

We are typically attracted to (that is, we tend to like) those persons who are similar to us. It stands to reason, then, that a relationship between two people who are dissimilar in significant respects (for example, a devout Republican and devout Democrat, an active athlete and a passive lout) may develop quickly through a relatively strong integrative stage without the partners being aware of these dissimilarities. Later, when their perceptual anesthesia is overcome, they experience a severe decrease in their levels of intensity, intimacy, and commitment. Those dissimilar intrapersonal characteristics were present all along (preexisting), and discovery of these dissimilarities was always a risk. Serious incompatibility of the relational partners dooms the relationship.

Mere differences between relational partners, though, do not automatically lead to termination of the relationship. In fact, you probably know more than one happy couple who seem to be very different but continue to enjoy a happy relationship. How come? The tired saying that "opposites attract" just doesn't seem to be a satisfactory explanation. On the other hand, other explanations are apparent. For instance, dissimilar partners may continue to enjoy a happy relationship without ever becoming aware of the differences that allegedly doom their relationship. Or they may discover their dissimilarities and find that their relationship is more important than the differences between them. Or one or both of the partners may actually change their self-concepts to reflect the relationship. We have a saying for this possibility, too: "This thing is bigger than both of us."

Generally speaking, no relationship that results in termination will fit neatly into one of these pigeonholes—passing away, sudden death, or pre-existing doom. But many relationships that "die" will have many of the characteristics of one of these models. The important point to remember is that none of these models lists causes of relational termination. Relationships that have many of the characteristics of each model do not always end and may be maintained for a long time. Moreover, a relationship that does reflect the characteristics of one of these models will probably evolve into a redefined relationship that may be stronger or weaker. And many relationships that die do not stop completely but continue with greater interactional distance (more frequent and longer gaps between periods of face-to-face communication) and with a different definition (typically much less intensity, intimacy, trust, and commitment). Each of these models is best understood as a general pattern that accounts for how most terminated relationships evolve to the point of termination.

RELATIONAL BREAKDOWN—"THE GATHERING STORM"

Imagine that you are a scholar interested in understanding how people dissolve their relationships, particularly relationships that have developed a relatively high degree of integration. In order to understand relational termination, you would have to observe and study interpersonal relationships that are in the process of terminating. But to do so is virtually impossible. Do you search for people who are about to break up, give them a tape recorder, and ask them to record their interpersonal communication while they are breaking up? Do you ask people whether they are about to break up and, if so, whether you can follow them around for a few months and observe them while their relationship disintegrates? Not very likely.

About the only available information we have concerning relational termination comes from surveys of people who have experienced a terminated relationship or who are asked to imagine one. Unfortunately, this information is subject to people's interpretations and perceptions of people. Their perceptions, particularly those expressed as answers on some survey form, are likely to reflect the attribution processes with which they protect their self-concepts, often placing blame on the other person or the situation. In other words, our understanding of relational termination is likely to be of questionable validity, but it is all we have to go on. The information from such surveys typically concerns what people have experienced (or perceived to have experienced) during the periods of time immediately preceding and immediately following relationship termination. The following pages will discuss those perceptual experiences during the breakdown of the relationship, the period immediately preceding relational termination. We will then discuss the aftermath of relational termination, the period immediately following relational termination.

Intrapersonal Factors

A close interpersonal relationship exerts a powerful impact on the individuals who participate in it. In fact, the effect of a highly integrated relationship is psychologically similar to mutual "addiction." When the relationship terminates or breaks down, the partners often experience "withdrawal" symptoms. Our interest focuses more on the emotional, psychological, and behavioral symptoms of relational termination. These symptoms are evident during the period of time in which the integrated relationship is suffering breakdown.

Steve Duck (1982, pp. 16–25) describes breakdown as the dissatisfaction of the participants with their interpersonal relationship. He has speculated that this period immediately preceding actual termination of the relationship psychologically affects each partner in the relationship. Of course, the breaking down of the relationship does not affect both partners in precisely the same way or to the same degree. But, according to Duck, all individuals in dissolving relationships experience four general phases of relational breakdown: the *intra-psychic phase*, the *dyadic phase*, the *social phase*, and the *grave-dressing phase*.

The intra-psychic phase focuses on the internalized feelings of each partner in terms of an emotional reaction to the other. Foremost in the individual's mind is an "I can't stand this any more" feeling. This is a time of emotional strife and internal struggle. The partner seriously questions the rewards or benefits of being in this relationship and is filled with anxiety, stress, self-doubt, and guilt. This early phase of relational breakdown may not be observable in the partner's actual behaviors, but if it is, that behavior is likely to reflect increased hostility, more value judgments, and the seeking of advice from friends and associates as to what to do. In fact, many of the letters to "Ann Landers" or "Dear Abby" read as though they were written by people in the middle of an intrapsychic phase of relational breakdown. This is essentially a problem-solving or decision-making stage for the relational partner and ends with the partner's decision to confront the other and tell her or him about the dissatisfaction.

The dyadic phase of relational breakdown begins with that confrontation. The participant tells the partner, in essence, "I'd be justified in withdrawing from this relationship. What should we do about it?" The interaction during this phase is likely to be rather negative, hostile, argumentative, and competitive. The issue at hand is no longer a matter for one individual to decide but is the joint decision of both relational partners: "Do we try to patch things up or go our separate ways?"

The dyadic phase of relational breakdown may be lengthy or relatively brief and will typically include a marked increase in the amount of personal talk and private discussion between the partners. They may seek the services of a third party (such as a counselor) to assist them, but their discussions remain highly personal. If the talks become too painful, the partners will avoid talking with each other altogether. When they do, they make the decision to dissolve their relationship by default. That is, in the absence of attempts to repair it, their relationship remains broken. This period may also include a trial separation in which the partners experiment with relational withdrawal. They may also attempt some experimental repair and see whether that works. The outcome of the dyadic phase is agreement on the response to the critical issue. That is, the partners either patch things up or split. If they patch things up, the phases of relational termination end (at least temporarily), and the relationship continues, although redefined. If they decide to split, the partners end the third phase.

The social phase of relational breakdown involves some serious soul searching by the relational partners. They may have decided to terminate their relationship, but they aren't sure they've made the correct decision. During this period, they wonder what it will be like not to be together any more. They may go through periods of vacillating back and forth between reconciling and withdrawing, experimental repairs and experimental separations. They wonder about the future, and they are frightened about the unknown. They wonder what other people will think about their decision to break up and often avoid interacting with other friends and being exposed to their potentially negative reactions. At the same time, they feel the need to tell other people just why and how they have decided to break up.

The social phase is a period of great uncertainty and stress. To compensate for that psychological discomfort, the partners will begin to assess blame for the breakup—typically attributing the fault to the other partner or the situation (rarely the self). The social phase of relational breakdown ends with the partners acknowledging to other people the impending death of their relationship. As this phase ends, the "whole world" learns of their relational breakdown.

The grave-dressing phase of relational termination is a period of coping with the fact that the relationship is over. The individuals need to get their relationship behind them. They may have told other people one story, but they now find the need to create an acceptable story of the breakdown for themselves. This is a period of psychological reinterpretation and reperception of past events. It involves a great deal of retrospective analysis of the past relationship, but the purpose is not to make sense of the past. Rather, it is to arrange the memories of the relationship so that each partner can live with them in the future.

Grave dressing involves a great deal of imagination and creativity. Former partners must rationalize their past emotions and feelings so that they decrease the significance of their past relationship. This is not a period for attributing blame for the relational breakdown; it is a period of protecting the self-concept and associated feelings of guilt and doubts of self-worth that naturally arise from the death of a close relationship. And that requires some rationalization that will help the partners explain their entire relationship from beginning to end. Partners who have trouble completing the grave-dressing phase will experience continued psychological stress and depression. If the outcome is not a successful protection and rebuilding of their self-concepts, they may find they need professional help from a psychotherapist.

The withdrawal symptoms experienced by individuals during the period of relational breakdown are often devastating to the partners. The impact is greater to the extent that the relationship was very well integrated and had achieved high levels of intensity, intimacy, trust, and commitment. Whether the relationship slowly passes away or dies suddenly does not particularly lessen the psychological stress felt by the relational partners during the period of relational breakdown. Keep in mind that these phases involve intrapersonal factors. They affect the interaction as the hostilities or self-doubts are expressed by the participants.

Interpersonal communication is insignificant in the intra-psychic phase, but it is extremely important during the dyadic phase. In this second phase, the strategies of relational termination come into play. This is the phase during which the participants determine whether they will indeed terminate their relationship, and it demands the highest degree of competence in interpersonal communication. Interpersonal communication skills are not necessarily used in attempts to repair the damage done to a relationship. Rather, they help the partners to arrive at the most beneficial and appropriate decision in regard to termination. The decision that is best for the partners may well be to terminate their relationship.

Contextual Factors

The situation itself may exert a significant impact on whether and how rapidly a relationship terminates. Often the relational partners are victims of a changing context, and the relationship terminates even though the partners themselves make no decision to end it. We have already discussed contexts that enforce a greater interactional distance. That is, the context—such as moving to a new home or neighborhood, taking a different job in a different city, being away from home a lot—forces a physical separation on the partners. A number of factors can explain why the physical separation takes place. Keeping a relationship active requires communication, actual interaction in a face-to-face setting. When the opportunities for interaction decrease and a greater discontinuity of interaction occurs, the relationship has no opportunity to grow, change, and sustain itself. It eventually dies through disuse; it decays.

Surveys of factors leading to divorce have consistently placed environmental pressures on the marriage at or near the top of the list. Newly married partners, for example, face problems they never encountered during their integrative stage. Day-to-day financial pressures—paying for groceries, rent, automobile, clothing, health care, and so on—are probably chief among them. The birth of children creates significant pressures on the marriage too. Not only is the need for more money greater, but the couple experiences a significant decrease in the amount of free time they have. Without the time or the money to go on vacations or to have regular evenings out, they are confined to home for longer periods of time. That feeling of confinement is often transferred to the relationship itself, laying the groundwork for relational breakdown.

Norms and changes in society may also affect the relationship negatively. Several years ago a newly divorced friend told me that her divorce was a classic outgrowth of the changing social norms created by the women's movement. For the first years of her marriage, she was the typical housewife who stayed at home, cleaned the house, made the meals, and supported the rising career of her husband. Later, she felt the need to continue her education, did so, and landed an excellent job. While she was working to advance her career, her husband (who had earlier encouraged her to go back to school) came to resent the fact that she had less free time to spend with him. The erosion of their relationship over several years ultimately led to termination and divorce. They parted amicably but were still the victims of changing social norms.

As society encourages women entering the work force to pursue careers, more marital relationships will include spouses in separate but equal careers. Society's norms are gradually changing to accommodate these changes. But individuals who are members of those relationships may not have come to accept those changes. The traditional husband may resent and even be jealous of his wife's career, especially if it is more successful than his. The traditional wife may resent and even be jealous of her husband's career or, conversely, of her husband's insistence that she get a job. These resentments are seeds of the intrapsychic phase of relational breakdown. Furthermore, as the number of dual-career marriages increases, the time for free interaction between husbands and wives decreases. Thus, through no fault of their own, their relationship does not have as much opportunity to grow and develop and sustain itself. The pressures of society on such couples place additional strain on the relationship and may lead to relational breakdown.

Every interpersonal relationship exists within a network of other social relationships. Each partner has friends, relatives, acquaintances, and other relationships of his or her own. The partners together have friends and acquaintances they share in common. We often call this network of interpersonal relationships a "support system" for each or both of the relational partners. But these systems of social support are not support to both partners equally. Alfred's friends are likely to be Betty's acquaintances, and Betty's friends are likely to be Alfred's acquaintances. And they will both have friends and acquaintances as a relational pair. When these contextual social relationships are in conflict with one another, though, the relationship suffers.

The most common contextual support system comprises the kinship relations of each partner. Alfred's family may or may not like Betty, but they will tend to be more supportive of Alfred. Betty's family will similarly be more supportive of Betty. When these two support systems are in conflict, they strain the relationship. If it is a severe strain, the conflicting support systems will lead to relational breakdown. The fact that the support systems are in conflict does not, of course, necessarily "cause" relational breakdown, but it does exert pressure on the relationship.

Elements of the context may affect the relationship, but they can do so only when they are displayed in the form of actual communicative actions. Human beings have a remarkable resiliency when placed in an unfavorable context. Struggling young married couples look forward to a better future and proceed to strengthen their relationship while trying to survive an unpleasant present. People hear their friends tell them evil things about their relational partners and then compartmentalize those conversations so that they don't affect the interaction they have with their partners. In other words, humans have a remarkable ability to adapt to the situation in which they find themselves. When contextual pressures do lead to a relational breakdown, the explanation is not so much that the pressures were too great but that the partners' ability to adapt and cope was not great enough.

Interpersonal Factors

In some ways, ending a relationship is easier than beginning a relationship. For example, the beginning stages of relational development involve a great deal of uncertainty reduction—that is, acquiring information about the other person and controlling the kinds of information you give the other. The stage of relational breakdown requires no such effort. And you certainly don't need to "lose" information in order to end the relationship. To build a relationship requires effort at communicating. To end a relationship requires little effort; you can just stop communicating.

Unlike any other stage of relational development, one person can terminate a relationship. The integrative stage of relational development requires that both partners work to build and strengthen the relationship. One person cannot strengthen a relationship; it requires a minimum of two people working together in concert—*inter*action. However, one person has little control over the continuance of a relationship if the other person decides unilaterally that it is over. *Inter*action is necessary only to sustain the relationship and keep it moving along the stages of evolutionary development. Mere *action*, an intrapersonal decision by either one of the relational partners, is enough to terminate it.

The entrance of a competing third person may also lead to relational breakdown. In this case, one of the partners "chooses" between two alternatives—friend one or friend two. And that choice is necessary in closely bonded relationships, such as marriage or best friends. The third person may also function as a "medium of change," according to John LaGaipa (1982, p. 196). That is, one of the partners wants to end the relationship and initiates some interaction with a third person as a way of breaking it off. LaGaipa discovered, in a survey of adolescent dating relationships, that when a boy wished to break off with his girlfriend, he would start dating another girl. After the breakup, the girl would typically insist that the relationship was stable until the other girl came along. However, the boy would suggest a different interpretation—that he wanted to break up, and the easiest way to do it was to start dating someone else. Of course, the girl could start dating someone else in order to break up with her boyfriend, but adolescent dating rituals provide much more opportunity and freedom for boys to initiate dates with third persons. Adolescent boys generally have the option of initiating the date, and they typically avoid asking "someone else's girl" for a date.

The most significant interpersonal factor of relational breakdown is the rules or interaction patterns developed by relational partners during integration. Every interpersonal relationship is unique to the extent that it develops, through continued interaction, its own rules and rituals defining that specific relationship. The partners may have pet names for each other. They may create their own special language to refer to particular things, and no one outside their relationship would have those same definitions. As their relationship begins to break down, their interaction includes fewer and fewer of these rituals and patterns. As the termination of their relationship nears, they tend to nullify these patterns, which have made their communication and their relationship unique. Failing to observe their own interaction patterns is virtually the same as failing to recognize the value of their relationship.

Some participants in relationships that are in the process of breaking down realize that something is wrong when they notice that their communication seems more "formal." They typically interpret that interaction in terms of their partner's becoming more "distant." Actually, they are recognizing the fact that the old familiar interaction patterns are missing. They no longer seem to be observing the rules established during their relational development. Their interaction isn't special any more; it isn't as close as it used to be. In other words, it's no longer different from that of other relationships, and those differences are what made their relationship special. The partners then wish they could go back to the way it used to be.

Whatever the circumstances leading to relational breakdown, relationships don't terminate on their own. They terminate when the communication between the partners changes. Communication may cease or be drastically reduced in amount. It may reflect new communication patterns that are destructive to the relationship. It may reflect interaction patterns that nullify the rules and rituals established earlier. In all cases, relationships don't terminate in people's heads or in the environment, although intrapersonal and contextual factors may precipitate the breakdown. Relationships terminate in the process of communication, the interaction patterns themselves. In fact, all phases in the evolutionary development of relationships are present in the patterns of interaction.

THE AFTERMATH—RESIDUES OF RELATIONSHIPS

Communication creates, intensifies, and sustains a relationship; it also ends one. And we all know that communication occurs in time, and that time always "marches on." As the relationship moves into the past, then, what are the residues that remain in the present? One axiom concerning interpersonal relationships is often neglected in the knowledge of common sense: *Close relationships do not "end"; they merely change.*

After the partners terminate their relationship, the relationship continues to exist in several forms. One, partners often continue to carry on some kind of relationship, to talk with one another, and to interact after they have terminated an intimate relationship. Of course, their interaction is quite different from what it once was, and they now define their relationship very differently. Their past interaction patterns are events that continue to exist in the form of memories. No one can deny that those events in the past did, in fact, happen. Unlike a computer, human memory cannot easily be erased. A computer can "forget" a memory when the file is erased, and it will function as though the erased file had never existed. The memory of humans, though, works quite differently.

A close relationship will leave a deeply embedded stamp in the individual memories of the partners after relational termination. Humans cannot erase memories of significant events in the past, but they can "change" their memory of events. Humans have the power to perceive, and perception allows them to create new memories or to redefine past events so that the remembered event is often very different from the event that actually happened. When computers change their memory, we say they have made an error. When humans do it, we say they are coping.

When close relationships end, the partners must go through a "getting over it" stage. This residue of the relationship is primarily a psychological reordering of memories and exists within the individual's psyche. But it has an interpersonal element, too. Besides rationalizing and redefining the past relationship so that it decreases in significance, the individual also moves the memory of the once close relationship from the top of the stack to the bottom. In order to render the memory less easily accessible, the individual may seek out a variety of different partners to fill the void left by the partner's departure. As the person accumulates a variety of new relational partners, the memory of the formerly close relationship is submerged. It will never be erased completely, of course, but it will be brought to the top of the cognitive deck less often with each additional relational experience.

When a relationship ends, people often cultivate other relationships with friends or acquaintances.
(Mark Antman/The Image Works)

Seeking new and different relational experiences is a second coping mechanism, one that attempts to acquire so much relational information that the memory banks tend to overload. Soon all the relational partners begin to blur, so that the partner in the terminated relationship becomes just another blurry face in the crowd. In this way, the teenager breaks up with his or her "steady," for example, and proceeds to go on many dates with a variety of different people. But the coping teenager avoids going steady with any single one.

The emotional pain following the end of a close relationship is uncomfortable, and the idea is not to let it happen again—at least, not right away. Of course, the individual runs the risk of having a "rebound" relationship. In the eagerness to fill the void left by the departed partner, the individual may attempt to replace the "steady" with another as soon as possible. This coping mechanism short-circuits the time necessary for a close relationship to evolve through a lengthy integration phase. Consequently, rebound relationships are often quite unsatisfying and typically lead to another termination. After having failed twice, the partner's emotional pain is even greater and the damage to feelings of self-worth is even more severe.

A third way that individuals deal with the aftermath of relational termination is to seek out other relationships, but not as substitutes for the absent partner. Recall that each interpersonal relationship exists within a large network of overlapping social relationships. Recall that some of those overlapping relationships include the friends and acquaintances (social-support systems) of each partner. When a close interpersonal relationship dissolves, the other social relationships remain and become even more important for the individual partner. In times of psychological stress, human beings seek out interpersonal means to ease their intrapersonal discomfort.

Often those relationships that serve as support systems become even closer as a result of their usefulness in these times of stress. In some ways, partners who function as support systems during the aftermath of relational termination do become substitutes for the other relational partner. Their continuity of interaction—as well as the trust and commitment of their interaction—increases. Although the relationships are not precisely the same, the "good friend" who is there in time of need becomes an even better friend as a result.

For the most part, we know more about what happens during times of relational termination in terms of intrapersonal or psychological factors than of interpersonal ones. We have noted the difficulty of securing information about what actually occurs in interpersonal communication during periods of relational breakdown. Interestingly, when Katherine Adams (1985) was conducting her research on relational communication strategies, she discovered that one of the persons assisting her was going through a period of relational breakdown with his wife. Even though the opportunity was available, she never considered asking that person to record his discussions with his wife as they were arguing about their relational future. As a result, though, we understand termination only by relying on the memories of people responding to surveys some time after they have experienced relational termination. Their responses are bound to reflect their psychological or intrapersonal feelings, which are often an inaccurate portrayal of their actual communication.

RELATIONAL STRATEGIES

Within the past decade, several communication scholars (including Baxter, 1979, 1982, 1983, 1984; Baxter & Philpott, 1982; Cody, 1982; and Ragan & Hopper, 1984) have become interested in the strategies used by people to terminate their relationships. They experienced the same problem, however, in attempting to observe how people interact when they are breaking off. They could not invade the privacy of people actually in the process of relational breakdown and observe their patterns of communication. Consequently, the information concerning disengagement strategies is largely in the form of responses to surveys asking people what they would do or say if they were in the situation of relational breakdown and wanted to end the relationship. This information concerning communicative strategies may be as suspect as the psychological information concerning relational breakdown. We have already discussed the fact that people tend to reinterpret their relationships after they have ended so that their memory of terminated relationships is generally quite different from the reality. Furthermore, people tend to respond to questions asking what they *would* do in a given situation with answers that reveal what they think they *should* do. As a result, the information from such surveys may confirm commonsense beliefs rather than reveal actual communicative behavior. The following discussion summarizes information from a variety of scholarly studies and attempts to separate fact from fiction whenever the invalidity of the information seems evident.

For the most part, relational strategies used for the purpose of breaking off a relationship occur during the dyadic phase of relational breakdown, discussed earlier. Most of the interpersonal communication occurs during this phase of relational termination. The issue, of course, is whether to terminate the relationship or try to repair it. Communication during the dyadic phase is a process of negotiation as the partners decide the fate or future of their interpersonal relationship. During this phase the partners use some specific negotiation strategies directed toward resolving the issue of whether the relationship is "to be or not to be."

Direct Strategies

Several years ago singer Paul Simon suggested, "There must be fifty ways to leave your lover." Each "way" was a brief rhyming one-liner that gave advice to the person to end the relationship without fuss and without beating around the bush. "Drop off the key, Lee" was the favorite one-liner of my oldest daughter whose name is, of course, Lee. Simon's lyrics advocated the use of relational strategies that told the partner directly that their relationship was over. In her studies of disengagement strategies, Leslie Baxter (1982) identified two kinds of direct strategies: manipulation and open confrontation.

A manipulatory strategy attempts to get the other person to agree with or take the initiative in breaking off the relationship. For example, you might suggest to your partner that you always considered that your relationship was only temporary, that "all good things must come to an end," or that "it's time to move on." Manipulation involves letting the other person know of your desire or intention to break up. You might also engage a third party, a mutual friend perhaps, to convey the information to your partner that you want to break off the relationship. The point of manipulation is to get your partner involved in communication that actually addresses the issue of whether your relationship should continue. It is a direct strategy in the sense that you are communicating for the purpose of conveying to your partner information that is directly relevant to the issue of termination.

An open confrontative strategy seeks to lay the issue of termination "on the table." Such a strategy brings the issue out in the open by encouraging conflict. In essence, you try to "pick a fight" with your partner. You might tell your partner openly that you want to break off the relationship. You explain to your partner the reasons for wanting to disengage. You tell your partner that it's all over. An open confrontation does not introduce the issue by suggesting that you want to patch things up. Rather, the confrontative strategy proposes a specific solution to the problems in the relationship—"let's end this relationship."

The open-confrontation strategy openly invites the other person to disagree and suggest some repair. If the partner fails to disagree with the proposal to terminate the relationship, the only thing to talk about is the alternative to break up. Confrontative strategies include assertions and reasons for terminating the relationship. The only way to consider possible repairs of the relationship is to respond to a confrontative strategy by disagreeing with it. Hence, confrontative strategies lead directly to relational termination or to interpersonal conflict.

Indirect Strategies

The purpose of an indirect strategy of relational termination is to behave in such a manner as to force the partner to realize that something is wrong. If an indirect strategy is successful, the partner soon gets the idea and brings up the issue of potential relational problems and the question of breaking off. An indirect strategy gets its point across by changing the interactive behaviors that have typified the communication in the past. The object is to withdraw from the relationship, to show your partner that some of your commitment to the relationship has been lost.

The most common indirect strategy for disengagement is to reduce the amount of interaction with the partner. You want to let your partner know that your relationship is in trouble, so you don't interact as much. In fact, you go out of your way to avoid interaction. When opportunities to talk arise, you make excuses for not talking. As one respondent to Baxter and Philpott (1982) said of a dating relationship, "I would just start seeing less and less of her until she got the message." The frequency of interaction between close friends is quite high. When that frequency decreases drastically, both partners become aware that something is going wrong.

Even when you are engaged in interaction with your partner, you can also use indirect strategies that tell your partner that something is wrong. You "withdraw" from the relationship by restricting your talk to topics of trivial importance. You don't ask your partner to do favors for you, and you find excuses not to do favors when your partner asks them of you. When you interact, you don't follow the rules that you and your partner have established during relational integration. You don't call your partner by any special name. You don't follow the patterns that have become familiar in the past. In essence, you are indirectly giving your partner a message by being "polite." That is, you talk to your close friend as though he or she were merely an acquaintance. Soon your partner will get the idea.

Positive-Tone Strategies

Baxter (1982) also identified what she called *positive-tone* strategies. The message that this kind of strategy intends to convey is "Things aren't working out, but we can still be friends." The object of this strategy is to disengage from the relationship while expressing some concern for the partner's feelings. A positive-tone strategy might include telling the other person that you have really enjoyed your relationship and will always have fond memories of it. But you are really sorry that things just didn't work out. In other words, you attempt to tell your partner that the relationship was a good one, a positive one, and you regret that it must end.

Along with assuring your partner of the positive aspects of your relationship, a positive-tone strategy will also explicitly avoid laying any blame on the partner. In other words, you attribute the fault of relational breakdown to some other factor (typically an element of the situation) beyond the control of either of you. "I really hate to leave, but this new job is just too good to pass up." "We've really had fun together, and I'll really miss you." "We can still be good friends even if we are 1,500 miles apart." Both you and your partner know that the relationship is over. The physical separation and subsequent lack of interaction will ultimately lead to progressively less interaction in the passing-away model of termination. But the purpose of the strategy is satisfied because you both leave the relationship on a positive note and believe that "if only things had been different. . . ." Attributing the relational disengagement to the situation attempts to avoid letting the other person have any hard feelings about breaking up. The relationship continues to have a positive tone, but that tone will continue to exist only in your memories. And we all know that memories fade with the passage of time.

Misunderstanding Strategies

Normal communication occurs with few problems because the relational partners implicitly understand what is going on in the interaction, even though the precise meaning is not explicit. On the other hand, one of the partners always has the option of violating taken-for-granted understandings and appear to misunderstand. Whenever someone violates a norm or rule of interaction, the partner recognizes that violation as a departure from the ordinary.

The failure to understand what is typically understood very easily signifies that something is wrong with the interaction and, hence, with the relationship. For example:

A: Hi. How ya doin'?
B: Whaddya mean, how'm I doin'? You know I don't feel good.
A: Well, I didn't mean to . . . .
B: You never "mean" to. You're so exasperating sometimes.
A: How come you're so touchy?
B: I'm not touchy. I just don't feel good, that's all.
A: Well, excyooooooze me!

Poor Alfred! He doesn't know what's going on. He was just making conversation, and Betty responds by violating all the rules of polite conversation. He can't understand why Betty is so touchy and finally gives up trying to understand. If something wasn't wrong with the relationship before, it is now.

Any violation of a norm, idiosyncratic or contextual (as in this instance), signifies a violation of the cooperation that is implicit whenever two people communicate with each other. A rule violation makes explicit a problem in communication. And when people have problems interacting with each other, they have problems in their relationship. After all, communicating is relating. To let the partner know that a problem exists in the relationship, a misunderstanding strategy makes that problem explicit by making it evident in the pattern of interaction.

Another misunderstanding strategy is to interact as though you just don't understand what your partner is telling you. The topic can be about anything: the relationship, the other's personal experience, the TV show you saw last night, or anything else. The strategy is to fail consistently to understand what your partner is trying to tell you. You are implicitly telling your partner that your relationship is in trouble. You are talking, but you just aren't "understanding" each other. Consider the following hypothetical interaction:

A: Did you hear what happened to Jackie?

B: Jackie who?

A: How many Jackies do we know? Jackie Smith, of course.

B: Jackie Smith? Oh yeah. What about her?

A: She just won the big contest at Burger King.

B: What contest?

A: The Burger King contest. The cards that you scrape off.

B: What do you mean "scrape off?"

A: You take a coin and scrape the gray stuff off. You know.

B: At Burger King? What are they giving away?

A: The big prize is a trip to Hawaii.

B: She's going to Hawaii? Really? That's great!

A: No, that's the grand prize. She won $100.

B: I thought you said she won a trip to Hawaii.

A: No. I said . . . Oh, just forget it.

Betty is making the conversation very difficult for poor Alfred. She just fails to understand and continually asks questions, often of the "What do you mean" kind. After a while Alfred decides it isn't worth the effort any more and quits trying to tell the story.

If Alfred and Betty have very many of these labored conversations, Alfred will soon get the idea that they have a relational problem. They used to get along so well, he thinks, but now they seem to be incompatible. They just "don't seem to communicate" any more. If and when Alfred comes to that conclusion, Betty will know that her "I just don't understand" strategy has worked. She has successfully disengaged herself from her relationship with Alfred.

Preferred Strategies

According to research by Baxter (1982) and Cody (1982), people say to researchers that they prefer to use positive-tone strategies when they want to break up with friends or other close relationships. In general, they report that they would tend to avoid using the more negative strategies, particularly those involving open confrontation. The extent to which this preference holds true in "real life," though, is unknown. We can speculate that people responding to questionnaires would typically report that the best type of relational termination is one in which the partners leave without a "sour taste in the mouth." They want to part as friends and with no hard feelings. This is the kind of strategy that people think they *should* use, whether they actually use it or not. After all, feeling good about relational termination is probably preferable to feeling bad. And when people are given a choice about whether they want to feel good or bad, they are likely to say they would rather feel good.

But the end of a close relationship usually does include a period of "feeling bad." If the relationship has been close, it is only natural that partners will feel *withdrawal symptoms*, an empty feeling after the relationship breaks up. Some close relationships will involve partners who remain friends and have pleasant memories about the past. But we have little reason to believe that such "let's remain friends" endings are typical of most relationships that terminate. In fact, we have more reason to believe that most relational breakdowns will have much less happy endings.

The research findings also suggest that people prefer the use of indirect to direct strategies in initiating discussion of the issue of whether to terminate their relationship. The idea behind this strategy, remember, is that you let the other person think that something is wrong with the relationship. Furthermore, using an indirect strategy doesn't invite conflict or argument about breaking off the relationship. Continued use of indirect strategies, if successful, leads gradually to the belief that both partners would be better off if they did break up. It's just too much hassle to continue. The problem, of course, is that the persistent use of indirect strategies will extend the time required to end the relationship. The discussions may drag on and on and on, when direct strategies might have led to a "swift and merciful" decision to break up.

When Baxter asked her respondents to express any regrets they had about their disengagement strategies, she found that reliance on indirect strategies was most frequently mentioned. There's no getting around it. Breaking off a close relationship with your partner is likely to be a painful process, no matter what strategies are used to end it. If the choice comes down to enduring the pain for a long or a short time, people will undoubtedly prefer that the pain last as briefly as possible. In that case, the direct "let's get it over and done with" strategy may be most effective in breaking off.

To summarize, no two relationships are exactly alike. We know that relationships evolve differently and that one friendship is different to some extent from every other. We also know that no two relationships are likely to end in the same manner (see Baxter, 1984). Some relationships will terminate as a result of the actions of only one of the partners; others will terminate from the actions of both. Some relationships will terminate with the involvement of a third party, who may be a reason for the breakdown of the relationship or a strategy used by one of the partners to force a termination; others will involve no third person at all. Some relationships will terminate after a long period of relational breakdown and much discussion of the issue; others will terminate swiftly with little discussion. Some relationships will terminate on a positive note; others will terminate with bitter feelings. The differences among terminated relationships are large and varied. Some general similarities are also apparent.

One, relational termination takes time. It is a process, a part of the evolutionary process of relational development. Part of the process involves interaction, and part involves psychological or intrapersonal conflict and reinterpretation of memories. Whether long or relatively brief, though, relational termination is a stage in a longer process and takes time.

Two, relationships don't merely "end"; they change. When relationships have evolved to a state of integration, they often continue to exist, though in a redefined form. That redefinition will typically include lowered levels of intensity, intimacy, trust, and commitment. Certainly the frequency and amount of interaction will decrease, and greater discontinuity of interaction will inevitably lead to gradually lower levels of interactional quality. Of course, some relationships terminate on a negative note and lead eventually to a total absence of communication between the partners. But even these relationships continue to exist in the memories of the partners, again after a process of intrapersonal redefinition and reinterpretation of the past events.

Three, ending an integrated relationship will inevitably leave some psychological scars on the individual self-concepts of the partners. No one can break off with a close friend and experience no aftermath, namely "withdrawal symptoms." The passage of time is necessary for the individuals to cope successfully with these withdrawal symptoms. Symptoms of relationship withdrawal may appear in the form of too much time available (the "empty" feeling), doubts about self-worth, lowered self-esteem, or other psychological scars. Humans have no way to eradicate memories of past events, but they can retrospectively change their perceptions of those events and wait for the memories to fade. The psychological aftermath of relational termination is also a process and requires time for its completion.

Four, in the absence of contextual changes (such as forced physical separation of the partners), relational termination rarely results from a reduction in the amount of interaction. When partners complain that they "just don't talk with each other any more," they are probably saying that they are becoming bored with their communication. Rarely does such a statement reflect a decrease in the actual amount of time spent in talking with each other. If it did, then partners in long-term continuing relationships would have the same complaint.

It is undoubtedly more accurate to say that communication stagnates rather than stops during relational breakdown and termination. Too much of the "same old thing" in the interaction (regardless of what it is) leads to boredom. Partners wonder what's wrong and feel that their relationship is not progressing. Relationships that fail to progress don't just stand still; they actually slide backward. Fresh water, if left to stand without being replenished with additional fresh water, will eventually turn into stagnant water. Relationships are just like that; they will stagnate if they are not revitalized by change.

Stagnation is also a process that takes time. It takes time for the partners to look back on their relationship and make sense of their interaction retrospectively. We are much better communicators when we are *developing* our relationships to high levels of intensity, intimacy, trust, and commitment. We are much less adept at *maintaining* our relationships at those levels. Maintaining interpersonal relationships at high levels involves the continuing process of *becoming* in the evolutionary development of interpersonal communication. And that is the subject of our discussions in the next chapter.

Summary

Popular music of the past several decades offers conflicting advice on the stage of relational termination. According to Neil Sedaka, "Breaking up is hard to do," but Paul Simon disagreed when he sang "There must be fifty ways to leave a lover." Breaking up with a formerly well-integrated partner is a process that develops over time. It may include a gradual erosion of the relationship that "passes away," or it may entail a "sudden death" of the relationship when new and damaging information about one of the partners comes to light. Or the seeds of "pre-existing doom" may be present throughout the entire relationship and finally result in breaking up.

The process of relational breakdown leading to termination typically goes through several phases. The *intra-psychic phase* involves intrapersonal struggle within one or both of the partners about whether to break off the relationship. During the *dyadic phase*, the partners discuss the issue of whether they want to break up. The partners let other people in their social network know about their relational breakdown in the *social phase* and then find the need to rearrange and reinterpret their terminated relationship intrapersonally again during the *grave-dressing phase*.

Relationships may break down for various reasons that exist within the minds of one or both partners, within the social context, and within the interpersonal interaction of the partners. The reasons for relational breakdown are difficult to pinpoint and typically include a variety of factors within all three sources. More important than the apparent reasons for relational breakdown is the process of interaction that leads to and results in relational termination, including the residues of the relationship left within the partners themselves and members of their social support systems.

Relational strategies used during the process of termination revolve around the issue of whether to end the relationship or try to patch things up. Whether the relationship terminates or is repaired, the definition of the relationship will change rather than simply end. Relational strategies include *indirect strategies, direct strategies, positive-tone strategies,* and *misunderstood strategies.* Whereas most people report their preference for *positive-tone* and *indirect* strategies, the more effective strategy in actual practice may be the direct ones. Under any circumstances, however, the strategies people prefer may reflect what they think they should do rather than what they actually do when breaking up with someone. The use of positive-tone strategies, for example, is much more socially acceptable than open confrontation.

Differences among terminated relationships are much more common than their similarities. Only a few general similarities are evident. One, relational termination takes time and is part of the process of relational development. Two, relationships don't end so much as they change. Three, relational termination leaves psychological scars on the relational partners. Four, communication stagnates rather than stops, leading up to relational breakdown and termination.

CHAPTER 14

"Becoming" Relationships— Maintenance, or "For Better or Worse"

Friendship is a very taxing and arduous form of leisure activity.

—Mortimer J. Adler

The better part of one's life consists of his friendships.

—Abraham Lincoln

If someone were to ask you why that special someone was such a good friend, you would probably experience great difficulty in answering that question. In fact, the best answer to such a question may be "I don't know. She just is." But what precisely makes someone a good friend is difficult to put into words. Many good friends confide in each other their innermost secrets, but others don't. Many good friends are together constantly and seem to do everything together, but others interact much less frequently. Many good friends seek each other out for practical help and advice, but others don't. Why are good friends such good friends? The answer is that they just are.

As difficult as it is to define the word "friend," though, it is even more difficult to explain what makes some friendships last while others don't. Some friendships last for years, and other friends grow apart from each other. How come? How do some friends maintain their relationships over such a long time? What is the secret of maintaining and keeping close relationships? Unfortunately, there are no simple answers to such questions. About the only thing that we can say without fear of being wrong is that there is no secret to keeping close relationships, but it does take a lot of work. Moreover, people who maintain close friendships often have no idea why. They just do.

Several years ago, a friend and I were commiserating with each other about the fact that so many of our mutual friends seemed to be getting divorced. He suggested that the basic reason *our* marriages remained intact was that we just never realized we had any option in the matter. We married "for better or worse" and assumed that whatever happened, we were in it "for the duration." He intended the comment as an attempt at humor (a feeble attempt, to be sure), but he was *really* talking about the fundamental basis for maintaining a relationship.

Close relationships endure because the participants *choose* to make them last, even if choice is not based on a rational consideration of alternatives. That is, we don't necessarily stay in a relationship because of the "rewards" we receive or because we are aware of strong reasons for maintaining it. We maintain our relationships because we *choose* to maintain them. This is not really an answer to why people maintain their relationships as much as it is a statement about *how* they do so. In the words of Robert Bell (1981), "Sometimes friendships are maintained simply because they have existed for a long time" (p. 24).

In this chapter we will attempt to shed some light on the "how" and the "how come" of enduring relationships. I hasten to add, though, that no one can claim to have a list of strategies that guarantee to keep every relationship together or to cure relationships that are deteriorating. If you expect to find some secret formula for maintaining relationships in this chapter, you will be sorely disappointed. No such formula exists. On the other hand, we do have some understanding of what characterizes relationships that "have existed for a long time," of what communication strategies are likely to characterize a long-term relationship, and of factors associated with long-term relationships.

In the following pages we will discuss the specific kinds of interpersonal relationships that have existed for a long time. We will discuss what it means to "maintain" a relationship in terms of its evolution over time and, specifically, the impact of the past on the present and future relationship. The evolving relationship is not a constant and steady progression but more like a roller-coaster ride of ups and downs.

Our discussions in this chapter will conclude with a description of some characteristics associated with very close relationships and the communicational strategies that typically occur in them. We won't know for sure that these strategies will guarantee how to keep a satisfying relationship, but we do know that using these strategies will enable us to improve our communication skills when we are involved in the process of maintaining a satisfying relationship. Even highly competent communicators will sometimes break up with their friends. Being competent in interpersonal communication will not guarantee success every time, but it will certainly shift the odds in your favor.

THE NATURE OF RELATIONSHIP MAINTENANCE

Precisely what do we mean when we use the term "relationship maintenance?" What does it mean to *maintain* a relationship? Is a relationship maintained if it merely exists for a long time? And just how long is a long time, anyway? Certainly some relationships exist for a long time and require little work to keep them going. For example, I have had close acquaintances—colleagues in communication departments at other universities—for years. I see them one or two times a year at professional conferences but never talk with them at any other time. We may write letters to each other a few times during any given year, but we rarely write folksy letters—

just business letters. And we have been acquaintances for over ten years. It doesn't take much effort to keep these acquaintanceships going. Neither person goes out of their way to do so. Is this what we mean by the term "relationship maintenance"?

Naturally, some relationships (such as long-term acquaintances) can exist for a very long time, even an entire lifetime. But these relationships, though they have existed for a long time, have never evolved into a highly integrated relationship. The fact that they have been maintained is more a matter of coincidence than anything else. My long-distance professional colleagues are acquaintances because we happen to attend the same professional conferences. Similarly, we develop acquaintanceships with people at work and keep them only because we happen to keep the same job for a long time. We see these people every day and can hardly avoid interacting with them, but we don't necessarily develop friendships with them. We live next door to people and develop acquaintanceships with them, but the relationship is based only on the coincidence that we happen to be neighbors. We may be on a first-name basis with the clerk at the checkout counter of the neighborhood grocery store, but that relationship exists only when and because we happen coincidentally to meet in the business of shopping for groceries.

Many relationships exist because the partners just happen to be in the same physical context at the same time. That context virtually requires interaction; hence, a relationship forms. But the relationship itself remains restricted to that physical context and does not typically extend into other contexts. Consequently, such relationships are simply a matter of coincidence: two people happen to be in the same place at the same time. If the context is one that the partners maintain for a long time, the relationship is "maintained," in a sense. But the relationship is bound to that context. The clerk gets a different job (that is, moves to another context), and the relationship ends. Relationships that are restricted to a coincidental context may be long-term relationships, but they are not very significant ones. As a result, we will not be considering them in this chapter's discussion of relationship maintenance.

Our primary concern is with those relationships that have evolved through the process of interpersonal communication to a relatively high level of integration. Rather than being based on mere coincidence, these relationships are maintained because the partners choose to maintain them. They exist for a long period of time because the partners want them to exist. Our interest is in those long-term relationships that have undergone a process of change—from initial acquaintanceship and small talk to highly developed levels of interactional quality. Maintaining these relationships requires that the partners work to maintain them in their communication. Friends, if they choose to remain friends, must choose to put forth the effort necessary to maintain their interaction (and, hence, their interpersonal relationship) as friends.

We already know that the relationship known as friendship may include a wide variety of different kinds of relationships. A friendship may be an extremely close relationship with a high degree of intensity, intimacy, trust, and commitment (as in "best friends" or "close friends"). Or it may be a relationship with only a mediocre level of intensity, intimacy, trust, and commitment (as in "just friends"). Our discussions will emphasize those relationships that reflect a rather high level of these characteristics. In fact, our primary concern is with all interpersonal relationships with high interaction quality. These relationships include kinship and family relations, marital partners, and lovers under the general category of "very close relationships."

Remember that the very close interpersonal relationship is not the same as "liking" or "attraction." An interpersonal relationship is a bond that develops through and is defined by the communication or interaction patterns of the partners. We may like an acquaintance because that person has an attitude similar to our own, is physically attractive, lives near us, and is of nearly the same age and social status as we are. (You will recall that these are some of the factors associated with interpersonal attraction.)

But merely because we like a person does not mean that we have a close relationship with that person. I like many of my acquaintances and many people whom I have never met. But I do not have a close relationship with these people. We maintain close relationships with people by maintaining interpersonal communication, by talking with them frequently and consistently. We will also probably like them. But please don't confuse the intrapersonal emotion of liking with the interpersonal communication of relating. When relationships begin to fall apart, the emotion of liking also begins to decrease. The emotion of liking that the partners feel is a *result* of the relationship, but it is not the relationship itself.

THE IMPACT OF "HISTORICITY"

Don't be too disturbed by the term "historicity." It is purely jargon, but the concept is an important one to keep in mind. We have consistently emphasized the fact that relationships evolve over a long period of time. During this evolutionary process, the relationship changes toward greater or less integration; but it is always changing. Occasionally we have referred to this evolutionary process as a constant state of *becoming*. Every set of relational partners, then, may be interacting at a particular point in time, but their interaction (and hence their relationship) at every point in time also reflects the entire history of their past interaction. The term used to describe how past history of interaction contributes to their present interaction is *historicity*. (If you are familiar with general system theory, you will recognize that we are using this term to embody the evolutionary characteristics of equifinality and multifinality.)

"Historicity" does not mean precisely the same as "history." As products of an educational system that trained us to think in linear terms, we tend to think of history as a linear sequence of events. That is, we tend to see events as a chain reaction, each influencing each other, like dominoes falling in a long row. The bombing of Pearl Harbor, we think, "caused" World War II. The discovery of the burglary of the Democratic headquarters in the Watergate apartments, we think, "caused" Richard Nixon to resign as president of the United States. Asking a question "causes" the other person to provide an answer. This linear approach— where one event leads to and influences the next—is the way we typically think of the "history" of chronological events.

The term "historicity" implies that a historical event does not necessarily influence another event to occur. In fact, the historical influence may actually move backward in time so that an anticipated future event actually influences a given event in the present. In this way, an event is influenced by another event that has not yet occurred. For example, "history" might explain that you experience hunger pains; therefore, you eat. "Historicity" might explain that you eat because you anticipate the enjoyable taste of the food—an event (experiencing the sensation of taste) that has not yet occurred!

So what does "historicity" mean? Essentially, it implies that the relationship at any point in time has evolved to its present state through past interaction patterns. However, there is absolutely no way of predicting, when those events occur, what that relationship is going to become. Many very close relationships began when two people hit it off immediately. They were attracted to each other right from the first and developed their friendship quickly and without difficulty. Other very close relationships, however, evolved from a rocky beginning. In fact, some good friends actually didn't like each other at first. But after they got to know each other, they became good friends. Other people were attracted to each other in a "love at first sight" beginning but grew to dislike each other after they got to know each other. We already know, therefore, that all or even most very close relationships do not begin in the same way. It logically follows, then, that we really can't predict what a relationship is likely to become on the basis of how it begins.

Research has demonstrated convincingly that it is virtually impossible to predict, on the basis of behaviors during the early stages of the relationship, how the relationship will turn out. For example, some people fervently believe that a more satisfying and lasting marriage is likely to develop when the couple live together for a time before they are married. Other people believe just as fervently that a more satisfying and lasting marriage is likelier to develop when a couple abstain from sexual activity until after they are married. Despite what anyone might believe, research results indicate that the early pattern of sexual activity (traditional, sexually moderate, or sexually liberal) provides absolutely no basis for predicting what the future relationship is likely to be. Researchers (Przybyla & Byrne, 1981) have concluded that "Individuals in each type of couple were equally likely to have broken up, continued dating, or married each other. There was no evidence that early sex inhibits the development of lasting commitments nor that a lasting relationship is necessarily facilitated by sexual abstinence or moderation" (p. 118).

So how does the history of past interaction contribute to the outcome of the relationship—that is, how the relationship turns out? First of all, the history of the interaction *is* the relationship. But the *meaning* of that relationship (and, hence, the meaning of the past interaction) is created through a process of retrospective sense-making. We make sense of the interaction *after* we have interacted. We also know that we can even *re*define the meaning of the interaction (and, hence, the relationship) and thereby change what it means at any point in the process. Moreover, we are constantly making sense of the relationship/interaction throughout our history of interaction. We can't change the interaction patterns that have occurred in the past, but we can change the meaning or sense that we have of that interaction after it has occurred. Furthermore, that meaning is also likely to change as the patterns of interaction continue to occur.

This is what is meant by "historicity." Every relationship is a product of the past history of the interaction patterns that have been enacted by the participants.

Those interaction patterns, though, are constantly changing, and their retrospective meaning is also constantly changing. Interpersonal communication or relationship contains more than mere history; it contains historicity.

Continuity—Not Consistency

There is an old saying that "The more things change, the more they stay the same." Although old sayings rarely have much value, this particular one is highly significant. The relationship is in a constant state of becoming, always changing and always different from one point to the next. The relationship is a process that is constantly occurring throughout time. We know that time does not and cannot stand still. It, too, is always moving, always changing and always different from one point to the next.

Let me illustrate this notion of the process of change through time. I buy a new car. It is beautiful. It is stylish. It runs beautifully. It has a shiny finish on the outside and gorgeous upholstery on the inside. It even smells like a new car. If time could stand still, that automobile would remain "new" forever. But times does not stand still. Eventually the shiny finish grows dull. The body becomes dented, and rust forms. The upholstery shows worn spots. The engine starts to use oil and develops a funny sound when it runs. The style of the car becomes outdated. And the smell of the car is often unpleasant. What happened? The car is the same car that it was when I bought it. It has the same engine, the same paint job, the same style, the same upholstery. But it has turned into an old clunker.

As the owner of the old clunker, I have several choices open to me. One, I can get rid of the old car and buy another new one. But I know that it will also grow old and wear out. Two, I can continue to drive the old clunker and be forever disappointed with it. But I know that I won't be enjoying myself as long as I'm driving it, and I still may have to get rid of it eventually. Three, I can maintain the present car. I select the third option and take the car to the body shop to have the dents and rust removed. I give the car a shiny new paint job. I have the engine repaired. I put seat covers on the upholstery. Soon I have the same old car, but it is now nearly the same as it was when it was brand new. Oh, the style may not be completely contemporary, but I like the style and am comfortable with it even though others (with brand new cars) may think it is out of date. In short, the only way I can maintain the car like a new car is to keep changing it and repairing it. And the more I keep changing it, the more it stays the same as it was when it was new.

Relationships are just like that car. The only way to keep the relationship fresh and new is to keep changing it and repairing it. And the more I keep changing that relationship, the more it is likely to remain the same as it was. In order to "live happily ever after," I need to make sure that the relationship continues to change. Certainly the things that make us happy at ten years of age are not the same things that make us happy when we're twenty. And the things that make us happy at age twenty will change considerably if we remain happy at age thirty and forty and so on.

To keep a very close relationship from disintegrating and perhaps even terminating, we need to keep changing the interaction patterns that define the relationship.

To illustrate, the interaction patterns of a very close relationship during the newlyweds' honeymoon are certainly not going to characterize a very close relationship during the couple's silver wedding anniversary. To maintain a satisfying marital relationship, the husband and wife must continually change their interaction patterns so that they maintain their level of satisfaction.

When the couple is first married, one or the other of them may work late or be absent from home in the evening hours or on weekends. They may not mind those periods of absence in the early years. After the birth of a child, however, the absent spouse is not present to help in the interaction patterns involved in raising a family. The partner may come to resent the absenteeism of the spouse and even redefine the past absenteeism (during the early years of the marriage) as a sign that the spouse never "really" cared about the marriage. To maintain the marriage as a very close relationship, the husband and wife must continually change their patterns of interaction.

The key to maintaining a relationship, then, is continuity rather than consistency. If you consistently do the same things over and over, regardless of how good they seemed at one time, they will soon become old and boring. Too much of a good thing will eventually turn into a bad thing. To be too consistent is to be boring. To resist change and keep the same interaction patterns indefinitely is to allow the relationship to decay. But unlike the process of biological decay, the process of decay in relationships can be reversed. A relationship that has started to deteriorate can, through appropriate changes in interaction patterns, get better and eventually be maintained as a good relationship once again.

We sometimes think that achieving the goal of a very close relationship is the most important part of the evolutionary process. That is simply not true. Achieving such a relationship is only a beginning; maintaining it is the next step. And maintenance is a never-ending part of the process of relational development. It requires constant attention on the part of both participants. They need to be aware of their communication at all times and be on the lookout for signs of its growing stale. According to psychologist, I. L. Mangam (1981), "All shared understandings lack permanence and must be continually reaffirmed or renegotiated through personal means; rules, procedures, structure and order itself are not automatic occurrences (however taken for granted they may appear) but rather must be worked at and sustained by the repeated acts of participants in the relationships that they create and maintain" (p. 200).

When a very close relationship starts to go wrong, the partners' first reaction is to return to the good old days when they were happy. They think that if they could just repeat the interaction that was instrumental in making their relationship satisfying, they would be happy again. This kind of remedy is probably doomed to failure. The couple does not have the same relationship that they once had. They can't go back; they must move forward. In other words, they must maintain the *continuity* of their relationship, their evolutionary process through time and into the future. If they can't repair the old relationship, then (just like the old car) they will probably decide to terminate it and go looking for a new one.

Keeping the relationship moving and changing (continuity)—not constant repetition (consistency) of the same old interaction patterns—is the key to successful maintenance of a relationship. Consistency leads to habits, and habits eventually become boring. Continuity leads to change. And the more things change, the more they stay the same.

Complexity—Not Simplicity

It is axiomatic that progress in evolutionary development leads to increasing complexity. Phrased simply, as something evolves or develops, it becomes more complex—that is, more differentiated. Evolution leads to greater variety. Let me illustrate the principle of complexity. When you developed your skill in using the English language, you became more complex. As your proficiency in the use of the language increased, you developed a larger vocabulary (more and different words and terms). You also learned more and different ways of saying the same thing, more and different ways of interpreting what other people said, more and different meanings of the same words or terms. In other words, your use of the English language became more complex as your language proficiency evolved.

Throughout your career in the American system of education, you have been trained to believe that complexity is a problem that needs to be solved. You were given mathematical problems in your first year of algebra that involved simplifying equations or fractions in order to reduce the number of parts you were required to handle. The fewer parts you had to consider, the more easily you could find the answer. As a member of our culture, you have come to expect and even demand straight (that is, simple) answers to straight questions. You dislike "beating around the bush." A reverence for the importance of simplicity is a norm that pervades our entire society. Unfortunately, real life is not simple; it is highly complex. To demand simple solutions to real-life problems is to be disappointed when you discover that there aren't any.

Interpersonal relationships, during their beginning stages of development, are rather simple. The rules for doing small talk and carrying on polite conversations are relatively few. We can master them rather quickly. As a relationship evolves and becomes closer, though, we become less sure of the rules guiding our behavior. More importantly, we are confronted with a great deal of new information about the other person and, perhaps, about ourselves. Whether we like it or not, we must learn to deal with an incredible variety of information and with the fact that we cannot easily predict where the relationship is going or guarantee how it will turn out. In short, we must learn to deal with a much higher level of complexity.

What do we mean when we say that the interaction in a very close relationship is more complex? Well, for one thing, we know that people in close relationships use a greater variety of themes and topics when they interact (Owen, 1981). We also know that people in close relationships have already discovered vast quantities of psychological information about the other person through earlier self-disclosing communication. After they have evolved to a close relationship, their uncertainty about each other is no longer an issue. At this point, they continue their interaction on other issues and topics. Hence, the issues and topics of interaction in very close relationships are more complex. That is, there are many more of them.

We also know that people in close relationships are aware that their relationship

As a relationship develops, the participants learn a great deal about each other.
(Fredrik D. Bodin/Stock, Boston)

is fragile and subject to decay if they don't keep doing something about it. People in close relationships have lived through that period of disappointment "after the honeymoon is over" and are aware of the failure of other close relationships. The partners know that merely expressing commitment to each other is not enough. The more serious problem is to cope with the difficulties of maintaining their commitment.

The strategies of relationship maintenance are really coping strategies. People in a very close relationship are typically aware of the problems facing them in their attempts to keep their relationship together. As Owen (1984) found in his study of people in different relationships, "We can expect that everyone at one time or another discusses how relationships are, as some put it, 'washed-up,' 'hurting,' 'hopeless,' and 'scary' . . ." (p. 283). He found, "For dating individuals [relationships in early stages of development], fragile relations are a real and present threat" (p. 283). But married couples tended to think that their own satisfying relationship was different from other relationships that were in trouble. They felt theirs was a unique relationship.

Maintaining your own close relationship when you know that those of your friends are floundering is a little like being in a lifeboat in shark-infested waters. You know that you are safe in the boat, but the risk is always there. You can stay in the lifeboat and run the risk of not being saved. But that risk seems better than jumping overboard and swimming for safety. In your relationship, you cope with the situation by believing that you are unique (compared with other relationships that haven't made it), and that very uniqueness is what maintains your relationship.

In short, you cope with the difficulties that you know are present. If your attempts to maintain your relationship are not successful, you have failed to cope. The strategies associated with terminating relationships (Chapter 13) were also coping strategies to decide whether and how to end your relationship with another person.

If you decide not to use the disengagement strategies and try to salvage the relationship, then the coping strategies attempt to repair damage that had been done.

But the coping strategies of relational maintenance do not attempt to repair past damage. Rather, maintenance strategies cope by not allowing damage to occur and not allowing the relationship to grow stale. To maintain a relationship, a strategy attempts to provide continuity—looking ahead to a brighter (or continued bright) future, rather than looking back to problems that have occurred in past interactions.

ROLLER-COASTER RELATIONSHIPS

We typically think of evolution or developmental change as constant and steady, like walking up a flight of stairs. You take one step at a time and eventually reach the top of the stairs. But a natural process of evolutionary change doesn't happen in a consistent manner. Rather, evolutionary change is a start-and-stop process of progress and regress, of spurts of change and lulls of no change. Biologically, for instance, your body developed from that of a small baby to its current adult size, but that development undoubtedly came in spurts of growth and in frustrating (to the child reaching puberty) periods of no growth at all.

When I was in the eighth grade, I was one of those adolescents who matured early and was shaving on a semiregular basis when my male classmates were still looking in the mirror for any trace of a whisker. I was singing songs two octaves below my classmates, who were still trying to keep their yodeling, breaking voices at the same pitch. I played forward on my eighth-grade basketball team; but when I graduated from high school, I was a guard (and a short one at that). I had my spurt of growth early and then watched as my other classmates passed me by. The center on my high school basketball team, for instance, sat on the bench in the eighth grade because he was too short.

Anyone who has ever tried to diet is fully aware of the uneven process of weight loss. You lose weight quickly at first, and then comes an agonizing period of no weight loss. In fact, while you are suffering on the diet, watching skinny people eat all they want, you step on the scales one morning and discover that you have actually gained weight overnight. Dieting is typically an evolutionary process of weight loss, weight gain, constant weight, weight loss, weight gain, and so forth. If dieters were to place the fluctuations of their weight on a line graph, that line would go up and down on a track similar to that of a roller coaster. To a dieter (just like the roller-coaster rider), the downward plunge is a time of great glee and the upward climb is boring and frustrating, made bearable only by the anticipation that there will be another exhilarating dive just ahead.

The evolutionary process in interpersonal relationships is like that roller coaster. The only difference is that the upward swing is the exhilarating part, while the downward plunge is frustrating and often unbearably depressing. There are, in a sense, forces that affect the relationship in opposite ways. Each participant, for example, has individual goals and motives that are not necessarily the same as those of the relationship. In fact, the responsibilities of being a member of the relationship may even conflict with the desires and goals of the individual participant.

Whenever individual people (with individual selves and self-interests) become members of an interpersonal relationship, they become subject to the tension between conflicting forces. Changes in the environment (such as the birth of a baby, loss of job, the apartment building going condo, moving to a new town, and so on) create tension and conflict with the present state of the relationship. The relationship then becomes a roller-coaster ride of rising and falling tension, increasing and decreasing conflict, good and bad times. The participants in the relationship cope with reality and quickly come to the realization that "happily ever after" really is a fairy tale.

Peaks and Valleys

Alan Alda described his marriage as moving between periods of boredom and monotony in which he and his wife hardly paid any attention to each other and periods of "puppy love" in which they gloried in waves of emotional intimacy. The key to understanding this notion of waves or peaks and valleys is to be aware that the relationship undergoes the waves; individual members don't. The individual self is not undergoing any evolutionary change. The individual self is a member of the relationship that undergoes the change and is, therefore, caught up in the change. Certainly the individual will experience the change, and his or her self-concept will undoubtedly change along with it. But the peaks and valleys of the relationship are part of the *normal* process of evolutionary change and not the fault of one of the members. The soap opera romances and fairy tale fiction of the popular media have provided us with the notion that a very close relationship is a matter of interpersonal "chemistry." One individual is so suited to the other that their relationship will just "happen" as a matter of course. If it doesn't work out, then the "chemistry" must have been bad or they had a "personality conflict." At the same time, we hear occasionally about someone giving up a career or a huge inheritance for the sake of a romantic relationship, and we tend to distrust the intelligence of that person. When Edward VIII gave up the British throne because of his love for Wallis Simpson (an American divorcée), the world applauded the strength of this love but not so secretly wondered whether he was quite sane.

Oddly enough, we simultaneously hold the beliefs that (1) very close relationships are made in heaven but that (2) most of them don't work out that way in real life. We wait for the time when we can become involved in one of those relationships but know that it probably won't happen to us. Two psychologists, Arthur Colman and Libby Colman (1975), describe this frustration with the reality of "love" and our cultural ideal of it:

> Each of us becomes aware of love for another in brief, intense moments. Love peaks and then passes. Rarely can it be continuously experienced, for the traffic of our daily lives distracts us from the ecstasy of our relationship with another. We seem to acknowledge the peak moments of love as a great good, as something that gives meaning to life and brings us our most exquisite pleasures, but we are at the same time distrustful of its reality. . . . We rarely think of love as something requiring work or discipline. (p. 3)

Maintaining a very close relationship with another person is not an easy task, but it *is* a task that requires work and effort. The relationship is rarely a matter of personal chemistry or personalities that are suited to each other. Maintaining a very close relationship in real life is much more likely to be the result of the participants' hard work at keeping their relationship going. They cope with the tensions that result from the clash of intrapersonal and interpersonal motivations or environmental changes. They change their interactional patterns in order to cope with these tensions. They enjoy the peaks of those "brief, intense moments" of emotion and don't become unduly depressed or frightened during the valleys of relational monotony or boredom. In every case, though, they are constantly aware that the rising and falling periods during the relationship are part of the normal evolutionary process of relationship maintenance. And the emotional highs are always worth waiting for.

Tension and Conflict

Most of us tend to distrust comments from people who say of their close friend or spouse, "We are so much alike, we never disagree with each other. In fact, we have never had an argument." Our first reaction is probably that the speaker is lying. If the speaker is telling the truth, we probably think that the relationship must be very dull indeed. It is hard to imagine a very close relationship that doesn't include some disagreement, conflict, and tension. If the relationship actually is entirely without tension, then it is also probably incapable of dealing with any conflict or tension that might arise. And the opportunities for conflict and tension to occur in a very close relationship are so numerous as to be virtually unavoidable.

Consider what a very close relationship is likely to be. These people spend a lot of time together. They have talked with each other so much and have self-disclosed so much that they know a great deal about each other, including those things that they don't particularly like. They have laid their selves on the line. They have risked a large portion of their self-concepts and invested their selves in this interpersonal relationship. In such a relationship, even a minor annoyance is likely to take on exaggerated importance. Even a little conflict can become a big argument.

In other words, the likelihood of tension and conflict in a very close relationship is much greater than in one that has not developed to such a high degree of intensity, intimacy, trust, and commitment. For members of a close relationship not to experience any conflict, they must actively avoid or ignore sources of conflict when they do arise. If they do so, though, they will actually be making matters worse. Sooner or later a situation over which they have no control will arise (such as a change in the environment). When it does, they simply won't be prepared to deal interactionally with the resulting tension.

A relationship actually needs some tension and conflict in order to survive for a long time. Maintaining a relationship clearly implies that the participants have developed their own ways of dealing successfully and normally with conflict. Relationship maintenance, then, involves the *management*, not the *absence*, of conflict.

Let me warn you that I am about to introduce another piece of academic jargon— *cultural schismogenesis*. Now I could easily discuss the idea of schismogenesis without actually using the term itself. However, this term is often useful in answering that frequently asked question, "What did you learn in college today?" If you are asked this, you can come back with a word that has five (count 'em) syllables and impress all your friends and neighbors. First, you need to know how to pronounce it correctly: skiz'-moh-jeh'-nuh-sis. Now for the definition.

"Schismogenesis" is a combination of two terms: "schism" and "genesis" A schism is a split or separation between two things—in this case, between two people in a relationship. "Genesis" means beginning. Hence, "schismogenesis" means the beginning of a split between the two participants in an interpersonal relationship. Try using this term in a normal conversation sometime, preferably in an off-the-cuff manner, and you will be the hit of the party. You can even say that the noted anthropologist Gregory Bateson (1972) first used the term. (Rest assured that others will recognize your intellectualism when you attribute what you say to some experts and casually drop their names into the conversation.)

Bateson describes cultural schismogenesis (the beginning of a breakup in the culture or social relationship) as coming from either of two different sources: conflict or absence of conflict. In other words, conflict can certainly create tension between the relational partners and result in their splitting up. Common sense tells us that conflict between the partners can disrupt their relationship. But common sense might also tell us that the happiest and healthiest relationship is one that has no conflict at all. And this is where the principle of cultural schismogenesis becomes significant.

Schismogenesis is as much a threat to a relationship with no conflict as one with too much conflict. When two people in a relationship have absolutely no problems, tension, or conflict, they are just as likely to break up as those who have too much conflict. The total absence of tension characterizes a relationship that is monotonous, boring, and tedious. It is a relationship characterized by consistency (not continuity) and by simplicity (not complexity). It isn't going anywhere and will eventually decay.

Partners maintain their relationships and fight the threat of schismogenesis through the normal evolutionary process of peaks-and-valleys of development. Some research into communication patterns in developing relationships has illustrated how partners maintain their relationships through conflict-management peaks and valleys. Fisher and Drecksel (1983) observed the interaction patterns of male friends over an extended period of time and discovered that they alternated between periods of competition or conflict and periods of virtually no conflict. Apparently these male friends fluctuated between conflict and cooperation without realizing that they were doing so. In fact, if they had been asked whether they had any conflict, they might very well have responded that they got along beautifully and experienced none at all. When they interacted with each other in their competitive periods, they did so as a part of the normal process of their developing relationship. Because it was "normal," their conflict did not disrupt their relationship, and they probably moved in and out of competitive interaction patterns without thinking about it.

In other words, partners in a very close relationship interact with each other long enough to develop their own patterns and rules. They then come to recognize these patterns as the definition of their relationship. Probably without realizing it, they don't allow schismogenesis of either kind (too much or too little conflict) to develop. They have periods of conflict interaction, and they also have interaction without conflict. In fluctuating between these two periods, they develop their own methods of managing conflict. They don't let conflict get out of hand, and they don't avoid it when it occurs normally. By managing conflict in this way, they maintain their relationship and avoid falling victim to cultural schismogenesis.

The success of partners in developing their very close relationship is a direct result of the rules and norms that they have enacted and come to expect from their interaction with one another. Contrary to popular opinion, perhaps, research has consistently demonstrated that people's satisfaction with their close relationships is rarely associated with the "fit" of their individual personalities but is consistently associated with the way in which they interact, particularly in how they manage conflict situations (see Burgess, 1981, p. 189). Precisely how their conflict is managed will vary considerably from one couple to another. However, some interactional strategies and patterns (to be discussed later in this chapter) can be associated with many couples who are successful in their attempts to maintain very close relationships.

Work and Play

Maintaining a close relationship is very serious business. It requires work and discipline. And in order to get the maximum amount of work accomplished, the relational partners have to play, too. Because they have been together for so long and interacted with each other so frequently, they are fully aware when their interaction is work and when it is play. When it's play, they can relax and release any tension they might have. When their interaction involves work, they are resolving their conflicts and further defining their relationship.

Only partners in relatively close relationships know how to play in their interaction. People who haven't developed a rather high level of relational quality (intensity, intimacy, trust, and commitment) during their past interaction are less sure how the other will respond. They will be more likely to interact in patterns that demonstrate politeness and respect for the other person. They follow the norms of the larger social context or the culture—norms that tell people it is better to be "nice" than "not nice." But play in interpersonal communication is often "not nice," at least when compared with norms of the larger society.

For instance, good friends kid each other a lot; acquaintances don't. Good friends insult each other a lot; acquaintances don't. Good friends can call each other names and tell them they are wrong about something; acquaintances can't. Good friends frequently disagree and argue with each other; acquaintances don't.

People in close relationships often develop regular times in which they interact with each other as a form of relaxation. In some situations, this interaction time is called "banana time" (Roy, 1973). They don't need to say it, but both partners realize that this is a time for playing. Both partners realize that they need to interpret what they say to each other quite differently from the way they would at other times. Obviously they can't interpret each other's comments literally. After all, they're kidding each other.

Interactional play sometimes takes the form of insulting one another. Comments during such times may sometimes appear, on the surface, to be devastatingly rude and even cruel. During insulting play, partners kid each other about things that don't really matter, but they tacitly agree that some topics (central to their self-concepts) are not appropriate. Partners in each very close relationship develop their own specialized topics of play and their own idiosyncratic patterns of interactional play. Hence, no particular sample of interaction would characterize the general kidding that most (or even very many) relationships would use. The key is not what kind of interactional play is used but rather the repetition of the same kidding themes used by specific partners.

Let me provide an example of a repeated kidding theme that is unique to a particular relationship. I have a friend who is an M.D. He, by virtue of his degree in medicine, is known as "Doctor" to the members of our society. I have a Ph.D. by virtue of my education in the field of communication. A few people may call me "Doctor Fisher," but they are limited to the university community. For years, we have carried on a running theme of kidding each other about the title of "Doctor." I have consistently referred to him as an "NRD" (which stands for "not a real doctor" and is pronounced "nerd," of course). I have, over the years, reminded him of his "real" status by giving him a T-shirt emblazoned with the declaration "World's #1 NERD," a poster describing the characteristics of a nerd, candy with the brand name Nerds, and a multitude of other less-than-subtle reminders. His wife has a large button that says "I'm with the nerd."

He, of course, has retaliated with his own feeble attempts to equate my Ph.D. with "NRD-ness." On one occasion he responded to my reference to a bathroom as a "john" with one of the cleverest insults in our long-standing repartee. You see, his first name is John. Without cracking a smile and without batting an eye, he replied, "We call them 'Aubs' in our house." Although there is no "winner" in our interaction involving this kidding theme, I shall let you (the reader) decide the comparative merits of Ph.D. versus M.D. One additional piece of information is probably relevant. My birthday is November 27, which falls on Thanksgiving Day about every fourth year. His birthday, on the other hand, is April 1! (No kidding!)

What are the characteristics of play in communication? First and foremost, the same kidding themes occur and recur frequently during the history of the relationship. Second, both partners are aware of the "rules of the game." No one gets upset or bothered by the play but, instead, enjoys it. In fact, if one person gets tired of the theme, it will cease to exist and the partners will probably develop a new one. Third, the game involves a high degree of reciprocity. If Alfred proceeds to kid Betty, the game will undoubtedly involve kidding from Betty in response. I called John a NRD, so he called me a NRD, too. Fourth, the interactional episodes of play include only a small part of the entire interaction of the relational partners. Play is recreation and occurs as a break from the monotony of serious interaction in the relationship. Thus, the partners move back and forth between episodes of interactional play and periods of serious interaction. But periods of serious interaction undoubtedly make up most of the interaction in very close relationships.

Another type of interactional play is called *shmoozing*. Two people can "shmooze" with each other by talking about absolutely trivial, unimportant, and insignificant topics. What they say and what they talk about is absolutely irrelevant and unimportant. They are just killing time with their interaction. But individuals can also shmooze by themselves. Even in a very close relationship, partners need a break from each other from time to time.

One way for partners to keep their relationship vital and fresh is to allow individual shmoozing time for each of them. They can get away by themselves for some period of time and do something for themselves, without any thought of the relationship. Individual shmoozing doesn't necessarily involve interaction with someone else; it refers to discretionary time in which the individual is alone. For many people, jogging is a form of shmoozing—an individual activity performed by an individual for purely individual purposes. The interaction in a very close relationship is extremely important for intrapersonal growth. And occasional breaks from the interaction or shmoozing is also important for the growth of the interpersonal relationship.

SPECIAL FRIENDSHIPS

You have probably noticed that our discussions in this chapter have frequently included the term "very close relationship." Some counselors use this term to refer to a specific kind of relationship with very high levels of intensity, intimacy, trust, and commitment. These relationships are not merely friendships; they are friendships that are extremely close—as in the case of "best friends." These relationships often (but not necessarily) include marital spouses and some family or kinship relations between, for example, brothers and sisters or parents and children.

Characteristics

What does a very close relationship look like? More accurately, perhaps, how do you go about creating one? After all, a special friendship does not magically come into being because people marry or are born into a close-knit family. Partners create and enact their very close relationship through the evolving historicity of their interaction. You just can't have such a relationship without working at it. Every marriage, for instance, is not a very close relationship. Mere conjugal love is not enough. Marital spouses or any other partners have this special kind of relationship only when they develop it through the process of interpersonal communication.

The first and most obvious characteristic of a very close relationship is that it endures. It is a special friendship that has lasted for a long time. But not all enduring relationships are special. Psychologist John Reisman (1981) has described three types of enduring friendships: "associative," "receptive," and "reciprocal" ones. The first two have endured but not necessarily because they are very close. An *associative friendship* endures because of circumstances that bring the partners together. Associative friendships include relationships with colleagues at work, at church, at school and members of the same club, athletic team, fraternity, or sorority. The sense of commitment that each partner feels toward the other is due to the situation (belonging to the same club). A *receptive friendship* is based on a difference in status or control. One member is the giver and the other is the taker. Leaders and followers create receptive friendships, as do instructors and students, mentors and trainees, masters and apprentices, or any set of people whose relationship is based on a relational difference of complementary roles in which one person is the giver and the other is the receiver.

A very close relationship is most likely to be a *reciprocal friendship* rather than an associative or receptive one. Partners in a reciprocal friendship feel a commitment specifically to their interpersonal relationship. Moreover, reciprocal friends tend to consider themselves as equals (symmetrical) in the relationship. They will switch back and forth between giving and receiving roles and will typically not maintain one role throughout the relationship.

To illustrate, a marital relationship is more likely to be a reciprocal relationship if the partners share their roles fairly equally. Husband and wife will both, at various times, take on the role of babysitter, housecleaner, meal preparer, lawn mower, furniture arranger, grocery shopper, and breadwinner. This is not to say that the "traditional" marriage (in which the husband goes off to work and the wife takes care of the house and children) cannot be a very close relationship. But it is a receptive friendship based on role differences. It is much easier for partners in a reciprocal friendship to create the interaction patterns of equality that are more typically the basis of a very close relationship.

A second characteristic of a very close relationship is the deep emotional attachment each partner feels toward the other and to the relationship itself. That emotion is typically called "love," even though partners in same-sex relationships generally don't use that specific term. But what does love look like in the interaction patterns of partners in a very close relationship? That question is difficult to answer. We might normally suppose that very close friends would self-disclose to each other or would seek out the very close friend for help in times of trouble. But we already know that very close friends self-disclose to each other much less than they did when they were in the earlier stage of integration. And some close friends turn to each other for help, but probably just as many others do not. (See O'Connor & Brown, 1984, especially p. 172). So how do partners exhibit "love" in very close relationships?

Obviously one very close relationship may be quite different from another. People use close friends quite differently. For some, a close friend is a person who can always be there when needed. For others, a close friend is a person who will listen to anything they want to tell them. For still others, a close friend is a person who is always ready to share favorite activities. In all cases, though, a close friend is a person who makes life more enjoyable—one who, when absent, leaves an empty place in the life of the other. The emotional attachment felt by one friend for another is the feeling that exists within the self of the individual communicator. It is best understood as a residue or aftermath or result of the interpersonal relationship. It is an intrapersonal symptom of a very close relationship, but it is not a defining characteristic of that relationship.

Moreover, love means something different to the partners at different stages in the evolution of a very close relationship. In the early stages, the feeling is one of excitement and anticipation of the good things that the future will bring. In the middle stages, the feeling is one of exhilaration and happiness because the partners have confronted, struggled with, and solved their problems. Anticipation of the future is still bright. As people grow older in a very long-term friendship, however, their feeling of love looks very different.

When he observed long-term married couples, Olson (1981) discovered that these partners seemed to regard love as a feeling of being very comfortable in the relationship. They felt no need to talk with each other as much as they once did. Their feeling toward the relationship may have reflected less excitement and anticipation, but it was probably no less intense. In the later stages of an enduring very close relationship, partners are comfortable in the presence of each other. They are comfortable in the relationship and would continue to experience a great feeling of emptiness if the partner were absent. The relationship itself continues to reflect high communalism, or oneness, but the emotional symptom of love internalized within each of the partners is different. But change is a normal occurrence in the evolutionary development of a relationship. And change in the emotional attachment of friends is another symptom of the continuity of the relationship. Recall that continuity (and change) is part of maintaining a relationship.

Gender and Very Close Relationships

In our earlier discussion of this topic we reached the conclusion that we typically perceive and believe that men and women communicate differently. When the gender issue is examined at the interpersonal level, however, the conclusion is quite the contrary. Generally, whether one is male or female does not have much influence on the process of interpersonal communication or the development of interpersonal relationships. Although the impact is slight, gender probably influences communication most when the partners are members of a very close relationship. Close male friends do interact differently than either close female friends or close male-female friends. In most cases, those differences tend to be somewhat superficial—for instance, different topics, different experiences, different expectations. But they are differences nonetheless.

As in every discussion that attempts to make some generalizations about friendships, we must keep in mind that each very close relationship has its own unique historicity. There is a considerable amount of variation among interpersonal relationships and patterns of communication. Nevertheless, some observations about what is typical of certain kinds of relationships are possible. The following discussion of the influence of gender on interpersonal relationships refers only to those typical characteristics. Any friendship involving specific individuals is likely to differ in some respects from the typical male friendship, female friendship, or male-female friendship.

Male Friendships. One thirty-five-year-old male has described his friendships with other males in the following manner: "There is a special quality to being friends with men and it wouldn't be the same with women. With my male friends there is something special—I don't know what, but it isn't there with women" (Bell, 1981, p. 78).

Some years ago, Betty Friedan wrote a book with the provocative title, *The Feminine Mystique*. Its counterpart for males (the "masculine mystique") is more commonly known by the Spanish word, "machismo." It is the social stereotype of males in Western society and goes something like this: The "real man" is strong and brave. He is athletic, aggressive, and never reveals his emotions; he is "cool," doesn't cry, and never eats quiche. Of course, machismo is a myth believed by some members of our culture rather than a realistic description of how men behave. For one thing, many masculine men like quiche and have been seen to cry on numerous occasions. Most men probably behave in a manner quite unlike the machismo myth. Nevertheless, some elements of machismo influence the interaction of males in very close relationships.

Males learn the mystique of machismo just by being members of our society. Small boys are given guns, footballs, and toy trucks as their first toys. They are expected and encouraged to participate in athletic teams even before they go to school and are rewarded for this. Most schools now have both boys' and girls' basketball, soccer, and track teams; but "everybody knows" that the boys' teams are really "where it's at." Girls are rarely allowed to be members of "macho" athletic teams that involve physical contact, such as football, wrestling, or hockey. We occasionally read stories in the newspapers of girls who have to go to court to earn their right to participate in such sports. Boys are expected and encouraged to be athletes; girls are actively discouraged.

The result is that boys have the frequent experience of being members of a team. They learn quickly the value of teamwork and becoming a good team player. Consequently, boys come to associate friendships with team membership, activity, role relations, and "doing." Boys learn to suppress their emotions (to "play with pain") and individual goals for the sake of the team. Athletics and the team dominate the socialization of males in American society.

Not surprisingly, adult males develop friendships with other males around organized activities. Male friends participate in games, go bowling, go fishing or hunting, play poker. Each has a role to play in the "game" of friendships. Hence, the interaction in male friendships often revolves around kidding themes, insults, verbal aggressiveness. That aggressiveness even takes the form of physical aggression. Male friends often develop aggressive greeting rituals that involve hitting each other with clenched fists, slapping each other on the back, clapping each other on the shoulders. Talk between male friends is often loud and boisterous. Their interaction is very similar to that of a "game"—reciprocated aggressive activities.

One theme characterizing the interaction of male friends is "locker-room talk." Allegedly, this kind of interaction frequently occurs in the informal communication of men when they are in locker rooms, but the term is more likely to refer to any all-male talk. Locker-room talk typically includes profanity, telling of dirty stories, verbal aggression, and a lot of needling or kidding exchanges. One favorite topic of conversation is (of course) women. The stereotypical rating system (from 1 to 10) that men apparently use to rate women is typical of the way locker-room talk treats the topic of women. This kind of interaction is crude and consistent with the mystique of machismo. Most males have undoubtedly participated in locker-room talk, even if they have never seen the inside of a locker room. But they know it is a game, and talk is the way to play the game. Furthermore, they would be very embarrassed if such talk were overheard by females.

Because of the cultural influence of team membership, males often have friendships in groups of three or more. Moreover, males often prefer to interact with their friends in groups. I often (but not as often as I would like) go fishing or skiing with three or more people. In planning such activities, we typically attempt to get three or more people to participate, but only two people is okay, too. Male friends are not necessarily uncomfortable in pairs, but the presence of three or more males in friendly activities or interactions is quite typical.

It has been said that male friendships are not as close as those of male-female or female-female pairs. To a large extent, this is probably true. At least, it is more difficult for males to develop very close relationships with other males for several reasons. One, the games that males play in their interaction are frequently competitive, and competition is rarely the principal basis on which very close relationships are built. Two, the team aspect of male friendships encourages partners to relate with each other in terms of roles, and roles lead to receptive rather than reciprocal friendships. Three, because male friendships often occur in groups of three or more, males don't have as many one-on-one interactional opportunities. Consequently, the closeness of their friendship is diluted by sheer numbers. Male friendships can certainly develop into very close relationships, but it's probably more difficult.

Female Friendships. One forty-year-old woman described her friendships with other women in the following manner:

> Womanness does matter because of the same socialization. All of us have experienced being crapped on. But I don't think it is any sort of basic femaleness. But I certainly have become aware of women as sisters. Sisters in the sense of so many common experiences. I have also come to really feel good about my women friends. (Bell, 1981, p. 63)

If male friendships are commonly thought to be less "personal," less "revealing," and less emotionally "attached," the common view of female friendships is just the reverse. We think of women friends as being more expressive and more intimate. Women, we believe, tend to reveal more of their selves to other women, to confide more in other women, and to express their emotions more freely with other women. Women, according to some "feminine mystique," are much more likely to have very close relationships with each other.

In one sense, though, our culture tends to think friendships among women are somehow inferior to friendships among men. Our society sees conversation among women as involving topics of decidedly trivial importance. Meredith Wilson immortalized women talk in the musical comedy *The Music Man*, by comparing such talk with that of chickens in his song, "Pick a Little, Talk a Little." "Hen talk" allegedly deals with such topics as exchanging recipes, the latest soap operas, giving birth to babies, what store is having a sale, the latest fashion in clothes, and gossip. On the other hand, "rooster talk" treating such topics as automobiles, sports scores, and hunting season can hardly be considered very profound.

The past few decades have strongly influenced the relationships of women in our society. The women's movement has engendered a sense of sisterhood among many women, a sense that is explicit in the woman's earlier description of her friendships. Latest census figures indicate that about 50 percent of the workforce comprises women. Dual-career marriages, with both husband and wife working in equivalent jobs, are commonplace. No longer can society expect that a married woman's most significant relationship will be with her husband. Most women today, like most men, have very close relationships outside marriage. If men have a unique bond of maleness that comes from being team members, women also have a unique bond that comes from their being women in a male-oriented society. Men have their mystique of machismo, and women have their mystique of sisterhood.

Are friendships between women more expressive and self-disclosing than male friendships? Certainly female friends do not typically engage in the verbal and nonverbal aggressiveness demonstrated in the interaction of male friends. Hugging and kissing constitute a typical greeting ritual of female friends, just as hitting and backslapping are typical greeting rituals of male friends. During a conversation, women are also more apt to touch their partners. This is typically a casual touch in which one friend might lay her hand on the other's arm. Further, women will often sit closer together when they are interacting with women friends. Consequently, we tend to think that the interaction characterizing typical female friendships is more expressive and more intimate than that typical of male friendships.

Intimacy and expressiveness are also more easily demonstrated with just two people in a one-to-one situation. Women typically do not have "team" friendships. Rather, females typically have one-on-one friendships. When only two people are involved, the interaction tends to be more personalized, more oriented to the self of the individual communicator. Hence, women tend to perceive their friendships as being more intensely personal. In the two-person interaction, women are more likely to express their emotional attachment to the other person.

Whether women's friendships are "closer" as a result of their expressiveness will probably never be totally clear. But expressions of emotion are probably more explicit in the interaction patterns of female friendships than in those of males. And the interaction patterns of women (for example, touching and sitting close together) will "look like" they are closer and more expressive.

Male-Female Friendships. The following comment comes from a forty-year-old male: "I have always felt I could be much closer to a woman as a friend than to any man. It is a real gut feeling I have. I feel that in general women care more about their friends than men do" (Bell, 1981, p. 111). And this comment from a twenty-six-year-old female: "Some of my male friendships have had to end because of attempts to move it into the bedroom. I have never had one male friend who accepted the friendship without wanting to move into sexual involvement" (Bell, 1981, p. 106).

An unfortunate but probably true comment on our culture is that very close relationships (outside marriage) are overwhelmingly between members of the same sex—both males or both females. As the above comment illustrates, a male-female friendship is expected to focus on sexual relations. When a boy and girl are friends in high school, for instance, all their other friends (both male and female) assume they are "going together." When fire and police departments went "coed" across the country, some of the most vocal critics of the change were the wives of policemen and firemen who feared there would be "hanky panky" between their husbands and female work partners. For some reason, our society assumes that males can be good friends and females can be good friends, but a male and female together will inevitably be lovers.

The culture in which we live has certainly encouraged the belief that friendships

Close friendships may evolve between spouses.
(Joel Gordon)

between males and females are expected to lead to some bonded relationship, principally marriage. Popular romantic novels, TV soap operas, and movies confirm the cultural expectation that boys and girls grow up to be husbands and wives. In fact, the recent avalanche of movies focusing on adolescents (probably beginning with *Porky's* and all the subsequent ripoffs) lead the audience to believe that sex is the only thing on the minds of adolescent boys (and probably girls).

Probably the most significant single factor accounting for the comparative rarity of male-female friendships is the sex-role stereotyping prevalent in our society. When a man and woman (of virtually any age from junior high on up) meet for the first time, their typical first response to each other is on the basis of sexual attractiveness. Adolescent girls are as likely as boys to rate specimens of the other sex on a scale from 1 to 10. Hence, unlike same-sex friendships, a male-female relationship begins its evolutionary development from initial interaction that is heavily influenced by the sexual dimension. These cultural expectations lead the partners to be aware at all times that the potential for sexual involvement is always there. And that potential gets in the way of the developing relationship.

The expectations and stereotypes of relational partners in a male-female friendship are also in the process of change as society slowly changes its views of sex roles. Indeed, a decade-old study at a midwestern college indicates that males tend to have greater confidence in their nonromantic friendships with females than in their male friendships, a finding that would have been unthinkable not too long ago. Nevertheless, the number of nonromantic friendships between males and females, compared with same-sex friendships, is extremely small. But, in the words of Bob Dylan, "the times they are achanging."

So far, we have said little about very close relationships when the members are married. Certainly, marital spouses can also be friends, but the mere exchange of marriage vows does not automatically create a very close relationship. Yet spouses do spend a great deal of time interacting with each other and thus have a greater opportunity to develop an extremely close relationship. It also stands to reason that sheer amount of interaction does not create a very close relationship, but it does provide an opportunity for development significantly greater than most other relationships. More important to the relationship than the amount of time spent interacting are, of course, the strategies used to maintain the relationship and the pattern of interaction when the relational partners are actually communicating with each other. And that is the topic for discussion in the next and final section of this chapter.

To repeat, the actual communication of males and females (with each other and with individuals of the opposite sex) is not all that different, though we often think it is. Males and females may be quite different biologically, but they probably aren't very different when it comes to how they communicate in interpersonal situations. Despite what we might believe from the conventional wisdom of our society, communication scholars (for example, Baxter, 1979; Ayres, 1980 & 1983; Fisher, 1983) have consistently discovered little difference in how males and females communicate. There are differences, to be sure, but those differences are often trivial and insignificant, such as using different topics of conversation. When it comes to strategies and patterns of interaction, the gender of the communicators apparently just isn't a very significant factor.

RELATIONAL THEMES AND STRATEGIES

The following descriptions of very close relationships come from people in Adams's (1985) study of relational strategies:

> My favorite person, lover, friend, and pal. Carl is also my biggest pain and frustration. I absolutely adore him. Our relationship is warm, loving and understanding. Carl and I have come a long way together. We've had our share of hardships and easy times. Now our relationship is eternally oriented because we are both determined to make it so.

What sort of strategies are used by people in very close relationships when they are engaged in normal communication with one another? What are the interaction patterns that characterize the process of communication of people trying to maintain their very close relationship? As you might imagine, questions such as these are very difficult to answer, since it is not easy to record people's everyday conversations. Furthermore, the interaction patterns of people in such relationships are constantly changing in order to maintain continuity. Recall the earlier discussion of roller-coaster relationships.

Our discussions of relational issues and strategies in Part 3 of this book have relied heavily on the observations of Katherine Adams (1985). The relational themes and interactional strategies discussed in the following pages are primarily very close relationships of marital couples in her study. The descriptions of two of these relationships that introduced this discussion are from wives describing their relationships with husbands.

Some of these couples are in the early years of their marriages; some have been married for decades. The thing they all have in common is the fact that their relationship is very close, in addition to being bonded through an exchange of marriage vows. The following discussion, then, treats typical interactional patterns relevant to themes and strategies. What it lacks is the evolutionary development of continuity—the changes in the interaction patterns the partners enacted in order to maintain their relationship. That continuity of change undoubtedly is different for each couple. Even though we will not be able to grasp that notion of "the more it changes, the more it stays the same," we can still gain some understanding of how people in very close relationships maintain their relationship in typical patterns of interaction.

Self-as-Relational Issues

An individual in a very close relationship will typically define much of his or her own self-concept in terms of the relationship. Consequently, each partner creates and enacts a self that is bound up in the relationship and, to a great extent, defined by it. Following are some comments from several typical interactions that reflect the self-as-relational theme:

> I think I'm ready to go to bed, you mind?
> It would be nice if you could go with me, and we could spend a day or two.
> That's another couple we should have over real soon.
> Have we decided which ones we want?
> We need at least a four-seater, though.
> We don't want to go without a charge card.

Each of these comments begins implicitly from the speaker's assumption that "I define my own individual activity in terms of what you do." In fact, what is really an individual activity becomes defined as a joint activity involving the partner. For example, the first comment tells the other person about an individual activity (going to bed) but still asks the other person for "permission" ("you mind?"). Now the partner is not *really* asking for permission to go to bed, but he does seem to be defining his own individual activity in terms of a joint activity. In asking "you mind?" he is implicitly defining his individual activity in terms of what they do together and acknowledges the fact that he is doing it alone.

Many of the comments define personal wants, desires, or motives in terms of wants and desires and motives which they both have as a single relationship. "We need" and "we don't want" are statements about what are essentially individual and intrapersonal notions—needs and wants. But the partner defines his or her own intrapersonal needs and wants as though they "belonged to" them both together. Each partner thus serves to define his or her individual self-concept and individual activities in terms of what they mean in the context of the relationship.

In this way, the partners create and enact a relationship that is as "real" as their own intrapersonal selves. Each of them has an entire system of intrapersonal wants, needs, motives, and desires, but they also attribute those same wants, needs, motives, and desires to the relationship (the "we"). Precisely to whom those wants and needs belong (to the two selves coincidentally or the relationship as a whole) is difficult to say. The result is that the theme of the interaction pattern tends to blur any real distinction between the things that belong to the individual self and those that belong to the relationship—in other words, self-as-relational issues.

Strategies

People in very close relationships probably use more strategies than communicators in any other kind of relationship. And in maintaining their relationship, they probably use a greater variety of strategies (complexity) in their interaction than at any other time of their relationship. If maintenance requires change and continuity of their interaction, then it stands to reason that people will use everything at their disposal to keep a very close relationship going. And the more strategies you have in your repertoire of communicative behaviors, the more choices you have at your disposal to interact appropriately. Recall, too, that maintaining a relationship involves continuity, not consistent use of the same strategies and interaction patterns for an extended period of time.

Interdependent Selves. Individuals maintain a very close relationship by using strategies that encourage interdependence, the sense of unity or togetherness of the partners. Of course, they can achieve interdependence by doing things together— that is, planning and participating in a joint activity. The following hypothetical conversation demonstrates the interdependence that comes from doing things together:

A: Let's do something this weekend. Whaddya say?

B: Yeah. I'd like that. Maybe we could take in a movie or something.

A: I was thinking of making a real night of it. I could pick you up after work and we could get something to eat. You know, a nice restaurant and. . . .

B: That sounds good. I've always wanted to go to that new French restaurant on Third. I've heard it's good.

A: Well, okay, but I was sorta looking forward to a good steak.

B: Then let's go to Angelo's. We haven't been there for a long time. And the food is good.

B: That's not far away from the Orpheum, either. I wonder what's playing.

A: How about a play, instead? The Acting Company's got a new play on right now.

B: Where do they put their plays on? I know they used to be in the Capitol building, but. . . .

A: I think they're in that old school on the north side now. They probably use the stage in the old gym or something.

B: What time you off work? I can get there by 5:30 at least, even if the traffic is bad.

This conversation logically progresses from the first suggestion of "doing something together" to making complete plans for an entire evening. The conversation focuses on a single activity in which both people will engage. Their strategy is based on doing one activity, a common activity involving both partners.

Partners can also achieve interdependence of their individual selves through coordinating their otherwise individual and independent actions. The following is the conversation of two people who have different things to do but synchronize their individual activities in order to maintain their interdependent relationship:

A: The boss told me today that he wants me to work late tomorrow night. I'm afraid I won't be home until late.

B: Really? When will you be through?

A: I'm not sure. I really don't know what he wants me to do. I suppose by seven at least.

B: I can pick you up when you're through. I can spend a little extra time at the office, myself.

A: If you're at the office, I could call you when we're through. That's better than trying to set a definite time.

B: No problem. I'll just be sitting at my desk working.

A: On second thought, why don't I take the bus? Or someone can give me a ride. There's a lot of people who live out in that direction.

B: It's no problem, really. I can use the extra time at work.

A: Well, this way you don't have to worry about leaving something in the middle. And you don't have to go out of your way to pick me up.

B: Okay, but I bet we leave work about the same time.

Interdependence so strongly characterizes the interaction of people in a very close relationship that one partner typically doesn't consider planning any activities without considering the plans of the other. Whether the activity is one in which both will participate or one that is essentially independent of the partner, the interaction will consider both partners in planning.

In a way, interdependence implies that each partner recognizes a sense of "being accountable" to the other. What one person does will affect what the other does, and each partner recognizes that fact of their relationship. Even when the partners do not attempt to coordinate their individual activities, they will probably inform each other what they are doing or plan to do. They don't necessarily ask for each other's permission or approval, but they do recognize the interdependence and mutual accountability of their actions to each other. In a very real sense, the actions of each partner take on meaning only with respect to the other person.

Responsive Strategies. People in virtually every relationship, from acquaintance to "very close relationship," will respond to the comments of the other. But the nature of that responsiveness will be different, depending on the level of interaction quality (intensity, intimacy, trust, and commitment). Partners in acquaintanceships (or any relationship relatively low in interaction quality) respond to each other in a parallel or coincidental manner—similar to "That same thing happened to me, too." In a "very close relationship," partners are responsive within the feeling of interdependence—similar to "If it happens to you, it's just like it happened to me." Occasionally this interdependent responsiveness seems like "empathy," but it is really much more than that. This responsiveness goes beyond "feeling" empathy and involves "acting" interdependently.

One way in which partners in very close relationships demonstrate responsiveness is in "advising" or offering advice to the other. On some occasions, one of the partners will request the advice:

A: I just can't seem to get rid of this headache. You think I should see a doctor?
B: You've been taking aspirins for days, and they haven't worked. You ought to get it taken care of.

On other occasions, the partner offers advice even when the other person has not requested any:

A: Sometimes I just hate to go to work in the morning. It just isn't fun anymore.
B: Why not quit? With your skills you can get another job easy. I sure wouldn't keep a job that made me so unhappy. It's not worth it.

A second way for people in a very close relationship to demonstrate their responsive interdependence is by "supporting" and "showing approval." Perhaps the strongest form of providing support is that of being an advocate for the other. Betty's comment above, for instance, is really a statement that supports Alfred by being his advocate. Betty expresses her advocacy with the line, "With your skills you can get another job easy." Partners can also serve as each other's advocates by defending and rationalizing the other's actions or feelings:

A: I don't know why, but I just couldn't make myself concentrate. I just know I flunked that test, and I knew the answers, too.
B: I bet you didn't flunk it. You just didn't do as well on it as you wanted. You're too smart to flunk it.
A: Oh, I flunked it all right. I know what answers I missed and what ones I left blank.
A: You just blanked, that's all. Remember you didn't get much sleep the night before. You were tired.
B: Yeah, but I still flunked it.
A: Your other scores are good, aren't they? And you've still got the final coming up. I bet you ace the final.
B: Well, I suppose. That test is only 10 percent of the grade. But still. . . .
A: Don't worry about it. Ace the final and you're home free.

A partner can also be supportive of the other person by providing assistance by "reproaching" or "repairing" the other's comments or actions. When you feel that the other person in a very close relationship has made a mistake or an error in judgment, you feel that you have made the mistake yourself. Hence, you respond by correcting the error. The correction may be as simple as making a minor repair in the information:

A: The color was kinda pink like that sweater of yours.

B: You mean my angora? I'd call it a light orange.
A: Yeah, kinda light orange. It was really pretty.

Sometimes the partner asks for the repair so that the story being told is really a joint activity:

A: It happened last week sometime, wasn't it, Betty?
B: Tuesday night I think. Right after the news was over.
A: That's right. Tuesday, and it was pretty late at night.

Individuals in a very close relationship experience no problem in correcting the other or offering reproaches when they feel they are needed. Neither partner wants the other to make a mistake. Hence, the partner will offer a reproach in response to what is considered an error. Consider the following interaction:

A: Can you believe that guy? He voted for that idiot when he knew the guy was crooked.
B: What makes you think he was crooked? You certainly liked his stand on the environmental protection bill last session.
A: But that was different. He's just trying to protect all those defense contractors. He'll vote for anything with big bucks for more bombs.
B: Maybe he's just voting in the best interests of the people who elected him. After all, those contractors provide a lot of jobs for people in the state. And what would happen to the state taxes if they didn't get that contract?
A: Yeah, well maybe. I'm still not convinced, though.

The point of the responsive strategy is not that each partner always approves or supports the other. Rather, the responsive strategy is a contribution to the interaction that consistently recognizes the worth of the other individual's opinion, desire, or self (a form of confirmation). Sometimes that strategy translates into a response that explicitly supports the partner, and sometimes it means that the appropriate response is a reproach or repair. The individuals in a very close relationship do not take the attitude of "my partner—right or wrong." Instead, they adopt the responsive attitude of "my partner—always be appropriately responsive."

Remember schismogenesis—creating a relational problem through a too consistent and monotonous interaction pattern? Always expressing support and approval of the partner's actions indiscriminately and too consistently is likely to lead to schismogenesis. In fact, too much supportiveness will eventually lead to a comment such as "Just once I'd like to hear you disagree with me!" Of course, finding fault with the other all the time is equally as destructive—"All you ever do is nag, nag, nag!" Before the interaction gets to the point of disrupting the relationship, though, one of the partners in a very close relationship is more likely to point out the potential harm of that action to the relationship, as in the following interaction:

A: You should stand up for your rights more often. Tell him what you really think.
B: I wish you wouldn't always tell me what I oughta do. I'm not a kid any more, you know.

A: Oh, I didn't mean to tell you what to do. I just get so mad sometimes when people don't respect who you are.

B: I know. And I really want your advice sometimes. It's just that some things I have to work out for myself.

A: Okay. I don't want you to think that I'm dictating to you. You gotta make your own decisions.

B: It's okay. It's just that sometimes. . . .

A: I understand. I won't give you advice unless you ask for it. But remember you can ask for my help anytime. I really do want to help.

B: And I appreciate that. I really will ask you, too, when I can't do it by myself.

The most appealing element of the interpersonal communication pattern that maintains long-term relationships is the fact that the partners feel no inhibitions in interacting with each other. They feel almost absolute freedom to say what they want whenever they want without fear of doing something wrong. In fact, they also realize that the partner will maintain the very close relationship even when they are wrong. They don't have to worry about arguing or being in conflict with each other, because they know that mere disagreement will not damage their relationship. They've worked out their differences in the past, and they are confident they will work them out in the future. The lack of inhibitions in their interaction may be the most significant part of relationship maintenance: the partners are totally comfortable in their interaction with each other.

The last line of the novel *Love Story*, popular a decade ago, has become almost a cliché: "Love is never having to say you're sorry." I have never fully understood that line and have never really believed it. The line could probably be rewritten, though, to describe more accurately the interaction patterns which serve to maintain a very close relationship. "Love is never *having* to say you're sorry or anything else. Love is *being comfortable* in saying you're sorry or anything else."

Summary

Maintaining interpersonal relationships is often little more than staying together for an extended period of time. Although many acquaintanceships last for years, those relationships require little maintenance and continue largely as a matter of coincidence—both partners are in the same place at the same time. Maintenance is a stage in the evolutionary development only when the relationship has evolved to a relatively high level of intensity, intimacy, trust, and commitment.

Every relationship is a product of its "historicity." The outcome or later developmental stage of a relationship can rarely be predicted on the basis of the way it started. Nevertheless, every relationship evolves to what it has become through the stages of its earlier patterns. To maintain interpersonal relationships at their high level of development is to ensure continuity, rather than consistency, in the developmental pattern. Relationships that continue to maintain themselves continue to change in order to remain the same. Long-term friendships are also characterized by complexity, rather than simplicity, in their interaction patterns.

The evolution during the maintenance of long-term relationships is like a roller coaster in that it tends to fluctuate back and forth between different patterns of characteristic interaction. The partners experience emotional highs in brief, intense moments after long periods of monotony and boredom. They fluctuate back and forth between periods of conflict and periods of total cooperation. They intersperse periods of serious interaction with periods of play. Throughout these peaks and valleys, ups and downs of interaction, the partners in very close relationships ward off the potential breakdown of their relationship that comes from too much of the same thing—the monotony of "cultural schismogenesis."

Very close relationships are often thought to include high levels of self-disclosure, with the partners confiding innermost secrets to each other and turning to each other for help in times of trouble. In real life, though, individuals in very close relationships do not need to self-disclose to each other. They have done most of this during earlier periods, when their relationship was becoming more integrated. Participants experience a feeling of closeness to each other, though, and are comfortable with each other during their interaction. The interaction of very close relationships differs somewhat on the basis of whether the partners are both males, both females, or male and female. The expectations and stereotypes of our society affect friendships on the basis of gender, particularly when the close friends are of different sex. Generally speaking, though, the influence of gender on the interaction patterns of members in very close relationships is believed to be much stronger than it actually is.

The interactional theme that characterizes the maintenance stage of close friendships focuses on the interdependence of the relational partners. Typically, individual communicators in the process of maintaining a very close relationship discuss self-as-relational themes and emphasize the interdependence of their individual selves—in planning and performing joint activities or synchronizing their independent and individual activities with each other. Relational strategies used to maintain close friendships involve the support and approval of the other person as well as offering reproaches and repairs. All types of these strategies could be generalized as "responsive strategies," in which each individual responds to the other individual with respect and self-interest. Strategies used to maintain close friendships are also very numerous. The greatest variety of strategies is used to maintain close relationships, and the partners feel comfortable in using as many of them as they want or need.

PART 4

Outcomes of Relationships

CHAPTER 15

Increasing Competence and Satisfaction

Relational competence: The ability to make someone think that both of you are pretty wonderful.

—Anonymous

Relational satisfaction: The realization that even though you don't get everything you want, you also don't get more of the things you don't want.

—Anonymous

There are basically only two views of any human activity: a consummatory view and an instrumental view. Now if you adopt the consummatory view, you tend to judge what you do on the basis of how much pleasure it gives you. But if you adopt an instrumental view, you tend to judge what you do on the basis of what you get out of it personally. Imagine taking a trip somewhere. If you view the trip as a consummatory activity, you "consume" the activity of traveling—that is, you "eat it up." You derive pleasure from looking out the window at the scenery, talking with your traveling companions, relaxing with a good book—from the sheer pleasure of traveling. On the other hand, if you see the trip as instrumental, then traveling is merely something you have to do in order to get where you want to go. I've always thought that people who like to travel by train take a consummatory view. Instrumentalists travel by plane.

You might say that the difference between *being competent* in interpersonal communication and *deriving satisfaction* from it is the difference between a consummatory (the doing of interpersonal communication) and an instrumental (the outcome or goal of interpersonal communication) view. When we stop to think about it, though, the more reasonable answer is to see competence and satisfaction as fundamentally the same. People who are competent in interpersonal communication derive satisfaction from their interpersonal relationships. I have heard several experts in salesmanship express the same idea when they suggest that the most effective sales representatives (the ones who make the "million-dollar club") are those who enjoy selling, enjoy meeting new people—and they're good at it.

I have always enjoyed the comment attributed to the author Lillian Hellman when she was asked whether she liked writing. She is alleged to have responded, "I hate writing, but I really enjoy having written." Some people have interpreted this statement to mean that she hated the consummatory activity of writing (competence) but enjoyed having achieved her goal (satisfaction). Another interpretation of her comment is that while she was writing, she had no way of assessing the value of what she had done, of determining whether what she was writing was good or not. But after she had finished, she could look back on what she had done and make an appropriate evaluation. (If this sounds like retrospective sensemaking to you, you have indeed learned something from reading this book.)

But we should know by now that retrospective sensemaking is an unavoidable part of the same process as doing the activities that you later make sense out of. How can you separate the two? Hence, we will take the position in this chapter that competence in interpersonal communication is essentially the same thing as achieving satisfaction from having communicated interpersonally—that becoming skilled in interpersonal communication is equivalent to gaining satisfaction from your relationships with other people.

What does it mean to be a competent communicator? If you were to read all the popularized "how to" books on being effective in interpersonal communication, you would discover hundreds of different answers to this question. But this material is also confusing, because much of the advice on how to improve your communicative effectiveness is in direct conflict with other advice. Our discussions in this chapter will attempt to make sense of the material (and there is a *lot* of material) concerning competence in or satisfaction with interpersonal communication.

Our first step in this sensemaking process is to identify the myths surrounding competence. I use the term "myths" because our society has established hundreds of beliefs about the nature of human communication that have proved to be false in actual practice. Much of what we believe to be true about competent communication makes good, sound common sense. But it often doesn't work that way in real life.

The second step in our discussions of increasing competence and satisfaction in interpersonal communication is to define precisely what we mean by the terms. We will discover that a simple definition of communicative competence is not immediately apparent. Interpersonal communication is much too complex to be understood in terms that are overly simple. For instance, does competence in interpersonal communication mean being a competent communicator (the personal view)? Or does it mean participating in a competent relationship (the interpersonal view)? In this chapter, we will be discussing both views.

If you are expecting to discover "the ten easy steps to becoming a competent communicator" in this chapter, you will be sorely disappointed. If you think that the ten (or twenty or thirty) easy steps actually exist, you are probably one of those who has a subscription to *The National Inquirer* and believes all the claims about the miracle diets (as in "How to lose 20 pounds in just 2 days without dieting or exercising—guaranteed"). Our discussions will conclude, however, with some reasonable (though not guaranteed to succeed and not necessarily "easy") guidelines to follow if you are seriously interested in becoming a more competent communicator and a more satisfied participant in your interpersonal relationships.

SOME MYTHS ABOUT COMMUNICATIVE COMPETENCE

There is an old saying that "Fifty thousand Frenchmen can't be wrong." The sentiment underlying this adage is the notion that what most people believe must be correct. That sentiment is pure and totally unadulterated "horsehockey" (to use a favorite expression of *M*★*A*★*S*★*H*'s Colonel Potter). For centuries, entire societies have believed many things about phenomena they did not fully understand. Such beliefs have extended from "the earth is flat" to "moonlight causes people to go insane" (the derivation of the word "lunacy"). Commonly held beliefs concerning communication and specifically communicative competence are numerous and fervently held. The tenacity of the general belief in them, however, is not a measure of their truth.

Why do we believe so many of the myths about communicative competence? One reason is the quite understandable confusion between what we think we *should* do and what we *actually* do. Our intentions are in the right place, even if our actions aren't. Another reason for the many myths about communicative competence stems from the inaccuracy of how we perceive the world around us. As you recall from our earlier discussions, we perceive things selectively and often inaccurately in order to protect our self-concepts, our former beliefs, our stereotypes, and so forth. Thus, we see what we want to see and base our beliefs on what we want to experience rather than what we actually do experience. The reasons why we have developed an entire mythology concerning communicative competence are not particularly significant, though. The fact that we do have myths is more important.

In order to understand what it means to be a competent participant in interpersonal relationships, we need first to recognize the myths surrounding competence. To be aware of what we "know" and dispel such false knowledge is the first step on the road to understanding. The following items provide only a partial listing of myths of communicative competence, phrased in the form of "good advice" to would-be interpersonal communicators:

1. Be honest.
2. Be yourself.
3. Express your true feelings.
4. Be open in communicating with others.
5. Believe in yourself.
6. Do not give advice to others, even when asked.
7. Avoid evaluating the other person.
8. Develop good listening habits.
9. Be attentive.
10. Think before you speak.
11. Develop effective communication skills.
12. Study communication.
13. Relax.

For different reasons, most of these statements are myths. Some are patently false. Some are probably good ideas but aren't very practical or even possible to put into practice. Some are based on truth but overstated and need to be qualified. Some are so general and vague as to be totally impractical.

The Myth of Openness

Each of the first five statements listed above reflects the myth of openness. According to it, the best relationships are those with "open" communication in which the partners confide in each other their innermost secrets and intimate details of their lives. Sometimes the myth of openness is phrased as an admonition to "really communicate" instead of "just talking." A cartoon in a national magazine some years ago derived humor from this myth. The cartoon depicted a marriage counselor with a couple, obviously his clients, sitting on the other side of the desk. The husband (or the wife) is saying to the new counselor, "But if we were to 'really communicate' with each other, our marriage would be in even more trouble!"

The myth of openness is not that those five "good advice" items are somehow wrong. To the contrary, being open with your partner is beneficial to the evolving relationship *at some times*. But being open at all costs is not beneficial. We discussed in Chapters 12 and 13 how partners get to know each other through being open and self-disclosing to each other. In fact, this open communication is one of the principal characteristics of a relationship in its integrating stage. Each of the partners needs to reduce uncertainty by gaining information about the other person's self. In Chapter 14, however, we discussed how couples who have already established a rather high level of interactional quality (intensity, intimacy, trust, and commitment) don't really self-disclose to each other very much. In other words, openness and self-disclosure in communication characterize an *integrating* relationship but do not play a significant part (and, indeed, are often harmful) in *maintaining* a close relationship. Nevertheless, we tend to accept the myth that all good interpersonal relationships are always open. Only bad relationships are not open. This myth ignores the process of evolutionary development in interpersonal communication.

There is another view concerning openness in interpersonal communication. One communication scholar, Mac Parks (1982), has warned against what he calls the "ideology of intimacy." He illustrates (with supporting evidence from research studies) that "Most of us tell lies and most of our statements are less than completely honest" (p. 90). He also suggests:

> Interpersonal relationships are established as much by privacy, secrecy, and deception as by self-disclosure, empathy, and openness. . . . Privacy and secrecy maintain relationships by allowing individuals to hide their inadequacies, thereby making themselves more attractive to their partners. . . . Moreover, deception can promote intimacy by protecting others, helping maintain a focus in conversations, and by avoiding tension and conflict. (pp. 90–91)

Another communication scholar, Bill Rawlins (1983), also refers to the unquestioned belief in openness as "problematic." He discusses how communicators are constantly caught in the dilemma of deciding when to be open and to what degree and when and how much to lie to their partners. Moreover, a group of communication scholars discovered that, when communicating, "People lie a lot, and they justify their white lies with ease—especially in certain social contexts" (Camden, Motley, & Wilson, 1984, p. 321). They even went so far to suggest that, since communicators often view "white lies . . . as a practical effective way to cope with certain situational demands," perhaps we should "view lying [as well as openness] as a particular sort of communicative competence" (p. 321). Few people, though, are willing to accept the precept "When in trouble lie to your partner" as one of the "ten easy steps" to developing effective skills in communication.

So what's the "real story" concerning openness in interpersonal communication? Certainly most close relationships have evolved through periods of high-self-disclosure and openness, and partners will maintain some degree of openness in their communication. But these same partners are very selective about the areas in which they choose to be open with one another. By *not* being open in ultrasensitive areas, particularly those in which one of the partners is vulnerable and could be hurt, the communicators actually enhance their relationship and keep the quality of interaction high.

Sometimes (and undoubtedly more often than we might think), partners in a very close relationship actually lie to each other and deceive their partners in some way. Lying, when the situation is appropriate, can also enhance and maintain a very close relationship. Openness in the process of interpersonal communication is often helpful to the evolution of a close relationship. But when we think of openness as a noble ideal toward which we should constantly strive, we contribute to the myth of openness.

The Myth of Objectivity

Items 6 and 7 in the list of "good advice" statements foster the myth that we should look at other people (and the entire world, for that matter) with an objective eye. It is better, we think, to avoid making judgments. Therefore we shouldn't evaluate other people or give them advice on what they should do. As in the case of openness, the myth is not that objectivity is wrong per se. However, there are times when being objective is not only problematic but absolutely impossible. And communicating with another person is one of those times.

We know that every time we perceive something, we inevitably evaluate it. When we perceive another person, we automatically evaluate that person. We wonder whether our relationship with this person will evolve into something more than casual acquaintance. We judge other people on the basis of how much we like them, and we apply our implicit personality theory to them. We cannot avoid making evaluative judgments of other persons. And certainly when our relationship has developed beyond casual acquaintance, we have already evaluated the other person as a person whom we like. To tell people to avoid evaluating others is to tell them to avoid doing something that is impossible to avoid.

More importantly, though, you shouldn't avoid evaluating your partner in an interpersonal relationship. If the relationship is going to get off the ground, you *must* evaluate the other person. Developing a relationship and continuing interpersonal communication is a matter of judgment. You don't continue interacting with someone unless you have judged that the other person is worth it. The only exception is the environment (such as your place of work) that requires interaction. But even in such an environment, you will still be making judgments about your acquaintance in order to determine whether you want the relationship to develop into something more than work acquaintance.

Recall that one of the strategies used by communicators in maintaining their very close relationship is to offer advice to the other person. Sometimes relational partners will ask for or encourage you to give them advice; sometimes you give your partner advice even when you are not asked. People in close relationships want to help each other when possible. Furthermore, they expect their partners to help them when they need help. To advise someone to avoid giving advice to a relational partner and to call this a skill in interpersonal communication is absurd. Such advice perpetuates the myth that making evaluations and judgments of other people is bad and objectivity is good.

The Myth of Listening Techniques

Engaging in interpersonal or face-to-face communication requires the use of communicative skills involving both sending and receiving messages. We send messages with verbal and nonverbal behaviors, and we receive messages through our five senses. Hearing, of course, is one of those senses. Items 8 and 9 in the above list encourage the practice of using the sense of hearing. No one will deny that listening is an important and valuable communicative skill. In fact, we will be discussing listening skills later in this chapter. The *myth* of listening techniques assumes that competence in listening is simply a matter of learning and practicing certain techniques.

For instance, what does being attentive mean to you? Does it mean to focus your mind in total concentration on what the other person is saying? Does it mean looking into the eyes of the other person and having an interested expression on your face? These are techniques that should not be confused with the skill of listening in interpersonal communication. Listening in a relationship is not merely paying attention or maintaining eye contact. In fact, it is a mistake to separate listening skills from speaking skills in the process of interpersonal communication. Listening and speaking together involve the use of verbal and nonverbal communication skills in being a partner in the interpersonal relationship.

Perhaps an example might best illustrate the point of what we might call "relational listening." The following hypothetical conversation might occur between (who else?) Alfred and Betty:

A: I just can't believe that guy.
B: What guy?
A: My English prof. I spent hours on that paper, and he only gave me a "C."
B: Really?
A: Yeah. I went to his office and showed him my notes and everything. He didn't even look at them hardly.
B: Is that right?
A: And after all that work, too. I just gotta get a higher grade than that. I could lose my scholarship if I don't get a 3.3 this semester.

B: Don't worry, you'll make it up in the other classes. You interested in a cuppa coffee or something?

Betty may be very attentive to what Alfred is saying and may even be practicing excellent techniques of good listening. But her comments do not demonstrate very good relational listening. See what happens in the following conversation:

A: I just can't believe that guy.

B: What's wrong? You seem upset about something.

A: Well, I am. My English prof gave me a "C" on my term paper, and I spent hours on it.

B: Oh, no. That's terrible. How could he give you a "C"? You always get the highest grade in the class. If I were you, I'd go see him. Maybe he made a mistake.

A: I already did. I showed him my notes and everything. I don't even think he looked at them.

B: Oh boy! That doesn't sound good. How are your other grades in the class? With a good final, you might still pull your grade up.

A: Well, I did pretty good on the midterm. And the final is worth about 30 percent of the grade.

B: Okay, you can't do anything about the term paper now. The thing to do is ace the final. I can help you study if you want. Throw questions at you or something. I only have one final, and I don't really need to study for it.

A: Yeah, maybe you're right. No use crying over spilled milk. I really need to study for that final, though. I could lose my scholarship.

B: No way! We're gonna show him on the final. Let's go get a cuppa coffee and talk about when we get together to study.

In the second conversation Betty is demonstrating effective skill in relational listening. She is not merely being attentive or using good listening techniques. She *contributes* (speaking) to the interaction on the basis of her listening. Every one of her comments is *responsive* to the needs and feelings expressed by Alfred. She listened for what Alfred was feeling and thinking and responded as a relational partner, not just as an attentive receiver of messages. She goes beyond the appearance of being sympathetic; she reaches out to offer assistance and advice. She acts (speaks) on the basis of the relationship. In fact, the relational listening she demonstrates serves to define the relationship as a rather close one. On the other hand, the listening skills she demonstrated in the first conversation point more to a relationship of casual acquaintance. In other words, Betty exhibited casual listening. Perhaps that kind of listening was appropriate to that relationship, but it certainly doesn't serve to enhance it.

Listening is too important to be treated so casually, as a mere collection of learned techniques. When we think of listening as a skill different from the entire process of interpersonal communication and practiced independently of it, we are missing the point of how listening functions in interpersonal relationships. Many people discuss the notions of "empathic listening" (interpreting intrapersonal feelings

It is important for partners in a relationship to develop relational listening.
(Joel Gordon)

of the speaker) or "active listening" (decoding messages accurately with full comprehension of their meanings). But the more important ability of listening in interpersonal communication is relational listening, or being responsive to the other person in terms of how the relationship has been defined in the historicity of past interaction patterns.

The Myth of Formula Answers

The final four statements in the list of communication skills are my favorites. They say everything without saying anything. They are solutions to all problems without providing any direction or guidance for solving the problems. Telling a nervous or apprehensive person to relax is like saying "Don't drown" to a person who doesn't know how to swim. It's good advice, but it isn't very helpful. We need to know more than the formula for solving the problem. We need to know how to use the formula, how to put it into effect. We need to know what the formula means in practice.

Let me illustrate. A few years ago I was talking with an advisee just before she was to take an oral examination. She was a very good student who tended to get excited in the situation of an oral exam and to talk herself into a hole that was difficult to crawl out of. Basically, she needed to relax and allow her abilities and intelligence to work for her. I advised her ("commanded," actually) never to answer any question immediately but to pause for a minimum of two seconds before she replied. Two seconds is about the time needed to take a single deep breath, but it seems like an interminable length of time during a normal conversation. The two-second pause was a practical way of telling her to relax and to think before she provided an answer. She passed her exam with flying colors and confided to me afterward that she had never felt so much confidence, so much in control of the situation.

There is certainly nothing wrong with the final four comments on the list. In fact, I endorse every one of them. But formula answers simply aren't very specific and certainly aren't very practical as a way to enhance your competence in interpersonal communication. On the other hand, item 12 ("Study communication") may be the single most important guideline in developing your competence and skills in interpersonal communication. In a very real way, this entire book deals with developing communicative competence.

To understand the process of interpersonal communication fully is to know what and when to communicate appropriately and effectively. Acquiring an understanding is the best way to achieve competence. Practice based on understanding may be the most useful and practical definition of competence. Getting rid of myths (which are really misunderstandings) is the best way to begin acquiring that understanding. All that remains is practice.

DEFINING COMPETENCE

Competence or skill in interpersonal communication is easier to recognize than to define. You know people, I am sure, who are very competent or skilled communicators. But you probably have a difficult time putting your finger on precisely what makes them competent. Some things come to mind that might be included in your definition. For instance, the competent communicator seems poised or at ease, appears natural, is articulate or fluent, uses grammar correctly, has a pleasing voice, coordinates verbal and nonverbal behaviors, and so forth. We typically tend to define competence in terms of the interactive behaviors produced by the communicator, although sometimes we define it quite differently.

Definitions of communicative competence will differ on the basis they use to assess competence. The following definitions vary because each uses a different basis for assessment:

Individual ability: Competent communication is "the ability to engage in appropriate and effective interpersonal interaction" (Spitzberg & Cupach, 1984, p. 14).

Individual goals: Competent communicators "accomplish tasks successfully" (p. 53) or are successful in "exerting control over the environment to achieve certain outcomes" (p. 54).

Instrumental behaviors: "Interactive skills are the skills you or I use in face to face encounters to arrange our behavior so that it is in step with our objectives. . . . Our behavior is a means that can, depending on our skill, either help or hinder us in achieving our ends" (Honey, 1976, p. 13).

Adaptation: "Persons who are able to adapt to different relational situations are 'rhetorically sensitive' and seen by others as competent communicators" (Wilmot, 1980, p. 194).

Whatever the basis used to define communicative competence, any definition (such as those given above) includes two essential features: knowledge and performance. The focus must be on interactional behaviors, but the competent communicator must not only be able to perform appropriate behaviors but also must know what behaviors to use and when to use them. Interactive behaviors that are appropriate in one relationship may be quite inappropriate in another, and no two interpersonal relationships are exactly alike. Behaviors that are appropriate during one stage in the evolutionary development of a relationship may be quite inappropriate during another.

Performing behaviors to achieve your goals or objectives is also problematic, especially when your goals change during the developmental process of the relationship. A behavior that was instrumental to one objective may turn out to be detrimental in the long run. That is, your retrospective sensemaking may lead you to revise your goals or objectives in the relationship.

The obvious truism concerning communicative competence is, perhaps, expressed by two authors (Rathjen & Foreyt, 1980) who wrote an entire book on defining social competence. They introduced this work with the statement that "the choice of which behaviors should be included in the repertoire of a socially competent person is not clear" (p. 1). Few people will deny the obvious truth, however frustrating, of such a statement.

Despite the problem of providing that clear definition, we still know that communicative competence is a powerful force in the process of enacting interpersonal relationships. Research into communicative competence (for example, Spitzberg & Hecht, 1984) has consistently demonstrated the fact that skills or competence in interpersonal communication will significantly affect how satisfied we are likely to be with our interpersonal relationships. Even without a satisfactory definition of communicative competence, though, we still have a relatively clear understanding of what communicative competence looks like when it occurs during the process of interpersonal communication.

Dimensions of Competence

According to two leading researchers (Wiemann & Kelly, 1981) into communicative competence:

> The interpersonally competent communicator is seen as responsible not only for being able to perform appropriately, but also for choosing relationship partners who will find satisfaction . . . with the performance options the individual has in his or her repertoire. . . . Interpersonal competence then becomes more a matter of avoiding errors or traps that lead to relational distress (or impasse) than of getting things just right communicationally. . . . The relationship is the context in which communication takes place (and in which meaning emerges). (p. 289)

Competence in interpersonal communication, then, is not any one thing or one list of things to do when communicating. Rather, it involves a number of different dimensions, ranging from having a repertoire of behaviors to choosing appropriate relational partners and even to deciding which relationships to continue and which to terminate. It involves having the ability to perform appropriate behaviors, having a repertoire of behaviors from which to choose, having appropriate partners, having realistic goals to be realized in the relationship, and so forth. Generally speaking, though, communicative competence boils down to two fundamental dimensions: capacity (that is, knowledge) and performance.

Interpersonal Capacity. All people are not created equal; some people have more ability than others. Some people have more athletic talent than others, some are more intelligent, some are more physically attractive. And some have a greater capacity for competence in interpersonal communication. The term "interpersonal capacity" refers generally to the level of ability or knowledge that a person possesses, enabling him or her to engage in interpersonal communication. Like most of your abilities, you can improve your capacity for communicative competence—within limits, of course. You can improve in any or all of the three components of this capacity: temporal frameworks, categorization devices, and interpretive procedures.

Temporal frameworks refers to the ability to make associations in time. Throughout the evolutionary process of relationship development, communicators are constantly making sense out of their past interaction and projecting appropriate links to what is likely to occur in the future. Some people are remarkably adept at seeing associations in time; others are remarkably poor.

Your capacity for temporal frameworks is essentially your ability to see events *as events* connected in time. People who have mastered the ability to see temporal-frameworks are able to discover the connections among communicative actions in the sequence of conversation, to see the *pattern of events* as they occur. Your temporal framework allows you to search for and discover meaning in the connections between events and to avoid interpreting prematurely some meaning in a single behavior. This skill allows you to place events in the context of a stream of events and to interpret meaning.

Categorization devices are the raw materials of meaning. To give meaning to an experience is to classify or place that experience into some category of experiences that are similar to each other. Everyone has an entire repertoire of categorization devices. Your capacity for categorizing is in direct proportion to the number of categories (specifically, the number of "appropriate" categories) you have at your disposal to be used to classify your experiences. The greater the variety of your categories, the greater your capacity to categorize and make finer discriminations of meaning.

Interpretive procedures include your ability to assume a number of different viewpoints in order to interpret the meaning of a given experience. Your interpretation of any experience is essentially the result of seeing your experience within some perspective. If you see your relationship as the result of the "chemistry" of two personalities, that will be how you will understand interpersonal communication. That interpretation will not necessarily be a competent one, however. Competence in applying interpretive procedures involves the ability to apply a number of different criteria, different procedures, different perspectives in order to understand the meaning of a given pattern of interaction.

The greater your interpersonal capacity for interpretive procedures, the more meanings you are able to interpret in the interaction and, hence, in the interpersonal relationship. Essentially, the interpretive procedure that is most competent is the one that chooses the most appropriate context (relationship type or relationship stage, for instance) in which to make your interpretation. The more procedures you have at your disposal for interpretation, the more likely you are to be able to make a competent one.

Interpersonal Performance. All the ability in the world will never be enough if you don't demonstrate that ability in actual performance. If you have the ability to get a 4.0 grade point average and exhibit mediocre performance in your classes, you will probably have an academic record that is closer to a 2.0 GPA. You may have the capacity to be a competent communicator; but unless you actually perform communicative behaviors competently, you will not be judged as very competent in interpersonal communication. In all cases, the actual performance of communicative competence is what counts as most important. Your capacity to be competent will never appear "on the record." At best, we can say that you don't communicate to the level of your ability.

Regardless of the level of your ability, the amount of satisfaction you receive from your interpersonal relationships will rest almost exclusively on how competently you perform behaviors when engaged in interpersonal communication. For that reason, the discussions throughout the remainder of this chapter will focus on the significance of interpersonal performance—the actual behaviors you perform (in concert with your partner) during the process of interpersonal communication.

Perceiving Competence in Others

Several years ago Peter Sellers starred in a movie called *Being There*. The character portrayed by Sellers was a gardener by trade and a bumbling idiot in his behavior (perhaps even mentally retarded). Despite his almost total ineptitude in communicating, nearly everyone around him *perceived* him to be a genius. He even became an adviser to the president of the United States. This movie dramatized one of the persistent problems associated with perceptions of competence—the fact that such perceptions are often irrelevant to either ability or performance of competent communication. Nevertheless, as we have already pointed out, one persistent finding in research is that we tend to be satisfied in our interpersonal relationships to the extent that we perceive the other person to be a competent communicator. Therefore, our definition of competence should probably take into account the perceptions of competence in others as well as the person's abilities and behaviors.

From what we already know about the nature of perception, we are aware that perceiving competence in other people is likely to be problematic. For one thing, we aren't really sure just what the perceiver is looking for. People will generally agree with each other on an overall evaluation of how competent or skilled the other person is, but they are likely to disagree on the components or definition of just what competence is (see, for example, Wiemann, 1977; Rubin, 1985). But this should not be too surprising. Remember that we have little difficulty in knowing competence when we see it, but we have problems providing a clear and concise definition of it. Our perceptions work the same way. We know competence (or lack of competence) when we see a person communicating, but we have difficulty in putting into words just what makes that person a competent communicator.

A second problem in perceiving competence in others concerns the "fit" between what we perceive and what the other person is actually doing. Rubin (1985), for example, is not alone in her discovery that people's perceptions of competence are often unrelated to the behaviors they have observed. Certainly the people who thought Peter Sellers competent in *Being There* exhibited little correlation between their judgment and his communicative behaviors. Hence, if capacity (as well as performance) is an important characteristic of the definition of competence, then the communicator's ability is of little importance when people perceive competence in others.

A final problem with perceptions of competence in other people is the nature of "person perception" itself. Recall our earlier discussions in Chapter 8. We tend to see other people in terms of ourselves. That is, we view other people by comparing them with ourselves. If they are similar, for example, we tend to view them as more attractive and more competent. In other words, when we perceive other people as being competent communicators, we perceive them more in terms of our own feelings than what they are actually doing when they are communicating. Perceiving our relational partners to be competent communicators may be a significant factor affecting how satisfied we are with our relationships, but the perceptions we have of their competence may have little to do with their abilities or performance in interpersonal communication.

THE COMPETENT COMMUNICATOR

The individual communicator is competent to the extent that he or she possesses the capacity or the ability to be competent, demonstrates skill in actually performing communicative behaviors, achieves the goals or outcomes desired in the communication, and is perceived by the partner to be communicating competently. We might say that the communicator is *really* competent if all four bases of communicative competence are present in the communicative situation. Of course, any one of the four ways of defining competence (capacity, performance, outcome, and perception) may lead to an assessment of competence that does not agree with the judgment from any of the other ways of assessing competence. In other words, judging the communicative competence of the individual communicator is not a simple task.

Communicative Style

Everyone does not communicate in exactly the same way. We can easily detect differences among our relational partners in terms of how they communicate in an interpersonal situation. To some extent, of course, we change our styles to adapt to the specific situation. We tend to be more formal or polite when the situation demands it (as when we meet people for the first time, when we attend a "dressy" occasion, or when we dine in a fancy restaurant). We tend to be more informal and looser when the situation demands it (as when we see old friends again, when we are with our family, when we attend a keg party, or when we eat in a fast-food restaurant). Generally, other people come to associate each of these situations with a certain way of communicating—a certain style of communicating that belongs to the individual communicator.

The number of different communicative styles is huge. They range from formal to informal, aggressive to passive, friendly to aloof, assertive to acquiescent, dominant to submissive, self-confident to ill at ease, competitive to cooperative, conversational to stiff, intellectual to anti-intellectual, natural to stilted, intimidating to respectful, and so on and so on. My own communicative style has been described (by others, of course) in the following terms: "natural and at ease," "practiced incompetence," "self-deprecating," "insulting," and "conscious bumbling," among other even less complimentary adjectives. (Now you know why I think that other people's perceptions of communicative competence are so unreliable.)

The point is that each of us, during our years of experience in interpersonal communication, develops some habits and consistent mannerisms that other people come to recognize as our own peculiar style of interpersonal communication. Of course, your description (perception) of your own style may differ from what others perceive it to be. (If that is the case, point out to these people that perceptions are often inaccurate. In other words, tell them that their perceptions are wrong!)

Every person's style of interpersonal communication changes considerably from one situation to the next. The influence of the social context, the identity of the relational partner, and past interactions will lead you to change your style somewhat so that it is appropriate to the situation, the stage of relational development, and the occasion for communicating. We will generally know when and how to adapt our style so that it will not appear to be out of place. But knowing what is appropriate in a given communicative situation also results from our having learned it during our years of experience in interpersonal communication.

Communicative competence is more than simply having a style of communicating. After all, everyone has a communicative style. Competence is adapting the particular style so that it is appropriate to the communicative situation. The greater the variety of communicative situations you have experienced, the more likely you are to judge what communicative behaviors (or styles) are appropriate. The person who has a single communicative style and uses it in every communicative situation is a communicator who is not able to adjust to the situation, is not able to judge the appropriateness of communicative behaviors and, in short, is incompetent. In terms of your communicative style, then, *adaptability* is a dimension of communicative competence.

Relational Strategies

In the last four chapters, we have emphasized that everyone uses relational strategies when communicating and forming interpersonal relationships with other people. It follows, then, that the competent communicator will use relational strategies in a competent manner. By demonstrating competence in using relational strategies during the process of interpersonal communication, the communicator is demonstrating an ability for competence, is giving the other person information that can then be used to perceive competence, and is adapting the communicative style that is appropriate to the situation. Using relational strategies while communicating is, perhaps, the central element of communicative competence. The competent use of relational strategies requires both capacity and performance.

To understand how to use relational strategies competently, we need to look at what people actually do when they communicate in the "real world." To be practical, we need to discover what researchers have discovered in their observations of interpersonal communication. John Wiemann and Cliff Kelly (1981), two of the foremost researchers in communicative competence, have summarized the research findings and indicate two primary and four secondary characteristics of communicative competence. When people use relational strategies competently, then, they demonstrate (primary characteristics) *control* and *empathy* as well as (secondary characteristics) *affiliation/support*, *behavioral flexibility*, *social relaxation*, and *goal achievement*. Now we need to translate these terms (jargon) into what competent communicators actually do when they communicate with other people.

Primary Characteristics. To use a strategy of *control*, you perform an action that implicitly defines your relationship or your interaction in terms of which relational partner is in control. (Recall the discussion of control modes in Chapter 10.) A control strategy is an implicit relational definition. For example, you might say to your partner, "What do you want to do tonight?" In essence, you have used a relational strategy that gives control of your future plans for the evening to your partner. On the other hand, you might use a relational strategy that defines yourself in control: "Let's go bowling tonight." The following conversation defines control clearly in the hands of Betty:

B: Let's go bowling tonight.
A: Okay. Where do you want to go?
B: I like those new computer alleys at Cottonwood Lanes.
A: Sounds good to me. I haven't bowled in ages.
B: Neither have I, but it should be fun. Pick you up at 8?
A: Sounds good. I'll be ready.

This conversation reflects what is known as a *complementary* pattern of relational control. Both persons agree on the definition of their relationship in terms of who is in control. Betty uses control strategies that indicate she is planning their activities, and Alfred agrees with Betty's plans and thereby defers to her control. The complementary pattern of relational control is based on a difference between the partners. That is, Betty is the controll*er*, and Alfred is the controll*ee*. Betty uses strategies to control their interaction, and Alfred uses strategies that agree with and accept her control strategies.

On the other hand, a control pattern may be based on equality as well as difference. When the interaction pattern defines the partners in equal control of the relationship, it is called *symmetry*. The following hypothetical conversation is symmetrical. Alfred uses strategies that define the relationship with himself in control of the interaction. Betty's strategies define herself in control. Both define themselves as controllers, a relational equality. However, they disagree on who is in control. The result is an interaction pattern of relational control known as *competitive symmetry*:

B: Let's go bowling tonight.
A: Naw, bowling is no fun. Let's go to a movie.
B: I don't like any of the movies playing. Bowling is fun.
A: That new Eastwood movie sounds good. Let's go see it.
B: I don't like him. Besides, I want to *do* something.
A: I just wanta relax, like in a movie. Bowling is for nerds.

Both Alfred and Betty try to gain control over the interactional topic and their evening plans. But neither relinquishes control to the other. The result is an interaction pattern that exhibits not only equality but also competition in terms of who is in the position of control in their interaction.

The type of control pattern that reflects communicative competence is not necessarily either symmetrical or complementary. You will recall that most relationships develop by evolving through patterns that include both symmetrical and complementary interaction. That fluctuation, you will recall, is one of the characteristics of relationship maintenance (Chapter 14) and helps the partners to avoid cultural schismogenesis. Communicative competence, then, is not an issue of who is in control but whether the control patterns "follow the rules" established in the interaction.

Competent communicators know the rules and interact with their partners while observing the rules they have developed during the evolutionary process of the relationship. Some of those rules, of course, come from the larger society and deal with such social customs as how to take turns in interaction. Although rules of control patterns will vary from one relationship to another, a general rule is that relational partners take turns at being in control. Competence, then, is knowing the rules for when to enact a symmetrical control pattern and when to enact a complementary one.

The second primary characteristic of communicative competence, *empathy*, borrows a psychological term referring to a person's ability to understand and mimic the feelings of another. If you're sad, I feel sad, too. If you're happy, I feel happy, too. When empathy is used to characterize communicative competence, though, it goes beyond the psychological feeling. It includes the strategies that the competent communicator contributes to the pattern of communication.

Empathic communicators are probably sensitive to the emotions and internalized feelings of their relational partners. But knowing when your partner is sad or depressed, for example, does not make you a competent—that is, an empathic—communicator. Competence requires performing your empathy in the interaction patterns. The empathic *person* knows when the partner is sad or depressed; the empathic *communicator* attempts to cheer up the relational partner who is sad or depressed. The empathic communicator probably has good empathic skills and is able to detect or be sensitive to the partner's feelings. But that's not really the point when empathy is a relational strategy.

The competent empathic communicator participates in the communication (acts or behaves) *as though* he or she is able to detect or be sensitive to the partner's feelings. In interpersonal communication, feelings or intrapersonal levels are not enough. The competent communicator must act, or participate in the interaction, as though the intrapersonal level were present.

Secondary Characteristics. The secondary characteristics of communicative competence are called secondary not because they are less important but because they derive from the characteristics of control and empathy. Communicators who exhibit affiliation and support demonstrate empathy. Communicators who exhibit social relaxation are probably in control of their selves during the process of communication. When they achieve goals, they are also probably using control strategies competently, so that their relationships with other people are consistent with their personal goals.

Behavioral flexibility may be the most important characteristic of communicative competence. The truly competent communicator undoubtedly possesses a large repertoire of relational strategies to use in communicative situations. Furthermore, the truly competent communicator has experienced a variety of different communicative situations with a variety of relational partners and has thus developed the ability to judge what strategies are most appropriate in which situations and with which relational partners. Being able to adapt and communicate appropriately is the flexibility that the communicator has in choosing strategies and adapting them to specific interpersonal relationships. The truly competent communicator is more than merely skilled, but is capable of knowing what "skill" means in a specific situation. In other words, the truly competent communicator has the ability to perform competently and to define competence for each specific situation.

Interpersonal Listening

We will probably agree that hearing is not the same as listening. That is, we may hear some sounds that we don't pay much attention to. As a result, we may hear these sounds but basically ignore them or don't listen to them. Why do we listen to some sounds and not others? The most obvious answer is that we pay attention to some more than others. And when we pay attention, our listening skills are much better than when we don't. The question now becomes, "Why do we pay attention?"

Two basic reasons for paying attention are confirmed over and over when people do research on listening behavior: *motivation* (see, for example, Kelly, 1967) and *incentives* (see, for example, Smeltzer & Watson, 1984). In other words, when we *want* to (motivation) pay attention, we will be much better listeners than when we don't want to pay attention. And when we have some *reason* to (incentive) pay attention, we will be much better listeners than when we don't have a reason to pay attention. For example, if the speaker is giving me directions on how to get back to the main highway when I'm lost, I have an incentive to pay attention and I'll be a pretty good listener. If the speaker is a person I like very much, I will be a pretty good listener because I *want* to pay attention. In short, our listening skills are often affected more by the motivations and incentives in the communicative situation than by any skills we might have.

Our listening abilities are also associated very closely with our general mental ability and memory (see, for example, Bostrom & Waldhart, 1980). In other words, people with high IQs will tend to be better listeners and remember more information for a longer period of time than people with low IQs. There isn't much we can do to improve our general mental ability and, thus, improve our listening skills. But we can do something about our memory.

Our memory works in unusual ways. For one thing, we don't remember details as well as we remember overall impressions. Most people remember very few specific details about information discussed in conversations only moments after the conversation is over (see Stafford & Daly, 1984). One reason is that informational details in interpersonal communication are less important than our memories of the relationship itself, the overall impression. In closer relationships, we remember not only informational details but also the general feeling we have when we are in each other's presence. With that overall impression in which to organize our memories, we tend to remember more information about conversations in close relationships. When the overall impression is forgettable (as in a casual acquaintance), we remember fewer details. Because the relationship is close, we also pay more attention and have a greater incentive to remember the details of the conversation. In other words, we are much better listeners when we are in relationships having higher interactional quality.

The point is that it is difficult to know precisely how listening skills contribute to a person's overall communicative competence. On the one hand, listening is significant in the exchange of messages that are a part of interpersonal communication. But that skill is affected more by motivations and incentives than in the level of skill or ability the individual listener possesses. Further, the amount of motivation and incentive will depend to a large extent on the nature of the relationship. The higher the interaction quality (intensity, intimacy, trust, and commitment) in the relationship, the more closely each partner will pay attention to what the other is saying and the more they will remember. Hence, the higher the interaction quality, the higher the level of listening skills exhibited by the communicators.

The bottom line is this. We can do little to improve our general mental ability and thus improve our listening skills. We are subject to incentives and motivations present in the specific interpersonal relationship. Our memory works better when we are interacting in close relationships. In other words, when the interactional quality (intensity, intimacy, trust, and commitment) is high, the communicators are better listeners.

The quality of the interaction in the interpersonal relationship exerts the most profound impact on the participants' listening abilities, and the interactional quality is high when the participants are competent communicators. Therefore, competent communicators will tend to have good listening skills. It remains unclear whether trying to develop your listening skills will increase your communicative competence. But trying to develop your skill in using relational strategies, for instance, will probably increase your listening skills. It is virtually impossible to separate speaking skills from listening skills.

THE COMPETENT RELATIONSHIP

If one of the participants in interpersonal communication is competent but the other is not, is the relationship likely to succeed? If both of the communicators are not highly competent, is the relationship doomed to failure? If both of the participants exhibit a high level of communicative competence, is the relationship assured of a long and healthy existence? Or is the relationship itself competent? Is it possible for two incompetent individuals to enact a competent relationship? Can two highly competent individuals enact an incompetent relationship? What on earth is meant by a "competent relationship"? Will the following pages provide the answers to all these questions?

Our discussions throughout this book have consistently emphasized that the relationship is different from either or both of the communicators individually. Neither communicator, as an individual, can determine what the relationship is or will be. Each individual communicator participates in and becomes part of the relationship, but the individual communicators cannot define the relationship by themselves. The whole relationship, because it is a whole, is likely to be quite different from the sum of its parts. A competent relationship may result from the interactive combination of two participants who are individually quite incompetent. Conversely, two individually competent people may not be able to create a relationship that is competent. The relationship may be more or less than the sum of its individual participants, but it almost certainly will be different from them.

Remember that competence is a judgment, assessment, or evaluation of what somebody is or does. But those judgments of competence occur after the communication has taken place—not prior to communicating. When one contributes to communication, the action or behavior becomes an event that fits together with the actions and events of the partner to create the pattern of interaction. According to anthropologists Orvis Collins and June Collins (1973), "In the knife-edged present in which we all live, none of us knows at that moment when he issues an act exactly how that act is to fit into the emergent future of interaction sequencing" (p. 122).

Competence is a judgment made on the basis of retrospective sensemaking and characterizes the interpersonal relationship. When you participate in interaction, you don't know what the pattern or "interaction sequencing" will be. At some point in the future, though, you look back on the interaction that you've already enacted and make sense of what the interaction pattern (and, hence, the relationship) means. In this way, the partners evaluate the competence of the interpersonal communication patterns (the entire relationship) as they evaluate each other's competence. The following discussion, then, shifts our focus from judging the competence of the individual communicator to judging the competence of the entire interpersonal relationship in which the individual communicators are members.

Relationship Rules

Whenever you learn a new game, your first reaction is to ask, "What are the rules?" In order to play the game, you must first be aware of what you can do and what you can't do. The rules of the game provide the information that is necessary to play the game. There are basically two kinds of rules: those that define the game itself and those that you use to play the game. (Recall the earlier discussion of constitutive and regulative rules in Chapter 4.) Chess, for example, is a game that has certain rules that define the game. The game is played on a square board divided into sixty-four smaller squares. Each player begins with the same sixteen pieces arranged in the same way at either end of the board. Each piece can move in only one way, and so forth. But some people are much better chess players than others. Why? After all, they all follow the same basic rules. The difference is that all chess players use another set of rules that guide what they do during the playing of the game. And this second set of rules—rules that regulate the playing of the game—is a central characteristic of relationship competence.

When you communicate with someone else, you follow rules that define how you communicate. You are rarely aware of following rules, but you follow them anyway. You use the same language. You follow the same norms of your culture. You take turns when speaking. In short, you follow the rules that define the game (or culture) itself. Following those rules doesn't mean you are a highly competent communicator, though. It means only that you have been acculturated within a society and have learned the customs and traditions of that society. That is, you are influenced by the social context. As in the game of chess, you can be aware of all the rules that define the game and still play it poorly. To be a good chess player, you need to learn rules that enable you to play the game well. To be a competent communicator, you need to learn rules that guide what you do when you are engaged in the game of interpersonal communication.

Unlike the rules that define the game, rules that regulate the game don't exist until and unless they are created by the players. Furthermore, one person cannot create rules to play the game, because interpersonal communication is not a game of solitaire. It takes two (or more) people to play the game, and it takes two (or more) people to create the rules. Hence, the rules for playing the "game" of interpersonal communication are enacted by the "players" (the communicators themselves) during the process of developing their relationship. Rules are, in essence, the patterns of interaction that you have developed in cooperation with your partner during the process of communication. The rules of your relationship are the sequential patterns of interaction that you (and your partner) come to identify with your relationship. They are the interaction patterns that make your relationship different from other interpersonal relationships.

John Van Maanen (1979) has suggested six "characteristics associated with all rules" of a relationship:

> *First*, rules cannot transcend the situation in which they are applied (though we often try). . . . *Second*, and relatedly, all rules have exceptions. . . . *Third*, rules not only change over time, they are also selectively enforced at any given time. . . . *Fourth*, rules, like all meaningful aspects of the social world, are negotiated. . . . *Fifth*, rules serve as resources to justify behavior after the fact as well as to guide behavior before the fact. . . . *Sixth*, shame more so than any form of direct punishment is the great enforcer of the rules. (pp. 74–76)

The first characteristic indicates that the interaction patterns of a specific interpersonal relationship *belong to* that relationship and even to that particular stage of the relationship. Even though we may try to mimic the interaction patterns that proved to be so successful in one relationship, we soon learn that we can't do so successfully. Each relationship is different and has its own rules. Furthermore, when a relationship starts to go sour, we may want to go back to the way it used to be. But we soon learn that you can't go back. It's just never the same. You need to move forward and create new rules to invigorate your relationship.

The second characteristic indicates that interaction patterns that define your relationship do not constitute the entire interaction you have with that person. Those patterns happen frequently, but they don't occur all the time. If they did, you would soon find them monotonous and dull. The interaction patterns occur *as a rule*, but all rules have exceptions. That's what makes the relationship interesting. The interaction patterns don't violate the rules, they just aren't typical or normal in your relationship. Rules are the defining characteristics of your interpersonal relationship. The rest of your interaction is part of your relationship but not as important to defining it.

The next three characteristics of relationship rules emphasize the evolutionary development of relationships and, thus, of rules also. Rules change over time (a fundamental characteristic of the evolutionary development and constant state of becoming) which means, of course, that rules do not have the same strength all the time. You may have one set of relationship rules with your very close relational partner that applies when you are all alone and another set that applies when you are in public. The fourth characteristic emphasizes the process of negotiation, also a fundamental characteristic of the pattern of relationship development that has been discussed in earlier chapters. The fifth characteristic suggests that rules help to provide guidelines for behaving in any given situation, but they still come about through the process of retrospective sensemaking.

The final characteristic suggests how people in a relationship "enforce" the rules or interaction patterns that guide their interpersonal communication. Certainly relational partners do not conform to the rules of their relationship because they have to but rather because they choose to. It is not fear of punishment that guides their interaction patterns but rather the free choice of partners to use the relationship rules to guide their participation in communication. When a partner breaks or violates one of the relationship rules, the individual is not punished by the partner so much as he or she becomes intrapersonally aware of having broken a rule. The individual, then, provides his or her own punishment. The rulebreaker feels shame or embarrassment at having done something wrong in the relationship.

A competent relationship, then, is interpersonal communication in which the interaction patterns are clearly established and demonstrated in the interpersonal communication of the relational partners. The more competent the relationship, the easier it is to see the relationship rules in the interaction patterns of the participants. Partners in a competent relationship know what the rules are (even though they may not realize it) and interact accordingly. They experience the intrapersonal pangs of shame or embarrassment when they break the rules. They negotiate changes in the rules in order to maintain the continuity of the relationship. The stronger the relationship rules in the interaction patterns, the more competent the interpersonal relationship.

Levels of Intimacy

You will probably not be surprised to learn that communication researchers (for example, Hecht, 1984) have discovered that partners are more satisfied with more intimate relationships than with less intimate ones. Somehow, that makes sense. You care more about your relationships with people you like and who like you, and you care less about your relationships with people you don't like and who don't especially like you. Not very startling, but it is certainly believable. But what about the "ideology of intimacy" we discussed earlier?

A relationship can possess a relatively high level of intimacy and low levels of intensity, trust, and commitment (the other components of interactional quality). An intimate relationship may involve friends who work together and never see each other away from the work setting. An intimate relationship may involve members of the same club or organization who enjoy their interaction when they get together but who don't get together very often.

Some people may have an "intimate acquaintanceship," in the sense that they find the relationship very satisfying. However, they place rather severe limits on the amount of their interaction, the continued development of their relationship, and the amount of intensity allowed to develop in their relationship. And these types of intimate relationships (in addition to those of lovers and marital partners) may also be included within a general classification of competent relationships. In other words, a highly competent relationship does not necessarily have to be a very close relationship.

Stages of Evolutionary Development

You will also find it credible, but hardly newsworthy, that communication researchers (for example, Wheeless, Wheeless, & Baus, 1984) have discovered that people tend to be most satisfied with relationships that have evolved to a stage of advanced development. In other words, people tend to find relationships with people they know very well more satisfying than those with people they don't know very well or know only slightly. This finding is again not an astounding piece of news, but it is certainly believable. A very close relationship is, by definition, a competent relationship.

Remember what happens in a relationship that has progressed in its evolutionary development. For one thing, the partners know each other better than they did earlier. They have reduced much of their uncertainty about who the partner is and what to expect from the relationship and in the communication process. Then, too, the partners have a considerable amount of "historicity." They are more comfortable in their communication and find the interaction itself rather enjoyable. They have developed a certain amount of emotional residue (such as liking) as a result of all this past interaction. It is hardly surprising, then, that we can refer to a highly developed relationship as a competent one.

In a relationship that has developed to an advanced stage, the partners know each other better and are comfortable with each other.
(Joel Gordon)

Characteristics

At this point, we can summarize what we mean when we say that a relationship is competent. A relationship is competent to the extent that:

1. It endures.
2. It is continuous.
3. It meets the expectations of its partners.
4. It serves various functions.

A competent relationship endures. Simple endurance or longevity may not be a sufficient reason to call a relationship competent. On the other hand, a competent relationship is likely to be a long-term relationship. The fact that the relationship has lasted a long time is a sign, though not a necessary sign, that it is a competent one. If it were less competent, it probably wouldn't have lasted as long.

A competent relationship is continuous. Recall that continuity is a key factor in maintaining a close relationship. Partners who maintain the closeness of their relationship keep the interaction from stagnating, from becoming too monotonous and repetitive. They maintain their relationship by constantly changing it to something new. The continuous relationship remains in a constant state of becoming. It remains fresh, vital, and new—regardless of how old and enduring it has been.

A competent relationship meets the expectations of its partners. No one is really sure which comes first—the expectations individuals have of their relationship or the relationship itself. Perhaps individuals enter a relationship expecting it to be a particular kind. When interaction fulfills those expectations, the individuals are satisfied with it. On the other hand, the process of interpersonal communication may provide the individual participants with some sense of what the future of their relationship will be. In that case, the process of interpersonal communication (the relationship) serves to create or guide the expectations of the relational partners. In either case, to the extent that retrospective sensemaking results in the partners' feeling that their relationship is consistent with their expectations, the relationship is competent.

A competent relationship serves various functions. Every interpersonal relationship that endures for any length of time does something to and for the participants or society. A family, for example, serves the social function of raising children for the next generation and of teaching that new generation the cultural norms and traditions of the society. The family also serves the intrapersonal functions of providing affection, support, and companionship for participants in the kinship relation. The competent interpersonal relationship may serve recreational, spiritual, economic, sexual, or any of a variety of other social functions. But it is functional.

SOME GUIDELINES FOR IMPROVING COMMUNICATIVE COMPETENCE

Despite the claims of some people to the contrary, no one has any way of knowing precisely what to do in order to ensure effective and enduring interpersonal relationships. Too much depends on the specific relationship, the specific situation, the specific relationship stage, the specific person to guarantee confidence in any list of "things to do" in order to demonstrate competence in interpersonal communication. Our discussions in this chapter have strongly suggested that competence is just as much a characteristic of the relationship as of the individual communicator. The eight recommendations discussed in the remaining pages of this chapter are certainly no guarantee that you will have happy, healthy, and successful interpersonal relationships from this time forward. They are intended only as principles of good advice that, given what we know about the nature of interpersonal communication, seem to be practical and to make sense.

1. Avoid generalizing from one interpersonal relationship to another. It is a common human tendency to analyze, to break something down into its parts, in order to understand it. When we have a relationship that goes sour, our first reaction is likely to be to try to find out what went wrong. When we have a relationship that is good, our first reaction is likely to be to try to find out what made it that way. Then we tell ourselves to avoid the wrong things and do the right things in our other relationships. Unfortunately, no two relationships are exactly the same. Generalizing from one relationship to another often leads to a false understanding based on what has been called the *error of assumed essence*.

We commit the error of assumed essence when we observe a difference between two things (in this case, two different relationships) and then assume that the difference we observed is the "reason why" the two relationships are different. But although the difference we observed is probably genuine, it is often not the critical distinguishing factor. We often hear of athletes who wear "lucky socks" or "lucky jackets" or do "lucky behaviors" in order to keep a winning streak going. An athlete might, for example, have begun wearing those socks on the first day of his winning streak. But only a superstitious fool would believe that wearing those socks was the critical factor that brought about the winning streak. In other words, just because two relationships are different, don't assume that the observed difference makes any difference.

2. Develop and practice a wide variety of relational strategies. Using one strategy does not guarantee that the relationship will develop in the way we want it to develop. Nor does using a lot of strategies guarantee the outcome we want. After all, the relationship will evolve over a long period of time. We can't guarantee what will happen in the future any more than we can guarantee how our partner will respond to a particular strategy. On the other hand, if the relationship evolves slowly, it stands to reason that we need to be prepared for whatever happens in the future— both the expected and the unexpected. The more strategies we have in our repertoire of communicative behaviors, the more likely we are to have an appropriate strategy for whatever situation develops in the future.

How do we know what strategy is appropriate? The answer to that question is simple. Use the "scientific method" to determine appropriateness—trial and error. In other words, try something. If it doesn't work, try something else until it does work. Of course, the success of the trial-and-error method in interpersonal communication depends on the number of items in our repertoire of strategies. The more strategies we have to try, the more likely we are to find one that is effective in any given situation of interpersonal communication.

3. Avoid confusing relational outcomes with emotional residues. This point has been made repeatedly in previous discussions. The emotion you feel toward the other person is not the same thing as the relationship. You may love the other person even though the relationship is a lousy one. Battered wives, for example, do not have "good" relationships with their sadistic husbands. Paradoxically, though, they often express an emotional love toward the partners who use them as punching bags. The emotion felt by relational partners is a residue resulting from the process of retrospectively making sense of the interaction patterns that create the relationship. Two people may have the same emotions about their relationships, even though the relationships are very different. Conversely, two people may have very different emotions, even though they are participants in the same relationship.

Every relationship that progresses to a rather high stage of development proceeds through different emotional stages. There is excitement and anticipation during courtship; emotional bliss during the honeymoon; an emotional roller-coaster ride during the ups and downs of relational development; and comfort and ease of the long-term familiar relationship. The relationship is the same, even though it is constantly in a state of becoming and changing, but the emotions felt by the participants vary widely from one stage to the next.

Two people in the same relationship with the same relational outcome may have differing emotions. Their interpersonal relationship (and don't forget there's only one relationship) has only one outcome; their intrapersonal emotions (at least two people are included) may have a variety of outcomes. The intrapersonal feeling is simply not the same thing as the interpersonal relationship. Despite all the directives of common sense, we should never confuse these two quite different elements of interpersonal communication.

4. Know the relationship rules, and follow them. The key to all relationship rules is appropriateness. When you participate appropriately in interpersonal communication, you are following the rules that define the relationship. To participate appropriately also implies a sense of timing. To participate in interpersonal communication appropriately is not only to perform the appropriate behavior but to perform it at the appropriate time. As long as you follow the rules, you will keep the relationship at its current stage of development. Of course, when you know that the relationship is beginning to get stale, you know that you need to change the rules. And sometimes, for purposes of maintaining continuity in the evolving relationship, you will find it appropriate to break the rules. Of course, timing is again the crucial factor in knowing and following the rules of the interpersonal relationship.

5. Be a relational gambler. Some years ago Kenny Rogers taught us, through the medium of popular music, that living is similar to gambling. In interpersonal relationships as in playing poker, the "secret to surviving is knowing what to throw away and knowing what to keep." All relationships are not good ones, and some relationships are never going to be good ones. If a relationship is incompetent, then why keep it? Being competent, then, is being able to distinguish competent relationships from incompetent ones. When relationships are competent, the gambler decides "to hold 'em." When they are incompetent, the gambler decides "to fold 'em." The secret to being a competent relational gambler is simply knowing when to do which.

You might think that a person who terminates a relationship rather than trying to work out the problem is probably not a competent communicator. In other words, I suppose, people who are competent communicators never have unsuccessful relationships. Such a belief is quite absurd. Anyone and everyone can and does have unsuccessful relationships. Sometimes, as we know, relationships terminate as a result of circumstances that are beyond the control of either participant. More importantly, though, let's take seriously the notion that the *relationship* itself is competent, rather than the notion that competent individuals participate in a relationship.

When the relationship is competent, then neither individual can guarantee what the outcome of the relationship is likely to be. The development of the relationship is the pattern of interaction enacted by both participants together, not by any single person. When we view the relationship as the source of communicative competence, then the individual participant can take neither credit for a successful relationship nor blame for an unsuccessful relationship. The key to being a good relational gambler is working at potentially successful relationships and ending unsuccessful relationships. Under no circumstances does the relational gambler feel guilty when a relationship doesn't work out. After all, you have to play the cards that are dealt to you.

6. Participate in a variety of different relationships. An acquaintance once told me of the difficulties she had experienced following her divorce. According to her story, she had really had only one boyfriend throughout her high school years. They were together constantly, so her friendships with other people (such as girlfriends) were very limited. She married her long-time "steady" shortly after high school graduation and was divorced a few years later. She was, according to her self-analysis, relationally naive. She didn't know how to act with other people. She didn't know how to act on dates. She didn't know how to make friends. In fact, she wasn't even sure what friendship meant. She suffered from low self-esteem and had little self-confidence. She proceeded to remarry (twice, in fact) and get divorced (also twice). At the time we talked, she was just beginning to solve her relational problems.

This woman's problem, perhaps more than anything else, was a lack of relational experience. That is, she had years of relational experience, but she had very little variety in these experiences. The same experience repeated over and over is still a single experience. Variety comes from having had many different kinds of experiences.

The more different kinds of relationships you have, the greater the variety of relational strategies you learn and the more likely you are to have encountered whatever relational experience may be in your future. We often talk about a "well-rounded" person without really knowing what we mean. One significant part of being well-rounded is the variety of interpersonal relationships you have experienced and from which you have learned. After all, relationships with other people probably exert the most significant impact on the development of an individual's personality. Want to be a more well-rounded individual person? Then participate in a greater variety of interpersonal relationships.

7. Manage the tension created by opposing forces in the relationship. The development and maintenance of a competent relationship involves a series of roller-coaster changes. Participants in every relationship are constantly being faced with dilemmas and choices between what to do and what not to do. Interpersonal communication during the evolutionary development of a relationship involves a constant effort to establish some equilibrium or balance between forces that are in opposition with each other. For example, how open should you be in disclosing private information about yourself to your partner? You want to be open, but you also want to protect your self. How involved should you get in the relationship? The more you identify with your partner in the relationship, the greater the risk you run of changing your unique self or personality. Throughout the process of relational development, each of the partners is torn between such opposing forces: conflict versus cooperation, openness versus self-protection, involvement versus privacy, integration versus differentiation, monotony versus mystery.

If you are successful in establishing a competent relationship, you will have devised ways of managing the tensions created by these opposing forces. You will have learned to take the good things with the bad. You will have experienced the ups and downs of relational maintenance. You will have balanced your private life with your relational life (by "shmoozing," for example). You will have discovered what you want to disclose and what you want to conceal about your self. In other words, you will have learned to cope with tensions.

Under no circumstances will you have an absence of tensions in a competent (or incompetent) relationship. To experience no tensions in a relationship is to have a lousy relationship, one that you couldn't care less about. Participants in competent relationships manage tensions; they learn to cope with the problems created by tension. In short, despite their ever-present tensions, participants in competent relationships "keep on truckin'."

8. Stop and smell the roses. Some years ago Irene and I (marital partners in a very close relationship) were struck with the fact that so many of our friends were getting divorced. Not only were neighbors getting divorced, but colleagues at work, friends from graduate school, friends from high school years, nearly everybody in the world (or so it seemed at the time) was getting divorced. If it could happen to them, we thought, then it could happen to us. We began to watch carefully the "seven danger signals" of marital unhappiness. We assumed that this relational unhappiness was like a virus. Without proper immunization, we were vulnerable to the disease and wondered when it would strike. Apparently we came to the conclusion that we weren't getting anywhere trying to "psych out" other people's unhappy relationships or our own happy one. Without thinking about it, I guess, we just quit worrying about it.

In trying to decide why your relationship is the way it is, you are wasting your time using your critical-thinking skills. You probably won't ever know the reasons for your happy relationships. Moreover, even if you did know why your relationship was happy, you wouldn't be any happier. The only possible conclusion, then, is to quit worrying about it. Stop and smell the roses while they are in bloom. Whatever makes your relationship a good one just isn't very important if searching for it takes all your energy. Don't analyze your relationships so much. Enjoy them.

Summary

Competence in and satisfaction with interpersonal communication are difficult to define separately. The outcome of communication is so closely linked with the process of communication that competence and satisfaction are often considered two sides of the same coin. Defining competence, however, is problematic because of the commonsense myths that surround it. The myths of communicative competence include those of openness, objectivity, listening techniques, and formula answers. Any definition of competence takes into consideration the communicator's capacity, performance, and adaptability as well as other people's perceptions of enacted behavior.

The competent individual communicator possesses social skills, is able to adapt a personal style to a variety of situations, and uses relational strategies with appropriateness and timing. Although listening skills are important, the competent communicator is more likely to use effective listening skills than to become competent as a result of having used effective listening skills.

The entire relationship, jointly created by the participants through their interaction patterns, may also be considered a source of competence. A competent relationship has clear relationship rules and is affected by levels of intimacy and stages of evolutionary development. A relationship is said to be competent to the extent that it endures, is continuous, meets (or guides) the expectations of its participants, and serves various functions. Although no list of "things to do" can guarantee effective interpersonal relationships, some good advice for improving communicative competence can offer guidelines for improving their effectiveness.

REFERENCES

Adams, K. L. 1985. *Communication as negotiation: A study of strategic interaction in social relationships.* Ph.D. dissertation, University of Utah.

Altman, I. 1975. *The environment and social behavior.* Monterey, CA: Brooks/Cole.

Altman, I., & Taylor, D. A. 1973. *Social penetration.* New York: Holt.

Andreyeva, G. M., & Gozman, L. J. 1981. Interpersonal relationships and social context. In S. Duck & R. Gilmour, eds., *Personal relationships 1: Studying personal relationships.* New York: Academic Press, pp. 47–66.

Ardrey, R. 1970. *The territorial imperative.* New York: Atheneum.

Ayres, J. 1980. Relationship stages and sex as factors in topic dwell time. *Western Journal of Speech Communication, 44,* 253–260.

Ayres, J. 1983. Strategies to maintain relationships: Their identification and perceived usage. *Communication Quarterly, 31,* 62–67.

Bateson, G. 1972. Culture contact and schismogenesis. *Steps to an ecology of mind.* New York: Chandler.

Baxter, L. A. 1979. Self disclosure as a relationship disengagement strategy: An exploratory investigation. *Human Communication Research, 5,* 215–222.

Baxter, L. A. 1982. Strategies for ending relationships: Two studies. *Western Journal of Speech Communication, 46,* 223–241.

Baxter, L. A. 1983. Relationship disengagement: An examination of the reversal hypothesis. *Western Journal of Speech Communication, 47,* 85–98.

Baxter, L. A. 1984. Trajectories of relationship disengagement. *Journal of Social and Personal Relationships, 1,* 29–48.

Baxter, L. A., & Philpott, J. 1982. Attribution-based strategies for initiating and terminating relationships. *Communication Quarterly, 30,* 217–224.

Baxter, L. A., & Wilmot, W. W. 1984. "Secret tests": Social strategies for acquiring information about the state of the relationship. *Human Communication Research, 11,* 171–202.

Bell, R. R. 1981. *Worlds of friendship.* Beverly Hills, CA: Sage.

Bennis, W. 1979. Toward better interpersonal relationships. In W. Bennis, J. Van Maanen, E. H. Schein, & F. I. Steele, eds., *Essays in Interpersonal Dynamics.* Homewood, IL: Dorsey, pp. 182–205.

Berger, C., & Calabrase, R. 1975. Some explorations in initial interaction and beyond: Toward a developmental theory of interpersonal communication. *Human Communication Research, 1,* 99–112.

Bernstein, B. 1972. Social class, language and socialization. In P. P. Giglioli, ed., *Language and social context: Selected readings.* New York: Penguin, pp. 157–178.

Bertalanffy, L. von. 1967. *Robots, men and minds.* New York: Braziller.

403

Birdwhistle, R. 1959. Contributions of linguistic-kinesic studies to the understanding of schizophrenia. In A. Auerbach, ed., *Schizophrenia: An integrated approach*. New York: Ronald Press, pp. 99–123.

Bochner, A. P. 1982. On the efficacy of openness in close relationships. In M. Burgoon, ed., *Communication yearbook 5*. New Brunswick, NJ: Transaction, pp. 109–124.

Booth, A. 1972. Sex and social participation. *American Sociological Review*, 34, 183–192.

Booth, A., & Hess, E. 1974. Cross-sex friendship. *Journal of Marriage and the Family*, 36, 38–47.

Bostrom, R. N., & Waldhart, E. S. 1980. Components in listening behavior. *Human Communication Research*, 6, 211–227.

Brown, P., & Levinson, S. 1978. Universals in language usage. Politeness phenomena. In E. Goody, ed., *Questions and politeness*. Cambridge, England: Cambridge University Press.

Burgess, R. L. 1981. Relationships in marriage and the family. In S. Duck & R. Gilmour, eds., *Personal relationships 1: Studying personal relationships*. New York: Academic Press, pp. 179–196.

Burgoon, J. K., & Hale, J. L. 1984. The fundamental topoi of relational communication. *Communication Monographs*, 51, 193–214.

Camden, C., Motley, M. T., & Wilson, A. 1984. White lies in interpersonal communication: A taxonomy and preliminary investigation of social motivations. *Western Journal of Speech Communication*, 48, 309–325.

Chelune, G. J., ed. 1979. *Self-disclosure*. San Francisco: Jossey-Bass.

Chomsky, N. 1965. *Aspects of the theory of syntax*. Cambridge, MA: MIT Press.

Cissna, K. N. L., & Sieburg, L. 1981. Patterns of interactional confirmation and disconfirmation. In C. Wilder-Mott & J. H. Weakland, eds., *Rigor & imagination: Essays from the legacy of Gregory Bateson*. New York: Praeger, pp. 253–282.

Cody, M. J. 1982. A typology of disengagement strategies and an examination of the role intimacy, reactions to inequity and relational problems play in strategy selection. *Communication Monographs*, 49, 148–170.

Cohen, J. 1969. *Sensation and Perception. I. Vision*. Chicago: Rand McNally.

Collins, O., & Collins, J. M. 1973. *Interaction and social structure*. The Hague: Mouton.

Colman, A. D., & Colman, L. L. 1975. *Love and ecstasy*. New York; Seabury.

Conville, R. L. 1983. Second-order development in interpersonal communication. *Human Communication Research*, 9, 195–207.

Crable, R. E. 1981. *One to another: A guidebook for interpersonal communication*. New York: Harper & Row.

Cunningham, J. D., & Antill, J. K. 1981. Love in developing romantic relationships. In S. Duck & R. Gilmour, eds., *Personal relationships 2: Developing personal relationships*. New York: Academic Press, pp. 27–51.

Cupach, W. R., & Spitzberg, B. H. 1983. Trait versus state: A comparison of dispositional and situational measures of interpersonal communication competence. *Western Journal of Speech Communication*, 47, 364–379.

Denzin, N. K. 1970. Rules of conduct and the study of deviant behavior. In G. J. McCall, M. M. McCall, N. K. Denzin, G. D. Suttles, & S. B. Kurth, eds., *Social Relationships*. Chicago: Aldine, pp. 62–94.

Duck, S. W. 1973. *Personal relationships and personal constructs: A study of friendship formation*. New York: Wiley.

Duck, S. 1977. *The study of acquaintance*. Westmead, England: Saxon House.

Duck, S. 1982. A topography of relationship disengagement and dissolution. In S. Duck, ed., *Personal relationships 4: Dissolving personal relationships*. New York: Academic Press, pp. 1–30.

Festinger, L. 1954. A theory of social comparison processes. *Human Relations*, 7, 117–140.

Festinger, L., Schachter, S., & Back, K. 1950. *Social pressures in informal groups: A study of human factors in housing*. New York: Harper & Row.

Fisher, B. A. 1978. *Perspectives on human communication.* New York: Macmillan.

Fisher, B. A. 1983. Differential effects of sexual composition and interactional context on interaction patterns in dyads. *Human Communication Research*, 9, 225–238.

Fisher, B. A., & Drecksel, G. L. 1983. A cyclical model of developing relationships: A study of relational control interaction. *Communication Monographs*, 50, 66–78.

Fitzpatrick, M. A., & Winke, J. 1979. You always hurt the one you love: Strategies and tactics in interpersonal conflict. *Communication Quarterly*, 38, 618–628.

Furnham, A. 1983. Research in social skills training: A critique. In R. Ellis & D. Whitington, eds., *New directions in social skill training.* London: Croom Helm.

Gamble, T., & Gamble, M. 1984. *Communication Works.* New York: Random House.

Garfinkel H., & Sacks, H. 1969. On formal structures of practical actions. In J. C. McKinney & E. Tiryakian, eds., *Theoretical sociology: Perspectives and developments.* New York: Appleton-Century-Crofts.

Gibb, J. 1961. Defensive communication. *Journal of Communication*, 11, 141–148.

Giglioli, P. P., ed. 1972. *Language and social context: Selected readings.* New York: Penguin.

Goffman, E. 1959. *The presentation of self in everyday life.* Garden City, NY: Doubleday.

Goffman, E. 1963. *Behavior in public places: Notes on the social organization of gatherings.* New York: Free Press.

Goffman, E. 1971. *Relations in public: Microstudies of the public order.* New York: Basic Books.

Gottman, J. M. 1982. Emotional responsiveness in marital conversations. *Journal of Communication*, 32, 108–120.

Gouldner, A. W. 1960. The norm of reciprocity: A preliminary statement. *American Sociological Review*, 25, 161–171.

Graziano, W. G., & Musser, L. M. 1982. The joining and the parting of the ways. In S. Duck, ed., *Personal relationships 4: Dissolving personal relationships.* New York: Academic Press, pp. 75–106.

Hall, E. T. 1966. *The hidden dimension.* New York: Doubleday.

Hanson, N. R. 1967. Observation and interpretation. In S. Morganbesser, ed., *Philosophy of science today.* New York: Basic Books, pp. 89–99.

Hart, R. P., & Burks, D. M. 1972. Rhetorical sensitivity and social interaction. *Speech Monographs*, 39, 75–91.

Harvey, J. H., Weber, W. L., Yarkin, K. L., & Stewart, B. E. 1982. In S. Duck, ed., *Personal relationships 4: Dissolving personal relationships.* New York: Academic Press, pp. 107–126.

Hayward, G. D. 1977. *An overview of psychological concepts of "home."* A paper presented to the annual conference of the Environmental Design Research Association, Urbana, IL.

Hecht, M. L. 1984. Satisfying communication and relationship labels: Intimacy and length of relationship as perceptual frames of naturalistic conversations. *Western Journal of Speech Communication*, 48, 201–216.

Heshka, S., & Nelson, Y. 1974. Interpersonal speaking distance as a function of age, sex, and relationship. *Sociometry*, 35, 92–104.

Hinde, R. A. 1979. *Towards understanding relationships.* London: Academic Press.

Honey, P. 1976. *Face to face: A practical guide to interactive skills.* London: Institute of Personnel Management.

Jones, E. E., & Nisbett, R. E. 1971. *The actor and the observer: Divergent perceptions of the causes of behavior.* Morristown, NJ: General Learning Press.

Jones, S. E., & Yarbrough, A. E. 1985. A naturalistic study of the meanings of touch. *Communication Monographs*, 52, 19–56.

Jourard, S. 1964. *The transparent self.* New York: Van Nostrand.

Kelley, H. H. 1979. *Personal relationships: Their structures and processes.* Hillsdale, NJ: Erlbaum.

Kelly, H. H., & Thibaut, J. W. 1978. *Interpersonal relations: A theory of interdependence.* New York: Wiley.

Kelly, C. M. 1967. Listening: Complex of activities *and* a unitary skill? *Speech Monographs,* 34, 455–466.

King, R. G. 1979. *Fundamentals of human communication.* New York: Macmillan.

Kitchens, J. T., Heron, T. P., & Behnke, R. R. 1976. *Effects of visual environmental aesthetics on interpersonal attraction.* A paper presented to the annual meeting of the Southern Speech Communication Association, San Antonio, TX.

Knapp, M. L. 1984. *Interpersonal communication and human relationships.* Boston: Allyn & Bacon.

Krivonos, P. D., & Knapp, M. L. 1975. Initiating communication: What do you say when you say hello? *Central States Speech Journal,* 26, 115–125.

Kuhn, M., & McPartland, T. S. 1954. An empirical investigation of self-attitudes. *American Sociological Review,* 19, 58–76.

Kurth, S. B. 1970. Friendships and friendly relations. In G. J. McCall, M. M. McCall, N. K. Denzin, G. D. Suttles, & S. B. Kurth, eds., *Social relationships.* Chicago: Aldine.

Labov, W. 1972. The logic of nonstandard English. In P. P. Giglioli, ed., *Language and social context: Selected readings.* New York: Penguin, pp. 179–215.

LaGaipa, J. J. 1981. A systems approach to personal relationships. In S. Duck, & R. Gilmour, eds., *Personal relationships 1; Studying personal relationships.* New York: Academic Press, pp. 67–89.

LaGaipa, J. J. 1982. Rules and rituals in disengaging from relationships. In S. Duck, ed., *Personal relationships 4: Dissolving personal relationships.* New York: Academic Press, pp. 189–210.

Lewis, R. A. 1978. Emotional intimacy among men. *Journal of Social Issues,* 34, 108–121.

Luft, J. 1970. *Group process: An introduction to group dynamics.* Palo Alto, CA: National Press.

Mangam, I. L. 1981. Relationships at work: A matter of tension and tolerance. In S. Duck & R. Gilmour, eds., *Personal relationships 1: Studying personal relationships.* New York: Academic Press, pp. 197–214.

Marwell, G., & Schmitt, D. R. 1967. Dimensions of compliance-gaining behavior: An empirical analysis. *Sociometry,* 30, 350–364.

Maslow, A. H., & Mintz, N. L. 1956. Effects of esthetic surroundings: I. Initial effects of three esthetic conditions upon perceiving "energy" and "well-being" in faces. *Journal of Psychology,* 41, 247–254.

McCall, G. J., McCall, M. M., Denzin, N. K., Suttles, G. D., & Kurth, S. B. 1970. *Social relationships.* Chicago: Aldine.

McFall, R. M., 1976. *Behavioral training: A skill-acquisition approach to clinical problems.* Morristown, NJ: General Learning Press.

Mead, G. H. 1913. The social self. *Journal of Philosophy, Psychology and Scientific Methods.* 10, 374–380.

Miller, G. A. 1956. The magical number seven, plus or minus two: Some limits on our capacity for processing information. *Psychological Review,* 63, 81–97.

Mintz, N. L. 1956. Effects of esthetic surroundings: II. Prolonged and repeated experience in a "beautiful" and "ugly" room. *Journal of Psychology,* 41, 459–466.

Newcomb, T. M. 1948. Autistic hostility and social reality, *Human Relations,* 1, 69–86.

Newman, H. 1981. Communication within ongoing intimate relationships: An attributional perspective. *Personality and Social Psychological Bulletin,* 7, 59–70.

Nofsinger, R. E., Jr. 1975. The demand ticket: A conversational device for getting the floor. *Speech Monographs,* 42, 1–9.

O'Connor, P., & Brown, G. W. 1984. Supportive relationships: Fact or fancy? *Journal of Social and Personal Relationships.* 1, 159–176.

Olson, C. D. 1981. *Artifacts in the home and relational communication: A preliminary report.* M.S. thesis, University of Utah.

Owen, W. F. 1981. Interpretive themes in relational communication. *Quarterly Journal of Speech*, 67, 274–286.

Parks, M. 1982. Ideology in interpersonal communication: Off the couch and into the world. In M. Burgoon, ed., *Communication yearbook 5*. New Brunswick, NJ: Transaction, pp. 79–108.

Patton, B. R., & Giffin, K. 1981. *Interpersonal communication in action*, 3rd ed. New York: Harper & Row.

Pearce, W. B., & Sharp, S. M. 1973. Self-disclosing communications. *Journal of Communication*, 23, 409–425.

Pendell, S. D. 1976. *The influence of room design on small group communication*. Ph.D. dissertation, University of Utah.

Phillips, G., & Wood, J. 1983. *Communication and human relationships: The study of interpersonal relationships*. New York: Macmillan.

Przybyla, D. P. J., & Byrne, D. 1981. Sexual relationships. In S. Duck & R. Gilmour, eds., *Personal relationships 1: Studying personal relationships*. New York: Academic Press, pp. 67–89.

Ragan, S. L., & Hopper, R. 1984. Ways to leave your lover: A conversational analysis of literature. *Communication Quarterly*, 32, 310–317.

Rathjen, D. P. 1980. An overview of social competence. In D. P. Rathjen & J. P. Foreyt, eds., *Social competence: Interventions for children and adults*. New York: Pergamon, pp. 1–23.

Rathjen, D. P., & Foreyt, J. P., eds. 1980. *Social competence: Interventions for children and adults*. New York: Pergamon.

Rawlins, W. K. 1983. Openness as problematic in ongoing friendships: Two conversational dilemmas. *Communication Monographs*, 50, 1–13.

Reisman, J. M. 1981. Adult friendships. In S. Duck & R. Gilmour, eds., *Personal relationships 2: Developing personal relationships*. New York: Academic Press, pp. 205–230.

Robert, M. 1982. *Managing conflict: From the inside out*. San Diego, CA: Learning Concepts.

Rodin, M. J. 1982. Non-engagement, failure to engage, and disengagement. In S. Duck, ed., *Personal relationships 4; Dissolving personal relationships*. New York: Academic Press, pp. 31–49.

Roloff, M. 1981. *Interpersonal communication: The social exchange approach*. Beverly Hills: Sage Publications.

Rosegrant, T. J., & McCroskey, J.C. 1975. The effect of race and sex on proxemics behavior in an interview setting. *Southern Speech Communication Journal*, 40, 408–420.

Ross, R., & Ross, M. 1982. *Relating and interacting: An introduction to interpersonal communication*. Englewood Cliffs, NJ: Prentice-Hall.

Roy, D. F. 1973. "Banana time"—Job satisfaction and informal interaction. In W. G. Bennis, D. E. Berlew, E. H. Schein, & F. I. Steele, eds., *Interpersonal dynamics: Essays and readings on human interaction*, 3rd ed. Homewood, IL: Dorsey, pp. 403–417.

Ruben, B. 1984. *Communication and human behavior*. New York: Macmillan.

Rubin, R. B. 1985. The validity of the communication competency assessment instrument. *Communication Monographs*, 52, 173–185.

Sacks, H., Schegloff, E. A., & Jefferson, G. 1978. A simplest systematics for the organization of turn taking for conversation. In J. Schenkein, ed., *Studies in the organization of conversational interaction*. New York: Academic Press, pp. 7–56.

Saussure, F. de. 1916. *Course in general linguistics*, trans. W. Baskin. New York: McGraw-Hill.

Scheflen, A. E. 1968. Quasi-courtship behavior in psychotherapy. In W. G. Bennis, E. H. Schein, F. I. Steele, & D. E. Berlew, eds., *Interpersonal dynamics: Essays and readings on human interaction*, rev. ed. Homewood, IL: Dorsey, pp. 182–196.

Scheflen, A. E. 1972. *Body language and social order: Communication as behavioral control*. Englewood Cliffs, NJ: Prentice-Hall.

Scheflen, A. E. 1974. *How behavior means*. Garden City, NY: Doubleday.

Schutz, W. C. 1958. *FIRO: A three-dimensional theory of interpersonal behavior.* New York: Holt, Rinehart & Winston.

Shannon, C. & Weaver, W. 1949. *The mathematical theory of communication.* Urbana: University of Illinois Press.

Sheehy, G. 1974. *Passages: Predictable crises of adult life.* New York: Dutton.

Sillars, A. L. 1980. Attributions and communication in roommate conflicts. *Communication Monographs,* 47, 180–200.

Sillars, A. L., Pike, G. R., Jones, T. S., & Murphy, M.A. 1984. Communication and understanding in marriage. *Human Communication Research,* 10, 317–350.

Simon, R. J., Crotts, G., & Mahan, L. 1970. An empirical note about married women and their friends. *Social Forces,* 48, 520–525.

Smeltzer, L. R., & Watson, K. W. 1984. Listening: An empirical comparison of discussion length and level of incentive. *Central States Speech Journal,* 35, 166–170.

Smilowitz, M. 1985. *Confirming communication in supervisor/subordinate dyads.* Ph.D. dissertation, University of Utah.

Snyder, M. 1974. Self-monitoring of expressive behavior. *Journal of Personality and Social Psychology,* 30, 526–537.

Sommer, R. 1969. *Personal space: The behavioral basis of design.* Englewood Cliffs, NJ.: Prentice-Hall.

Spitzberg. B. H., & Cupach, W. R. 1984. *Interpersonal communication competence.* Beverly Hills, CA: Sage.

Spitzberg, G. H., & Hecht, M. L. 1984. A component model of relational competence. *Human Communication Research,* 10, 575–600.

Stafford, L., & Daly, J. A. 1984. Conversational memory: The effects of recall mode and memory expectancies on remembrances of natural conversations. *Human Communication Research,* 10, 351–378.

Sunnafrank, M. J., & Miller, G. R. 1981. The role of initial conversations in determining attraction to similar and dissimilar strangers. *Human Communication Research,* 8, 16–25.

Thibaut, J., & Kelly, H. 1959. *The social psychology of groups.* New York: Wiley.

Ting-Toomey, S. 1983. An analysis of verbal communication patterns in high and low marital adjustment groups. *Human Communication Research,* 9, 306–319.

Van Maanen, J., 1979. On the understanding of interpersonal relations. In W. Bennis, J. Van Maanen, E. H. Schein, & F. I. Steele, eds., *Essays in interpersonal dynamics.* Homewood, IL: Dorsey, pp. 13–42.

Villard, K. L. & Whipple, L. J. 1976. *Beginnings in relational communication.* New York: Wiley.

Warriner, C. K. 1970. *The emergence of society.* Homewood, IL: Dorsey.

Watzlawick, P., Beavin, J. H., & Jackson, D. D. 1967. *Pragmatics of human communication.* New York: Norton.

Wheeless, L. R. Wheeless, V. E., & Baus, R. 1984. Sexual communication, communication satisfaction, and solidarity in the development stages of intimate relationships. *Western Journal of Speech Communication,* 48, 217–230.

Wiemann, J. M. 1977. Explication and test of a model of communicative competence. *Human Communication Research,* 3, 195–213.

Wiemann, J. M., & Kelly, C. W. 1981. Pragmatics of interpersonal competence. In Wilder-Mott & J. H. Weakland, eds., *Rigor & imagination: Essays from the legacy of Gregory Bateson.* New York: Praeger, pp. 283–298.

Wilmot, W. W. 1980. *Dyadic Communication,* 2nd ed. Reading, MA: Addison-Wesley.

AUTHOR INDEX

SUBJECT INDEX